D0436078

# Eisenhower's War of Words

## Rhetoric and Leadership

# Eisenhower's War of Words

## Rhetoric and Leadership

Edited by Martin J. Medhurst

Michigan State University
East Lansing
1994

All Michigan State University Press books are produced on paper which meets the requirements of American National Standard of Information Sciences—Permanence of paper for
printed materials ANSI Z23.48-1984.

Printed in the United States of America

Michigan State University Press
East Lansing, Michigan 48823-5202

02  01  00  99  98  97  96  95  94  1  2  3  4  5  6  7  8  9  10

Library of Congress Cataloging-in-Publication Data

Eisenhower's war of words : rhetoric and leadership / edited by Martin J. Medhurst
          p.        cm. — (Rhetoric and public affairs series)
     Includes bibliographical references and index.
     ISBN 0-87013-340-3
     1. Eisenhower, Dwight D. (Dwight David), 1890-1969—Oratory. 2. Eisenhower, Dwight
D. (Dwight David), 1890-1969—Literary Art. 3. Rhetoric—Political aspects—United
States—History—20th century. 4. Communication in politics—United States—History—
20th century. 5. United States—Foreign relations—1953-1961. 6. United States—Politics
and government—1943-1961. 7. Cold War.
     I. Medhurst, Martin J. II. Series.
     E836.E43  1994
     973'.921'092—dc20                                        93-47650
                                                              CIP

For

Julia Marie, James, and Monica

May you grow up in a world where

> . . . peoples of all faiths, all races, all nations, may have their great human needs satisfied; that those now denied opportunity shall come to enjoy it to the full; that all who yearn for freedom may experience its spiritual blessings; that those who have freedom will understand, also, its heavy responsibilities; that all who are insensitive to the needs of others will learn charity; that the scourges of poverty, disease and ignorance will be made to disappear from the earth, and that, in the goodness of time, all peoples will come to live together in a peace guaranteed by the binding force of mutual respect and love.

Dwight D. Eisenhower<br>
January 17, 1961

# Contents

| Martin J. | **Introduction** |
| Medhurst | |

Dwight D. Eisenhower was a warrior. Behind the broad smile and twinkling blue eyes, behind the upraised arms and immense personal magnetism lurked a Cold War strategist of the first order. To understand anything about President Eisenhower, one must keep constantly in mind that he was first—and last—General Eisenhower. Neither with the end of World War II nor with his election to the presidency did Eisenhower ever cease to think and act like the military man he was trained to be. From the years immediately following his graduation from West Point in 1915, to his brilliant performance at the Command and General Staff School in 1925, to his historic rout of the Second Army during the Louisiana maneuvers of 1941, Eisenhower built his career as a strategist and tactician. That the majority of those years from 1915 to 1941 were spent in staff positions where he worked for such notables as Fox Connor, John J. Pershing, and Douglas MacArthur should not obscure the fact that Ike was trained as a warrior, not a paper pusher. When war came, Ike was ready to wage it and to employ any and all tools at his disposal, including psychological warfare, black propaganda, and deception.

Upon his election to the presidency in 1952, General Eisenhower purposed not only to continue the Cold War that he had inherited from the Truman administration; he decided to win it, even though he was under no illusions that victory would come quickly or easily. Eisenhower understood that the nature of that war was essentially rhetorical—that is, that it was a war of words, images, perceptions, attitudes, motives, and expectations. It was a war in which the battlefield was in the hearts and minds of people, both in America and throughout the world, especially in those areas ripe for communist exploitation because of poverty, internal turmoil, or political corruption. From his first inaugural address of January 1953 until his farewell address of January 1961, Eisenhower operated from the premise that "The future shall belong to the free."[1] Far from merely announcing this sentiment, Ike set about to make it a reality. Foremost among Eisenhower's weapons in this war was rhetorical discourse—"discourse intentionally designed to achieve a particular goal with one or more specific audience."[2] This book is about such discourse.

For Eisenhower, rhetoric was a weapon with which to wage Cold War. Too often, scholars write about Cold War as though the crucial component is to be

1

found in the adjective. To Ike, the Cold War was not first and foremost "cold," it was first and foremost "war," though a kind of war requiring special means and striving toward a particular end—a "peace" that was neither peace nor war, but something in between. When Ike spoke of this war, he always took as his focus the end desired rather than the means used to pursue that end. He thus spoke of "the chance for peace," "waging peace," and "the price of peace," even titling the second volume of his White House memoirs, *Waging Peace, 1956-1961*. That the Cold War was not ended nor true peace achieved during Eisenhower's eight years in office has led some to label his administrations a failure. But careful study of Eisenhower's speeches and writings makes clear one thing: Ike never believed that "victory" would come quickly, but he did believe it would come. He believed that it would come not with a bang, but with an internal collapse of the Soviet Union. The goal, therefore, was to outlast the opponent. The Cold War would not be a sprint, but a long-distance race in which the side that could keep itself in "balance"—a crucial concept for Eisenhower—would be most likely to win in the end.

The central role for rhetoric, therefore, was to promote balanced perceptions and actions at home, instigate imbalance and frustration in the enemy, and induce neutrals to view the Western allies as their best hope for political and economic advancement. To Eisenhower, effective rhetoric had almost nothing to do with style or delivery. The lilting tones of a Roosevelt or the balanced parallelisms of a Kennedy impressed Eisenhower not at all. Instead, rhetoric was thought of as a strategic art of selection, invention, arrangement, word choice, nuance, tone, implication, timing, and audience adaptation. Most centrally, rhetoric was purposive; it existed to accomplish goals in the real worlds of international diplomacy and domestic debate. It was a weapon in the arsenal of the Cold War, one that could be employed selectively, and as the situation required, to effect particular strategic ends.

This collection of essays is about Eisenhower's strategic use of rhetoric. It is organized around significant moments in the Eisenhower presidency, moments when rhetorical discourse was brought into play in an effort to effect change or modification in the existing situation. Such moments were often ones of crisis—McCarthyism, Indochina, Suez, Little Rock, the U-2 affair. At such times the strategic use of rhetoric became the primary means by which Eisenhower sought to influence the beliefs, attitudes, and actions of audiences, both foreign and domestic. Study of such moments allows one to learn more about Eisenhower as a strategic communicator as well as about the nature, possibilities, and limitations of rhetoric as a medium for the conduct of public business.

Chapter one opens with a overview of "Eisenhower as Cold Warrior." Robert L. Ivie finds in Eisenhower "a powerful rhetorical agent of Cold War acculturation" who helped to "institutionalize an age of peril." By providing an overview of Eisenhower's speaking during his eight years in office, Ivie demonstrates how "Eisenhower portrayed the communist threat as pervasive, persistent, global, and total—a conflict that would continue indefinitely until either slavery or freedom prevailed." The author finds two conceptual metaphors that drive Eisenhower's rhetorical vision and that function to instantiate a "cultural pathology of peril."

Mark J. Schaefermeyer devotes chapter two to an analysis of "Dulles and Eisenhower on 'Massive Retaliation.'" The author finds the doctrine of massive retaliation effective "as a *rhetorical* strategy" because it was "masterfully conceived in its indirection." Neither Dulles nor Eisenhower alone can be credited with originating the concept of massive retaliation, according to Schaefermeyer, though both assisted in its formulation and both subscribed to its tenets. By embracing the concept, the president and his secretary of state "sought to make ambiguity their ally."

In "'Keeping the Faith': Eisenhower Introduces the Hydrogen Age," Rachel L. Holloway argues that when "faced with uncertainty and public anxiety" over the H-Bomb, President Eisenhower drew on a "long tradition of religious interpretations of American experience" both to neutralize potential opposition to the bomb and to create a "definitional orientation toward nuclear weapons" in general. In so doing, Eisenhower secured four rhetorical advantages but also, in Holloway's judgment, raised significant questions about "the power of language to subvert public participation and democratic debate."

Nowhere was the power of language to subvert democracy more pronounced than in "The Case of Eisenhower Versus McCarthyism." In the fourth chapter, Thomas Rosteck explores both the content and form of Eisenhower's public rhetoric about McCarthy, McCarthyism, and internal subversion. Rosteck argues that "Eisenhower created an inconsistent rhetorical world" because the president's arguments showed "an acceptance of the *form*" of McCarthyism. Utilization of this argumentative form had certain rhetorical advantages, Rosteck argues, but in the end promulgated "the vision of a world starkly divided" and thus helped to "legitimate" the "paranoia of the McCarthy movement."

In chapter five, "Eisenhower and the Indochina Problem," Gregory A. Olson traces Dwight Eisenhower's thinking on the problem of Vietnam using both public and private sources. He finds that Eisenhower "expressed belief in the domino theory" some "two years before assuming the presidency," but that his thinking throughout his eight years in office was affected more by the situational demands of the moment than by adherence to any particular theory or a priori belief system. By taking rhetorical refuge in the "miracle" of Diem, the "Eisenhower administration trapped itself and future administrations," says Olson, "into a commitment to prove the veracity of that rhetoric."

J. Michael Hogan investigates "Eisenhower and Open Skies: A Case Study in 'Psychological Warfare'" in chapter six. He argues that scholars have failed "to appreciate Eisenhower's concern with 'psychological strategy,'" and offers Eisenhower's Open Skies proposal at the 1955 Geneva Conference as "a classic expression of that strategy." Far from being a failure, Open Skies, according to Hogan, "did precisely what it was *designed* to do: it recaptured the propaganda offensive from the Soviet Union and cultivated favorable world opinion."

In "The Rhetoric of Distancing: Eisenhower's Suez Crisis Speech, 31 October, 1956," Richard B. Gregg shows how historical and contemporary situational factors shaped Eisenhower's response to the coordinated attack by Britain, France, and Israel on the Suez Canal. Working from the premise that "all public addresses constitute a form of symbolic inducement," Gregg finds Eisenhower's speech to be "a strategic enterprise" that functioned to "direct intention and reaction" in such a way as to "distance the events Eisenhower refers to from the United States and thus from any major concern of the American public."

From the crisis at Suez the book next turns to the "Crisis at Little Rock: Eisenhower, History, and Mediated Political Realities." Steven R. Goldzwig and George N. Dionisopoulos seek to create a "richer understanding of the rhetorical dimensions of the mass media" as the events in Little Rock were refracted through the analytical lenses of newspapers, magazines, radio, and television. Viewing both the mediated reports and the subsequent history of those reports as "rhetorical constructions," the authors conclude that Eisenhower's "public style" was "incommensurate with the mediated imperatives" he faced.

In chapter nine, "Eisenhower and Sputnik: The Irony of Failed Leadership," David Henry argues that the Eisenhower administration made "severe miscalculations" in developing a rhetorical strategy to counter the launching of the first earth satellite by the Soviet Union. Henry finds that Eisenhower made "a poor initial assessment of the situation and audience" and that such a miscalculation "led to weak strategic choices" at the inception of the campaign to recapture public confidence. Such strategic errors raise questions, says Henry, about "the potential of rhetorical leadership in the age of a television presidency."

Lawrence W. Haapanen discusses "The Missed Opportunity: The U-2 and Paris" in chapter ten. By tracing the "rhetorical trajectory" of Eisenhower's comments throughout the month of May 1960, the author argues that the president's rhetoric was designed "to bolster his public image" rather than to inform or explain. Eisenhower's 25 May 1960 address to the nation is examined in detail and found to provide "the calming appearance of stability and continuity rather than the complexion of an abrupt and foreboding break" in superpower relations.

Chapter eleven sheds "New Light on Eisenhower's Farewell Address." Charles J. G. Griffin argues that the warning about the military-industrial complex "illlustrates Eisenhower's 'hidden hand' rhetorical style at work." The author suggests that Eisenhower "saw his own farewell as an opportunity to emulate the rhetorical precedent of his hero," George Washington, "by striking back at his foes without compromising, indeed, while enhancing, his stature as a man of principle." The farewell address thus became a vehicle for both political and programmatic ends.

The volume concludes with "Eisenhower's Rhetorical Leadership: An Interpretation." Based on the literature concerned with presidential leadership, studies of Eisenhower's leadership abilities, personal interviews and archival data, and the evidence adduced in chapters one through eleven, Martin J. Medhurst offers an overview of Eisenhower as rhetorician. In so doing, the author explores both the strengths and weaknesses of Eisenhower's rhetorical leadership and reveals the conceptual foundations from which that leadership emerged.

Over thirty years ago, Richard Neustadt wrote that presidential power "is the power to persuade."[3] While many scholars have repeated that assessment, it has only been within the last dozen years that historians, political scientists, journalists, and scholars of speech communication have begun to unpack the implications of Neustadt's insight. The idea of a "rhetorical presidency,"[4] first introduced in 1981, has now become a recognized, if not always valued, construct for evaluating presidential leadership. Eisenhower scholarship, too, has begun to reflect the importance of rhetoric as a tool of statecraft, starting with Fred I. Greenstein's *The Hidden-Hand Presidency: Eisenhower as Leader* (1982) and extending most recently to Martin J. Medhurst's *Dwight D. Eisenhower: Strategic Communicator* (1993) and *Eisenhower's War of Words: Rhetoric and Leadership* (1994).

As the first volume in a new series on Rhetoric and Public Affairs, *Eisenhower's War of Words* raises as many questions as it answers. In so doing, it acknowledges rhetoric to be as much a method of inquiry as a set of propositions about how to compose effective orations or essays. More than a set of techniques or the theory of stylized discourse, rhetoric is a way of thinking about and acting in the world as we know it, a world replete with problems, imperfections, competing interests, and strategic goals. By examining this world of "symbolic inducement,"[5] the series in Rhetoric and Public Affairs seeks to enter the ongoing conversation in which, to paraphrase one of the ancients, people in community make decisions concerning the good of that community. So defined, both rhetoric and community take on expansive roles. That is what we intend this new series to do—to expand our understandings of both rhetoric as a method of inquiry and our sense of what constitutes a community concern or public affair, and in so expanding to illuminate our understanding of ourselves, our neighbors, and our world.

## NOTES

1. "Inaugural Address," *Public Papers of the Presidents of the United States: Dwight D. Eisenhower, 1953* (Washington, D.C.: Government Printing Office, 1960), 1-8.
2. Martin J. Medhurst, Robert L. Ivie, Philip Wander, and Robert L. Scott, *Cold War Rhetoric: Strategy, Metaphor, and Ideology* (Westport, Conn.: Greenwood Press, 1990), 19.
3. Richard E. Neustadt, *Presidential Power: The Politics of Leadership, With Reflections on Johnson and Nixon* (1960; rpt. and expanded New York: John Wiley and Sons, Inc., 1976), 78.
4. James W. Ceaser, Glen E. Thurow, Jeffrey Tulis, and Joseph M. Bissette, "The Rise of the Rhetorical Presidency," *Presidential Studies Quarterly* 11 (1981): 158-171. See also Jeffrey K. Tulis, *The Rhetorical Presidency* (Princeton: Princeton University Press, 1987).
5. On the relationship between rhetoric as a method of inquiry and symbolic inducement see Richard B. Gregg, "The Criticism of Symbolic Inducement: A Critical-Theoretical Connection." In *Speech Communication in the 20th Century*, ed. Thomas W. Benson (Carbondale: Southern Illinois University Press, 1985), 41-62.

Eisenhower with cold warrior C. D. Jackson

Robert L.
Ivie

# Eisenhower as Cold Warrior

The common image of Dwight Eisenhower—as a benign
warrior for peace who dedicated his presidency to a failed quest for détente
with the Soviet Union—severely underestimates his impact as an agent of Cold
War acculturation. This misleading perception of Eisenhower as a peaceful
rather than cold warrior persists within a confluence of otherwise divergent
historical assessments of his administration. Initially, historians considered
Eisenhower a weak, passive president who, disaffected by politics and befud-
dled by the complexities of government, delegated the daily conduct of foreign
affairs to his secretary of state, John Foster Dulles. The president thereby
remained above the fray while speaking benignly of peace, unity, and cooperation. Later, Robert A. Divine's revisionist account of Eisenhower and the Cold
War made "Ike's pursuit of peace . . . the dominant feature of his presidency,
and the failure to secure it his greatest disappointment."[1] Revisionists in general credited Eisenhower with a strategic use of executive power to minimize
America's involvement in international conflict. Recently, a postrevisionist
view has emerged to portray Eisenhower as a skilled leader nevertheless confounded by the complexities of his circumstances. Thus, according to Chester
J. Pach, Jr. and Elmo Richardson, the president proved to be "better at assessing the shortcomings of past policies than at devising new ones" and, despite
his "longing for peace," had to adopt dangerous methods of "waging Cold
War."[2]

Each of these perspectives overlooks the lasting influence of Eisenhower's
Cold War presidency on the nation's political culture largely because of three
distracting factors. First, from the beginning of his initial term until his final
days in office, and consistently thereafter, Eisenhower cultivated the image of
an aspiring peacemaker; he entitled the second volume of his memoirs *Waging
Peace, 1956-1961* and, in his farewell address, expressed disappointment that
permanent peace ultimately had eluded him.[3] In reality, these were sincere but
strategic reaffirmations of the nation's mythic quest for absolute security from
foreign threats, a goal not only unattainable but also misleading in its implication of the criterion by which to evaluate Eisenhower's presidency.[4] Measured

by the standard of perfect peace, his administration was at best a partial success and at worst a complete failure. Understood, however, as a strategic commitment to sustaining an international peace offensive, Eisenhower's rhetoric of unrequited devotion to worldwide cooperation and global harmony takes on new significance as an instrument for bracing public morale over a prolonged period of Cold War.

A second distracting factor was Eisenhower's relationship to John Foster Dulles, who provided a bellicose counterpoint to the president's crusade for peace, which created the impression of an administration at odds with itself and raised in turn the false issue of who controlled foreign policy, the chief executive or his secretary of state? Instead of discordant voices competing for control of the national agenda, Eisenhower's and Dulles's nominal differences were rhetorical counterparts in an integrated campaign to underscore Soviet intransigence.[5] They amounted to a useful variation on the twin themes of unfulfilled aspirations for peace and continuing threats to the national security. Together, these two themes constituted a crusade for peace premised on the dawn of universal freedom.

Third, Eisenhower's evident limitations as an orator distracted attention from the rhetorical sophistication of his presidency. As Richard E. Crable has observed, judgments of the president's "oratorical ability are consistently unfavorable."[6] When speaking from manuscript, his delivery regularly appeared halting, dull, and uninspired, while his choice of words frequently sounded benign and convoluted. When speaking impromptu, his verbiage could befuddle the most alert listeners. Thus, the sound of Eisenhower's presidency, according to Roderick P. Hart, was that of a "wordy, fuzzy, somewhat arcane speaker."[7] Yet, as Martin J. Medhurst has argued, Eisenhower was a far more strategic communicator than his public persona would otherwise suggest.[8] He was, in fact, according to Crable, one of "the nation's great political communicators."[9] The public not only liked Ike, they trusted the sincerity of his appeals to their deepest fears and fundamental values.

Looking beyond the illusion of Eisenhower as a sincere but uninspired and outflanked crusader for peace in his own time helps clarify his contribution to what, in another context, David L. Anderson has called the "pervasive pathologies in American society."[10] Eisenhower—himself a product of American political culture—became a powerful rhetorical agent of Cold War acculturation through the medium of his presidency, thus leaving a permanent mark on a national psyche already obsessed with absolute security. In short, Ike's rhetorical legacy as a cold warrior was to institutionalize an age of peril. As he said in his radio address to the nation on 19 May 1953, "The truth is that our danger cannot be fixed or confined to one specific instant. We live in an age of peril."[11]

The strategic framework erected by Eisenhower to prolong indefinitely Soviet-American rivalry consisted of three interlinked parts; each merits discussion as a reflection of the president's political and rhetorical craftsmanship. His grand plan integrated: (1) a foreign policy that relied on nuclear weaponry to achieve "reasonable security" at an affordable cost with; (2) a coordinated program of psychological warfare to sustain an American peace offensive which; (3) was based on a rhetorical strategy that totalized the Communist threat and thus blocked the road to "true peace." Understanding Eisenhower's leadership requires a keen appreciation of how his policy, program, and strategy were contrived to commit the nation to a protracted period of perceived imperilment.

## REASONABLE SECURITY THROUGH NUCLEAR DETERRENCE

The first part of the president's plan for institutionalizing an age of peril was to adopt the cost-effective policy of nuclear deterrence in order to achieve what he termed "reasonable security." Maintaining an "organized, effective resistance" to Soviet communism "over a long period of years," he told his old friend General Alfred M. Gruenther, was "possible only with a healthy American economy."[12] Six months later, on 30 October 1953, Eisenhower approved NSC 162/2; this basic national security policy endorsed "a strong military posture, with emphasis on the capability of inflicting massive retaliatory damage by offensive striking power."[13] The administration's New Look amounted to a gamble that Soviet aggression would be deterred by the fear of nuclear retaliation, a bluff that could save defense expenditures and keep the economy strong if it succeeded, but would destroy civilization if it failed. Ike, who loved the game of bridge, was holding a nuclear trump he hoped never to have to play.

Eisenhower's positive view of reasonable security, conveyed to the public as the best they could expect in an imperfect world, necessarily invoked the negative corollary of lingering insecurity. National insecurity was the unspoken residue of reasonable security. "We want adequate security. We want no more than adequacy. But we will accept nothing less," Eisenhower declared.[14] Spending $200 billion over a five-year period to maintain the nation's military strength "can give us no more than relative security; only true peace can give us true security." Peace preserved by arms alone produced "merely a precarious security."[15]

Even reasonable security, achieved at the risk of nuclear annihilation, could not be sustained without also gambling on the availability of collective and mutual security through alliances, accompanied by military and economic aid. The president insisted, in the face of strong opposition, that the nation's own defense would be enhanced by relying on the conventional forces of those other countries willing to help contain communism. By reducing America's armed forces, especially its army, to effect substantial savings, Eisenhower increased the nation's dependence on collective security. In his words, "The policy we pursue will recognize the truth that no single country, even one so powerful as ours, can alone defend the liberty of all nations threatened by Communist aggression from without and subversion within. Mutual security means effective mutual cooperation. For the United States, this means that, as a matter of common sense and national interest, we shall give help to other nations in the measure that they strive earnestly to do their full share of the common task."[16] The United States could no longer insure its safety in isolation as an island fortress nor alone as a military colossus.[17] "We live in a shrunken world," Eisenhower observed, which requires collective security through "voluntary association" with diverse and developing nations.[18]

Reliance on mutual and collective security suggested a degree of vulnerability. As Eisenhower explained to the public, "We could not possibly station our troops all over the world to prevent the overflow of Communism. It is much more economical and vastly more effective to follow and strengthen our system of collective security."[19] Mutual security programs formed "a saving shield of freedom" at an affordable price.[20] Thus, the insecurity associated with increasing America's dependency on its allies was motivated by an even deeper fear that capitalism would defeat itself by requiring more spending on defense than the nation could afford.[21]

The nation's dependency on Eisenhower's cheap, but perilous, New Look policy of nuclear deterrence, augmented by collective and mutual security, served more to bring the United States to the brink of war around the world—in Lebanon, Quemoy and Matsu, Berlin, and Indochina—than to promote peace positively and actively. A precarious peace was preserved by rattling nuclear sabers; by extending America's alliance system beyond NATO to include regional defense pacts such as SEATO and CENTO, both of which drew artificial new lines of confrontation with international communism; and by direct intervention in the affairs of nations, including the CIA's covert operations in Iran and Guatemala.

Nuclear brinkmanship on a global scale not only "codified" containment as the nation's basic Cold War policy, as Cecil V. Crabb, Jr. and Kevin V. Mulcahy have noted, but also precipitated what H. W. Brands has called "the age of vulnerability" in which the administration was forced to conclude that "national security no longer existed. The best they could hope for was a policy that would minimize national insecurity."[22] The safety of the United States depended as never before on the rationality and good behavior of its mortal enemy. The nation thus risked nuclear suicide to defend global interests not necessarily vital to its security.[23] National safety required continuing faith in the superiority of American technology over that of its nuclear rival—a faith severely shaken in 1957 when the Soviet Union launched its Sputnik satellite into earth orbit. These were the conditions that led to the "permanent armaments industry of vast proportions" which, in his farewell address, Eisenhower claimed he had been "compelled to create." Although the president warned that this new "military-industrial complex" entailed "grave implications" the nation could ill afford to ignore, his administration nevertheless had established a structural imperative for escalating the arms race and perpetuating nuclear fear.[24]

Eisenhower was a cold warrior by design, not a man who left the presidency disappointed over his failure to achieve a lasting peace. As Stephen E. Ambrose has observed, Eisenhower "made foreign policy. . . . He ran the show," and he "accepted the risk of an expanding arms race over the risk of trusting the Russians."[25] What Ambrose and others seem not to have recognized, however, was Eisenhower's willingness to take short-term calculated risks to increase the chance of achieving true peace sometime in the distant future, after communism's eventual defeat. He did not anticipate success for his crusade for true peace and universal freedom after only eight years in the White House; instead, he led the nation down the long and perilous path of reasonable security, mustering America's material and psychological resources for a sustained and uncompromising conflict with atheistic communism. "We must be ready to dare all for our country," the president proclaimed in his first inaugural address, "for history does not long entrust the care of freedom to the weak or the timid. We must acquire proficiency in defense and display stamina in purpose."[26]

## PSYCHOLOGICAL WARFARE AND EISENHOWER'S PEACE OFFENSIVE

In order to sustain the nation's stamina in the face of a prolonged risk of nuclear holocaust, Eisenhower committed his administration to a program of psychological warfare designed to promote a coordinated peace offensive. Explaining his Cold War aim of securing freedom by peaceful means in the 1952 presidential campaign, candidate Eisenhower endorsed psychological warfare as a "struggle for the minds and wills of humanity." In his view:

> Every significant act of government should be so timed and so directed at a principal target, and so related to other governmental actions, that it will produce the maximum effect. It means that our government in this critical matter [of psychological warfare] will no longer be divided into air-tight compartments.

> It means that, in carrying out a national policy, every department and every agency of government that can make a useful contribution will bring its full strength to bear under a coordinated program. We shall no longer have a Department of State that deals with foreign policy in an aloof cloister; a Defense Establishment that makes military appraisals in a vacuum; a Mutual

Security Administration that, with sovereign independence, spends billions overseas. We must bring the dozens of agencies and bureaus into concerted action under an overall scheme of strategy. And we must have a firm hand on the tiller to sail the ship along a consistent course.

In practice, this "peaceful tool" of psychological warfare would be employed not only to "render unreliable, in the minds of the Kremlin rulers, the hundreds of millions enslaved in the occupied and satellite nations" but also to bolster "the spirit, the resolve, the determination with which we [the American public] bend to our tasks." Thus, Eisenhower promised to appoint "a man of exceptional qualifications to handle the national psychological effort," a man who would have "the full confidence of and direct access to the Chief Executive" and would work "through a revitalized and reconstructed National Security Council."[27]

C. D. Jackson, the man whom Eisenhower appointed as his advisor on psychological warfare, assured Walt W. Rostow (a fellow psychological warrior) that the president-elect grasped the concept of political warfare and its relationship to high-level diplomacy and that, once Eisenhower was inaugurated, he would seize the initiative through a "long term *plan* to persuade friend and foe that we are for peace."[28] The plan began to take shape quickly after Eisenhower took office. Within the first year, an Operations Coordinating Board was established as an arm of the National Security Council to plan and implement the psychological warfare offensive. The stated purpose of this "sustained program"—initially designed in March to be launched, following Stalin's death, by a speech Eisenhower eventually delivered on 16 April to the American Society of Newspaper Editors—was fourfold: (1) to undermine the fragile unity among the new Soviet leaders; (2) to associate the aspirations of the Soviet and satellite peoples more closely with a "clear and fresh vision of American purposes"; (3) to unify the free world around an American-led campaign for peace; and (4) "to provide a new and more firm base *within the United States* for the pursuit of American interests and objectives." Henceforth, propaganda was to be integrated with diplomacy and foreign policy at the highest levels of government, and foreign policy was to be linked to the president's message, strategically entitled "The Chance for Peace."[29]

The "adequate merchandising" of the president's speech, according to C. D. Jackson, would require the completion of numerous tasks. The domestic press, radio, and television would have to be prepared for the message, as would foreign press representatives in Washington. A full text of the speech would be cabled to the heads of U.S. missions abroad, with a covering memorandum from the State Department to explain the text's importance and to insure that it would be called to the attention of colleagues in the diplomatic corps as well as the foreign and prime ministers of host countries. "Our Ambassadors and Ministers must be made to understand that they are responsible for an immediate merchandising-in-depth of this Message to friend and foe," Jackson emphasized, and they must "firmly and immediately" dismiss any "psychological warfare overtones or implications." Furthermore, USIS missions and the public affairs or press attachés of the U.S. missions would be instructed to have the full text of the speech translated and distributed widely in pamphlet form throughout each country. U.S. ambassadors would hold press conferences emphasizing the essential points of the president's message, and the International Information Administration would prepare editorials and feature articles "to be fed to foreign journalists who may want to make these ideas their own." Further steps were envisioned to coordinate with Henry Cabot Lodge, Jr., the U.S. Ambassador to the United Nations, as well as the Voice of America, Radio Free Europe, the CIA, all of Eisenhower's cabinet officers, the information chiefs of the various government departments and agencies, and others.[30] Films of the president's speech were distributed worldwide, and motion pictures were produced to explain and dramatize Eisenhower's essential points.[31]

The president concurred with the strategy of merchandising his words, even when it required covert means. Telling America's story, he wrote confidentially, would require in most instances concealing the hand of government, including "arrangements with all sorts of privately operated enterprises in the field of entertainment, dramatics, music, and so on" as well as "clandestine arrangements with magazines, newspapers and other periodicals, and book publishers."[32] Thus, the basic pattern of Eisenhower's peace offensive was established early in his presidency with events surrounding "The Chance for Peace" speech. The pattern would be repeated throughout his tenure to capitalize fully on his "Atoms for Peace" speech, his "Open Skies" proposal, and other official communications designed to bolster public opinion by characterizing America's Cold War policy, including its dangerous dependency on nuclear deterrence, as the only option remaining after several good-faith initiatives for peace were rebuffed by an intransigent and untrustworthy adversary.[33] The basic goal of psychological warfare was to win the peace on America's terms over the long haul—while minimizing the chances of war in the short term—through the skillful exploitation of opportunities that "might advance the real disintegration of the Soviet Empire."[34] As Eisenhower stressed to the members of the National Security Council on 5 March 1953, any presidential statement following the death of Joseph Stalin would be "a psychological and not a diplomatic move."[35] He also understood, as Richard A. Melanson has noted, that his foreign policy could not succeed without cultivating a domestic consensus.[36]

## EISENHOWER'S RHETORICAL STRATEGY

To achieve the goals of the psychological warfare program, Eisenhower employed a rhetorical strategy with two key themes. Both were chosen to reconcile his professed aspirations for peace with his calculated reliance on nuclear deterrence and willingness to engage in brinkmanship. The age of peril would have to be extended indefinitely, Eisenhower suggested, because (1) the global tide of Communist barbarism that threatened to engulf civilization (2) had blocked the road to true peace, thus condemning the world to travel the dark and perilous road of nuclear deterrence until communism receded. Together, these themes drew upon culturally sanctioned imagery to reinforce deep national anxieties and inspire unwavering courage in the face of ceaseless danger. Thus, the Cold War was conducted rhetorically as a profound struggle between absolute good and evil, with the enemy's unconditional surrender as the only acceptable result. The president's crusade for peace contemplated no compromise with freedom's nemesis, even at the risk of nuclear annihilation, for true peace required a degree of cooperation that aggressive communism was incapable of providing.

### Totalizing the Communist Threat

Early in his campaign for the presidency, General Eisenhower spoke bluntly of the absolute threat to civilization posed by "Communist barbarism." Addressing the American Legion in Madison Square Garden on 25 August 1952, he lamented the tragedy of lost opportunity following the great victory over fascism in 1945. "Hope for peace among men disappeared under the monstrous advance of Communist tyranny," he declared. One evil foe had been vanquished only to be replaced by an even more virile enemy of freedom. "This tyranny is primitive in its brutalism. It is insatiable in its lust for conquest. It is committed to subversion and revolution and war until the Continents are its slave camps and all humankind are its chattel."

Eisenhower called the roll of "captive peoples" who, once independent, were "now suffocating under the Russian pall." The victims of Communist barbarism included not only Poles, Czechs, and other Eastern Europeans who were "blood kin to us," but also "more than five hundred million human beings" held captive on the Kremlin's Asiatic periphery. America would never quit searching, he proclaimed, "for the peaceful instruments of their liberation."

These captive nations, which had been "propagandized, beaten, terrorized into a uniform, submissive mass," provided "harsh evidence that dire peril stalks every free nation today. Tyranny must feed on new conquests—or wither." An objective of the "Red Cancer" was the "gradual strangulation of industrial America." Hence, the present "threat posed by the Soviets" placed the United States "in greater peril" than at any time in its history. Americans could never "rest content until the tidal mud of aggressive Communism [had] receded within its own borders." In the meantime, they must steadfastly "preach" against "this paganism" the values of human dignity, freedom, and brotherhood "under the fatherhood of God."[37]

Thus, Eisenhower's campaign rhetoric totalized the threat to freedom by relying on the timeless image of civilization imperiled by savagery.[38] Communism was portrayed as primitive, barbaric, monstrous, and brutal. Communist pagans captured, enslaved, terrorized, beat, and strangled free peoples, reducing them to mere chattel. An insatiable lust for conquest goaded the Communist predator to stalk its prey relentlessly and to feed on each new victim, much like a cancer consumes its host. Freedom could never be safe in such an uncivilized world.

This was the image of relentless danger that carried over into Eisenhower's presidential speeches. In his first inaugural address he observed that the "forces of good and evil are massed and armed and opposed as rarely before in history." America's enemies "know no god but force, no devotion but its use. They tutor men in treason. They feed upon the hunger of others. Whatever defies them, they torture, especially the truth." Freedom, he proclaimed, was "pitted against slavery" and charged with the responsibility of saving humanity "from preying upon itself."[39] Six months later, the president warned that "the struggle in which freedom today is engaged is quite literally a total and universal struggle. It engages every aspect of our lives. It is waged in every arena in which a challenged civilization must fight to live," confronting the free world with no less than a military, economic, political, scientific, intellectual, and spiritual struggle "for the soul of man."[40] America would forget only at its own peril, Eisenhower again cautioned, the fundamental truth "that the Communist dictatorship, ruthless, strong, insatiable, is determined to establish its sway over all the world" by using "force and the threat of force" along with "bribery, subversion, and sabotage" as well as "propaganda."[41]

The warning was renewed in the president's second inaugural address. "Rarely has this earth known such peril as today," he declared. The whole world was split by the "divisive force" of "International Communism and the power that it controls. The designs of that power, dark in purpose, are clear in practice. It strives to seal forever the fate of those it has enslaved. It strives to break the ties that unite the free."[42] One year later, Eisenhower's 1958 State of the Union address featured a strong admonition against ignoring a Soviet threat that was "unique in history" because of "its all-inclusiveness."[43] The next month, he reminded his countrymen that the Soviet Union had "swallowed up its neighbors" and had deployed tanks "to crush attempts to gain freedom."[44] In July, he reiterated that "the free nations of the world are under constant attack by

International Communism. This attack is planned on a broad front and carefully directed. Its ultimate goal is world domination."[45] America provided a necessary "shield for freedom" against the "predatory force" of "atheistic imperialism."[46] Even Eisenhower's 1961 farewell to the nation underscored the need of free peoples to remain forever alert: "We face a hostile ideology—global in scope, atheistic in character, ruthless in purpose, and insidious in method. Unhappily the danger it poses promises to be of indefinite duration."[47]

Thus, using language employed by Harry S. Truman to inaugurate the Cold War, Eisenhower portrayed the Communist threat as pervasive, persistent, global, and total—a conflict that would continue indefinitely until either slavery or freedom prevailed. The symbolism of civilization pitted against savagery was compelling but unsettling to those who preferred the hope of peace over the despair of perpetual friction and the eventuality of nuclear war. At the very least, they wanted reassurance that the administration was trying to avoid war with the Soviet Union and that peace remained a goal worthy of pursuit. Fear alone was not enough to sustain the public through an age of peril. They needed more than images of Communist brutality, enslavement, and atheism to bolster their courage and preserve their faith in a prolonged Cold War. Without assurances, their misguided fear might necessitate costly preparations for a hot war to quell the Communist threat.

Eisenhower understood better than anyone that fear could degenerate into despair or foster desperation unless faith was restored in the quest for peace. The positive vision of a crusade for peace was required to convert fear into courage and to uphold the national spirit over the long and treacherous course of Cold War. Even while campaigning for election to the presidency, Eisenhower had warned the nation not to panic at the sight of Communist barbarism:

> Fear, induced by peril, is a climate that fosters militarism and the conversion of a nation into an arsenal for war. Fear is a climate that nourishes bankruptcy in dollars and morals alike. Those afraid seek security in the heedless extravagance that breeds waste of substance and corruption of men. Fear is a climate that, if long endured, is as costly in its toll on material resources, on lives, on the spirit of men as defeat in war. In an era of chronic fear can be heard the death rattle of a nation.
>
> From this time forward, we Americans cannot tolerate the preparation and execution of our program in a climate of fear and hysteria. Day by day we must follow a course which all our people may understand and support with confidence; and we must not abate our efforts until we have banished from the free world the last probability of Communist aggression.
>
> The course to peace is the establishment of conditions that will abolish fear and build confidence.[48]

After his election, Eisenhower continued to counsel against despair and desperation and to preach faith in the future. In his first State of the Union address, he observed that the free world could not "indefinitely remain in a posture of paralyzed tension" and that his administration, therefore, had begun to define "a new, positive foreign policy" which was "dedicated to making the free world secure" while "envision[ing] all peaceful methods and devices."[49] Five years later, Eisenhower used the same occasion to reiterate his commitment to peace and to warn that "we could make no more tragic mistake than merely to concentrate on military strength. For if we did only this, the future would hold nothing for the world but an Age of Terror. And so our second task is to do the constructive work of building a genuine peace."[50]

The road to genuine peace, however, was made rhetorically inaccessible by the president even as he held it up to the nation as a symbol of hope in an extended era of nuclear peril. Eisenhower's rhetorical strategy not only totalized the Communist threat but also made the Cold War self-perpetuating by fabricating tests of peaceful intent the Soviets could only fail. The genius of Eisenhower's Cold War rhetoric was its capacity to promote a crusade for freedom as a quest for peace.

### Blocking the Road to Peace

Two conceptual images are the keys to Eisenhower's strategy of promoting Cold War as a quest for peace. One is the imagery of two roads; the other is the image of light versus dark. Together, they constructed a motive for prolonging the Soviet-American rivalry indefinitely.

The image of two roads, one light and the other dark, was advanced systematically in Eisenhower's first major foreign policy address. Delivered on 16 April 1953, just over a month after Joseph Stalin's death, "The Chance for Peace" speech was designed to initiate the president's peace offensive. On 21 February, Eisenhower had commended to Dulles an idea advanced by Charles E. Wilson for a presidential "Peace Message" launched as "a new approach to a Peace Front."[51] Speech writers were instructed to draft a presidential statement that would serve as "the opening gun in the political warfare campaign" and thereby "exploit" the "vulnerability created by Stalin's death."[52] C. D. Jackson believed this was "the first really big propaganda opportunity offered to our side for a long time."[53]

The speech employed the contrast between light and dark to distinguish between the two roads—the inaccessible road to genuine peace and the dangerous road of Cold War. The well-lighted and safe road was held up as an alluring ideal, a timeless aspiration renewed with each cycle of life. "In this spring of 1953," the president began, "the free world weighs one question above all others: the chance for a just peace for all peoples."[54] The road to a just peace—"the way chosen by the United States"—was "plainly marked" by the principles of freedom, international cooperation, respect for inalienable rights, economic well-being, nonviolence, and an honest understanding of other nations. In short, genuine peace was premised on an absolute assurance of political and economic freedom. America aspired to lift the burden of arms and fear from the backs of humanity so that they would "find before them a golden age of freedom and of peace."

The free world, however, could not resume its "quest for a just peace" until some "genuine evidence of peaceful purpose" was forthcoming from the new leaders of the Soviet Union, since "the shadow of fear again has darkly lengthened across the world." The new Soviet leadership was presented with a "precious opportunity to awaken" and help "turn the black tide of events," an opportunity that amounted to a clear and simple "test" of their intentions as measured by their deeds. The "first great step" down the road of genuine peace would include the conclusion of an honorable armistice in Korea, an end to "the direct and indirect attacks upon the security of Indochina and Malaya," a "free and united Germany, with a government based upon free and secret elections," an end to the "unnatural division of Europe," and eventually progress on agreements to reduce the burden of conventional and nuclear weapons. If the new leadership was not willing to persuade through deeds, the president asked, "where then is the concrete evidence of the Soviet Union's concern for peace?"

Eisenhower's test of Soviet intentions was clear, but the outcome was rigged. As Ambrose has pointed out, the president understood his test consisted of demands that were unacceptable to the Soviet leadership. The Soviets would never consider withdrawing from Eastern Europe, any suggestion of reunifying Germany "gave them nightmares," and they were unalterably opposed to on-site inspections of military installations within their borders. Moreover, their ability to halt guerrilla warfare was questionable, even if they wanted to bring conflict to an end in Indochina.[55] Thus, Eisenhower's rhetorical trap was well set. "If we strive but fail" to seize this precious chance for peace, he concluded, "and the world remains armed against itself, it at least need be divided no longer in its clear knowledge of who has condemned humankind to this fate." The well-lighted path to genuine peace could not be traveled by the United States alone. It required the full cooperation of all parties, including the Soviet Union, united in freedom. Thus, the quest for peace could only resume when the Russians finally conformed to "our firm faith that God created men to enjoy, not destroy, the fruits of the earth and of their own toil."

With the road to genuine peace blocked by Soviet intransigence, Eisenhower left his listeners no option other than to tread down the "dread road," where the worst to be feared was atomic war and the best to be expected was "a life of perpetual fear and tension." This way of life, "under the cloud of threatening war," left "humanity hanging from a cross of iron" because the Soviet government insisted on seeking its security "not in mutual trust and mutual aid but in *force.* . . . Security was to be sought by denying it to all others." Nuclear deterrence, then, was a risk necessitated by the shadow of fear under which humankind had been forced to travel until it could someday resume again its journey down the road to true peace. Although "the hope of free men remain[ed] stubborn and brave" and rejected the "crude counsel of despair," "vigilance and sacrifice" were still the essential price to be paid for preserving liberty.

The editorial writer for *The Houston Chronicle* captured Eisenhower's point most vividly when he observed that the president had "extended to the rulers of Russia Thursday an olive branch held in a mailed glove that covered the hand of friendship. . . . [His address] put the blame for the cold war where it belongs—on the Soviet leaders." The president had succeeded in seizing the initiative and driving "a wedge between the people and rulers of Russia and the satellite states."[56] In short, he had given his people something to cheer about, including the hope of eventual victory, as they resigned themselves to a long and risky journey down the dreaded path of Cold War.

For the remainder of his presidency, Eisenhower's crusade for freedom continued to operate under the guise of a quest for peace. His peace offensive against communism served to bolster public morale, both by preserving hope of someday walking the high road of genuine peace and by providing carefully crafted demonstrations of continuing Soviet contempt for American gestures of reconciliation. The Cold War became rhetorically self-sustaining as the Soviets continued to fail each new test of peaceful intentions, thereby reinforcing Eisenhower's image as a sincere but thwarted champion of international harmony.

The president's "Atoms for Peace" address, delivered before the U.N. General Assembly on 8 December 1953, is a particularly revealing case in point. As Medhurst has demonstrated, it was an artfully designed exercise in Cold War rhetoric that, despite the administration's representations to the contrary, was aimed at advancing the American peace offensive and achieving a psychological victory over the Soviet Union. While designed to appear as a step toward nuclear disarmament, the speech was, in fact, aimed at preparing the American public for an age of peril while publicly placing the Soviets on the spot. In Medhurst's words, "Even if the American offer was sincere, it placed the U.S.S.R. in a position of either accepting the offer (and thereby implicitly testifying to America's long-professed desire for peace) or rejecting the offer (and thereby appearing to the world at large as an aggressor unwilling to explore a plan that, as presented by Eisenhower, would benefit directly the underdeveloped nations as well as the cause of international peace)."[57]

The president set his rhetorical trap with the same symbolism he had used in April. America's "quest for peace," he declared, was to help the world "move out of the dark chamber of horrors into the light, to find a way by which the

minds of men, the hopes of men, the souls of men everywhere can move forward toward peace and happiness and well-being."[58] The alternative to this
quest was "to confirm the hopeless finality of a belief that two atomic colossi
are doomed malevolently to eye each other indefinitely across a trembling
world." Thus, "every new avenue of peace, no matter how dimly discernible,
should be explored." One such avenue, he proposed, would be to seek, in cooperation with the Soviet Union, a solution to the atomic armaments race and to
create, again with the Soviet Union's cooperation, an internationally controlled
pool of fissionable materials to promote the peaceful uses of atomic energy.
The test of Soviet intentions, of course, was whether they would respond in
good faith to the president's gesture. "The United States is prepared to undertake these explorations in good faith," Eisenhower vowed. "Any [negotiating]
partner of the United States acting in the same good faith will find the United
States a not unreasonable or ungenerous associate." Thus, it was the Soviet
Union, not the United States, that doomed the world to travel the dark road of
nuclear peril.

Eisenhower reiterated this theme of forced imperilment often in his public
speeches. On 15 July 1955, for instance, he told the nation that, while the free
people of the world hate war and want peace, they could not expose their
rights, their privileges, their homes, their wives, and their children to the risk
of disarming their countries. "We want to make it perfectly clear," the president stressed, "that these armaments do not reflect the way we want to live.
They merely reflect the way, under present conditions, we have to live." He
would go to Geneva to do his best "to start the world on the beginning of a
new road, a road that may be long and difficult, but which, if faithfully followed, will lead us on to a better and fuller life."[59] Once again, the Soviets had
blocked the road to genuine peace.

Russia flunked Ike's test again in October 1956 when in Hungary and other
captive nations of Eastern Europe there was "the dawning of a new day" that
promised the "light of liberty soon [would] shine again in this darkness," if the
Soviet Union acted faithfully on its announced intention to withdraw its ruling
advisors, and perhaps even its occupying forces, from Poland, Hungary, and
Rumania. These acts, should they actually occur, would provide the world with
"the greatest forward stride toward justice, trust and understanding among
nations in our generation."[60] Failure to act on such promises, however, as in
Berlin two years later, added yet another "stumbling block that International
Communism has placed along the road to peace."[61]

Thus, it should have come as no surprise when Eisenhower concluded at the
end of his farewell address that lasting peace was not in sight. Although steady
progress toward the ultimate goal had been made, he suggested, the road to
true peace remained impassable. The best that could be said was that war had
been avoided.[62] The age of peril would persist indefinitely.

## THE PATHOLOGY OF PERPETUAL PERIL

The voice of a cold warrior behind the mask of peace coaxed America down a perilous path of nuclear deterrence in search of security. Eisenhower's hidden-hand presidency, as it has been characterized by Fred I. Greenstein, extended to his rhetoric.[63] The president carefully integrated rhetorical strategy with foreign policy through an extensive network of communications, resulting in a sustained peace offensive that symbolically transformed the nation's perennial quest for absolute security into a heroic crusade for universal freedom. Through the agency of his Cold War rhetoric, Eisenhower sanctioned—and thereby helped to perpetuate—a cultural pathology of peril, thus inhibiting any desire to seek a mutual accommodation of differences with the Soviet Union.

The culture of fear, to which Eisenhower contributed substantially, is itself problematic in any assessment of his leadership. From one vantage point, Eisenhower merely reiterated the reality of the Communist threat in terms the public could understand and appreciate. Cultivating the public's anxieties strengthened his nuclear hand enough to deter war in the short term and guarantee a Cold War victory over the Soviet Union thirty years later. Preparing the nation to endure an age of peril, therefore, was a profound exercise of presidential leadership. Eisenhower imparted courage and vision where a less adept chief executive might have allowed the ship of state to flounder on the heavy seas of Communist aggression. He was a realist who understood the importance of steering a middle course between "the Fortress America isolationism of Taft and the Keynesian internationalism of Truman."[64]

On the other hand, as an agent of Cold War acculturation, Eisenhower left a rhetorical legacy of fear that perpetuated the age of peril even after the captive nations of Eastern Europe broke free of the Soviet orbit. The Wilsonian ideal of a world made safe for democracy continued to define American expectations of a just and secure peace, just as images of Soviet barbarism dramatized democracy's possible demise. Other than the unpalatable alternative of realpolitik, America lacked any moral vision of security in an international environment of ideological diversity, competing national interests, shifting alliances, diminishing national power, and intermittent conflict. Freedom's perceived vulnerability made existence in an uncivilized world inherently dangerous. Therefore, Mikhail Gorbachev's declaration of *glasnost* and *perestroika* nearly three decades after Eisenhower left office was easily interpreted in the West as a rejection of Communist barbarism in favor of free speech and free markets—i.e., as an admission of Soviet defeat.[65] The "New World Order," proclaimed by President George Bush as a symbol of America's Cold War victory and renewed commitment to enforce global peace, simply reaffirmed the continuing quest for total security on American terms. This pathology of perpetual insecurity, while not Eisenhower's responsibility alone, became an institution in his time.

Whether one views the culture of fear as pathological or functional, Eisenhower played the role of cold warrior deftly, without undercutting his public image as a man of peace. His leadership was steady and purposeful, his rhetoric calculated and crafted, and his influence large and lasting. The impact of the Cold War on American political culture cannot be assessed adequately without taking into account Eisenhower's strategic application of psychological warfare to legitimize nuclear peril as the price of genuine peace. The commander in chief rallied his civilian troops under the flag of peace for a crusade against communism.

## NOTES

1. Robert A. Divine, *Eisenhower and the Cold War* (Oxford: Oxford University Press, 1981), 105.
2. Chester J. Pach, Jr. and Elmo Richardson, *The Presidency of Dwight D. Eisenhower*, rev. ed. (Lawrence: University Press of Kansas, 1991), 75-76.
3. Dwight D. Eisenhower, *Waging Peace, 1956-1961* (Garden City: Doubleday, 1965); "Farewell Radio and Television Address to the American People, January 17, 1961," *Public Papers of the Presidents of the United States: Dwight D. Eisenhower, 1960* (Washington, D.C.: Government Printing Office, 1961), 1037 (hereafter cited as *Public Papers*).
4. On America's traditional search for perfect safety, see James Chace and Caleb Carr, *America Invulnerable: The Quest for Absolute Security from 1812 to Star Wars* (New York: Summit Books, 1988).
5. For a thorough discussion of the collaborative relationship between the president and his secretary of state, see Cecil V. Crabb, Jr. and Kevin V. Mulcahy, *Presidents and Foreign Policy Making: From FDR to Reagan* (Baton Rouge: Louisiana State University Press, 1986), 156-97.
6. Richard E. Crable, "Dwight David Eisenhower," in *American Orators of the Twentieth Century: Critical Studies and Sources*, ed., Bernard K. Duffy and Halford R. Ryan (Westport, Conn.: Greenwood Press, 1987), 120.
7. Roderick P. Hart, *Verbal Style and the Presidency: A Computer-Based Analysis* (Orlando: Academic Press, Inc., 1984), 80.
8. Martin J. Medhurst, "Eisenhower's 'Atoms for Peace' Speech: A Case Study in the Strategic Use of Language," *Communication Monographs* 54 (1987): 204-20.
9. Crable, "Dwight David Eisenhower," 115.
10. David L. Anderson, *Trapped by Success: The Eisenhower Administration and Vietnam, 1953-1961* (New York: Columbia University Press, 1991), xii.
11. Dwight D. Eisenhower, "Defense of Our Country and Its Cost," *Vital Speeches of the Day 19* (1 June 1953): 482.
12. Eisenhower to Gruenther, 4 May 1953, Whitman File, DDE Diary Series, Box 3, DDE Diary, December 1952-July 1953 (3), Eisenhower Library, Abilene, Kansas (hereafter cited as DDE Library).

13. U.S. Department of State, *Foreign Relations of the United States: 1952-1954* (Washington, D.C.: Government Printing Office, 1977), 2, pt. 1:582 (hereafter cited as *FRUS*).

14. "Radio and Television Address to the American People on 'Our Future Security,' November 13, 1957," *Public Papers, 1957*, 816.

15. "Remarks and Address at Dinner of the National Conference on the Foreign Aspects of National Security, February 25, 1958," *Public Papers, 1958*, 178, 181.

16. "Annual Message to the Congress on the State of the Union. February 2, 1953," *Public Papers, 1953*, 14.

17. "Second Inaugural Address, January 21, 1957," *Public Papers, 1957*, 63-64.

18. "Address at the Cow Palace on Accepting the Nomination of the Republican National Convention, August 23, 1956," *Public Papers, 1956*, 712.

19. "Radio and Television Address to the American People on 'Our Future Security,' November 13, 1957," *Public Papers, 1957*, 813.

20. "Radio and Television Address to the American People on the Need for Mutual Security in Waging Peace, May 21, 1957," *Public Papers, 1957*, 385.

21. Walter LaFeber, *The American Age: United States Foreign Policy at Home and Abroad since 1750* (New York: W. W. Norton, 1989), 513.

22. Crabb and Mulcahy, *Presidents and Foreign Policy Making*, 159, 196-197; H. W. Brands, "The Age of Vulnerability: Eisenhower and the National Insecurity State," *The American Historical Review* 94 (October 1989): 964.

23. Brands, 973.

24. "Farewell Radio and Television Address to the American People, January 17, 1961," *Public Papers, 1960*, 1038.

25. Stephen E. Ambrose, *The President*, vol. 2 of *Eisenhower* (New York: Simon and Schuster, 1984), 10, 621.

26. Inaugural Address, January 20, 1953," *Public Papers, 1953*, 7.

27. "Extract from Address by Dwight D. Eisenhower, Delivered at San Francisco, Wednesday, October 8, 1952," C. D. Jackson Records, 1953-1954, Box 2, Robert Cutler, DDE Library.

28. C. D. Jackson to W. W. Rostow, 31 December 1952, C. D. Jackson Papers, Box 85, DDE Library.

29. "Draft for NSC: Proposed Plan for a Psychological Warfare Offensive," March 1953, C. D. Jackson Papers, Box 85, Stalin's Death, DDE Library. Emphasis added.

30. Memorandum from C. D. Jackson to George Morgan, 11 April 1953, C. D. Jackson Records, 1953-1954, Box 4, George Morgan, DDE Library.

31. Memorandum from Anthony Guarco to C. D. Jackson, 11 May 1953, C. D. Jackson Records, 1953-1954, Box 5, Movies, DDE Library.

32. Dwight Eisenhower to William Benton, 1 May 1953, C. D. Jackson Papers, Box 41, DDE Correspondence, 1956 (2), DDE Library. Regarding the hidden-hand theme, Eisenhower's words were as follows: "Another need is in the job of presenting the American story throughout the world, to friends and enemies alike. It is hopeless to do this by lecturing and pontification. It must be done in many ways. And in most of it the hand of government must be carefully concealed, and, in some cases I should say, wholly eliminated."

33. Medhurst, "Eisenhower's 'Atoms for Peace' Speech," and J. Michael Hogan, "Eisenhower and Open Skies: A Case Study in 'Psychological Warfare'," in this volume.

34. Memorandum from C. D. Jackson to Robert Cutler, 4 March 1953, C. D. Jackson Papers, Box 37, General Robert Cutler, DDE Library.

35. Minutes of the 135th Meeting of the National Security Council, 4 March 1953, Whitman File, NSC Series, Box 4, DDE Library.
36. Richard A. Melanson, "The Foundations of Eisenhower's Foreign Policy: Continuity, Community, and Consensus," in *Reevaluating Eisenhower: American Foreign Policy in the Fifties*, ed. Richard A. Melanson and David Mayers (Urbana: University of Illinois Press, 1987), 43.
37. This address is reprinted from the files of the Republican National Committee, 1932-1965, as the "Speech by General Eisenhower, New York City, August 25, 1952," in *The Eisenhower Administration, 1953-1961: A Documentary History*, ed. Robert L. Branyan and Lawrence H. Larsen (New York: Random House, Inc., 1971), 32-38.
38. Robert L. Ivie, "Images of Savagery in American Justifications for War," *Communication Monographs* 47 (November 1980): 279-94.
39. *Public Papers, 1953*, 1, 3-5.
40. The text of the speech delivered on 10 June 1953, in Minneapolis, Minnesota, is reprinted in "Military and Economic Security," *Vital Speeches of the Day* 19 (1 July 1953): 546-47.
41. Dwight D. Eisenhower, "The Free World Must Build on its Successes," *Vital Speeches of the Day* 20 (15 September 1954): 706.
42. *Public Papers, 1957*, 61-62.
43. "Annual Message to the Congress on the State of the Union, January 9, 1958," *Public Papers, 1958*, 3.
44. "Special Message to the Congress on the Mutual Security Program, February 19, 1958," *Public Papers, 1958*, 164.
45. "Statement by the President on Mutual Security and the Cost of Waging Peace, July 2, 1958," *Public Papers, 1958*, 519.
46. From a nationally televised speech by the president, delivered on 3 December 1959: Dwight D. Eisenhower, "Peace and Friendship, In Freedom," in *Representative American Speeches: 1959-1960*, ed. Lester Thonssen (New York: H. W. Wilson Co., 1960), 27-28.
47. "Farewell Address," *Public Papers, 1960*, 1038.
48. "Speech by General Eisenhower, New York City, August 25, 1952," in *The Eisenhower Administration*, 35.
49. "Annual Message to the Congress on the State of the Union, February 2, 1953," *Public Papers, 1953*, 13.
50. "Annual Message to the Congress on the State of the Union, January 9, 1958," *Public Papers, 1958*, 2.
51. FRUS, vol. 8, 1075-77.
52. Walt W. Rostow, "Notes on the Origin of the President's Speech of April 16, 1953," C. D. Jackson Papers, Box 85, DDE Library.
53. Minutes of the 135th Meeting of the National Security Council, March 4, 1953, Whitman File, NSC Series, Box 4, DDE Library.
54. All citations of this speech are from Dwight D. Eisenhower, "The Chance for Peace," *Public Papers, 1953*, 179-88.
55. Ambrose, *The President*, 94.
56. "Peace or War: A Great Address," *The Houston Chronicle and Herald*, 17 April 1953, 8.
57. Medhurst, "Eisenhower's 'Atoms for Peace' Speech," 204-5, 207-8.
58. "Address Before the General Assembly of the United Nations on Peaceful Uses of Atomic Energy, New York City, December 8, 1953," *Public Papers, 1953*, 813-22. All

subsequent citations of the speech are from this source, except where corrected as actually delivered.

59. "Radio and Television Address to the American People Prior to Departure for the Big Four Conference at Geneva, July 15, 1955," *Public Papers, 1955*, 703-5.

60. "Radio and Television Report to the American People on the Developments in Eastern Europe and the Middle East, October 31, 1956," *Public Papers, 1956*, 1060, 1062.

61. "Radio and Television Report to the American People: Security in the Free World, March 16, 1959," *Public Papers, 1959*, 278.

62. *Public Papers, 1960*, 1039-40.

63. Fred I. Greenstein, *The Hidden-Hand Presidency: Eisenhower as Leader* (New York: Basic Books, 1982).

64. Melanson, "The Foundations of Eisenhower's Foreign Policy," 49.

65. Robert L. Ivie, "A New Cold War Parable in the Post-Cold War Press," *Deadline* 5 (January/February, 1990): 1-2, 8-9.

Eisenhower with John Foster Dulles

Mark J. Schaefermeyer

# Dulles and Eisenhower on "Massive Retaliation"

On 20 January 1953, Dwight D. Eisenhower was sworn in as the thirty-fourth President of the United States. The situation on that day was bleak: wars raged in Korea and Indochina; Iran was close to falling into Communist hands; Red China was flexing its territorial muscle; and European economies were struggling to recover from World War II. Domestically, the United States faced a staggering and continuing deficit, the value of the dollar was dropping, numerous wage and price controls were in effect, and taxes were burdensome. These international tensions and economic difficulties soon would play a major part in the foreign policy strategies of President Eisenhower and Secretary of State John Foster Dulles.

Eisenhower had campaigned in 1952 on winning the peace in Korea and practicing fiscal conservatism at home. These were not political ploys but deeply held personal convictions. Ike was adamant that his administration would move toward a balanced budget and still provide the security necessary to keep America free. He was certain that the greatest danger to the United States was economic in nature. To meet this danger, Eisenhower proposed a reduction in defense spending to enhance the nation's economic strength. Early in his administration, Secretary of the Treasury George Humphrey and Budget Director Joseph Dodge were added to the National Security Council—a move clearly signaling Ike's belief that the domestic economy and national security were intimately linked. Furthermore, Eisenhower demanded that all military planning be evaluated in terms of budgetary realities.[1] These enhancements demonstrated the president's fiscal perspective which was "to make national security planning an efficient business, with the emphasis placed on organization and economy."[2]

Eisenhower was concerned that "[W]e cannot defend the nation in a way which will exhaust our economy."[3] He believed that the United States should be strong enough to prevent the further expansion of Communist aggression and to protect American strategic interests worldwide. What followed were revamped foreign and defense policies. The New Look involved a reduction of overall defense spending and a redistribution of military outlays. The U.S. Air Force and the development of strategic weapons were to be expanded while a corresponding decrease in conventional troop strength and Army/Navy materiel was to be effected.[4] With the New Look, named by the media as "more bang for the buck," the Eisenhower administration moved quickly to position the United States for the emerging thermonuclear age. It was in this set of circumstances that a new foreign policy premised on "massive retaliation" was formulated.

Despite numerous critics both then and now, as a strategy, massive retaliation seems to have met with some success during Eisenhower's administration. The nature of this success lay in the doctrine's effectiveness as a *rhetorical* strategy. The foreign policy rhetoric of the administration, as presented through the president and his secretary of state, was simultaneously vague and blunt. Its effect was to raise a "reasonable doubt" in the minds of Soviet and Chinese Communists as to exactly what America might do under varying degrees of provocation. This essay traces the origins of the concept of massive retaliation, presents its exposition in the rhetoric of Eisenhower and Dulles from January of 1953 through the spring of 1954,[5] and assesses the reasons for its apparent success, with special attention to the rhetorical nature of the doctrine and its implementation.

## ORIGINS OF MASSIVE RETALIATION

According to Dulles, the origin of the "peace through deterrence" policy occurred as early as 1950 when he responded publicly to a speech by Herbert Hoover. Hoover advocated a defense policy that would "fortress" America rather than expend effort in maintaining defenses around the perimeter of the Soviet sphere of influence. Dulles agreed with the premise—that the Soviet perimeter should not be allowed to expand—but offered an alternative policy. He advocated the buildup of a powerful deterrent that would maintain peace and could be used anywhere, at anytime. Though he would later consider this policy his greatest success as secretary of state, Dulles was not the only person to advocate such a strategy.

Prior to Eisenhower's election, elements of what would come to be labeled massive retaliation were discussed within the Truman administration. Harold E. Stassen, for example, proposed that the United States warn the Soviets that the next Communist incursion would bring war to Moscow. Truman's secretary of the air force declared in 1951 that the Strategic Air Command's ability to deliver atomic weapons was the "greatest deterrent" to keeping Russia from starting a war. General Omar Bradley, chairman of the Joint Chiefs of Staff, declared to a senate subcommittee that Russia was deterred from overrunning Europe by fear of American atomic retaliation.[6] Clearly, the basic concept was not a new one when Dulles rebutted Hoover.

In his speech of 29 December 1950, Dulles advocated what later came to be known as the "New Look." He began by arguing against two alternative defense policies. First, he refuted the concept of area defense—the idea that each nation could spread resources along a common border with the Soviets or Chinese and thus insure the common good. Second, he refuted the "fortress" concept as flawed, arguing that "[a]ny nation which at a moment of supreme danger sheds those of its allies who are most endangered, and to whom it is bound by solemn treaty, . . . is scarcely in a position thereafter to do much picking and choosing for its own account. It elects a dangerous course, for solitary defense is never impregnable."[7]

Instead, Dulles saw retaliatory power as the ultimate deterrent to Soviet attack. As outlined, his plan highlighted two features that would be key themes of the New Look: (1) capacity to counterattack, and (2) ability to take action of one's own choosing. The first requires little explanation. Dulles believed that the United States must be able to mount a swift retaliatory strike if she or her vital interests were the victims of aggression. The capacity to strike quickly and the will to do so would, he believed, deter potential aggressors. Second, experience with the Korean conflict convinced Dulles that the United States must be able to choose the place and means for retaliation rather than having to respond to locations chosen by the enemy. Dulles argued, "[We] do not want to be committed to a series of Koreas all around the globe. . . . The arsenal of retaliation should include all forms of counter-attack with maximum flexibility, mobility and the possibility of surprise."[8] So, by late 1950, Dulles was already on record as favoring something very similar to massive retaliation.

But was Dulles the sole architect of the new defense strategy? How much input did the new president have in developing the New Look as a defense policy? Eisenhower was immensely qualified to construct defense policy. He served as chief of planning and operations for the War Department in 1942; commander of the European Theatre from 1942-1945; Army chief of staff from 1945-1948; chairman of the Joint Chiefs in 1949 and NATO supreme commander from 1951-1952. These experiences gave Eisenhower ample ability and credibility to define defense policy as president. Recent analyses strongly indicate that the New Look that emerged in 1953 and 1954 was developed and implemented primarily by Eisenhower himself.[9]

Eisenhower was a formidable manager. He had learned how to motivate people to get the best out of those who worked for him. According to James D. Weaver, "most of the biographies, memoirs, congressional hearings, and interviews conducted with key executives in the Eisenhower administration overwhelmingly confirm the view that Eisenhower was a very self-confident, self-assured, and activist Commander in Chief—a man to whom command decisions were inbred."[10] The policies that emanated from the White House were Eisenhower's. But just when and how did Eisenhower arrive at the conclusion that the New Look based on nuclear deterrence was the means for keeping communism at bay?

Some scholars argue that his stance developed through his management of the Allied command in World War II. Others believe that it developed from his experience as the head of NATO. Whatever the source, it is clear that Eisenhower had specific ideas about how nuclear weapons should be used long before he ran for the presidency. As army chief of staff, Eisenhower wrote to Bernard Baruch on 14 June 1946, that the United States must establish a system for preventing aggression: "[t]here must exist for deterrent purposes, provisions for *retaliation* in the event other control and prevention devices should fail. . . . [T]o prevent the use of atomic weapons there must exist the capability of employing atomic weapons against the recalcitrant."[11] Eisenhower believed that the "existence of the atomic bomb in our hands is a deterrent, in fact, to aggression in the world."[12] As early as February 1951, while still commander of NATO, Eisenhower told the Senate Foreign Relations Committee and Armed Services Committee that he would use the atomic bomb "instantly" in a war if he thought the "net" advantage of its use would be on his side.[13]

Having been a career soldier, Eisenhower understood the need for strategy in peace as well as in war. While he abhorred the idea of using atomic or thermonuclear weapons, Eisenhower realized that the strategic thing to do was to avoid telegraphing any reluctance to utilize any weapon, including nuclear ones. Deception, surprise, and obfuscation had worked on 6 June 1944, at Normandy. Now it was time to employ those same techniques in peacetime to thwart the Communist threat. The availability of nuclear weapons combined with a weakening economic situation at home and a stalemate in Korea invited adoption of a policy such as massive retaliation. The New Look would feature scaling down conventional forces combined with a build up of atomic weapons; over time, the economy would be strengthened by cutting defense expenditures.

## EISENHOWER AND DULLES ON THE NEW LOOK

The source of the concept, development, and promulgation of the New Look with its corollary of massive retaliation was a joint effort between President Eisenhower and John Foster Dulles. The success of communicating the plan to the world relied very much on the relationship between the president and his secretary of state. To work, the concept had to be sufficiently credible to deter potential aggressors—it had to come from the highest echelons of the United States government. The administration's stance on world peace had to be viewed as equally credible.[14] In other words, the rhetorical goal emphasized peace without ruling out force as a response to aggression against free and sovereign nations. While the New Look may have been primarily an economic initiative for Eisenhower, its emphasis on strategic and tactical uses of nuclear weapons required a willingness to employ retaliatory strikes on aggressor nations. To ensure the success of this policy, Eisenhower had to work with someone he could trust, someone of like mind, someone like John Foster

Dulles. The working relationship Ike established with Dulles was a major part of the rhetorical strategy that lay behind the doctrine of massive retaliation.

Recent studies of Eisenhower's leadership style and *modus operandi* have shown that he was much more involved in the administration of his two terms of office than had been previously thought.[15] Further, Eisenhower had much more input into Dulles's public statements (especially concerning the New Look) than believed during the 1950s. Dulles routinely reviewed his major addresses with Eisenhower prior to delivery. In a memo to Dulles on 8 September 1953, the president commented on a draft of Dulles's upcoming speech to the United Nations. Having refrained from making editorial corrections (because Dulles had not yet done that himself), Eisenhower nonetheless offered comments on the general character of the speech. "I rather feel that it would be well to state flatly in the beginning that you have no intention of producing a Philippic," wrote Ike, "that your purpose is to advance the cause of conciliation and understanding and not to be concerned merely with excoriation."[16] Eisenhower not only was willing to make suggestions of substance but also of rhetorical practice, as this and many other memoranda prove.

No doubt Dulles sought the president's input because of the nature of his position, but the maturation of their relationship also contributed to the mutual trust and respect they held for each other. Indeed, the relationship, according to Eisenhower, began in 1952 as "an active association and exchange of views which was to grow in intimacy and breadth during the next seven years."[17] However, the major pronouncements and policies of the administration belonged to the president. As Arthur Larson put it, "[t]he main direction and tone of American foreign policy"[18] was Eisenhower's. In 1968, the former president provided further insight into his relationship with Dulles:

> Of all the men in my cabinet there was no one whom I respected more than Secretary of State John Foster Dulles. I depended greatly on his wisdom. Yet Foster made no important move without consulting the President. I reviewed in advance all his major pronouncements and speeches, and when he was abroad he was constantly in touch by cable and telephone. If we did not see eye to eye—and these instances were rare—it was, of course, my opinion that prevailed; this is the way it has to be.[19]

The basic policy of the New Look and its reliance on retaliation was one to which both men contributed, but the final decision on its implementation as a foreign policy and strategy of deterrence was the president's.[20]

Finally, while the secretary of state held his press conferences on Tuesdays, the president held his on Wednesdays, allowing Eisenhower the opportunity to affirm, and/or interpret any comments Dulles might have made a day earlier. Dulles's press conference comments were not to be quoted directly without special permission.[21] The administration could "reinterpret," if necessary, the secretary of state's reported comments. This practice augmented the rhetoric of vagueness that characterized the strategy of retaliation.

## Massive Retaliation as Deterrence

While a complete description of the New Look was not presented to the public until Eisenhower's second *State of the Union* address on 7 January 1954, there were statements by administration officials about the new policy well before that time. In a speech to the French National Political Science Institute on 5 May 1952, Dulles articulated what would become a key rationale. Decrying the current ability of the Soviet and Chinese Communists to "pick the time, place, and method of aggression," he declared that the free world possessed "the capacity to hit an aggressor where it hurts, at times and places of our choosing."[22] Dulles foresaw the immediate application of this concept in Indochina. If the Chinese Communists were to send their armies openly into Vietnam, they should know that "we will not be content merely to try to meet their armed forces at the point they select for their aggression, but by retaliatory action of our own fashioning." Dulles indicated an almost prescient understanding of the "No more Koreas" concern of the future president. More importantly, he articulated the main reason for the new policy—retaliation on the United States' own terms.

Perhaps the most notable of the early discussions was a *Life* magazine article, "A Policy of Boldness," written by Dulles and published two weeks after his Paris speech. Beginning with an indictment of the policies of containment[23] and "nation-as-fortress," Dulles outlined the essence of a new foreign policy that was less defensive in posture. He predicated his argument on the economic folly of attempting to maintain a line of defense around the entire twenty-thousand-mile border that the Soviet Union shared with the free world. Nor could the free world match the Communists man-for-man or tank-for-tank. In trying to do so, wrote Dulles, "we shall succumb to the twin evils of militarism and bankruptcy."[24] Dulles presented a single solution: "that is for the free world to develop the will and organize the means to retaliate instantly against open aggression by Red armies, so that . . . we could and would strike back where it hurts, by means of our choosing."[25] Following his reiteration of the free world's intent to respond at times of its choosing with massive force against targets, Dulles noted the importance of atomic energy "coupled with strategic air and sea power," as a new means to stop "open aggression before it starts."[26] Here, then, Dulles linked the destructive power of atomic weaponry with the inclination, if necessary, to retaliate.

This 1952 article presented the other crucial aspects of what would become the New Look: economic necessity and atomic deterrence. Without explicitly threatening to use atomic weapons, Dulles associated the power of free world community force with United States' atomic power. The ideas behind Dulles's article, expressed earlier that month in a Paris meeting with Eisenhower, became the blueprint for Eisenhower's foreign policy. The Republican Party platform for the November elections included a similar statement when it held that "we should develop with utmost speed a force-in-being . . . of such power as to deter sudden attack or promptly and decisively defeat it." Along with the requisite air, land, and sea forces, this defense should include "atomic energy weapons in abundance."[27]

In a speech to the American Legion on 25 August 1952, Eisenhower made clear his answer to containment: "We must have security forces of mobility, security forces whose destructive and retaliatory power is so great that it causes nightmares in the Kremlin whenever they think of attacking us." In this same speech Eisenhower previewed the link between the U.S. military posture and domestic economy when he stated: "We must keep America economically strong. . . . America's spiritual, economic and military strength is the corner-stone of the free world."[28]

Long before his election to the presidency, Eisenhower had considered— and largely adopted—the need for a doctrine similar to that of massive retaliation. Some historians still assert that Dulles and Admiral Arthur Radford, commander in chief of the Pacific Fleet, pressed the massive retaliation option on board the USS Helena on return from the president-elect's pre-inauguration trip to Korea, but the best evidence is that Ike was already leaning in that direction. Given Eisenhower's inclination to exhibit a tough stance to the Soviet and Chinese Communists, it is likely that Radford and Dulles merely confirmed or refined what the president-elect already was considering.

Eisenhower's first inaugural address, delivered on 20 January 1953, focused on freedom, a theme in keeping with the epideictic nature of the speech.[29] Eisenhower did, however, mention the specter of nuclear war—although without the words "atomic," "nuclear," or "weapons" ("armed" and "armament" each occurred once). He called them "devices to level not only mountains but also cities" and referred to them as having "the power to erase human life from this planet." In fact, after opening with a brief prayer, Eisenhower began his inaugural by alluding to the "forces of good and evil [that] are massed and armed and opposed as rarely before in history."[30] Even more indicative of his stance was the first of nine principles by which the nation would abide in its "labor for world peace." "Abhorring war as a chosen way to balk the purposes of those who threaten us," Ike intoned, "we hold it to be the first task of states-manship to develop the strength that will deter the forces of aggression and promote the conditions of peace."[31] The second principle was a strong state-ment against appeasement. This address, with its hope for a better world, sub-tly and indirectly sent a message not unlike that of the Reagan administration—peace and freedom through strength. The covert message was one of toughness; of standing one's ground. Eisenhower also presented the eco-nomic argument when he claimed that "economic health [is] an indispensable basis of military strength."[32]

In his first State of the Union address to Congress, Eisenhower developed more fully the essential economic argument supporting the New Look. "Our problem," he said, "is to achieve adequate military strength within the limits of endurable strain upon our economy. To amass military power without regard to our economic capacity would be to defend ourselves against one kind of disaster by inviting another."[33] Eisenhower accordingly declared that the new secretary of defense would draft and recommend changes to improve the effectiveness of the defense effort. The notion of defensive power had not yet been reformulated to include the reduction of conventional forces—a key feature of the New Look. "While retaliatory power is one strong deterrent to a would-be aggressor, another powerful deterrent is defensive power. No enemy is likely to attempt an attack foredoomed to failure."[34] Nowhere in this speech did Eisenhower take into account the fact that an aggressor may attack a powerful defense by relying on the element of surprise and swiftness. Such considerations would later lead to focusing on strategic air power and "instant" retaliation; but in January 1953 the evolving policy still centered on national defense instead of collective power as envisioned by Dulles.

In an address to the American Society of Newspaper Editors on 16 April 1953, Eisenhower again stressed the overt theme of freedom. As in the inaugural, Ike articulated elements of the New Look: "It [amassing of Soviet power] instilled in the free nations—and let none doubt this—the unshakable conviction that, as long as there persists a threat to freedom, they must, at any cost, remain armed, strong, and ready for the risk of war."[35] This motivational warrant supported the inferential leap of faith inherent in the doctrine of massive retaliation. The interests of free people around the world would be protected by a nation ready to go to (nuclear) war if necessary.

This passage also raised Eisenhower's central concerns: collective power and security. Free nations were compelled, said Ike, to "spend unprecedented money and energy for armaments," and to "develop weapons of war now capable of inflicting instant and terrible punishment upon any aggressor."[36] Eisenhower also focused attention on the economic problem of national defense for both sides. He reflected on the "burden of arms draining the wealth and the labor of all peoples," for every military expense represented "a theft from those who hunger and are not fed, those who are cold and are not clothed."[37]

By late April Eisenhower had laid out the essential threats to the maintenance of freedom—threats that would prompt him to seek a new military policy. In a top-secret memo of 30 April 1953, Eisenhower declared that the external threat was the Communists' intent to dominate the entire world; the internal threat was the expense of strengthening free world opposition to this external threat.[38] On the same day, Ike publicly emphasized the connection between a sound economy and effective defense: "Effectiveness with economy must be made the watchwords of our defense effort. . . . To protect our economy, maximum effectiveness at minimum cost is essential."[39]

In his press conference of 30 April, the president discussed the Department of Defense reorganization plan that had been sent to Congress. This plan included elements of the New Look without any specifics related to "massive" retaliation. Said Eisenhower:

> The program we are presenting is a long-term program . . . to present a position of genuine strength to any would-be aggressor. . . . We reject the idea that we must build up to a maximum attainable strength for some specific date [in the future]. Defense is not a matter of maximum strength for a single date. It is a matter of adequate protection to be projected as far into the future as the actions and apparent purposes of others may compel us. . . .
>
> Security based upon heavy armaments is a way of life that has been forced upon us and on our allies.[40]

Coupled with his announced plans to reorganize the Defense Department, Eisenhower couched future policy in economic terms—fulfilling the promise of his campaign and his long-standing belief that economic security was crucial to winning the Cold War and securing world peace. He also reinforced the image of the United States as a peace-loving nation regretfully compelled to take these steps.

Eisenhower introduced a new element in an address to the National Junior Chamber of Commerce on 10 June 1953. The president alluded to an idea earlier expressed by Dulles; that defense policy cannot "be a mere repetition of today's reflex to yesterday's crisis."[41] The defense of freedom must be a "powerful deterrent to any would-be aggressor" instead of a response to an enemy's offensive moves. This paralleled Dulles's argument that the free world should engage the enemy on grounds of the free world's own choosing rather than allowing the enemy to control the time and place of response.

In noting that the defense of freedom would require a common effort, Eisenhower asserted that "none can sanely seek security alone." Part of the economic necessity is that all free nations must "stand together or they shall fall separately. Again and again we must remind ourselves that this is a matter not only of political principle but of economic necessity."[42] Echoing Dulles's earlier assertions, Eisenhower recognized the importance of a collective effort that would share the economic burden of defense.

On 2 September 1953, John Foster Dulles spoke to the American Legion in St. Louis. While ostensibly discussing the recent armistice in Korea, he referred to the military power of the free nations then protecting Korea as a deterrent to new aggression. Claiming that peace was harder to win than war, Dulles returned to his earlier theme of anticipating enemy aggression: "Peace requires anticipating what it is that tempts an aggressor and letting him know in advance that, if he does not exercise self-control, he may face a hard fight, perhaps a losing fight."[43] In Dulles's view, Korea had taught the free world that foreseeing aggression and letting an aggressor know the potential consequences of its action beforehand would make the enemy reconsider hostile moves.

Dulles noted that the sixteen United Nations members who fought against the Communists in Korea had issued a declaration saying "if the armistice should be breached by unprovoked Communist aggression, then the sixteen nations" would be prompt to resist that aggression. Also, and more revealing, "the consequences of such a breach of the armistice would be so grave that, in all probability, it would not be possible to confine hostilities within the frontiers of Korea."[44] Not only did this declaration refer to the concept of collective security, but the passage seemed to suggest U.N. approval of a more powerful form of retaliation—actions more destructive than stop-gap reaction.

Although Eisenhower had yet to announce the specifics of his new policy, he was privately considering its potential ramifications. In a memo responding to an outline for reconsidering security policies, Eisenhower discussed Soviet atomic weapon development. Ike held that the United States no longer would be able to rely on a policy that merely attempted to avert disaster following surprise attack, but held that we would have "to be constantly ready, on an instantaneous basis, to inflict greater loss upon the enemy than he could reasonably hope to inflict upon us." For Eisenhower, "this would be a deterrent."[45] Eisenhower further discussed the importance of gaining the "enlightened support" of the American public as a necessary prerequisite to the success of any revised policy. After noting the importance of a coordinated effort on developing the policy, Eisenhower concluded by advocating a campaign. "[A] carefully thought out program of speeches, national and international conferences, articles, and legislation, would be in order," he held.[46] Apparently the administration was ever-mindful of the need to manage carefully the announcement of this policy to American voters—and to the world.

Over the next seven weeks Eisenhower made several statements about the soon-to-be announced policy, while continuing to practice the technique of sending intentionally vague mixed messages. For example, in his press conference of 30 September 1953, he proclaimed: "We don't want any war, and anyone who has had certainly the kind of experience with war that I have had can say this with such a passion, almost, as to put war at the very last of any possible solutions to the world's difficulties." Simultaneously, the president also maintained that the United States "will not quail from any sacrifice necessary" for national security.[47] In a speech to the United Church Women on 6 October, Eisenhower stated: "We are forced to concentrate on building such stores of armaments [atomic weapons] as can deter any attack against those who want to be free."[48] On 8 October, Eisenhower declared that the United States had a large number of atomic weapons "suited to the special needs of the Army, Navy, and Air Force for the specific tasks assigned to each service."[49] In the space of a few days, the administration appeared not only reluctant to resort to any violent solution but also well-prepared to release nuclear weapons if aggression were to occur.

## The New Look Emerges

On 30 October 1953 the National Security Council finalized its "Statement of Policy" (NSC 162/2) on basic national security. The policy presumed two basic requirements: (1) to meet the Soviet threat to U.S. security, and (2) to avoid seriously weakening the U.S. economy or undermining its fundamental values and institutions.[50] Most notably, the policy approved by the president outlined specific requirements for security against the Soviet threat:

a. Development and maintenance of:
  1. A strong military posture, with emphasis on the capability of inflicting massive retaliatory damage by offensive striking power;
  2. U. S. and allied forces in readiness to move rapidly initially to counter aggression by Soviet bloc forces and to hold vital areas and lines of communication; and
  3. A mobilization base, and its protection against crippling damage, adequate to insure victory in the event of general war.

b. Maintenance of a sound, strong and growing economy, capable of providing through the operation of free institutions, the strength described in a above over the long pull and of rapidly and effectively changing to full mobilization.

c. Maintenance of morale and free institutions and the willingness of the U. S. people to support the measures necessary for national security.[51]

In its policy conclusions, the document clarified what was meant by "massive retaliatory damage by offensive striking power" by stating that "[t]he risk of Soviet aggression will be minimized by maintaining a strong security posture, with emphasis on adequate offensive retaliatory strength and defensive strength. This must be based on massive atomic capability."[52]

Although this document was not for public consumption (special security precautions on a need-to-know basis were assigned to it), NSC 162/2 clearly outlined an administration commitment to use whatever force necessary to stop Communist aggression. It held that "[i]n the event of hostilities, the United States will consider nuclear weapons to be as available for use as other munitions."[53] With the completion of NSC 162/2 came the need to publicize its essential elements to the world, for only by publicly revealing the new doctrine could the administration hope to gauge its function as a deterrent. In truth, "massive retaliation" was as much a rhetorical strategy as it was a strategic doctrine, and Eisenhower knew it.

In his "Atoms for Peace" address before the General Assembly of the United Nations on 8 December 1953, Eisenhower advanced his vision of peace in an atomic world. Yet, for a speech that went through innumerable drafts, the emphasis was hardly on "Atoms for Peace."[54] Such phrases as "atomic danger," "destructive cargo," "devastating retaliation," "fearful material damage," "hideous damage," "fearful atomic dilemma," and "destructive forces" left no doubt as to the message of fear implicit in the age of atomic warfare. Moreover, Eisenhower strongly hinted at the New Look when he stated: "Atomic weapons have virtually achieved conventional status within our armed services. In the United States, the Army, the Navy, the Air Force, and the Marine corps are all capable of putting this weapon to military use."[55] Later in the speech, in case anyone missed it, Eisenhower again alluded to the new policy: "Second, even a vast superiority in number of weapons, and a consequent capability of devastating retaliation, is no preventive, of itself, against the fearful material damage and toll of human lives that would be inflicted by surprise aggression."[56] Overtly a message of peace, the speech was covertly a strong warning to the Soviets to reconsider any plans for aggression.[57]

On 7 January 1954, in his second State of the Union address, Eisenhower announced the development of a new initiative in foreign policy, one that would respond to "a great strategic change" in the past year. Premised on the belief that the United States would no longer limit itself to "mere reaction against crises provoked by others," the new policy, said Eisenhower, "is free to develop along lines of our choice."[58] In keeping with his speech of 8 December 1953, Eisenhower discussed atomic energy proposals for peaceful purposes before reviewing defense strategies. However, as before, and in line with NSC 162/2, he was quite clear about the nation's response if provoked. Noting the growth in U.S. military power, both to defend the continent and to deter aggression, Eisenhower declared that the allied nations would maintain a massive capability to strike back if they or their vital interests were the victims of aggression.

In outlining the administration's defense initiative, Eisenhower followed a carefully crafted rhetorical design. He first asserted the intention to use atomic power to serve the needs of peace. Then he immediately followed with another, more chilling, claim: "[W]e take into full account our great and growing number of nuclear weapons and the most effective means of using them against an aggressor if they are needed to preserve our freedom."[59] In addition, he pledged to share knowledge of the tactical use of nuclear weapons with the country's allies. As a major policy initiative, this emphasis on nuclear weapons as equal partners of conventional weapons and the willingness to share the new technology with allies were pointed and specific warnings to the Communist nations.

In his conclusion, Eisenhower repeated, in the same order, the basic ideas he had presented earlier: "A government can sincerely strive for peace, as ours is striving, and ask its people to make sacrifices for the sake of peace." But the United States will remain vigilant in the face of Communist aggression for "[i]t is our duty . . . to remain strong in all those ways—spiritual, economic, military— that will give us maximum safety against the possibility of aggressive action by others."[60] The president maintained a certain distance from any extreme form of saber rattling by arguing that the nation had first sought peace but had been forced into a more offensive-oriented posture because of past and likely future Communist aggression toward free nations. Eisenhower spoke softly. He left it for his secretary of state to show the stick. In a 12 January 1954 speech before the Council on Foreign Relations, Dulles echoed, in more detail, the arguments and conclusions of NSC 162/2. His initial line of argument returned to his "Policy of Boldness" essay. No longer would the United States hold back and respond only to emergencies, for such situations did not "necessarily make good permanent policies." "Emergency policies are costly," Dulles argued, "they are superficial and they imply that the enemy has the initiative. They cannot be depended upon to serve our long-time interests."[61] Rather, Dulles declared, the proper course was to rely more upon community deterrent power and less on local defensive power. As a local community depended on a security system equipped to deter criminals, so, likewise, the Eisenhower administration would seek a comparable international security system. "We want for ourselves and for others a maximum deterrent at bearable cost," said Dulles. "Local defense must be reinforced by the further deterrent of massive retaliatory power."[62]

Dulles then returned to the concept of response on grounds of allied choosing. "The way to deter aggression is for the free community to be willing and able to respond vigorously at places and with means of its own choosing," he argued. A necessary corollary to this concept was the economic equation that both lay behind and gave rise to the new doctrine. Given the inability to predict either the exact timing of Soviet aggression or the enormous cost of local defense, whether with conventional or "new" weapons, the doctrine of massive retaliation was a necessity. Thus was the basic decision of the NSC "to depend primarily on a great capacity to retaliate instantly by means and at places of our choosing . . . [permitting] a selection of military means instead of a multiplication of means [and] to get, and to share, more security at less cost"[63] announced to the world.

At face value, and in keeping with the president's assertions five days earlier, the New Look was cast in the most pragmatic terms. The new policy did not arise out of malice toward the Soviets or Chinese—it was not an offensive policy in its essential ingredients, though it did explicate an offensive strategy in the face of aggression. It was instead a new defense policy that carried foreign policy implications. It was also a rhetorical strategy that relied primarily upon the ethos of John Foster Dulles for its credibility.

Throughout the speech of 12 January, Dulles's focus was on the strategy of choice rather than on nuclear warfare. He did not, in fact, mention nuclear or atomic arms at all. Dulles took a more circular approach than did Eisenhower in his second State of the Union message by linking the terms *means* and *places* (of the allies own choosing), with *capacity, massive, retaliate,* and *instantly* to describe U.S. and allied response to Communist aggression. Yet the impression remained that "great" or "massive" meant nuclear response.

In the press conference after his speech to the Council on Foreign Relations, Dulles neither confirmed nor denied the impression that "great retaliation" meant atomic or hydrogen bombs.[64] However, when pressed in a subsequent press conference on 16 March 1954, Dulles reminded the reporters that he had advocated "a *capacity* to retaliate instantly. In no place did I say we *would* retaliate instantly, although we might indeed retaliate instantly under conditions that call for that."[65] Dulles mentioned a situation which certainly did have atomic implications—the fact that it took the United States four years to retaliate against Tokyo after Pearl Harbor. Certainly, this was a thinly veiled reference to the atomic bombs dropped on Hiroshima and Nagasaki.

Clearly, Dulles was being purposefully vague by never explicitly mentioning nuclear retaliation. He did, in fact, emphasize the importance of uncertainty as a deterrent.

> The question of circumstances under which you retaliate, where you retaliate, how quickly you retaliate, is a matter which has to be dealt with in the light of the facts of each particular case. . . . The whole essence of the program is that the actions should be an action of our choosing and he is not to know in advance what it is, and that uncertainty on his part is a key to the success of the policy.[66]

Cleverly stated to avoid the type of pronouncement that would create havoc with the Communist powers and the rest of the world, Dulles said no more than had already been expressed in NSC 162/2 or stated by the president of the United States.

To "clarify" further the U.S. position, Dulles subsequently revised and extended his speech to the Council on Foreign Affairs in an essay entitled "Policy for Security and Peace" published in the April 1954 issue of *Foreign Affairs*.[67] Having described the nature and scope of the Soviet threat, Dulles next discussed the concept of community defense and its necessity for the new defense initiative. "Without the cooperation of allies," he wrote, "we would not even be in a position to retaliate massively against the war industries of an attacking nation." The United States had to rely on the international facilities (air bases) of its allies for its strategic air power to be in a position to retaliate effectively. And while strategic air power may be, in the words of Winston Churchill, the "supreme deterrent," Dulles noted that "massive atomic and thermonuclear retaliation is not the kind of power which could most usefully be evoked under all circumstances."[68] Thus, Dulles indicated that releasing nuclear weapons required a special set of circumstances and was not to be the normative response to any and all forms of aggression.

After the storm of protest and criticism following Dulles's speech of 12 January, the administration had a crucial opportunity to explain the government's policies. Having been surprised by the "misinterpretation" of what he reportedly implied, Dulles offered a more definitive explanation.[69] First, to exploit the full potential of collective security, he argued, the "free world must make imaginative use of the deterrent capabilities of these new [atomic] weapons and mobilities. Properly used, they can produce defensive power able to retaliate at once and effectively against any aggression."[70] While Dulles thus raised the specter of atomic retaliation, he maintained that its use, nevertheless, would be purely *defensive*. He focused more attention, however, on the point that aggressors would be deterred by the potential for losing more than they could gain. Deterring attack with collective defense meant insuring that aggressors must understand they would suffer damage far in excess of what they might gain from their aggression. By drawing so much attention to this aspect of his argument, Dulles implied, without actually stating, that the "more to lose" *topos* was a reference to nuclear devastation. In spite of the public outcry, Dulles maintained his stance of deliberate vagueness. In trying to interpret this rhetoric of mixed signals, any potential aggressor had to weigh the possibility of receiving more than it had bargained for if it should engage in aggression against the United States or its allies.

Nor was Dulles's *Foreign Affairs* article the lone administration attempt to respond to criticism. At his press conference on 17 March 1954, the president characterized the arguments of his secretary of state as follows: "He [Dulles] was showing the value to America to have a capability of doing certain things, what he believed that would be in the way of deterring an aggressor and preventing this dread possibility of war occurring."[71] Elsewhere, Eisenhower argued that it would be criminal to respond with nuclear weapons to any act of aggression anywhere in the world. Speaking to the nation on 5 April 1954, Ike reminded the world of the Unites States' resolve to deter aggression: "As long as they [men in the Kremlin] know that we are in position to act strongly and to retaliate," said he, "war is not a decision to be taken lightly."[72] While the United States would not use the H-bomb to start a war, nothing could be greater "than the retaliation that will certainly be visited upon them if they would attack any of our nations, or any part of our vital interests, aggressively and in order to conquer us."[73] Once again, the president was equally and purposefully vague. Nuclear weapons would not be used as offensive weapons; the United States sought peace above all else; yet the response to Communist aggression would be instant and massive if necessary and, by implication, might or might not include strategic or tactical use of nuclear weapons.

## CONCLUSION

In retrospect, Eisenhower's and Dulles's rhetoric seems masterfully conceived in its indirection. While both took a hard line with the notion of instant and massive retaliation in the face of Communist aggression, both, especially

Eisenhower, maintained that the United States desired other, more peaceful, solutions. Both believed that retaliation, especially nuclear retaliation, should be a last resort, but neither wished to make that statement clearly. In so doing, they sought to make ambiguity their ally. At the time, Secretary Dulles seemed to receive much of the credit—and blame—for the New Look and the concept of "massive retaliation." Time has corrected this notion—Eisenhower and others had a significant hand in the development of the doctrine. The apparent autonomy of the secretary of state was part of the act. It simply did not exist. Secretary Dulles acted only with Eisenhower's approval and prior knowledge.[74] Dulles was given his role as the no-nonsense bureaucrat eager to stamp out evil by any available means. He played his role well, thus allowing Eisenhower to appear more reasoned and conciliatory. Both played parts, but Eisenhower was the director.

## NOTES

1. Robert A. Strong, "Eisenhower and Arms Control," in *Reevaluating Eisenhower: American Foreign Policy in the Fifties*, ed. Richard A. Melanson and David Mayers (Urbana: University of Illinois Press, 1987), 243.
2. Samuel F. Wells, Jr., "The Origins of Massive Retaliation," *Political Science Quarterly* 96 (1981): 33.
3. Stephen E. Ambrose, *Eisenhower: The President* (New York: Simon & Schuster, 1984), 224.
4. The Army would be cut back nearly half a million men over a four-year period while the Navy would lose a handful of combat ships and approximately 100,000 sailors. In contrast, the Air Force would increase from 115 to 137 wings and add 30,000 men. With the Air Force to act as primary deterrent against Communist attack, defense spending would be reduced from $35 to $31 billion a year. Robert A. Divine, *Eisenhower and the Cold War* (New York: Oxford University Press, 1981), 37.
5. This cutoff date was chosen for practical reasons. The essence of the New Look did not change after this point nor did the principal's rhetoric about retaliation as deterrent. For example, Eisenhower's subsequent State of the Union messages returned less and less over time to this theme.
6. Lester A. Sobel, *National Issues* (New York: Facts on File, 1956), 28.
7. John Foster Dulles, "Speech to the United Nations," *New York Times*, 30 December 1950, I4.
8. Ibid.
9. Duane Windsor, "Eisenhower's New Look Reexamined: The View from Three Decades" in *Dwight D. Eisenhower: Soldier, President, Statesman*, ed. Joann P. Krieg (Westport, Conn.: Greenwood Press, 1987), 148.
10. James D. Weaver, "Eisenhower as Commander in Chief," in *Dwight D. Eisenhower: Soldier, President, Statesman*, ed. Joann P. Krieg (Westport, Conn.: Greenwood Press, 1987), 141.
11. Eisenhower to Baruch, 14 June 1946, *The Papers of Dwight David Eisenhower: The Chief of Staff*, vol. 7, ed. Louis Galambos (Baltimore: Johns Hopkins University Press, 1978), 1126.
12. Eisenhower to Baruch, *Papers*, 1127.
13. Sobel, *National Issues*, 29.
14. This is perhaps one reason why the Shoemaker (1954-91) index of Eisenhower's public address contains so many more references to the word peace and its derivatives than to those

dealing with war, massive retaliation, and atomic or nuclear weapons. Given his experiences with World War II, it is no surprise that world peace was an important, if not the most important, goal for the Eisenhower administration. See Ralph Joseph Shoemaker, ed., *The President's Words, An Index* (Louisville, KY: E.D.G. Shoemaker and R. J. Shoemaker, 1954).

15. See John W. Sloan, "The Management and Decision-Making Style of President Eisenhower," *Presidential Studies Quarterly* 20 (1990): 308-17; Philip G. Henderson, "Organizing the Presidency for Effective Leadership," *Presidential Studies Quarterly* 17 (1987): 43-69; R. Gordon Hoxie, "Eisenhower and Presidential Leadership," *Presidential Studies Quarterly* 13 (1983): 589-612; Fred I. Greenstein, *The Hidden-Hand Presidency: Eisenhower as Leader* (New York: Basic Books, 1982); and James D. Barber, *The Presidential Character: Predicting Performance in the White House*, 3rd ed. (New York: Prentice-Hall, 1985).

16. Whitman File , DDE Diary Series, Box 3, Eisenhower Library, Abilene, Kansas (hereafter cited as DDE Library).

17. Dwight D. Eisenhower, *Mandate for Change: 1953-1956* (New York: Doubleday, 1963), 23.

18. Arthur Larson, *Eisenhower: The President Nobody Knew* (New York: Scribners, 1968), 74.

19. Dwight D. Eisenhower, "Some Thoughts on the Presidency," *Reader's Digest* (November 1968): 54-55.

20. See Greenstein, 87-88 and Richard H. Immerman, "Eisenhower and Dulles: Who Made the Decisions?" *Political Psychology* 1 (1979): 21-38, for more on how foreign policy decisions were made.

21. "The Secretary is not to be quoted directly, that is, not to use quotation marks unless special permission is given. Anything else he says can be attributed to him. You can say Secretary Dulles said so and so, and you can even use the word, but no direct quotation marks. . . . If the Secretary should say something as background, then his name is not to be used with the information at all. It can be used but leave his name out. And if he goes off the record, you tell nobody outside this room about it." Press and Radio News Conference, 18 February 1953, *Press Conferences of Secretaries of State*, Series III, No. 2, (February 1953-December 1957), 1.

22. John Foster Dulles, "Far-Eastern Problems: Defense through Deterrent Power," *Vital Speeches of the Day* 18 (1952): 494.

23. Dulles masterfully quoted a former ambassador of India, Minocher R. Masani: "'Defenses seem constantly improvised—a hole plugged here, a leak stopped there. . . . Clearly, mere containment is no longer enough.' The ambassador added to his reproach by recalling that of Demosthenes, addressed to the Athenians in 351 B.C.: 'Shame on you, Athenians . . . for not wishing to understand that in war one must not allow oneself to be at the command of events, but to forestall them. . . . You make war against Philip like a barbarian when he wrestles. . . . If you hear that Philip has attacked in the Chersonese, you send help there; if he is at Thermopylae, you run there; and if he turns aside you follow him to right and left, as if you were acting on his orders. Never a fixed plan, never any precautions; you wait for bad news before you act.'" See John Foster Dulles, "A Policy of Boldness," *Life* (19 May 1952): 146.

24. Ibid., 151.

25. Ibid.

26. Ibid.

27. Arthur M. Schlesinger, Jr. and Fred L. Israel, eds., *History of American Presidential Elections, 1789-1968*, vol. 4 (New York: McGraw-Hill, 1971), 3285. Actually, Eisenhower had struck out language from an earlier platform draft written by Dulles that was too provocative.

28. Dwight D. Eisenhower, "Speech by General Dwight D. Eisenhower, New York, August 25, 1952," in Schlesinger and Israel, *History* 4:3300.

29. The word "free" appears 21 times and the word "freedom" appears 10 times in Eisenhower's first inaugural address. This amounts to 1.3 percent of the total number of

words used. The frequency for this word in the English language is 43.5 (slightly more than one occurrence every million tokens). Two other words, "faith" and "peace," occur 13 (SFI=49) and 12 (SFI=57.3) times respectively. The measures are based on the American Heritage Intermediate Corpus which is a computer-assembled selection of 5,088,721 words drawn in 500-word samples from 1,045 published materials; see John B. Carroll, Peter Davies, and Barry Richman, eds., *The American Heritage Word Frequency Book* (New York: American Heritage Publishing, Inc., 1971). As a benchmark, a Standard Frequency Index (SFI) of 40 equals once every million tokens; an SFI of 90 equals once every 10 tokens.

30. *Public Papers of the Presidents of the United States: Dwight D. Eisenhower, 1953* (Washington D.C.: Government Printing Office, 1960), 1 (hereafter cited as *Public Papers*).
31. Ibid., 5. Interestingly, this enemy is never named; he never mentions the terms "Soviet(s)," "Russians," or "communists."
32. Ibid., 6.
33. Ibid., 17.
34. Ibid., 18.
35. Ibid., 181. In this speech, "free" occurs 21 times while "freedom" occurs 4 times—together accounting for .9 percent of the total words used. This time, however, references to the devices of destruction ("arms," "armaments," "weapons," etc.) occur a total of 22 times ("atomic" occurs 3 times: "atomic war," "atomic weapons," and "atomic energy"). Also, in contrast to the first inaugural, the enemies are named quite clearly. "Soviet" and "Russia" occur 21 times, "East(ern) Europe" occurs twice, and "China" once.
36. Ibid.
37. Ibid., 182.
38. White House Central Files, Confidential File, Box 45, National Security, DDE Library.
39. *Public Papers, 1953,* 227.
40. Ibid., 241-242.
41. Ibid., 387.
42. Ibid., 386.
43. John Foster Dulles, "Korea: Deterrents to New Aggression," *Vital Speeches of the Day* 19 (1 October 1953): 738.
44. Dulles, "Korea," 739.
45. Whitman File , DDE Diary Series, Box 3, DDE Library, 8 September 1953.
46. Ibid.
47. *Public Papers, 1953,* 617-18.
48. Ibid., 635.
49. Ibid., 645.
50. U. S. Department of Defense, *The Pentagon Papers: The Defense Department History of United States Decisionmaking on Vietnam,* vol. 1, Gravel Edition (Boston: Beacon Press, 1971), 413.
51. Ibid., 416.
52. Ibid., 424.
53. Ibid., 426.
54. Of the 31 occurrences of "atomic," 20 refer to weapons while only 11 references modify non-destructive nouns (i.e., energy, age, colossi, dilemma, realities). In fact, taken together, references to "weapons" (including "fissionable material") occurred 49 times—1.6 percent of the total word count. By contrast, "peace," "peaceful," and "peacetime" occur a total of 25 times—.8 percent.
55. *Public Papers, 1953,* 815.
56. Ibid., 816.

57. Martin J. Medhurst, "Eisenhower's 'Atoms for Peace' Speech: A Case Study in the Strategic Use of Language," *Communication Monographs* 54 (1987): 209-10.
58. Fred L. Israel, ed., *The State of the Union Messages of the Presidents: 1790-1966*, vol. 3 (New York: Chelsea House, 1967), 3027.
59. Ibid., 3029.
60. Ibid., 3038.
61. John Foster Dulles, "Foreign Policies and National Security: Maximum Deterrent at Bearable Cost," *Vital Speeches of the Day* 20 (12 January 1954): 232.
62. Dulles, "Foreign Policies," 233.
63. Ibid.
64. John Foster Dulles, "Press Conference of 19 January 1954," *Press Conferences of Secretaries of State*, February 1953-December 1957, Series III, 4-5.
65. John Foster Dulles, "Press Conference of 16 March 1954," *Press Conferences of Secretaries of State*, February 1953-December 1957, Series III, 2, emphasis added.
66. Ibid., 3.
67. John Foster Dulles, "Policy for Security and Peace," *Foreign Affairs* 32 (April 1954): 353-364. The editors of the journal, published by the Council on Foreign Affairs, requested the essay from Dulles. In his 16 March press conference, he described the article as "a somewhat more polished, I hope, restatement of my speech . . . [that] will elaborate to some extent the thesis which I expressed in my address of January 12." Dulles, "Press Conference of 16 March 1954," *Press Conferences*, 7.
68. Ibid., 356.
69. See Robert A. Divine, *Eisenhower and the Cold War* (New York: Oxford University Press, 1981), 38; Douglas Kinnard, *The Secretary of Defense* (Lexington, KY: University Press of Kentucky, 1980), 26-28; Lester A. Sobel, *National Issues* (New York: Facts on File, 1956), 29-31; and Samuel F. Wells, Jr., "The Origins of Massive Retaliation," *Political Science Quarterly* 96 (1981): 34-36. "Amazingly, he is known to have been completely taken aback by the flood of letters he received from the American clergy—men with whom, as a leading lay churchman, he had long worked closely—bitterly upbraiding him for his announcement of a policy of 'massive retaliation.' He was shocked that they construed his formula as immoral. He never anticipated it. He couldn't understand it. At the time, he remarked to one of these authors: 'But I never threatened *massive retaliation*. I only said we must have the *capacity for massive retaliation*.'" Roscoe Drummond and Gaston Coblentz, *Duel at The Brink: John Foster Dulles' Command of American Power* (London: Weidenfeld and Nicolson, 1960), 69.
70. Dulles, "Policy," 358.
71. *Public Papers, 1954*, 325.
72. Ibid., 72.
73. Ibid.
74. According to Dulles: "I've never take any major decision without full consultation with and approval by the President. . . . I also clear all my major addresses with the President. I invariably accept his suggestions. I consider it most important to let it be known that my speeches have received the President's approval." See Andrew H. Berding, *Dulles on Diplomacy* (Princeton, N.J.: Van Nostrand, 1965), 15-16. In a 1 December 1953 State Department Press Release, Dulles declared that the foreign policy principles by which the administration operated (and which, by this point, included those precepts established in NSC 162/2) were "agreed on by President Eisenhower and me before I took my present office. Those principles still stand." John Foster Dulles, "Statement by Secretary of State John Foster Dulles at his Press Conference December 1," *Press Conferences of Secretaries of State*, February 1953-December 1957, Series III, 645.

The Hydrogen Age Begins

Rachel L.
Holloway

# "Keeping the Faith"
## Eisenhower Introduces the Hydrogen Age

In *So Help Me God: Religion and the Presidency, Wilson to Nixon*, Robert S. Alley argues that Dwight D. Eisenhower's election marked the "total restoration of American 'Messianism'"; Eisenhower "touched the heart-string of the nation, which was in a religious mood."[1] Indeed, Eisenhower began his presidency with an inaugural prayer: "Almighty God, . . . May cooperation be permitted and be the mutual aim of those who, under the concepts of our constitution, hold to differing political faiths; so that all may work for the good of our beloved country and Thy glory."[2] Eisenhower instituted the White House Prayer Breakfast, established a national day of prayer, advocated the addition of the words "under God" to the pledge of allegiance and helped to raise "In God We Trust" to its status as the nation's official motto.[3] R. Gordon Hoxie notes that "with the exception of Lincoln, more perhaps than any other President, Eisenhower conveyed his views in moral and spiritual terms. The first of the modern presidents to do so, he added another dimension to Presidential leadership roles: moral and spiritual."[4]

Americans called on Eisenhower's moral leadership during a period of change and uncertainty. As Eisenhower took office, he inherited a growing Cold War, the Korean conflict, and an imminent French defeat in Indochina. On the domestic front, a growing budget deficit encouraged the administration to get "more bang for the buck." He controlled the world's most powerful military force and a development program designed to increase that power exponentially. Nuclear weapons were soon to become the centerpiece of American defense strategy. At the same time, Eisenhower was reticent to commit America to the use of nuclear weapons and favored easing tensions in the Cold War; he promoted "atoms for peace."

The situation was complicated further on 7 November 1952, two days prior to Eisenhower's election; the United States secretly tested its first thermonuclear device, the hydrogen bomb. The "Mike" shot exploded with a force one thousand times greater than the bomb which leveled Hiroshima.[5] Thus, at the beginning of the hydrogen age, Eisenhower's political challenge was to define the political situation in a way that would simultaneously reassure the public

47

and gain acceptance of policy positions which, taken at face value, appeared to heighten the uncertainty of the international situation.

Faced with uncertainty and public anxiety, Eisenhower turned to a rhetoric of "faith." In particular, Eisenhower created a definitional orientation toward nuclear weapons which emphasized America's purpose (the preservation of freedom) and which cast nuclear weapons (particularly the hydrogen bomb) as an agency of that purpose. Through that discourse, Americans were reassured. They needed merely to remain faithful to America's purpose in order to achieve peace, both as individuals and as a nation.

More specifically, Eisenhower's faith-centered terminology served multiple rhetorical functions in his management of the hydrogen bomb issue. The faith terminology: (1) encouraged the public to trust the president and discouraged public challenge to nuclear policy; (2) allowed citizens to participate in the nation's governance by praying for peace; (3) gave Eisenhower the rhetorical latitude necessary to promote disarmament and military superiority simultaneously; and (4) encouraged acceptance of the high levels of secrecy maintained during the Eisenhower years.

Eisenhower's faith-centered rhetorical strategies can best be understood by examining two major areas: the social and rhetorical contexts which contributed to the development of strategies; and the key terms and values that Eisenhower used to describe nuclear weapons, especially the hydrogen bomb, during the first eighteen months of his presidency.

## FAITH IN AMERICA: THE CONTEXT OF CIVIL RELIGION

Eisenhower's faith-centered discourse drew on a long tradition of religious interpretations of American experience. Arthur M. Schlesinger, Jr. identifies a "providential destiny" as one of two competing strands present in America's political identity.[6] From the Puritan's "City on the Hill" to concerns with a New World Order, Americans espoused a special status among nations; America was a "redeemer nation" which would lead the world toward freedom. Russel Nye characterizes American belief this way: "Deep within the American mythology lies the conviction that a new free form of government was introduced into this continent by people chosen of God, in order to found a society in which the individual would possess all that liberty to which God thought him entitled, far from the interferences of Europe, free from the burden of the prejudiced past, to serve as an inspiration and model to the world."[7]

Because Americans believed that they were a chosen people, they often described America's political purpose in religious terms. For instance, John Adams wrote: "I always consider the settlement of America with reverence, as the opening of a grand scene and design in Providence for the illumination of the ignorant and the emancipation of the slavish part of mankind all over the earth."[8] Thomas Jefferson once suggested that the Great Seal of the United States should portray the children of Israel led by a pillar of light.[9]Herman Melville described America as a savior: "We Americans are the peculiar, chosen people—the Israel of our time; we bear the ark of the liberties of the world. . . . God has predestinated, mankind expects, great things from our race; and great things we feel in our souls. The rest of the nations must soon be in our rear. . . . Long enough have we been skeptics with regard to ourselves, and doubted whether, indeed, the political Messiah had come. But he has come in us."[10] From its inception, America espoused and followed a God-given mission.

The merging of political and religious symbolism created an American civil religion. James David Fairbanks defines civil religion as "the basic symbols of transcendence which serve to unify the members of a political community and give meaning to their collective existence."[11] While few scholars agree about the exact nature of America's civil religion, most agree that religious symbols pervade American political discourse.[12] Roderick P. Hart notes that, whether America's transcendent symbols create a distinct and definable religion or not, American politics is religious in its rhetorical and symbolic practices: "We as a nation have fashioned our national anthems, insisted that our presidents take their oaths of office on the Bible, established Capitol prayer rooms, pro-claimed national days of prayer, brandished federal banners in our churches, and talked, talked, talked . . . of God's special love for America, of America's unique responsibility to God, of a New Israel and a Chosen People, of rededi-cating ourselves to the principles of basic, Christian Americanism, and so on."[13] In his commentary on the imperial presidency, Michael Novak insists that American political leaders increasingly play religious roles: "The chief officers of the state perform priestly and prophetic roles, conduct huge public liturgies, constantly reinterpret the nation's fundamental documents and tra-ditions, furnish the central terms of public discourse."[14] Fairbanks argues that the "priestly function" of the presidency is central to a president's success in motivating the American people.[15] Because America's orientation is guided by terms for purpose, presidential acts and words must conform in some degree to that orientation.

Perhaps at no time was America's commitment to its identity as a righteous nation greater than in the 1950s. Although the 1920s and 1930s found Americans as depressed religiously as they were economically, the New Deal and World War II signaled a reinvigorated religion in America. Church affilia-tion grew from 43 percent in 1920 to 55 percent in 1950 and reached its high-est point with 69 percent affiliation in 1960.[16] In 1952, 75 percent of Americans polled found religion "very important."[17] Individuals identified strongly with organized religion.

The prestige of religious leaders also grew during the 1950s. By 1963, a Roper poll reported that 40 percent of the American people identified religious leaders as the group "doing the most good" and most to be trusted.[18] That opinion perhaps reflected the increased visibility that religious leaders enjoyed. Reverend Billy Graham's mass-media ministry reinvented the Protestant tent-meeting and reached an unprecedented audience. By 1956, the Billy Graham Evangelistic Association, founded only six years earlier, reported an annual budget of two million dollars.[19]

Religion achieved a renewed intellectual status as well. Religious books populated the best-seller lists. Reverend Norman Vincent Peale offered Americans peace of mind through his *Guide to Confident Living* (1948) and *The Power of Positive Thinking* (1952). In 1949, Bishop Fulton J. Sheen gave Americans hope for *Peace of Soul*. In 1955, Will Herberg reported that the academy expressed renewed interest in religion as well: "Kierkegaard, Maritain, Reinhold Niebuhr, Buber, Tillich, Berdyaev, Simone Weil: these writers have standing and prestige with the intellectual elite of today in a way no religious writers have had for many decades. Religious ideas, concepts, and teachings have become familiar in the pages of the 'vanguard' journals of literature, politics, and art."[20] America's religious interests were "born again" in the 1950s.

While religious interest was pervasive, religious belief remained somewhat undefined. Sociologists and historians note that American religion in the 1950s was as much a "faith in faith" as it was a resurgence of religious doctrine. Herberg writes that "the American believes that religion is something very important for the community; he also believes that 'faith,' or what we may call religiosity, is a kind of 'miracle drug' that can cure all the ailments of the spirit. It is not faith in *anything* that is so powerful, just faith, the 'magic of believing.'" Herberg goes on to explain that the cult of faith evinced two forms: an introvert form in which faith was trusted to bring about mental health and peace of mind and the extrovert form in which faith became positive thinking. The traditional terms, "don't lose faith" and "have faith" originally meant to have faith in God but soon came to mean "have faith in yourself."[21] As an extension, when individuals faced political quandaries, to have faith meant to have faith in yourself *as an American* or, in other words, have faith in the American Way.

Kenneth Burke notes that purpose-centered terminologies tend to arise in periods of confusion or skepticism: "They are a mark of transition, flourishing when one set of public presuppositions about the ends of life has become weakened or disorganized, and no new public structure, of sufficient depth and scope to be satisfying, has yet taken its place."[22] This uncertainty pushes a purpose-centered terminology forward. Typical American explanations and orientations become transformed through a need to preserve a "way of doing things." Specifically, Burke explains that American pragmatism (to do things a particular way because it works) quickly gives way to American idealism (to do things a particular way because it is the American Way) and, if pushed further, the orientation becomes American mysticism (to do things a particular way because those acts fulfill the American Way as an ultimate and transcendent purpose.) "The 'American Way,'" he says, "is offered purely and simply as a purpose, our business pragmatism having thus been transformed into a mystical nationalism."[23]

The 1950s were fertile ground for the emergence of an American purpose-centered orientation. America's faith in faith responded to the insecurities created in America's economic, social, and political environments. Religion gave Americans a way to belong in a fragmented society. America was experiencing the age of affluence. Americans were more mobile than ever before, both economically and geographically, and as a result faced new social problems. Sydney Ahlstrom notes that "the organization man, 'the lonely crowd' and the suburban status seeker became new features of the religious situations."[24] Churches offered these disconnected individuals a sense of community and family.

Americans faced insecurity in areas beyond their work as well. The changing international scene, the challenges of new technologies, the new demands in a competitive work environment, the population boom, and other factors all contributed to a sense of uncertainty and rapid change. Herberg asserts that Americans were seeking security within the world's insecurities:

> Increasing numbers of younger people are turning to the security to be found in the enduring, elemental ways and institutions of mankind; in the family, they feel, they can find the permanence and stability, the meaning and value they crave amid a world falling into chaos. Religion, like the family, is one of the enduring, elemental institutions of mankind; indeed, the two have been closely linked from the very earliest times. The search for meaning and security in what is basic and unchanging, rather than in the fluctuating fortunes of social or political activity, is one of the major factors in the upswing of religion among the American people.[25]

Religion offered reassurance in a rapidly changing world.

Religion also provided reassurance in the face of *political* change and uncertainty. Religious explanations framed political issues and, to some degree, political terms merged into religious beliefs. Herberg reports that a *Ladies Home Journal* poll tested Americans' commitment to the "law of love"—"to love thy neighbor as thyself." Ninety percent reported they obeyed the law when the one to be loved was of another religion. Eighty percent said "yes" when the person was of another race. Seventy-eight percent would practice love toward a business competitor. However, the responses shifted dramatically when the survey raised political identifications. Only 27 percent said they would practice the "law of love" if the person to be loved was "a member of a political party that you think is dangerous." Sixty-three percent said "no" if the person addressed was "an enemy of the nation."[26] So while Americans reported an extremely loving self-perception, that generosity would not extend to the "Godless communists." Similarly, Ahlstrom notes that American responses to the Cold War and the Korean Conflict often blended political and religious terms:

> Consciously and subconsciously, with and without governmental stimuli, the patriotism of this "nation with the soul of a church" was aroused. Being a church member and speaking favorably of religion became a means of affirming the "American way of life," especially since the USSR and its Communist allies were formally committed to atheism. The other side of this process—and to a degree its result—was a long drawn out repetition of the Red Scare of 1919-20. Senator Joseph McCarthy of Wisconsin had his heyday, and being an active church member became a way to avoid suspicion of being a subversive influence.[27]

Faith in the American Way and its attendant patriotic values equaled personal and national security.

The social and political climate offered clear rhetorical resources to political leaders who could align themselves with America's faith. Yet, not just anyone could wield the rhetorical power offered by faith. Just as the phrase "trust me" often conjures the opposite response when employed by a suspicious character, only a political leader with a consistent ethos can effectively exhort others to have faith.

Not surprisingly, Eisenhower's own ethos matched the times in which he was elected. Eisenhower returned home a hero after World War II. His popularity among American voters was unchallenged. Richard E. Crable notes that Ike's public identifications as a successful military leader, a common, down-to-earth individual, and a humble, non-political man merged into two paradoxical and strategic images: the peaceful warrior and the duty-bound consensus builder. He became a hero, says Crable, "not because he was a warrior or a pacifist, a leader or a common man, a candidate or a nonpartisan, or a politician or a nonpolitician. He was a hero because he—simultaneously and paradoxically—was all of these things."[28] Eisenhower offered an insecure people experience, strength, and confidence.

Eisenhower also offered Americans spiritual guidance. As a candidate, Eisenhower offered greater hope and security. Herberg argues that Eisenhower cast his candidacy in terms of a moral crusade: "I am engaged in a crusade . . . to substitute good government for what we most earnestly believe has been bad government."[29] As president, Eisenhower embraced two central religious themes, according to Fairbanks. First, he insisted that "there is a God who stands over the nation." Second, he asserted that the nation's political strength came from its religious faith.[30] Like the American people, Eisenhower asserted that faith was a good in itself: "Our government makes no sense unless it is founded in a deeply felt religious faith—and I don't care what it is."[31] Eisenhower asserted that "recognition of the Supreme Being is the first, the most basic expression of Americanism. Without God, there could be no American form of government, nor an American way of life."[32] He further asserted that democracy is a spiritual conviction, "a conviction that each of us is enormously valuable because of a certain standing before our own God."[33] In 1953, Billy Graham, a national religious symbol in his own right, said, "The overwhelming majority of the American people felt a little more secure realizing that we have a man who believes in prayer at the helm of our government at this crucial hour."[34] Eisenhower gave voice to America's civil religion. In part because of his religious identifications, Americans not only liked Ike, but they trusted him. They placed their faith in his leadership and his vision of America.

Thus, Eisenhower's ethos not only was consistent with America's religiosity, America's religiosity was part of Eisenhower's ethos. Eisenhower's choice of the term faith was in character not only for Eisenhower, but for the nation as well.

Yet, faith was more than an expression of personal and national character. Faith provided a rhetorical strategy through which Eisenhower reassured Americans about threats to their peace of mind and security. The hydrogen bomb was a particularly troublesome issue. It was simultaneously a horrible destructive force and the centerpiece of American military security. Herberg writes, "the utter predicament of human existence is no longer simply a philosophical or theological proposition; it is the most patent of everyday facts. The hydrogen bomb, on which our survival depends, yet which threatens us with destruction, is the sinister symbol of our plight."[35] Given his commitment to its further development, Eisenhower needed to define the hydrogen bomb in positive terms consistent with America's present orientation. Eisenhower used faith to place the hydrogen bomb in an unthreatening, and indeed reassuring, definitional context. Rather than a sinister symbol, the hydrogen bomb became the primary means through which America remained at peace and secure. The sinister bomb became a saving grace.

## EISENHOWER'S FAITH AND THE HYDROGEN BOMB

In early November 1952, Secretary of the Atomic Energy Commission Roy Snapp met President-elect Eisenhower at Augusta National Golf Club. Snapp's mission was to brief Eisenhower about the most recent nuclear weapons test— the Mike shot. Snapp gave Eisenhower a letter from AEC Chairman Gordon Dean which described the first full-scale thermonuclear device. Its explosive power was a thousand times greater than the Hiroshima bomb. The island test site, Eugelab, disappeared, vaporized in an instant. Only an underwater crater of fifteen-hundred yards in diameter remained.[36] Eisenhower quickly grasped the implication of the breakthrough and expressed concern especially about apparent lapses of secrecy. He promptly scheduled a more in-depth AEC briefing for later that month.

The commissioners met secretly with the president-elect in New York on 19 November, with President Truman's full knowledge and support. They detailed the AEC's programs for research and development, both for nuclear weapons and nuclear power. Richard Hewlett and Jack M. Holl report that "it was clear that Eisenhower fully supported the Commission's efforts rapidly to enlarge the arsenal of nuclear weapons and to maintain that strength as the bastion of national security." At the same time, Eisenhower understood "the possibilities for human failure, misdirected ambition, intrigue, treachery, and death in the nuclear era."[37] Because of this, Eisenhower was passionate about secrecy and security.

The commissioners, too, desired intense secrecy. Originally the AEC hoped to keep the most recent nuclear tests secret long enough to prevent Soviet scientists from gathering information from the atmosphere. Unfortunately, security leaks confirmed the test, if not its specific results. Hewlett reports that the potential for thermonuclear weapons quelled even the commissioners: "A curious silence surrounded anything related to the hydrogen bomb. The enormous magnitude of its implications was almost too terrifying to contemplate. Even the Commissioners and those few members of the staff used to discussing the subject could not speak casually in the awesome presence of the bomb."[38] This "Super" weapon produced a qualitative surge forward into the nuclear age.

Thus, as Eisenhower was inaugurated, he and a very few others knew that the threat of nuclear weapons was about to escalate exponentially. Despite the changing nature of the situation, Eisenhower's inaugural address created not only a sense of urgency but a sense of hope. He described the world in the opposed terms of the growing Cold War: the United States and the Soviet Union, the forces of good and of evil respectively, stood opposed in the ultimate struggle over the future. Not surprisingly, given his knowledge of the hydrogen bomb, Eisenhower stressed that a critical moment had arrived and that the moment demanded an American response:

> The world and we have passed the midway point of a century of continuing challenge. We sense with all our faculties that forces of good and evil are massed and armed and opposed as rarely before in history. This fact defines the meaning of this day.[39]

Eisenhower's language might have seemed extreme to a public that knew little of the magnitude of thermonuclear power. In retrospect, Eisenhower's statements about international tension might seem understated, rather than exaggerated. Hindsight does not change analysis of his rhetorical response to that situation, however. His message was as clear then as it is now. Americans, Eisenhower counseled, must renew their faith in America's identity and purpose:

> We are summoned by this honored and historic ceremony to witness more than the act of one citizen swearing his oath of service, in the presence of God. We are called as a people to give testimony in the sight of the world to our faith that the future shall belong to the free.

In this critical hour, Eisenhower called the nation to fulfill its moral and spiritual duty. He asked the nation to renew its commitment to "freedom" and to its "faith" in America and the world's journey toward freedom. He asserted clearly that America's leadership was the outcome of neither choice nor accident; on the contrary, he declared that "destiny has laid upon our country the responsibility of the free world's leadership." What America must do to fulfill that destiny, he argued, was to renew and to enact "faith."

Eisenhower confessed that world events continually tested America's faith. Leadership was an uncertain and difficult proposition given the heated opposition between "freedom-loving people" and "Communist aggressors." Indeed, the forces of good and the forces of evil sometimes were difficult to distinguish. As he said in his inaugural:

> The promise of this life is imperiled by the very genius that has made it possible. Nations amass wealth. Labor sweats to create—and turns out devices to level not only mountains but also cities. Science seems ready to confer upon us, as its final gift, the power to erase human life from this planet.

Thus, within Eisenhower's definitional frame, the answer to the nation's (and the world's) problems and uncertainty was to proclaim and remain faithful to America's purpose as the "protector of and leader toward freedom." Indeed, he referred to the need for faith twelve times in the address. In his definition of the world's situation, faith defines and rules. Eisenhower asserted that Americans "shall remain free, never to be proven guilty of the one capital offense against freedom, a lack of staunch faith."

With freedom and its preservation as the terms adopted to describe America's purpose, all other acts were framed accordingly. In Eisenhower's terms, the explanation and evaluation of any situation was not determined by terms for acts *per se* but by terms which describe the purpose behind a given act. For Eisenhower, America's fundamental faith must guide all her actions. As he said at the close of his inaugural:

The peace we seek, then, is nothing less than the practice and fulfillment of our whole faith among ourselves and in our dealings with others. This signifies more than the stilling of guns, easing the sorrow of war. More than an escape from death, it is a way of life. More than a haven for the weary, it is a hope for the brave. This is the hope that beckons us onward in this century of trial. This is the work that awaits us all, to be done with bravery, with charity, and with prayer to Almighty God.

Eisenhower's choice of the broad term "faith" to encompass appropriate action left substantial room for policy maneuvering. Many, and even contradictory, policies could fall within the nation's faith in its destiny because Eisenhower never defined exactly what political acts constituted "faith."

American agencies also are defined in terms of America's purpose. Thus, for Eisenhower, the "power to level mountains" was inherently neither good nor bad. That power was only as good or bad as the purpose it fulfilled. Thus, if such power was used "to erase human life from [the] planet," the power was negative. But if the very same power could be used to preserve freedom, it would serve a good purpose and would be good power. Kenneth Burke has noted that the agency-purpose, or means-end, terminological relations leave the evaluation of means open to interpretation:

All means are necessarily "impure." For besides the properties in them that fit them for the particular use to which they are put, they have other properties (properties that would fit them for other possible uses, including hostile uses.) And their identity in themselves (as against their identity from the standpoint of some particular use) thus make them ambiguous from the standpoint of their possible consequences. That is, there is no one end exclusively implicit in them. And thus, from the standpoint of any given end, they are "impure." And we act by a progressive purification of them.[40]

Eisenhower "purified" America's primary agency of "security," nuclear weapons, by defining them in terms of America's pursuit and protection of freedom.

Eisenhower's discourse merged terms for purpose and terms for agents and agencies; an individual's purpose reflected character. A righteous purpose justified any means necessary to uphold or enact that purpose. In other words, Eisenhower proposed that to know the actor's purpose (and thus the actor) was to know the nature of the act and the agency. The fundamental assumption behind Eisenhower's message was that Americans, because they were guided by a righteous purpose, performed only "good" acts, if they remained true to their destined leadership role. To be American was to seek freedom in all circumstances.

As Eisenhower's administration began, nuclear weapons were defined as part of America's efforts to protect freedom. A belief in American destiny and

American righteousness legitimized the proliferation of nuclear weapons. Eisenhower's inauguration, in his own view, expressed "a purpose of strengthening our dedication and devotion to the precepts of our founding documents, a conscious renewal of faith in our country and in the watchfulness of a Divine Providence." He used polarized Cold War rhetoric to cast Americans as heroic "protectors of freedom" and the Soviet Union as villainous "Communist aggressors" whose goal was to destroy "freedom" at the first possible opportunity. Nuclear weapons in American control were a means to protect freedom; in Soviet hands, nuclear weapons became agencies of aggression. Thus, not the weapons, but the ideologies and purposes of each side defined the situation. The weapons themselves were not a threat. Indeed, in this definitional frame, nuclear weapons were no different than any other weapon. They were undeniably more powerful but they still were controlled by human purpose.

Eisenhower's Cold War rhetoric combined with his emphasis on the term "faith" created a strategic definitional frame for nuclear weapons issues. Cold War oppositions legitimized nuclear weapons as part of America's ongoing struggle for freedom, established an urgent threat which justified greater military force, and simplified a complex issue. The faith-centered oppositions inspired devotion and encouraged Americans to support their president's policies.

While Eisenhower's emphasis on terms for America's purpose and faith provided inspiration, it also contributed to strategic policy making. Despite Eisenhower's purification of nuclear weapons, their potential threat if held by other, less pure, hands always lurked in Eisenhower's policy. Ike resolved many apparent contradictions in policy through his identified purpose: America could seek peace and build more weapons simultaneously; America could, in theory, create peace through its ability to inflict harm; America could further freedom in the world through military intervention in the politics of other nations. As long as Americans remained true to their purpose, as long as their acts could be cast as efforts "to preserve freedom," those acts worked toward good. The means to achieve the purpose were sanctioned theoretically, even before they were identified.

A concomitant premise in this terminology was that all who opposed "American acts" were part of the "massed forces of evil" which would lead the world toward greater darkness. Given Eisenhower's identifications, those individuals who even subtly opposed the administration's policies challenged, or perhaps thwarted, America's destiny. With McCarthyism on the rise, Americans already were especially careful about their behavior. Eisenhower's orientation, intentionally or not, reinforced the country's growing paranoia.

Moreover, Eisenhower's terminology reassured the American people that a lack of detailed information was unimportant to their role. Faith was "unquestioning loyalty." Anyone who sought out details or questioned policy decisions demonstrated a lack of faith, which Eisenhower already had identified as the greatest sin against freedom. Much as a good Christian did not challenge God's will, so too must Americans not demonstrate a weak faith by asking the administration for more information. Faith encouraged the public quiescence necessary to extreme secrecy.

Eisenhower's key terms and identifications tapped into historically legitimate and presently invigorated American values—freedom, an American destiny, progress, and science. Eisenhower's ideas, therefore, drew from salient ideals. Yet, putting these ideals into concrete terms was difficult. Eisenhower spoke of military strength and nuclear superiority, yet privately he agreed to use only the psychological power of nuclear weapons.[41] At the same time, the United States was committed to the protection of free peoples throughout the world. Beyond these defense concerns, Eisenhower had promised to move toward a balanced budget. Nuclear weapons, especially the hydrogen bomb, promised "more bang for the buck."[42] Thus, Eisenhower's faith in freedom was reinforced by economic motives. To meet his international and domestic obligations, Eisenhower introduced a "New Look" in military preparedness.

The New Look committed the United States to a massive nuclear deterrent on land, sea, and air. Despite his personal reluctance, in October 1953, Eisenhower approved the addition of the following sentence to the nation's security policy: "In the event of hostilities, the United States will consider nuclear weapons to be as available for use as other munitions."[43] The Strategic Air Command's long-range bombers, planes equipped to deliver the U.S. nuclear force anywhere in the world, were identified as "the major deterrent" to Soviet aggression. Eisenhower's New Look responded to predicted Soviet nuclear capabilities. When the U.S.S.R. successfully detonated a thermonuclear device in August 1953, much sooner than American scientists had predicted, the threat, in terms of capability, became real.

Despite public statements to the contrary, America's military policy was not merely a matter of outpacing the Soviets. Expert predictions proposed that "nuclear superiority" soon would be a meaningless term, no matter the quantity or quality of the nuclear arsenal. Eisenhower's New Look faced imminent obsolescence.

## THE OPPENHEIMER PANEL CHALLENGES EISENHOWER'S TERMS

Late in his administration, President Harry S. Truman created a panel to advise him on the potential for international disarmament. Vannevar Bush, Allen Dulles, John S. Dickey, and Joseph E. Johnson comprised the panel. J. Robert Oppenheimer, the wartime director of the Los Alamos laboratory, served as the panel's chair. The essence of their report, usually called the

Oppenheimer Report, became public in July 1953. Oppenheimer summarized the panel's recommendations in a *Foreign Affairs* article, "Atomic Weapons and American Policy."[44]

Oppenheimer's discourse seemed to counter Eisenhower's hopeful definition of the nuclear situation. Oppenheimer painted a very bleak picture of world affairs. Despite what he described as overwhelming security constraints, Oppenheimer tried to communicate a very dangerous situation:

> What I can say is this: I have never discussed these prospects candidly with any responsible group, whether scientists or statesmen, whether citizens or officers of the government, . . . that they did not come away with a great sense of anxiety and somberness at what they saw. The very least we can say is that, looking ten years ahead, it is likely to be small comfort that the Soviet Union is four years behind us, and small comfort that they are only about half as big as we are. The ten-thousandth bomb, useful as it may be in filling the vast munitions pipelines of a great war, will not in any strategic sense offset their two-thousandth.[45]

Oppenheimer, in a single paragraph, stripped the United States of the "strategic superiority" on which its entire defense was built. While the Soviet Union's technology trailed American nuclear capability significantly, Oppenheimer offered little hope that the difference would be meaningful for long. Truman's and Eisenhower's policies were built on the assumption that the United States held an overwhelming lead in nuclear weapons development and production. Each time that lead had been eroded, the United States had responded with a major innovation; such was the case with the hydrogen bomb. Oppenheimer predicted a change in the course of the nuclear arms race. He did not challenge the superiority of American weapons; he did challenge the assumption that military superiority was meaningful to long-term security. Oppenheimer suggested that bigger and better and more weapons did not necessarily equal increased security. Moreover, he predicted that significant change was unlikely; a decrease in the mutual hostility between the United States and the Soviet Union was unrealistic. Oppenheimer insisted that the situation, therefore, only would worsen:

> Thus the prevailing view is that we are probably faced with a long period of cold war in which conflict, tension, and armaments are to be with us. The trouble then is just this: during this period the atomic clock ticks faster and faster. We may anticipate a state of affairs in which two great powers will each be in a position to put an end to the civilization and life of the other, though not without risking its own. We may be likened to two scorpions in a bottle, each capable of killing the other, but only at the risk of his own life.

Today, Oppenheimer's analysis is familiar and accurate. But, in 1953, as McGeorge Bundy notes, Oppenheimer's words were both "startling and chilling."

Bundy explains that Oppenheimer's argument "was presented when no Soviet thermonuclear explosion had yet occurred and when American superiority was overwhelming. In this situation it was daunting to be required to recognize the absence of any reason whatever for future complacency."[46] The president had very recently told the American people to "have faith" and to be hopeful about the international situation. He had told them that Americans had nothing to fear, if they maintained their faith in America's ability to lead the world toward freedom. Oppenheimer's predictions counseled that faith might be insufficient to meet this unforeseen challenge. The links between nuclear weapons and security were weakened by Oppenheimer's report.

Eisenhower accepted some of Oppenheimer's ideas and rejected others. Yet, in October 1953, Eisenhower reiterated his "faith"-ful nuclear rhetoric. In a speech to the national assembly of the United Church Women, Eisenhower said that the group's "three-fold faith" in "yourselves, in your country, and in God" was the "very basis of our society."[47] He said that "faith is evidently too simple a thing for some to recognize its paramount worth" and thus drew attention to its value:

> Now, of course, the cynic—the Marxist or the worshipper of machines and numbers—will scoff that faith is no armor against artillery, that the spirit weakens fast before the blast of the bomb. But your husbands and brothers and fathers can testify that in the terrifying nakedness of the battlefield, the faith and the spirit of men are the keys to survival and victory.

Eisenhower called on his high credibility as a military commander to assert that faith was more powerful than any weapon. And military weapons had no power without faith. Indeed, under threat of nuclear war, Eisenhower saw faith as a central factor in America's movement toward peace. After listing measures which must be taken to arrive at security, Eisenhower turned again to his underlying principle of faith:

> Now, these are some of the grand labors before us—the tasks and tests and problems that span the world. For the spirit that will resolve them, however, we need not seek the source in distant places. I deeply believe that one of the supreme hopes for the world's destiny lies in the American community: in its moral values, in its sense of order and decency, in its cooperative spirit. . . . [America's] leadership depends no less directly upon the faith, the courage, the love of freedom and the capacity for sacrifice of every American citizen, every American home, every American community.

"Faith in Freedom" defined American character. Finally, at the speech's end, after thirteen references to "faith," Eisenhower reiterated the ideal he professed in his inaugural address:

'Whatever America hopes to bring to pass in the world, must first come to pass in the heart of America.' I know no more plain or pure ideal to which we can pledge our lives. I know of no other way we can prove worthy of freedom.

In these passages, Eisenhower contended that the American people had the ability and the duty to have faith. With faith, America could preserve freedom and create peace. Without faith, America was, in Eisenhower's terms, lost. Indeed, a "faithless" American was no American at all. For Eisenhower, "faithless American" was an oxymoron.

At about the same time, the Eisenhower administration, for several months, pursued "Operation Candor" as a response to the Oppenheimer panel's recommendations.[48] Eventually, the administration adopted a much less extreme position than the panel proposed. Their compromise was made public in late 1953 in Eisenhower's famous "Atoms for Peace" address to the United Nations.[49] In that speech, Eisenhower proposed that all governments principally involved in nuclear weapons production should make contributions of fissionable material to an International Atomic Energy Agency. That material would be used to research and develop peaceful applications of nuclear power. A key function of the plan, Eisenhower asserted, was to open a discussion designed to answer the difficult problems posed by nuclear energy. His proposal stressed cooperation, discussion, and openness. He called for an international body to govern atomic energy.

Yet, "candor," as the Oppenheimer panel defined it, was not part of Eisenhower's terminology. Oppenheimer called for more open disclosure of nuclear weapons data. Eisenhower decided to encourage cooperation about peaceful applications of nuclear energy only. Information about atomic weapons development still was given the government's most stringent protection. Security required secrecy. And public faith made such secrecy possible.

Perhaps more telling, however, was Eisenhower's own lack of candor. He spoke as if the threat of nuclear weapons in 1953 were no more substantial than the danger immediately following World War II. He still spoke as if America enjoyed an overwhelming and un-threatened nuclear superiority, although scientists' predictions and military evidence suggested that the nation's superiority soon might be meaningless. Bundy maintains that "Eisenhower understood the somber conclusions of Oppenheimer's panel, and in many later words and actions he showed his broad agreement with them, but he was not willing to 'scare' people or to leave them without an upbeat message of hope."[50] Eisenhower mentioned the terrible danger posed by thermonuclear weapons. He confessed a concern about the "unfriendly hands" that held nuclear weapons. Yet, in the end, he claimed to be opening a new door to negotiation and world peace.

Martin Medhurst notes that while Eisenhower's explicit message remained positive and hopeful, the president and his key advisors never intended to pursue disarmament agreements. The president's goal was to engender other sorts of international cooperation. Medhurst argues convincingly that the speech was designed to put the U.S.S.R. on the defensive and to cast America as the leader toward peace.[51] Eisenhower's discourse inspired Americans to live up to their destined purpose and encouraged them to remain faithful. Unfortunately, that hope was based on a seemingly small prospect of cooperation.

Thus, by the end of 1953, Eisenhower's faith-centered rhetorical perspective was in place. He placed both constructive and destructive uses of nuclear power within his overall definitional frame. Because he asserted that America followed a righteous purpose, the nation's inability to disarm was only in response to the Communist villain, not a part of her innate character. America wanted to beat weapons into plowshares. But, according to Eisenhower, the United States had no choice but to develop a more powerful nuclear arsenal. Once America established security, then the nation was free to pursue peaceful uses for nuclear power and to work toward disarmament.

## EISENHOWER INTRODUCES THE HYDROGEN BOMB

Throughout 1953, the question of humanity's control of the forces of fusion rarely had been raised. Yet, the next year brought new challenges to Eisenhower in the nuclear realm. On 17 March 1954, the United States announced the success of Operation Castle. America had tested a *usable* hydrogen bomb. The "Super" was news.[52]

The Castle series produced unprecedented results. Not only was a practical weapon tested, but that weapon's explosive potential was incredible. Headlines on 18 March declared "2nd Hydrogen Blast Proves Mightier Than Any Forecast."[53] After days of official silence, Eisenhower admitted that the hydrogen blast was much bigger than anticipated; even the scientists were surprised by its magnitude. Because the scientists had underestimated the blast, fallout from the test irradiated twenty-eight Americans and 236 Pacific Island natives. A Japanese ship also was showered with radioactive fallout; all aboard suffered from radiation illness. Their cargo was dangerous and impounded upon their arrival in Japan. The ship had been well outside the government's designated test area. Although the government insisted that injuries sustained were minor, the tests seemed "out of control."[54] Uncertainty in this instance could be measured in megatons. The American public and its leaders were anxious. The Castle test raised questions about the security of nuclear weapons, in and of themselves, not as a means to some overriding purpose.

Congressional leaders called for more information. Two days later, Eisenhower released to the media the first film and color photos of a hydrogen blast. The photos showed only an earlier hydrogen bomb test. Information from the most recent tests was held in strict secrecy. Only the most general statements were allowed. Even in peacetime, a "candor" such as that proposed by the Oppenheimer panel was inimical to the country's interests, according to the Atomic Energy Commission and the White House. The AEC and others feared that the Soviets or others might glean important information from U.S. tests. Finally, under congressional and public pressure for full disclosure, Eisenhower called a press conference. He made a short opening statement and turned the explanative task over to AEC Commissioner Lewis Strauss. Strauss delivered the startling news that the hydrogen bomb could wipe out any city.

Strauss recounted the official story of the hydrogen bomb's development: America built the atomic bomb; the Soviet Union exploded a similar device in August 1949; America had to regain the lead in the arms race. Strauss adopted the administration's Cold War terminology and used it to explain America's most recent response to Soviet aggression: "Realizing that our leadership was therefore challenged and that our sole possession of the weapon which had been a major deterrent to aggression had been canceled, it became clear that our superiority would therefore be only relative and dependent upon a quantitative lead."[55] One obvious solution, Strauss reported, was to build greater numbers of atomic weapons. A second alternative was to achieve a qualitatively more powerful weapon. Truman had given the go-ahead to research that weapon, the Super. A successful test of a thermonuclear prototype was accomplished in November 1952. While America almost lost the lead in nuclear weapons development, Strauss noted that, luckily, America had responded well and regained nuclear superiority with the Castle series. To conclude, he reiterated the administration's position: The United States would develop peaceful uses of atomic power now that military security was once again assured. A successful test of the most destructive weapon ever known opened the avenue toward peace.

Strauss, like Eisenhower, expressed confidence, satisfaction, and hope, yet reporters asked questions that indicated concern. They wanted to know if the weapons could explode "out of control." They asked Strauss to comment on the weapon's "unbelievable" blast. America's faith was shaken. A final exchange between Strauss and reporters captured the public unease and the government's reticence to discuss nuclear capabilities:

> Reporter:  Many people in Congress, I think many elsewhere, have been reaching out and grasping for some information as to what happens when the H-bomb goes off, how big is the area of destruction in its various stages; and what I am asking you for now is some enlightenment on that subject.

Strauss:    Well, the nature of an H-bomb, Mr. Wilson, is that, in effect, it can be made to be as large as you wish, as large as the military requirement demands, that is to say, an H-bomb can be made large enough to take out a city.

Chorus:     What?

Strauss:    To take out a city.

Reporter:   How big a city?

Strauss:    Any city.

Reporter:   Any city? New York?

Strauss:    The metropolitan area, yes.[56]

The country was shocked. In order to reassure the American people, President Eisenhower discussed the problems of the Hydrogen Age in a radio and television address to the nation four days later.

Eisenhower spoke to the American people about what he called a "very big subject"; he spoke about America's "strengths, its problems, its apprehensions, and its future."[57] Eisenhower emphasized yet again the spiritual faith required for America to be secure:

> But I want to call your particular attention to spiritual strength. Now, I don't think it amiss, in this season of the year that has so many religious overtones, that we call attention to this fact: that in conception, our Nation had a spiritual foundation, so announced by the men who wrote the Declaration of Independence. You remember what they said? "We hold that all men are endowed by their Creator with certain rights." That is very definitely a spiritual conception. . . . I want to call your attention to this particular part of the American strength, because without all this everything else goes by the board. We must be strong in our dedication and our devotion to America. That is the first element of our entire strength.

In this opening section, Eisenhower again tied all American success—military, political, and social—to the ability and willingness of Americans to remain faithful to a "spiritual conception" of America. Having reiterated the spiritual duty of Americans, Eisenhower began to discuss the "threats coming from all angles—internal and external." The first threat came in the form of the hydrogen bomb:

> Now, this transfer of power, this increase of power from a mere musket and a little cannon, all the way to the hydrogen bomb in a single lifetime, is indicative of

the things that have happened to us. They rather indicate how far the advances of science have outraced our social consciousness, how much more we have developed scientifically than we are capable of handling emotionally and intellectually. So that is one of the reasons that we have this great concern, of which the hydrogen bomb is merely a dramatic symbol.

Eisenhower minimized the hydrogen bomb's destructive potential and drew attention away from its "uncontrollable" power demonstrated only days earlier. He asserted that the hydrogen bomb was "merely a dramatic symbol." Consistent with his earlier rhetoric, the bomb itself did not pose a threat. He contended that the threat resided in human beings, not weapons:

> Now, the H-bomb—the H-bomb and the Atomic Age. They are not in themselves a great threat to us. Of course not. The H-bomb is a threat to us only if a potential aggressor, who also has the secrets of the H-bomb, determines to use it against us. And against that, then, we have to make our provisions, to make certain that sensible men have done every possible thing they can to protect ourselves against that threat.

Thus, a military build-up and continued civil defense measures were justified. Eisenhower almost admitted that some concern might be justified as well, given that all people were not as spiritually motivated as were Americans:

> Sometimes you feel, almost that we can be excused for getting a little bit hysterical, because these dangers come from so many angles, and they are of such different kinds, and no matter what we do they still seem to exist. But underlying all of these dangers is one thing; the threat that we have from without, the great threat imposed upon us by aggressive communism, the atheistic doctrine that believes in statism as against our conception of the dignity of man, his equality before the law—that is the struggle of the ages.

While he accepted some worry as a natural response to the situation, Eisenhower also reassured Americans that they were equal to the challenge. He contended that America's problems were no more complex than the problems that Americans faced in their own homes every day:

> This is not greatly different from what the ordinary American family does. It has the problems of meeting the payments on the mortgage, paying for the family car, educating the children, laying aside some money for use in case of unexpected illness. It meets these problems courageously. It doesn't get panicky. It solves these problems with what I would call courage and faith, but above all by cooperation, by discussing the problem among the different members of the family and then saying: this is what we can do, this is what we will do, and reaching a satisfactory answer.

He argued that the nation's problems were of the same kind, just of a greater magnitude.

From the outset of this speech, Eisenhower sounded like a parent scolding a child who was frightened by a shadow in the dark. He talked of unwarranted panic and hysteria. This tone and his use of a family metaphor were not surprising, given his overall terminological orientation. Eisenhower's emphasis on faith created a parental, caretaker role. In Christianity, God is a loving, all-knowing father; in Eisenhower's rhetoric, the president and his administration take care of the American people. At another level, the people, like the family members, were to have courage and faith, they were to cooperate, and, although the premise was left implicit, they were to abide by and to support the family's decision. Eisenhower's terms discouraged private, let alone public, dissent against his nuclear policies. Clearly, without his own parental and "priestly" ethos, Eisenhower's admonitions might just as easily invite rebellion as quiescence.

Having scolded citizens for a lack of faith, Eisenhower rebuilt the public's flagging spirit. Eisenhower assured America that no need for worry existed, because Americans would live up to their destiny:

> Now, my friends, I should say that the one great aspiration of America is a free, peaceful, and prosperous world. To have a free, peaceful, and prosperous world, we must be ever stronger; we must be ever stronger not only in the things I have mentioned but particularly in this spiritual sense, in the belief— the faith that we can do certain things. We must have the faith that comes from a study of our own history, from the inspiration of leaders like Washington and Lincoln, and what our pioneering forefathers did.

Eisenhower again argued that as long as America stayed true to her purpose she had nothing to fear:

> There must be something in the heart as well as the head. So as we do this, as you and I approach our problems in this way, I assure you we don't have to fear. Of course there are risks, if we are not vigilant. But we do not have to be hysterical. We can be vigilant. We can be Americans. We can stand up and hold up our heads and say: America is the greatest force that God has ever allowed to exist on his footstool. As such it is up to us to lead this world to a peaceful and secure existence. And I assure you we can do it.

As in his earlier discourse, Eisenhower refused to scare the public. He continued to paint a world picture which was far from perfect but which also was far from hopeless. Communism was a problem but it was one that Americans could handle, both externally and internally, if they remained faithful and vigilant.

Eisenhower's speech did not quell all questions. *U.S. News and World Report* asked "Is the H-Bomb Going 'Wild?' *Newsweek* queried "Where Now, World?"[58] These articles and others reported the new questions and answers raised by the recent hydrogen bomb tests. In the end, however, the weapon's overpowering destructive capability was turned into a "good." One report said, "it all boils down to this: Both [the] U.S. and Russia now have a bomb that is far beyond anything anticipated when American scientists got the go-ahead four years ago. It cannot yet destroy the earth with one blast, or set off secondary reactions that could, but the trend seems to be in that direction. . . . Perhaps the destructive power of the H-Bomb has become so great that no nation will start a major war, which would inevitably involve its use."[59] *Newsweek* concurred: "H-Bomb Odds: 1 Million to 1—and That's What May Save Us."[60] The country gradually moved from the era of "massive retaliation" to embrace the era of "mutual assured destruction." While many European nations launched protests against the hydrogen bomb, Americans continued to have faith that America and freedom would endure the hydrogen age.

## CONCLUSION

Eisenhower's faith-centered Cold War rhetoric offered several rhetorical advantages. First, the definitions he proposed were broad enough to encompass what might appear to be conflicting policies. He could promote international cooperation and a national military build-up simultaneously . Moreover, his terminology easily accommodated changes in the overall situation. The Soviets' explosion of a hydrogen device and America's test of a feasible hydrogen bomb merely were extensions of events already explained by Eisenhower's orientation.

By emphasizing America's purpose to "preserve freedom" and identifying the hydrogen bomb as an agency of that purpose, Eisenhower placed the hydrogen bomb within an American rhetorical tradition and thereby changed it from a "threat" to a "savior." Eisenhower reassured America that the hydrogen bomb's destructive potential contributed to America's security. He reassured the American public that the hydrogen bomb posed no threat, as long as Americans controlled it. According to Eisenhower, the hydrogen bomb was merely a next step in America's destined quest to preserve freedom and create peace. Because America's purposes were noble, the hydrogen bomb in and of itself posed no threat.

Furthermore, Eisenhower's choice of the term faith tapped the rhetorical strengths of religious symbols. Such symbols provided an infinite time frame in which to accomplish goals and create a unity of apparently contradictory conclusions. As Ira Chernus notes:

> Religious symbols frequently (some would say always) mediate a reality that seems to be infinite—unlimited in power, in knowledge, in space, and in time. This reality transcends rational comprehension; . . . Simultaneously, though, the religious symbol represents coherence, structure, and order in the

world. It beckons with its assurance of all-embracing security. In a sense, it is related to the promise of continuing life.[61]

Thus, in choosing religious terms to define the hydrogen bomb, Eisenhower tapped powerful, existent symbols which identified the Super bomb as a means to gain security, hope, and even life, just when life on earth seemed most threatened.

At a pragmatic level, characterizations of the hydrogen bomb as savior and an emphasis on faith and America's destiny encouraged Americans to forestall judgment about the current administration's abilities to deal with the Soviet threat. During a quest, not even the hero can predict with certainty where the destined path will lead or where it will end. Thus, given this terminology, the public had no choice but to have faith and wait in hope that the triumphant end was near. Within this transcendent frame, events that might have been described as failures became merely temporary setbacks in the ongoing struggle. At each juncture, the rhetor again called the people to renew faith as the struggle continued.

The emphasis on faith also offered the public a means to participate psychologically or spiritually, without inviting them to participate in substantive discussions of policy or to challenge policy. To argue against Eisenhower's characterization of the hydrogen bomb was to argue against America's destiny. To argue against the hydrogen bomb was to demonstrate a lack of faith, an act Eisenhower identified explicitly as the greatest sin against patriotism. Eisenhower's terms, therefore, discouraged criticism of his New Look defense policy.

Beyond the broad strategic potential of religious symbols, Eisenhower applied that potential to a "religious" force in society and politics. Chernus argues that nuclear weapons are especially amenable to religious characterization. Because nuclear weapons are perceived as omnipotent, omniscient, and omnipresent, people respond to them religiously.[62] As with a god, people experience both awe and fear in the bomb's presence. It holds the power both to save and to destroy the world. In some sense, we are at its mercy. Thus, Eisenhower's religious characterization of the hydrogen bomb resonated with his audience's psychological experience of nuclear weapons.

Because faithful people do not question gods or a god's spokespersons on earth, faith also encouraged the public to accept the secrecy the Eisenhower administration deemed necessary to national security. While the president justified secrecy as a response to the Soviet threat, the secrets were not kept from the Soviets alone. The American public knew little of its own nation's strengths and weaknesses. Indeed, the Oppenheimer Report argued that the Soviets could gain little new information from the recommended disclosures to the American people.[63] Eisenhower, however, refused to "scare the people to death." He preferred that they remain confident, and ignorant, in their faith.

Eisenhower's emphasis on terms for American purpose also suggested that America need not take responsibility for the growing nuclear arms race. Guilt was placed elsewhere. Americans were responding to the Soviet threat. Despite Hiroshima, Americans were free from "nuclear sin" because they had no choice but to defend freedom. America's purpose legitimized a military build-up.

While Eisenhower's rhetorical choices were pragmatically strategic, they raise questions about the power of language to subvert public participation and democratic debate. A faith-centered rhetoric pacifies and reassures. While politically expedient, the terminological choices hold implications for democratic process and implicitly subvert the same values the "American Way" celebrates. Doris Graber and Murray Edelman note that the use of powerful, emotion-laden terms such as liberty, and freedom (and I would add faith), constrain the public's ability to question and respond to situations.[64] Graber notes the results of such "symbolic sanctions":

> If it is "patriotic" to fight in a war and "traitorous" to refuse to fight, the average person prefers risking his life to risking his reputation. The decision becomes a question of adhering to or rejecting the mores of one's community, rather than a question of weighing the situation on its merits.[65]

Thus, when Eisenhower labeled a challenge to the nation's military policy as a "lack of faith" and "unpatriotic," he limited the public to one response—faith and its explicitly designated enactments. In order to preserve freedom, Eisenhower, in effect, denied it.

No critic can draw a causal link between a rhetor's language choices and the public's response to a situation. However, criticism may note characteristics of discourse which hold implications for public action and for potential policy. Inasmuch as Eisenhower's discourse featured terms which encouraged a particular perspective toward nuclear weapons, he simultaneously advocated a public response to them as well. In the end, America "kept the faith" and, for good or evil, supported the nation's participation in a nuclear arms race.

## NOTES

1. Robert S. Alley, *So Help Me God: Religion and the Presidency, Wilson to Nixon* (Richmond, Virginia: John Knox Press, 1972), 82.
2. "Inaugural Address, January 20, 1953," *Public Papers of the Presidents of the United States: Dwight D. Eisenhower, 1953* (Washington, D.C.: Government Printing Office, 1954), 1 (hereafter cited as *Public Papers*).
3. Sydney E. Ahlstrom, *A Religious History of the American People* (New Haven: Yale University Press, 1972), 954.
4. R. Gordon Hoxie, "Eisenhower and Presidential Leadership," *Presidential Studies Quarterly* 13 (1983): 608.
5. Herbert York, *The Advisors: Oppenheimer, Teller and the Superbomb* (San Francisco: W. H. Freeman, 1976), 82-83.

6. Arthur M. Schlesinger, Jr., *The Cycles of American History* (Boston: Houghton-Mifflin, 1986), 1-22.
7. Russel B. Nye, *This Almost Chosen People: Essays in the History of American Ideas* (East Lansing: Michigan State University Press, 1966), 165.
8. Schlesinger, 14.
9. Ibid., 15.
10. Melville quoted in Schlesinger, 15.
11. James David Fairbanks, "The Priestly Functions of the Presidency: A Discussion of the Literature on Civil Religion and Its Implications for the Study of Presidential Leadership," *Presidential Studies Quarterly* 11 (1981): 215.
12. Fairbanks provides a comprehensive review and critique of literature on American civil religion. See Fairbanks, 216-29. For a rhetorical analysis of American civil religion, see Roderick P. Hart, *The Political Pulpit* (West Lafayette: Purdue University Press, 1977).
13. Hart, 12.
14. Michael Novak, *Choosing Our King: Powerful Symbols in Presidential Politics* (New York: Macmillan, 1974), 302.
15. Fairbanks, 218-19.
16. Will Herberg, *Protestant-Catholic-Jew: An Essay in American Religious Sociology*, 2nd ed. (New York: Anchor Books, 1060), 48.
17. George Gallup, Jr. and Sarah Jones, *100 Questions and Answers: Religion in America* (Princeton: Princeton Religion Research Center, 1989), 196.
18. Herberg, 51.
19. Ahlstrom, 957.
20. Herberg, 66.
21. Ibid., 103-4.
22. Kenneth Burke, *A Grammar of Motives* (1945; reprint, Berkeley: University of California Press, 1969), 288.
23. Burke, 310.
24. Ahlstrom, 951.
25. Herberg, 75.
26. Ibid., 89.
27. Ahlstrom, 951-952.
28. Richard E. Crable, "Ike: Identification, Argument, and Paradoxical Appeal," *Quarterly Journal of Speech* 63 (1977): 195.
29. Eisenhower quoted in Herberg, 79.
30. James David Fairbanks, "Religious Dimensions of Presidential Leadership: The Case of Dwight Eisenhower," *Presidential Studies Quarterly* 12 (1982): 264.
31. Eisenhower quoted in Herberg, 84.
32. Ibid., 258.
33. Fairbanks, "Religious Dimensions," 264.
34. Graham quoted in Alley, 86.
35. Herberg, 73.
36. Richard G. Hewlett and Jack M. Holl, *Atoms for Peace and War 1953-1961: Eisenhower and the Atomic Energy Commission* (Berkeley: University of California Press, 1990), 3.
37. Hewlett, 15.
38. Ibid., 12.
39. "Inaugural Address, January 20, 1953," *Public Papers, 1953*, 1. All subsequent quotations come from this source.
40. Burke, 309.

41. Bundy reports that despite his public statements about the possibility of employing nuclear weapons, Eisenhower wanted to avoid their use at all cost. Eisenhower resisted pressure to use nuclear weapons both in Korea and in Indochina. See McGeorge Bundy, *Danger and Survival: Choices About the Bomb in the First Fifty Years* (New York: Random House, 1988), 246-55.

42. John Newhouse, *War and Peace in the Nuclear Age* (New York: Alfred A. Knopf, 1989), 94-95.

43. Bundy, 246.

44. The article was reprinted in *The Bulletin of the Atomic Scientists*. See J. Robert Oppenheimer, "Atomic Weapons and American Policy," *The Bulletin of the Atomic Scientists* 9 (1953): 202-5. Commentary and an interview spawned by the article appeared as Gertrude Samuels, "A Plea for 'Candor' About the Atom," *The New York Times Magazine*, 21 June 1953.

45. Oppenheimer, 203. All subsequent quotations attributed to Oppenheimer come from this source.

46. Bundy, 289.

47. *Public Papers, 1953*, 634. All subsequent references come from this source.

48. Bundy, 287-95.

49. "Address Before the General Assembly of the United Nations on Peaceful Uses of Atomic Energy, New York City, December 8, 1953," *Public Papers, 1953*, 813-22.

50. Bundy, 292.

51. Martin J. Medhurst, "Eisenhower's 'Atoms for Peace' Speech: A Case Study in the Strategic Use of Language," *Communication Monographs* 54 (1987): 218-19.

52. For examples, see Hanson W. Baldwin, "Atom Tests Emphasize Stepped-Up Arms Race: New Series in Pacific will Include First Operating Model of H-Bomb," *New York Times*, 7 March 1954, D5; "Hydrogen Bomb Confirmed," *New York Times*, 17 March 1954, A9.

53. "2nd Hydrogen Blast Proves Mightier Than Any Forecast," *New York Times*, 18 March 1954, A1.

54. See "Fisherman Burned in Bikini Test Blast," *New York Times*, 16 March 1954, A19; Elie Abel, "Hydrogen Blast Astonished Scientists, Eisenhower Says," *New York Times*, 25 March 1954, A1; "Eisenhower Releases Movie of Superbomb," *New York Times*, 27 March 1954, A1.

55. "Text of Statement and Comments by Strauss on Hydrogen Bomb Tests in the Pacific," *New York Times*, 1 April 1954, A20.

56. Ibid., A20.

57. "Radio and Television Address to the American People on the State of the Nation," *Public Papers, 1954*, 372-89. All further quotations are from this source.

58. "Is the H-Bomb Going 'Wild'?" *U.S. News and World Report*, 9 April 1954, 21-25; "Where Now, World?" *Newsweek*, 29 March 1954, 19-23.

59. Ibid., 22.

60. "H-Bomb Odds: 1 Million to 1—And That's What May Save Us," *Newsweek*, 5 April 1954, 28.

61. Ira Chernus, *Dr. Strangegod: On the Symbolic Meaning of Nuclear Weapons* (Columbia, South Carolina: University of South Carolina Press, 1986), 8.

62. Chernus, 12-31.

63. Oppenheimer, 203.

64. See Doris A. Graber, *Verbal Behavior and Politics* (Chicago: University of Illinois Press, 1976), 310-15; and Murray Edelman, *The Symbolic Uses of Politics* (Chicago: University of Illinois Press, 1967), 125.

65. Graber, 311.

Eisenhower and McCarthy campaign in Wisconsin

Thomas
Rosteck

# The Case of Eisenhower versus McCarthyism

In November 1953 former President Harry S. Truman
defined McCarthyism:

> It is the corruption of the truth, the abandonment of our historical devotion
> to fair play and due process of law. It is the use of the "big lie" and
> unfounded accusation against any citizen in the name of Americanism and
> security. It lives on untruth; it is the spread of fear and the destruction of
> faith at every level of society.[1]

For many, Truman's definition seems to capture the essence of a troubled
era of recent American history. For in the decade following 1945 the anxieties
and tensions generated by the Second World War and exacerbated by the Cold
War created strains and dislocations throughout society. Symptomatic of those
strains was the rise of McCarthyism and the shadow it cast across American
politics.[2] This dissonant era has intrigued historians and social commentators,
perhaps because the controversies of the time are fundamental: how to negotiate the delicate relationship between the executive and the legislative branches
of government; how to preserve the nation's internal security and at the same
time safeguard civil liberty; how to determine a citizen's loyalty, or risk, to the
nation's security without curbing dissent.[3]

Eventually, of course—the story is well known and has entered the popular
lore—the nation did emerge from the factious years of McCarthyism. Finally,
after a time, politicians learned the lesson of responsibility, administrators
learned to temper judgment with restraint, and the courts infused new strength
into the struggle for civil liberties.[4] Yet for all that we now know about this fas-
cinating and disturbing era, the role of the thirty-fourth president of the United
States, Dwight D. Eisenhower, in the "downfall of McCarthyism" generates, even
today, considerable controversy.[5]

Some historians characterize Eisenhower's presidency as a "shrewd use of
political art and craft." Claiming that Eisenhower went to great lengths to conceal his political leadership, these scholars argue that a large share of the credit
for neutralizing or "finishing off" McCarthyism must go to Eisenhower.[6]

Others, however, tell a quite different version: one in which, at best, Eisenhower was aloof in the "movement against McCarthyism," his leadership (when it was apparent) a "failure." At worst, Eisenhower "exacerbated the problem" and "did about as little as could possibly be done" to control or combat McCarthyism.[7]

To join this debate over the role of Dwight D. Eisenhower in the movement against McCarthyism, I will examine Eisenhower's public statements on the issues of McCarthyism. Such rhetorical analysis has the potential to offer a distinctive vantage from which to reevaluate the controversy and perhaps to account for the contemporary, divided assessment of Eisenhower's leadership. My rhetorical analysis will neither look at Eisenhower's "hidden-hand strategies," nor merely locate his rhetorical techniques; instead, it will grapple with how the content and style of Eisenhower's discourse influenced the countermovement against McCarthyism.

While it is, of course, impossible to establish the precise role of Eisenhower's public argument in turning back McCarthyism, examining his rhetoric may prove instructive on several counts. First, Eisenhower's ambivalences over the relationship between the personal and public realms are salient. This rhetorical tension and Eisenhower's articulation of it sheds new light upon the rhetorical development of McCarthyism. Second, the study of McCarthyism and the rhetorical movement of its opposition suggests ways in which establishment rhetoricians such as Eisenhower, are able to confront, frame, and incorporate rhetoric from radical movements.[8] Third, the newly vivified scholarly interest in presidential discourse in itself warrants a further appraisal of Eisenhower as a "rhetorical president."[9]

The most compelling motive for studying the rhetoric of Eisenhower versus McCarthyism lies in what Eisenhower's rhetorical practice may tell us about the relationship between specific ideologies and their inherent rhetoric. Certainly, an ideology both organizes one's world view and constrains the arguments one engages.[10] What is less obvious is that an ideology also colors and shapes the presentation of those arguments.[11] Eisenhower's presentation of arguments against McCarthyism posed interesting rhetorical dilemmas. As a public opponent of McCarthyism, Eisenhower created an inconsistent rhetorical world. While his discourse certainly revealed an antipathy to the ideology of McCarthyism, the rhetorical action inherent in his discourse showed an acceptance of the *form* of that ideology. Close study of his rhetoric suggests, in the final analysis, a basic inconsistency between the content and style found in Eisenhower's arguments against McCarthyism. This inconsistency may account both for the divided judgment of history concerning Eisenhower's role in the rhetorical movement against McCarthyism and for the residues of McCarthyism that survived both the censure and subsequent death of the man behind the label, Senator Joseph R. McCarthy.

Any study of Eisenhower's public statements on McCarthyism is difficult and complicated from the beginning. First there is the apparent disparity between Eisenhower's private views on McCarthyism and his public statements. That Ike was "uncomfortable with," "opposed to" or even "appalled by" McCarthyism, there seems today to be little doubt.[12] Yet his public statements were circumspect and often evasive. Eisenhower refused to speak directly in public against Senator McCarthy, or even to "name" or sustain a "definition" of the movement in his discourse. While there is evidence that this was a deliberate strategy on Eisenhower's part, the critic who expects to see a clear clash and development of opposing argument is to be disappointed. In short, one finds in this case what might be described as the rhetoric of indirection or the rhetoric of allusion in which an opposition rhetor adopts a rhetorical strategy of indirect speech and argument through the medium of the national press. This strategy, though enjoying some distinct tactical advantages, also creates some obstacles in countering McCarthyism.[13]

Specifically, I argue that adopting McCarthy and cohorts' argumentative grounds compelled Eisenhower to present his opposition in a set of dualistic alternatives: ends versus means, principle versus policy, men versus measures, secrecy versus disclosure, and legislative versus executive. This rhetorical action mimicked and paralleled the dualistic rhetoric of McCarthyism in a way that undercut Eisenhower's arguments against the movement. Moreover, borrowing the form of McCarthyism, and filling that form with the content of anti-McCarthyism prevented Eisenhower from offering a satisfying counterstance.

## THE RHETORICAL SITUATION

As a new decade began in 1950 the public mood in the United States was unsettled and uncertain.[14] To a majority of Americans circumstances both at home and abroad were grim, foreboding, ominous. To most, communism appeared an evil shadow hanging over the world, an enemy threatening and powerful. The perceived danger was not only external but within the nation itself; it seemed to many in America that Reds, fellow travelers, and Communist sympathizers sought to undermine American democracy and institutions at every turn. The press and media fueled the national paranoia with stories trumpeting the exposure, dismissal, and trials of suspected Communists.[15] Both major political parties played upon the public's fear, trading accusations that seemed to "prove" the other coddled Communists in government, or tolerated subversion and infiltration, or were soft toward the Soviet Union or the Chinese Communists.

It was in this national mood that the politics of the era operated. But the issues of loyalty and security had a long history, one revealing how deep the roots of suspicion reached into the national psyche. The Truman administration first implemented a loyalty program for the executive branch of the federal government in 1947.[16] Even after several modifications that tightened provisions, charges that the Democrats permitted subversion in government were central to the cry "twenty years of treason" sounded in the 1950 and 1952 elections by anti-Communist zealots within the Republican Party.

The conservative right-wing of the GOP adopted the "commie issue" as potent political ammunition. Soon groups including a revitalized Special House Committee on Un-American Activities and a Senate standing committee on Internal Security were pioneering many of the techniques that would come to be labeled McCarthyism. They made wholesale accusations of Communist infiltration of the government; declared private citizens to be traitors because they had been seen in the company of or associated with suspected Communists; welcomed testimony from vengeful or deluded ex-Communists; bullied "unfriendly" witnesses; and for the purposes of slandering groups and individuals, did not hesitate to exploit ties to sensationalist newspapers.[17]

At the center of the movement, of course, was Joseph R. McCarthy, a heretofore unremarkable Republican junior senator from Wisconsin. Beginning in 1950, the senator and his varying charges dominated national attention and became the focus of the national fear. So significant was his presence that McCarthy gave his name to the entire decade. But Joseph R. McCarthy neither caused the era, nor invented its dominant attitudes.[18] Blacklisting, the distrust of anything liberal, the fear of so-called subversive groups, even the bullying of witnesses before congressional committees predated Joseph McCarthy's election to public office. Instead, as much as anything else, McCarthy was shaped by his times and its psychology. And, after a fashion, Joseph McCarthy came to embody it.[19]

It was into this situation that politician Dwight Eisenhower stepped. Despite the defeat of Robert Taft for the nomination of the Republican party in 1952, the anti-Communist McCarthyites maintained an influential position in the party. Candidate Eisenhower initially assumed the prescribed stance against the "disloyal," and for a period, accommodated himself in small, symbolic ways to the emotional thrust of the movement. In campaign speeches he, too, exploited the Communist issue, accusing the Democrats of "a toleration of men who take papers from our secret files and pass them on dark streets to spies from Moscow."[20] In an incident studied in detail, Eisenhower deleted praise of General George Marshall from a campaign speech in Milwaukee, Wisconsin, Senator McCarthy's home state.[21] Later as a newly inaugurated president, Eisenhower seemed obliged—by the demagoguery of the McCarthyites as well as by his own campaign promises—to be more anti-Communist than Truman.[22] President Eisenhower affirmed his determination to clear Communists out of government by instituting a broadened security program, encouraging the use of the FBI, cooperating with investigating committees of the Congress, and clearly implying the Truman administration had been remiss, if not treasonable, in dealing with the security problems of government.

In short, Eisenhower "did not avow belief in the McCarthyite conspiracy theory of the origin of the country's troubles yet to the dismay of supporters . . . neither did he disavow it."[23] To understand more fully how Eisenhower's arguments against McCarthyism soon took form and shape, we need to consider McCarthyism as constituting a set of rhetorical exigencies for Eisenhower.[24]

## McCarthyism as Political Problem

At the most immediate level, McCarthyism posed a problem for Eisenhower with respect to control of the Republican party—a party truly divided. On one side were the moderate, eastern establishment or Dewey Republicans; on the other, the conservative, neo-isolationist, midwestern or Taft Republicans who generally embraced McCarthyism, in part because rabid anti-communism was thought to pay enormous political benefits in flaying the Democratic party.[25]

Following Eisenhower's election many expected that the McCarthyite attacks on the new executive branch would cease. Yet within days of the inauguration McCarthy announced ten separate investigations into the State Department alone, Senators William Jenner and Pat McCarran announced their own inquiries into the executive branch, and the Eisenhower administration was left to ponder what had happened to "teamwork." From the perspective of the new Republican administration, the McCarthyites were acting as if there were still a Democrat in the White House.[26]

Early in 1953 the Republican party faced a difficult dilemma. To repudiate McCarthyism entirely would undercut the GOP contention that the Democrats had been soft on communism. To embrace him too eagerly would invite a backlash that might destroy Senator McCarthy and others, vitiate the Communist issue, and reduce the prospects for continued Republican success.[27] As an ally of Thomas Dewey and the moderates, Eisenhower could little afford to break openly with the Taft forces—he needed to handle McCarthyism with caution because of the power of the Republican right and fears of further splitting the party.

According to some historians, Eisenhower quickly came to terms with the McCarthyites as the price for this unity. The Harry Dexter White case, Executive Order 10450, and the Oppenheimer incident served as evidence of McCarthyism's influence with the new administration.[28] Yet while Eisenhower took steps that seemed to further the national concern with security interests, in his public statements he kept aloof from McCarthyism, and in private its tactics disgusted and infuriated him.[29]

Incidents were brought to a head in November 1953, when McCarthy charged that while the Eisenhower administration was doing somewhat better than Truman in combating subversives, there were "a few cases where our batting average is zero—we struck out." He criticized Eisenhower's remark to the effect that communism would not be an important issue in the fall congressional campaign, contending instead that the "raw, harsh, unpleasant fact is that communism will be an issue in 1954."[30] The administration was divided— some saw this as a direct challenge to the president and argued that Eisenhower was morally involved in the dispute and no longer could stand aside. According to this view, appeasing McCarthy was useless; sooner or later McCarthy was going to declare war on the administration. Staffers on the opposite side argued that Eisenhower's engaging in a personal quarrel with McCarthy could only make matters worse. The fight would sunder Republican ranks and jeopardize the president's leadership and his legislative program— Eisenhower, they said, could not hope to out brawl the McCarthyites.[31]

In sum, to preserve party unity, Eisenhower faced the problem of how to deal with McCarthyism. Should he directly challenge the McCarthyites? Or should he work indirectly in presenting an alternative rhetorical vision?

## McCarthyism as Constitutional Problem

McCarthyism also posed a constitutional dilemma for Eisenhower. The tactics and investigations of the McCarthyites invariably were directed against departments and organizations of the executive branch of government. Within the State Department, inquires were launched into the diplomatic corps, overseas libraries, and the Voice of America; within the Department of Defense investigators looked into the Signal Corps, Officer Candidate Schools, and the professional staff itself. McCarthyites sought to pressure American allies to avoid trade with China and Russia. In other words, the McCarthyites sought to influence precisely those areas that were strictly under the constitutional control of the president. So long as the president was a Democrat, the problems could be characterized as partisan, but with Eisenhower's election, the questions quickly became ones about the rights and privileges of coordinate branches of government.

Issues crystallized around McCarthy's call in May 1954 for all employees of the executive departments to ignore Eisenhower's order of confidentiality, and instead to come forward to the congressional investigators with evidence of subversion and infiltration. Convinced this was "an act of treason," Eisenhower approached the issue as one of constitutional scope. Believing that the president should not "mettle in the business of the Senate," Eisenhower argued for "mutual respect" between the branches.[32] Compounding the problem was the realization that Senator McCarthy was invulnerable to Eisenhower's public attack, and that such attacks might alienate sympathetic members of the Congress.[33] The need, as Eisenhower saw it, was to give all encouragement possible to established congressional leaders like Taft, Eugene Millikin, and Leverett Saltonstall in an effort to strengthen them in dealing with the extremists.[34]

The problem, then, was twofold: how to maintain the strength of the executive branch from incursions by the legislative or, how to respect the independence of the coordinate branches; and how to control the trouble generated by a member of the legislature.

### McCarthyism as Moral Problem

Anti-communism was not the only issue associated with McCarthyism. Dwight Eisenhower, the McCarthyites, and indeed most of the American people saw the possibility of domestic Communist subversion as a real and significant problem.[35] Moreover, as the visible symbol of the movement, Senator McCarthy was enormously popular and perceived by many to be an "effective, two-fisted fighter" of Communists.[36] Instead, in his memoirs, Eisenhower explained that in his opinion what McCarthyism stood for was violation of "personal liberties and constitutional process."[37]

Clearly, McCarthyism was at base both a moral and a morally complex issue. As a movement it furthered a view of America that had been officially endorsed and propagated during two world wars. In that view nationalism and loyalty to the state—to those in power—became the overriding test of true Americanism, while un-Americanism became synonymous with communism, socialism, and internationalism.[38] Communism became the symbol which united these concerns. Talcott Parsons has argued that this is an effective choice in the context of the "loyalty problem" because communism comes ready made with ambivalent attitudes, among them conspiratorial methods, foreign control, liberal/progressive elements, and a history of infiltration in the 1930s. Parsons noted:

> Those who are out of sympathy with the main tradition of American liberalism can find a powerful target for their objections in the totalitarian tactics of communism and can readily stigmatize it as "un-American." Then by extending their objections to the liberal component of Communist ideology, they can attack liberalism in general, on the grounds that association with Communist totalitarianism makes anything liberal suspect.[39]

As a moral issue communism represented the epitome of the alien world— atheism, immorality, destruction of the family, and socialism.[40] For the supporters of McCarthyism, concern over communism symbolized a basic uneasiness about the health of American institutions, about American identity, and about the American future.[41] Some have speculated that McCarthyism's emphasis upon communism was, for many, symbolic of inner threatening forces on the unconscious level.[42]

It is those fears and a general unease over secrecy itself that perhaps pushed many to endorse what today seem harsh remedies for suspected Communist infiltration. The exigency that Eisenhower faced was to recognize the strains symbolized by McCarthyism. How could these fears be assuaged in a way that did no damage to American self-image? How could subversion be defeated within the frame of American values? How to accomplish the ends of McCarthyism—the elimination of subversion in government offices—and yet do so in line with American standards of freedom of speech, fair play, and innocence until proven guilty?

## Primary Rhetorical Strategies

Eisenhower himself constructed an account of how he dealt with McCarthyism. Most are familiar with his oft-quoted remark, "I will not get in the gutter with that guy," uttered in response to the suggestion that he take on McCarthy directly.[43] In his memoirs, Eisenhower explained that his approach was to attack that for which McCarthyism stood, and he repeatedly used the term "ignore him" to describe his method of dealing with Senator McCarthy personally.[44] Yet today we know, through his personal diaries and letters, that Eisenhower disagreed with the tactics of both the senator and the movement. Instead, there is evidence that he worked behind the scenes wielding a low-key approach in taking on McCarthyism.[45]

But our focus is Eisenhower's public rhetoric. We are interested in what it might disclose of Eisenhower's means of dealing with the exigencies of McCarthyism, and with what that rhetoric might contribute to the public debate of the era. Four patterns recur throughout Eisenhower's statements on McCarthyism: the argument over values; the means argument; the argument over private and public; and the disclosure argument. Boundaries among them are sometimes fuzzy and the same evidence might support multiple arguments, but the fundamental inference made by each species of argument is distinct.

### Us versus Them: The Values Argument

Given the temper of the era, one who turns to Eisenhower's rhetoric should not be surprised to find at its heart a world view that holds benevolent American values in opposition to those of an evil Communist conspiracy. In Eisenhower's world view, there exists a divinely inspired creed that defines America's distinctiveness, establishes America's role as an example, and functions argumentatively as the foundation for opposition to McCarthyism.

These values—what Eisenhower calls America's basic ideals (man's dignity, brotherhood, man's freedom, faith in country and in a God who looks with favor upon America)—were handed down as the "creed of our fathers."[46] But for Eisenhower, these values are active and alive. Not only do they provide a ground for unity, but these "laws of spiritual strength generate and define our material strength."[47] As Ike said in 1954:

> Now exactly what do we mean by these spiritual values? We mean those characteristics of man that we call ennobling in their effect upon him—courage—imagination—initiative—a sense of decency, of justice and of right. All of which, in a very real sense, is a translation into a political system of a deeply-felt religious faith.[48]

Moreover, these values help to define the destiny of the United States. As this American creed is lived it serves as a lesson to the rest of the world. For "whatever America hopes to bring to pass in the world, must first come to pass in the heart of America."[49] It is our purpose, Eisenhower says, to "grow beyond our forebearers" and to realize their dreams in the whole of the world.[50] The American creed, divinely inspired, lived, and active in the world is the best antidote to atheistic communism. And it is this challenge that defines the universe of Eisenhower discourse.[51]

The values argument appears most eloquently in a speech candidate Eisenhower delivered to the American Legion convention in August of 1952. In addressing the future of the world and America's role, Eisenhower argues for the importance of values.

> Against the paganism [of communism], we must preach the truly revolutionary values of man's dignity, man's freedom, man's brotherhood under the fatherhood of God. These values have inspired generations. . . . All history testifies that these spiritual values are the ultimate source of every right, every privilege—for that matter every material advantage we enjoy in the modern world. To preach and practice them so that all the world shall once again find hope in them requires of each of us a genuine effort in daily life. . . . The world—all the world—will again recognize the United States of America as the spiritual and material realization of the dreams that men have dreamt since the dawn of history.[52]

Because these values are sacred, they must be zealously guarded. And as the creed is a shield against enemies, so too is it a weapon against them. The necessity of protecting our core values warrants action against "fellow travelers" as well as the protection of fundamental rights. We must not think we are protecting ourselves, Eisenhower warns, while at the same time we are attacking our values.[53]

> Let us tolerate nobody in our whole system who attempts to weaken and destroy the American system [sic]. Especially let us be watchful for those who by stealth attempt subversion and treasonable betrayal in government. At the same time, let us hew sharply to the fundamental American principle that every man is innocent until he is proved guilty. To do less is dangerous to our freedom at home and to our position of leadership in the world.[54]

Eisenhower amplifies this idea in two important statements. The first, in response to a request for a presidential message to the annual conference of the American Library Association, expands Eisenhower's remarks on "book-burners" to issue a warning about the effects of McCarthyism on the American system.[55] Eisenhower cautions that because American freedoms rest upon "freedom of inquiry, freedom of the spoken and written word, freedom of exchange of ideas," we must be "alert" to "zealots" who with "more wrath than wisdom" would "try to defend freedom by denying freedom." On the contrary, "we know that freedom cannot be served by the devices of the tyrant . . . and any who act as if freedom's defenses are to be found in suppression and suspicion and fear confess a doctrine that is alien to America."[56]

Scarcely a month later, amidst the publicity of the McCarthyites' charge that the "largest single group supporting the Communist apparatus in the United States today is composed of Protestant clergymen,"[57] Eisenhower again uses the occasion to promulgate the idea of shared values. In a telegram to the National Council of Christians and Jews, Eisenhower claims that such attacks "betray contempt for the principles of freedom and decency." Instead, churches are "citadels of our faith in individual freedom and human dignity. This faith is the living source of all our spiritual strength. And this strength is our matchless armor in our world-wide struggle against the forces of godless tyranny and oppression."[58]

Several implications of this argumentative cluster seem unmistakable. In Eisenhower's discourse the world is divided into two camps separated by conflict. One side acts in accordance with all that is good, decent, and at one with God's will. The other acts in direct opposition. Religious faith, moral insight, and a respect for God's laws form a set of virtues attributed to the nation which are called upon both to distinguish the United States from the "other," and to justify certain kinds of action both abroad and at home.[59] Such dualism may perhaps be anticipated, but it also suggests one element of Eisenhower's rhetorical strategy against McCarthyism. To undermine the movement, Eisenhower will re-frame McCarthyism as a question of its relation to the American creed. Eisenhower will attack McCarthyism on the "fair play" issues because these are common sense versions of the spiritual values that Americans hold in common and that unify the society.

This partially explains the predominance of what rhetorical scholars often identify as ceremonial address in Eisenhower's statements against McCarthyism.[60]

Part and parcel of what Eisenhower called his "positive approach," this discourse about American values has several distinct advantages. Contrasting abstract, fundamental American values with McCarthyism gives Eisenhower the chance to draw together the biggest portion of the audience, because in the abstract it was easy for most of Eisenhower's listeners to agree that McCarthyism was a perversion of values they found salient. Being in no fear of contradiction, Eisenhower can seek to increase adherence to the values he lauds; establish a sense of communion centered around these shared values; and convert his listeners into an audience suspended in opposition to McCarthyism by rallying them around unquestioned and supposedly unquestionable eternal values.[61] This unity is, itself, one of the rhetorical weapons Eisenhower uses against McCarthyism.

### Ends versus Means: The Morality of Anti-McCarthyism

The theme of American values directing American action is standard Cold War rhetoric. Certainly it is reflected in the argument over means versus ends, the second consistent cluster across Eisenhower's public statements. It first appears during the campaign in 1952, when Eisenhower announces: "The differences between me and Senator McCarthy . . . have nothing to do with the end result we are seeking . . . of ridding this government of the incompetents, the dishonest, and above all the subversives and the disloyal. The differences apply to method."[62] Later, in his first news conference, Eisenhower explains: "I have no doubt that most—say almost 100 percent of Americans—would like to stamp out all traces of communism in our country; it is methods of approaching it" that cause problems.[63]

Since our moral code functions as a weapon against communism, Eisenhower argues that we cannot destroy what we are attempting to defend. For in opposing "these ideologies that we believe will destroy our form of government" we must "do it under methods where we don't destroy it." We are not "protecting the United States, [when] at the same time destroying or attacking those values which have made it great."[64]

In November 1953, on a nationally televised awards ceremony where he received the B'nai B'rith's Democratic Legacy Award, Eisenhower exemplifies the argument over ends and means through the use of the American Western Myth.

Announcing his theme as "why are we proud?," Eisenhower rejects the usual reasons of national beauty or material wealth. Instead, "we are proud," he says, because from the "beginning of the Nation, a man can walk upright . . . and meet his enemy" face to face. Referring to his own upbringing in Abilene, Kansas ("a famous place in the West"), Eisenhower reminds his audience of the "code" that he was raised to prize: to "meet anyone face to face with whom you disagree." You couldn't "sneak up" on anyone, says the president. But you could get away with "almost anything" so long as "the bullet was in the front."

Returning to the present era, Eisenhower argues that all Americans "live by that same code." If someone "accuses you, he must come up in front." As for the future, he urges that there be no "weakening of the code . . . to meet your accuser face to face" if we are going to "continue to be proud we are Americans." Finally answering the question with which he began, Eisenhower concludes that the things that make us proud "are of the soul and of the spirit . . . the preserving of the code."[65]

To insure the protection of that "code," Eisenhower calls for "fair methods" in dealing with suspected subversion. All such programs must safeguard the rights of individuals and be conducted with methods all "right thinking" Americans could agree were moral.[66] Congress, too, should consider "moral" as well as legal and constitutional values in carrying out its investigations.[67]

This call for fairness may be seen most clearly in a speech delivered to the annual convention of the national Young Republicans organization in June 1953. Though famous for its middle section that describes what came to be known as Eisenhower's political philosophy—the "middle way"—the oration links American values with actions against Communist subversion.

After recounting the achievements of his administration's actions during its first six months in office, Eisenhower announces a second topic. Most important, he says, all future actions must be based on principles with "no compromise" and realized in programs that "conform to basic beliefs."

"We believe," he says "that the best way to defend the precious ideals of individual freedom is that middle way which avoids extremes in action." This means heeding "the inalienable liberties of the individual" as well as the demands for security.

> This middle way means guarding against those enemies who would claim the privilege of freedom to destroy freedom itself. It means guarding against any who would pretend to defend this freedom with weapons from the arsenal of the tyrant.[68]

Unless we have moral background for policy, that policy is antagonistic to America's basic precepts and therefore unacceptable.[69] It is "fixed principles that will guide us," he says.[70] For Eisenhower, the way to combat McCarthyism is to remain true to the principles that unite and that foster American strength.

Thus Eisenhower seeks to undermine McCarthyism by having it both ways. While never questioning the necessity of locating and removing subversives from government, Eisenhower tries to separate his methods from those of McCarthyism. However, in practice, given the difficulty of reconciling some actions (notably an executive order extending security provisions, the Harry Dexter White affair, and the Oppenheimer case) it is sometimes difficult to see the connection between Eisenhower's principle and his policies. Indeed, it might be argued that Eisenhower unwittingly nurtured the idea that "right intent is of the essence"—a position that permits isolation from his policies.[71] The solution of course is elegant: policy derives, yet is separate, from principle. The effect, of course, is that this dualism between methods and objectives, between policies and procedures, leaves the ends of McCarthyism unquestioned.

This suggestion is ominous. Perhaps a distinction between policies and carrying out those policies is simple-minded. Certainly the potential end-result is that day-to-day decisions do not matter; only the policy matters and it has an autonomous life independent of daily actions and judgments.[72] In short, the appearance of piety begins to take precedence over actual performance.

### Legislative versus Executive: The Constitutional Argument

The sets of antitheses, the dualistic pattern that we are beginning to discover beneath Dwight Eisenhower's public discourse is further manifested in arguments about the relationship between the Congress and the president. To some scholars one of the most lasting issues of McCarthyism is the constitutional question of the power of the executive branch to control its own affairs without interference from the legislative.[73] Eisenhower's views were announced early in his first campaign: the primary responsibility for "keeping the disloyal and the dangerous" out of government "rests squarely upon the executive branch." Unless each branch discharges its responsibilities and respects the rights and responsibilities of the others, "confusion and disorder" will result.[74]

This strategy of holding to a strict interpretation of the constitutional division of powers is also suggested in the circumspect manner in which Eisenhower withholds criticism of Congress. Quick to point out that the legislature is a "coordinate branch of government"[75] with its own rights and responsibilities, Eisenhower supports the right of Congress to investigate and argues that this is one of their constitutional duties that cannot be abridged.[76]

These themes are exemplified in the statement that Eisenhower read at his news conference of 3 March 1954—a statement that draws together the arguments on American values, on means and ends, and on the separation of powers. When Senator McCarthy, investigating what he called subversion in the Army Signal Corps, berated army officers for withholding evidence from his inquiries, Eisenhower uses the occasion to reinforce his sense of the division between the parts of government.[77] Admitting that the army made errors in the case, Eisenhower reaffirms his confidence in Army Secretary Robert T. Stevens, but authorizes no humiliation of executive branch employees. Moreover, while subversion must be guarded, we must also "use methods that conform to the American sense of justice and fair play." Having emphasized once more the values that embody Americanism, Eisenhower moves to address the constitutional issue. Responsibility for conduct of the executive branch rests with the president and may not be delegated to other branches, he argues. While Congress may investigate, "it is the responsibility of the Congress to see to it that its procedures are proper and fair." Indeed, what is needed, says Eisenhower, is an atmosphere of mutual respect.[78] It is only in this spirit of harmony between the "coordinate branches" that coherent and consistent policies can be advanced, and the major programs of the administration accomplished.[79]

In short, the constitutional argument is one that suggests a dualistic model of governmental relations. The branches of government, legislative and executive, committed to the same end are forever separate and distinct; neither may interfere with the other as a matter of principle. Thus, Eisenhower is able to retain control of the ends of fighting subversion and infiltration in the executive branch while denying the authority of Congress to cross into executive affairs.

### Public versus Private: The Disclosure Argument

It has been widely recognized that Eisenhower's public statements on McCarthyism are peculiar in one respect at least: there is no mention of Senator McCarthy or other personalities.[80] We may account for this in two ways. First, it is consistent with Eisenhower's stated policy of "no personalities." Yet it is also a strategy that retains the argumentative distinction between private opinions and public utterance. Second, issues of personality are displaced in the rhetoric by an emphasis upon Eisenhower's positive program. Both of these explanations have consequences for Eisenhower's arguments against McCarthyism.

In dealing with McCarthyism, Eisenhower emphasizes what he calls his "positive" program.[81] This enables him to presume to be taking action against the dangers of subversion and to be doing so in a way that preserves values, while at the same time diminishing the thrust of McCarthyism. The cornerstone of this approach, of course, is Eisenhower's own security program, one that extends Truman's tight security provisions to every government agency and to every type of job. Indeed, Eisenhower finds it expedient to refer now and again to the number of "security risks" detected, collared, and dismissed from the government as a result of his security program.[82] Because he can point to the Communist problem as taken care of, the president is in a position to urge getting to work on his programs for the country. For instance, at the height of the national obsession with the Army-McCarthy hearings in the summer of 1954, Eisenhower says, "I'm anxious to see it cease. Let's get the facts out and then let's go on about the important business of this government."[83] With this argument, Eisenhower diminishes the importance of McCarthyism and points to what he claims are the "real problems" of America. In addition, this permits Eisenhower to appear above the issues of the hearings by arguing for responsible procedures (disadvantaging McCarthy), not on the grounds of combating McCarthyism, but on those of resolving the hearings to get on with the business of governance.[84]

In addition to concentrating upon his own programs, Eisenhower steadfastly refuses to discuss personalities. His rule: "I never deal in my statements in terms of personalities" is one that he adheres to almost uniformly.[85] "It is inappropriate for me to comment specifically on individuals," Eisenhower would say; "I never talk personalities; I refuse to do so;" and "all disagreements with my opponents is always based on principles."[86] "I answer questions addressed to principles and ideas," he insists, "I am not engaged in argument with individuals."[87] Eisenhower's personal diaries and correspondence reveal that this was a conscious strategy, and we may speculate upon its advantages. First of all, it is certainly expedient to seem to argue more with abstract demagogues than with any real McCarthyite. In addition, as Fred Greenstein suggests, this strategy itself has the advantage of cutting McCarthyism from the publicity that nourishes it.[88]

However, rhetorically, it also serves Eisenhower as a strategy of diversion, allowing him to protect private opinions from public scrutiny. "It is not proper to discuss publicly certain matters," he would say; I "stand on my own private conscience;" these are my "personal opinions, my personal convictions," and are not for public statement.[89] At times, when questioned about McCarthyism, Eisenhower answers that he has ideas of what is right or wrong, but "I see no reason really for publicizing or explaining them."[90]

Clearly, Eisenhower maintains a universe of discourse that holds to the antithesis of private and public.[91] In his argument, not everything should be revealed; the individual retains the right to privacy and to guard his own personal secrets against unwarranted disclosure. Corresponding to this dualism of public and private, Eisenhower argues against turning over records of the executive to congressional investigators. Besides holding that these records are privileged, Eisenhower also claims, based on the principle of secrecy, that certain types of information cannot be exposed to view.[92] Despite the demands of the McCarthyites for complete disclosure, some documents are never to be released; thus Ike's assertion concerning "certain things I wouldn't give out to anyone."[93]

## EISENHOWER'S IDEOLOGICAL VISION AND RHETORICAL BLINDNESS

In general, operating with what we may call the rhetoric of separation, Eisenhower's purpose is not to deny the Communist-in-government issue but rather to separate Americans who believe in practicing "decent and fair" methods of anti-communism from the McCarthyites who, according to the president, do not.[94] Stressing the distinctions between ends and means, and urging policies based on principles consonant with spiritual and secular values are tactics designed to secure this objective.

To accomplish his positive program, Eisenhower undertakes to separate moderate Republicans from right wing anti-Communists. He hopes to accomplish this by taking the Communist issue away from the McCarthyites through his own security program, and by stressing in his own programs what he calls the real business of the country. This strategy is aided by Eisenhower's refusal to engage in personalities or to attack the members of the Congress, actions which might give publicity to the McCarthyites or force members of Congress to defend their colleagues. In never seeking to deny the right of a congressional committee to investigate the executive branch, Eisenhower insists only on a measure of mutual courtesy. We can speculate that this demonstration of mutual respect would be seen in a positive light by members of the coordinate branch of government.

As the foundation of his anti-McCarthyism discourse, Eisenhower celebrates the verities of an American creed and the abstractions of freedom of mind, fidelity to the Constitution, fair play, honesty, magnanimity, and divinely inspired brotherhood. Given the fearful era, such appeals would likely have considerable resonance for an audience weary of continued and outrageous charges of corruption and subversion.

Yet despite this potential, when we look closely at the discourse, Eisenhower's rhetorical strategies generate substantial rhetorical obstacles. For instance, we have found the predominant rhetorical form of Eisenhower's public discourse to be the antithesis. A series of oppositions structures Eisenhower's notion of good versus evil and their archetypal conflict in the world. This antithetical form is instantiated, in the moral realm, by the concept that means take precedence over ends and that principles and policies are autonomous and unconnected. It corresponds within the political realm to the sense that the executive branch and the legislative branch are coordinate parts of government—sovereign and separate. It is revealed in foreign and domestic affairs as a world divided into the free world and atheistic communism; into loyal Americans versus fellow travelers. Finally in his discourse, Eisenhower separates his private thoughts from his public utterance, a tactic that omits personality conflicts but one that also holds fast the distinction between secrecy and disclosure.

What we find in each component of Eisenhower's universe of discourse is a compartmentalization of thought and a dualistic world view. These distinctions hold throughout: manner and deed in political life are quite distinct and unrelated, secrets may be held in private when they serve no purpose, principles take precedence over policies, means over ends; all are quite like the legislature and the executive, held separate.[95]

## RHETORICAL IMPLICATIONS: THE IMPASSE OF MCCARTHYISM

This rhetoric of antithesis prompts a reexamination of Eisenhower's discourse compared with the rhetorical forms of McCarthyism. In its public discourse McCarthyism has been characterized as an ideology obsessed with morality. Its moral vision projects a world divided between loyal Americans and those with "un-American" tendencies.[96] For the McCarthyite, appearance conceals essence, and the motivating assumption of McCarthyism is a belief that people, motives, and institutions are not what they seem.[97]

In a prophetic analysis written in 1954, John Oakes suggests that McCarthyism relies upon the prurient interest in "stripping bare" what is hidden by position, education, and privilege, thereby "reducing complex and difficult questions to words having to do with secrets and the hidden."[98] Recently Edwin Black has agreed, arguing that in its rhetorical form, McCarthyism is inherently bound up with assumptions about secrecy and disclosure.[99] McCarthyism, Black argues, plays upon the set of half-acknowledged, either/or assumptions of the American public that concealment is bad, disclosure good; that openness is the ultimate term, concealment is guilt; that ends always fully justify means.[100]

In comparing the discourse of McCarthyism with that of Eisenhower, it is apparent that opposing ideologies compel movement and counter-movement rhetors to diametric positions on the issues. Where McCarthyism likely appealed to an audience which assumed that concealment is bad and which embraced disclosure and openness, the ideology of Dwight Eisenhower likely appealed to an audience who retained notions of privacy, of appearance, of order, and procedure.[101] On every issue, the two sides affirm contradictories.

But it is also apparent, though perhaps not so immediately noticeable, that both McCarthyism and the anti-McCarthyism of Dwight Eisenhower share the rhetorical form of the antithesis. Where Eisenhower's discourse proposes an individualistic society that entails respect for secrecy as opposed to disclosure, for "decent" means over expedient ends, for separation of executive and legislative influence, in retaining these bifurcations of McCarthyism Eisenhower doesn't call into question McCarthyism's implied antithetical world view.[102] In short, Dwight Eisenhower's anti-McCarthyism mimics the rhetorical form of the ideology he seeks to supplant.

What we have found, in the discourse of McCarthyism and in the discourse of Eisenhower's anti-McCarthyism, is a symbolic identity. In *The Political Unconscious*, Frederic Jameson suggests that the critic look at the formal processes of discourse as a sort of "sedimented content" which carry ideological messages quite apart from the manifest content.[103] This code, Jameson argues, is an index of a prevailing larger ideological unity of the social system, one, in the present case, shared by McCarthyites and anti-McCarthyites alike.[104]

We may speculate that in sharing the rhetorical form of antithesis, both movement and counter-movement promulgate for their audience the vision of a world starkly divided—one without middle ground, without compromise, a world view tending toward simplicity and compartmentalization. Both McCarthyism and Eisenhower's anti-McCarthyism therefore provide their audiences with cues that exclude transcendent alternatives. The antithesis shapes a style of discourse that saves an audience, both psychologically exhausted from a world war and accustomed to viewing the "other" as adversary, from contemplating the complexities of the Cold War and the ambiguities of morality and action in the world.

Given this, it seems difficult to imagine that Eisenhower could effect a complete "cure" for McCarthyism as long as he borrowed the forms of argument embodying its ideology. Advocating his anti-McCarthyism in the rhetorical form of antithesis likely perpetuated the distinctions between secrecy-disclosure, public-private, means-ends, legislative-executive.

This brings me to the question with which this essay began—the relationship between the rhetoric of Dwight Eisenhower and his role in the demise of McCarthyism. How can the two views of Eisenhower—as doing nothing or as destroying McCarthyism—both be sustained? Perhaps in retaining the rhetorical form of McCarthyism while wrapping it around an alternative ideology, Eisenhower found a way to appeal simultaneously to diverse publics. This strategy encourages the same message to be read in quite different ways by different audiences. Eisenhower could seem to be anti-Communist to some and at the same moment seem to be anti-McCarthyism by others. It certainly accounts for Eisenhower as an enigmatic phenomenon for whom private virtue is the measure of public action, and good will enough for successful leadership.[105]

At first glance, perhaps, maintaining an original rhetorical form and using it for the service of an alternative ideology seems a particularly effective strategy for the modern politician. But in the end, I suggest, our conclusion must be less charitable. Our analysis finally compels us to conclude that in seeking to "take the communist issue" from the McCarthyites, yet retaining its rhetorical form, Eisenhower unwittingly encouraged the psychological perspectives that gave McCarthyism rise to live in the margins of American political and social life. Rhetorically, in borrowing the form of McCarthyism, and filling that form with the content of anti-McCarthyism, Eisenhower likely legitimated the Cold War paranoia of the McCarthy movement. While this strategy helped to eliminate Senator McCarthy, it also had the unintentional effect of leaving the corrosive residues of McCarthyism firmly in place.[106] This residue continues to seep into our public discourse even to this day.

## NOTES

1. "Truman Accuses Brownell of Lying; Sees Office Debased in White Case; Says GOP Embraces 'McCarthyism,'" *New York Times*, 17 November 1953, 1.
2. Robert Griffith, "Senators Potter, Hennings, and McCarthy: A Review Article," *Wisconsin Magazine of History* 49 (Summer 1966): 336.
3. Peter Lyon, *Eisenhower: Portrait of the Hero* (Boston: Little, Brown and Company, 1974), 490.
4. Griffith, "Senators Potter, Hennings, and McCarthy," 336.

5. Eisenhower scholarship has progressed through several waves or eras of its own. Some contemporary accounts (for example, Lyon) treat Eisenhower's relationship with McCarthyism not as an exercise of leadership but rather as a failure to respond to a challenge to McCarthy's influence and authority. Even in the middle 1970s when scholars uncovered many primary sources that revealed heretofore unknown aspects of the period, the original impression remains. Greenstein argues that although Eisenhower in no way can be thought of as the agent of McCarthy's demise, he recognized the importance of defusing the senator. He formulated and summarized in his private diary a basic strategy for accomplishing just that—a strategy he continued to use, but adjusted and supplemented during McCarthy's seemingly unchallenged sovereignty in 1953 and rapid decline in 1954. Greenstein argues that throughout the period Eisenhower rejected courses of action urged on him by some of his closest allies that, it can plausibly be argued, would have perpetuated McCarthy's influence. See Fred I. Greenstein, *The Hidden-Hand Presidency: Eisenhower as Leader* (Basic Books: New York, 1982), 156.

6. See Greenstein, 7-9; Allen Yarnell, "Eisenhower and McCarthy: An Appraisal of Presidential Strategy," *Presidential Studies Quarterly* 10 (1980): 96; Richard Rovere, "The Untold Story of McCarthy's Fall," *New York Review of Books* 5 (28 October 1965): 4; John P. Rossi, "The British Reaction to McCarthyism, 1950-54," *Mid-America* 70 (January 1988): 16; Murray Kempton, "The Underestimation of Dwight D. Eisenhower," *Esquire* 63 (September 1967): 108-9, 156; Richard Rovere, "Eisenhower Revisited—A Political Genius? A Brilliant Man?" *The New York Times Magazine* (7 February 1971): 14-15; William B. Ewald, *Who Killed Joe McCarthy?* (New York: Simon and Schuster, 1984).

7. Lyon, 496, 523.

8. Many scholars have studied the way ideology and accommodation have shaped movement rhetoric, for example: John W. Bowers and Donovan J. Ochs, *The Rhetoric of Agitation and Control* (Reading, MA: Addison-Wesley, 1971); Herbert W. Simons, "Requirements, Problems, and Strategies: A Theory of Persuasion for Social Movements," *Quarterly Journal of Speech* 56 (1970): 1-11; Herbert W. Simons, Elizabeth W. Mechling and Howard N. Schreier, "The Functions of Human Communication in Mobilizing for Action from the Bottom Up: The Rhetoric of Social Movements," in *Handbook of Rhetorical and Communication Theory*, ed. Carroll C. Arnold and John W. Bowers (Boston: Allyn and Bacon, 1984), 792-867; David Zarefsky, "President Johnson's War on Poverty: The Rhetoric of Three 'Establishment' Movements," *Communication Monographs* 44 (1977): 352-73.

9. For the concept of the "rhetorical presidency," see James W. Ceaser, Glen E. Thurow, Jeffrey Tulis, Joseph M. Bessette, "The Rise of the Rhetorical Presidency," *Presidential Studies Quarterly* 11 (1981): 158-71.

10. Clifford Geertz, "Ideology as a Culture System," in *Interpretation of Cultures* (New York: Harper, 1973), 193-233; Michael C. McGee, "The 'Ideograph': A Link Between Rhetoric and Ideology," *Quarterly Journal of Speech* 66 (1980): 1-16.

11. Many scholars have studied the relationship between rhetorical characteristics and ideology, for example: Edwin Black, "The Sentimental Style," *Form and Genre*, ed. Kathleen Hall Jamieson and Karlyn Kohrs Campbell (Falls Church, VA: Speech Communication Association, 1978), 75-86; Edwin Black, "The Second Persona," *Quarterly Journal of Speech* 56 (April 1970): 109-19; Richard Hofstater, "The Paranoid Style in American Politics," in *The Paranoid Style in American Politics and Other Essays* (New York: Knopf, 1965); Roderick P. Hart, "The Rhetoric of the True Believer," *Speech Monographs* 38 (1971): 249-61; James W. Chesebro, "Rhetorical Strategies of Radicals," *Today's Speech* 20 (1972): 37-48; Brenda Robinson Hancock, "Affirmation by Negation in the Women's

Liberation Movement," *Quarterly Journal of Speech* 58 (1972): 264-71; Dale G. Leathers, "Fundamentalism of the Radical Right," *Southern Speech Journal* 33 (1968): 245-58; Kathleen Hall Jamieson, "The Metaphoric Cluster in the Rhetoric of Pope Paul II and Edmund G. Brown, Jr.," *Quarterly Journal of Speech* 66 (1980): 51-72.

12. Richard E. Crable, "Ike: Identification, Argument, and Paradoxical Appeal," *Quarterly Journal of Speech* 63 (1977): 192. William F. Crandell, "Eisenhower the Strategist: The Battle of the Bulge and the Censure of Joe McCarthy," *Presidential Studies Quarterly* 17 (1987): 488; Robert J. Donovan, *Eisenhower: the Inside Story* (New York: Harper, 1956), 243-57; Greenstein, 169; Emmet John Hughes, *The Ordeal of Power: A Political Memoir of the Eisenhower Years* (New York: Atheneum, 1963), 92; Lyon, 521; Yarnell, 91; James C. Hagerty, *The Diary of James C. Hagerty: Eisenhower in Mid-Course, 1954-55*, ed. Robert H. Ferrell (Bloomington, Indiana: Indiana University Press, 1983), 47.

13. I will not concentrate directly upon the personal accusation and defense between Eisenhower and Senator McCarthy. My focus will be more upon McCarthyism as a movement, one that predated the senator's arrival in the Congress and one that survived after his downfall. In addition, there exists both scholarly and popular work that summarizes the story of McCarthy and Eisenhower. See Martin J. Medhurst, *Dwight D. Eisenhower: Strategic Communicator* (Westport, Connecticut: Greenwood Press, 1993), 97-110.

14. The following is based upon Robert C. Goldston, *The American Nightmare: Senator Joseph R. McCarthy and the Politics of Hate* (Indianapolis, Indiana: Bobbs-Merrill, 1973); Edwin R. Bayley, *Joe McCarthy and the Press* (Madison, Wisconsin: University of Wisconsin Press, 1984); Thomas Reeves, *The Life and Times of Joe McCarthy: A Biography* (New York: Stein and Day, 1982); Cedric Belfrage, *The American Inquisition, 1955-60* (Indianapolis, Indiana: Bobbs-Merrill, 1973); David Caute, *The Great Fear: The Anti-Communist Purge Under Truman and Eisenhower* (New York: Simon and Schuster, 1978).

15. See Bayley, esp. 132-65.

16. This follows the account given in Caute, 274-6.

17. Several scholars trace the origins of the techniques of McCarthyism to the Dies Committee created in 1938 by the House of Representatives to investigate "un-American" activities. See for example, Reeves, 207; Goldston, 35.

18. While recognizing McCarthyism's disruptive force, revisionist historians have re-framed McCarthyism as a product of the normal political routine. For them, though McCarthy capitalized on popular concern over foreign policy, communism, and the Korean War, the animus of McCarthyism reflected the specific traumas of conservative Republican activists—internal Communist subversion, the New Deal, centralized government, left-wing intellectuals, and the corrupting influences of a cosmopolitan society. In such a view, the resentments of these Republicans and the Senator's own talents were the driving forces behind the McCarthy movement. See Michael Paul Rogin, *The Intellectuals and McCarthy: The Radical Spectre* (Cambridge: Massachusetts Institute of Technology Press, 1967), esp. 216.

19. Goldston, 13; also, Rogin, 45-65, and Seymour Martin Lipset, "Three Decades of the Radical Right," in *The Radical Right*, ed. Daniel Bell (Garden City, NY: Anchor Books, 1964), 373-446.

20. Eisenhower cited in Lyon, 491.

21. The story is widely reported. For one of the most complete versions, see Robert Griffith, "The General and the Senator: Republican Politics and the 1952 Campaign in Wisconsin," *Wisconsin Magazine of History* 54 (Autumn 1970): 23-29.

22. Lyon, 500.

23. William V. Shannon, "Eisenhower as President," *Commentary* 26 (November 1958): 394.
24. Lloyd F. Bitzer, "The Rhetorical Situation," *Philosophy and Rhetoric* 1 (1968): 12-13.
25. Caute, 345. Also Rovere, *Senator Joe McCarthy*, 102-5.
26. Lyon, 491.
27. Griffith, "The General and the Senator," 23.
28. Norman Graebner, "Eisenhower's Popular Leadership," *Current History* 39 (October 1960): 232.
29. Hagerty, 32, 47; Greenstein, 169-70.
30. Donovan, 246.
31. Ibid., 247.
32. Lyon, 521.
33. Crandell, 496; also, Ewald, 383.
34. Donovan, 243.
35. Ewald, 379; Reeves, 534-5, 562.
36. Aldric Revell, cited in Reeves, 421.
37. Dwight D. Eisenhower, *The White House Years: Mandate for Change, 1953-1956* (Garden City: Doubleday & Co, 1963), 320.
38. Philip Wander, "Political Rhetoric and the Un-American Tradition," in Martin J. Medhurst, Robert L. Ivie, Philip Wander and Robert L. Scott, *Cold War Rhetoric: Strategy, Metaphor, and Ideology* (Westport, Connecticut: Greenwood Press, 1990), 191.
39. Talcott Parsons, "Social Strains in America (1955)," in *The Radical Right*, ed. Daniel Bell (Garden City, NY: Anchor Books, 1964), 221.
40. Rogin, 220.
41. Ibid., 242.
42. Will Herberg, "McCarthy and Hitler: A Delusive Parallel," *New Republic* 131 (23 August 1954): 13-15.
43. This statement appears in a number of sources. For example, Donovan, 249 and Hughes, 92.
44. Eisenhower, *The White House Years*, 320.
45. Greenstein, 214-8.
46. "Remarks Recorded for the American Legion 'Back to God' Program, February 1, 1953," *Public Papers of the Presidents of the United States: Dwight D. Eisenhower, 1953* (Washington, D.C.: Government Printing Office, 1960), 11 (hereafter cited as *Public Papers*); "Inaugural Address, January 20, 1953," *Public Papers, 1953*, 3; "Address at Transylvania College, Lexington, Kentucky, April 23, 1954," *Public Papers, 1954*, 420.
47. "Inaugural Address, January 20, 1953," 7. Also, "The President's News Conference of May 28, 1953, *Public Papers, 1953*, 300.
48. "Address at Transylvania College," 417.
49. "Address at the Sixth National Assembly of the United Church Women, Atlantic City, New Jersey, October 6, 1953," *Public Papers, 1953*, 640.
50. "Address at the Sixth National Assembly of the United Church Women, 638.
51. "Inaugural Address, January 20, 1953," 4; Also, "Remarks Recorded for the American Legion 'Back to God' Program, February 1, 1953," 11-12.
52. "Speech by General Dwight D. Eisenhower to the American Legion Convention, New York City, August 25, 1952," in *History of American Presidential Elections*, vol. IV, ed. Arthur M. Schlesinger, Jr. and Fred L. Israel (New York: McGraw Hill Book Co., 1971), 3301-2. (Hereafter cited as "Legion Convention.")
53. "The President's News Conference of February 25, 1953," *Public Papers, 1953*, 67.
54. "Legion Convention," 3301.

55. Eisenhower's admonition "don't join the book burners" was widely interpreted as being critical of McCarthyism. "Remarks at the Dartmouth College Commencement Exercises, Hanover, New Hampshire, June 14, 1953," *Public Papers, 1953*, 411-15.

56. "Letter on Intellectual Freedom to the President of the American Library Association," *Public Papers, 1953*, 455-6.

57. J.B. Matthews, "Reds and Our Churches," *The American Mercury*, July 1953, 3.

58. "Message to the National Co-Chairmen, Commission on Religious Organizations, National Conference of Christians and Jews," *Public Papers, 1953*, 489.

59. Philip Wander calls this ideology "cold war dualism." Wander, "The Rhetoric of American Foreign Policy," *Quarterly Journal of Speech* 70 (1984): 157.

60. Of course, this might be explained by noting that most of Eisenhower's speaking experience prior to entering politics had been of this genre; he had very little deliberative speaking experience. See Malcolm O. Sillars, "The Presidential Campaign of 1952," *Western Speech* 22 (Spring 1958): 97.

61. Chaim Perelman and L. Olbrechts-Tyteca, *The New Rhetoric: A Treatise on Argumentation*, trans. John Wilkinson and Purcell Weaver (Notre Dame, Indiana: University of Notre Dame Press, 1969), 49-51; Lawrence W. Rosenfield, "The Practical Celebration of Epideictic," in *Rhetoric in Transition: Studies in the Nature and Uses of Rhetoric*, ed. Eugene E. White (University Park: Pennsylvania State University Press, 1980), 131-55.

62. Barton J. Bernstein, "Election of 1952," in Schlesinger, Jr. and Israel, eds., 3245.

63. "The President's News Conference of February 25, 1953," 63.

64. "The President's News Conference of February 25, 1953," 67; "The President's News Conference of November 11, 1953," *Public Papers, 1953*, 761.

65. "Remarks Upon Receiving the America's Democratic Legacy Award at a B'nai B'rith Dinner in Honor of the 40th Anniversary of the Anti-Defamation League, November 23, 1953," *Public Papers, 1953*, 798; Also, "Remarks at the Luncheon of the Republican Women's Spring Conference, April 24, 1953," *Public Papers, 1953*, 215.

66. "Annual Message to the Congress on the State of the Union, February 2, 1953," *Public Papers, 1953*, 25.

67. "The President's News Conference of February 25, 1953," 66; also, "The President's News Conference of December 2, 1953," *Public Papers, 1953*, 802.

68. "Address at the Annual Convention of the National Young Republican Organization, Mount Rushmore National Monument, South Dakota, June 11, 1953," *Public Papers, 1953*, 407-8. (Hereafter cited as "Young Republicans.")

69. "Address at the New York Republican State Committee Dinner, Astor Hotel, New York City, May 7, 1953," *Public Papers, 1953*, 272.

70. "Inaugural Address, January 20, 1953," 5.

71. Graebner, 231. This point is argued more forcefully and completely in Richard Sennett, *The Fall of Public Man: On the Social Psychology of Capitalism* (New York: Random House, 1976).

72. Shannon, 395.

73. The debate seemed to revolve around the question of who controlled the president's men. While this controversy was one that animated most of the decisions around the appointments of Charles ("Chip") Bohlen and others, it reached a head in early 1954 when Senator McCarthy suggested that employees of the various agencies of the civil service and appointments come forward with information about subversion in their agency in contradiction to the presidential order that restricted access to executive documents.

74. "Young Republicans," 407.

75. "The President's News Conference of February 25, 1953," 66.
76. "The President's News Conference of March 5, 1953," *Public Papers, 1953*, 88, 79; "The President's News Conference of November 18, 1953," 784; "The President's News Conference of February 25, 1953," 65.
77. Hagerty, 24.
78. "The President's News Conference of May 14, 1953," *Public Papers, 1953*, 288-91.
79. "The President's News Conference of March 3, 1954," *Public Papers, 1954*, 290.
80. Greenstein terms this Eisenhower's "no personalities policy." See Greenstein, 28-9, 160-61, 221-22, 224.
81. Greenstein, 174.
82. "The President's News Conference of November 18, 1953," 788; also "The President's News Conference of March 3, 1954," 289.
83. "The President's News Conference of June 17, 1953," *Public Papers, 1953*, 430; compare with "The President's News Conference of May 19, 1954," *Public Papers, 1954*, 496.
84. "The President's News Conference of March 3, 1954," 291; "The President's News Conference of March 10, 1954," *Public Papers, 1954*, 305. See Greenstein, 173.
85. "The President's News Conference of July 22, 1953," *Public Papers, 1953*, 506.
86. "The President's News Conference of February 25, 1953," 66; "The President's News Conference of June 17, 1953," *Public Papers, 1953*, 426.
87. "The President's News Conference of January 27, 1954," *Public Papers, 1954*, 206.
88. Greenstein, 170.
89. "The President's News Conference of March 5, 1953," 88; "The President's News Conference of July 22, 1953," 506; "The President's News Conference of November 11, 1953," 759.
90. "The President's News Conference of November 11, 1953," 763; also, "The President's News Conference of November 18, 1953," *Public Papers, 1953*, 784.
91. Other scholars have likewise noted Eisenhower's penchant for privacy and secrecy. For example, see Crable, 190.
92. "The President's News Conference of March 5, 1953," 82.
93. "The President's News Conference of May 12, 1954," *Public Papers, 1954*, 474.
94. My debt at this stage of the argument to Ewald, esp. 379-84, should be obvious.
95. Hughes, 133.
96. Rogin, 228-9.
97. Ibid., 242.
98. John B. Oakes, "Report on McCarthy and McCarthyism," *New York Times Magazine* (2 November 1952): 12.
99. Edwin Black, "Secrecy and Disclosure as Rhetorical Forms," *Quarterly Journal of Speech* 74 (1988): 133-150.
100. McCarthy announced in a speech to the 1952 Republican National Convention that he would continue to "fight dirty" whenever he saw fit, because "a dirty fight is the only fight the communists understand." McCarthy cited in Reeves, 424.
101. Black "Secrecy and Disclosure," 149.
102. Ibid., 148.
103. Fredric Jameson, *The Political Unconscious: Narrative as a Socially Symbolic Act* (Ithaca, New York: Cornell University Press, 1981), 39-99.
104. Ibid., 88.
105. Graebner, 230.
106. Crandell, 498.

Eisenhower  greets Ngo Dinh Diem upon his visit to America

Gregory A.
Olson

# Eisenhower and the Indochina Problem

**W**hile serving as Supreme Commander of the North Atlantic Treaty Organization (NATO) in 1951, Dwight D. Eisenhower made the following entry in his diary:

> . . . the French have a knotty problem on that one [Indochina]—the campaign out there is a draining sore in their side. Yet if they quit and Indochina falls to Commies, it is easily possible that the entire Southeast Asia and Indonesia will go, soon to be followed by India. That prospect makes the whole problem one of interest to us all. I'd favor reinforcement to get the thing over at once; but I'm convinced that no military victory is possible in that kind of theater. Even if Indochina were completely cleared of Communists, right across the border is China with inexhaustible manpower.[1]

Almost two years before assuming the presidency, Eisenhower expressed belief in the domino theory and support for U.S. military involvement in Indochina; yet he doubted that a military victory could be achieved. That philosophy influenced Eisenhower's thinking when he was forced to decide whether to intervene militarily in early 1954. Eisenhower's philosophy included another component: a strong distaste for colonialism. Eisenhower once said that in 1950, he had "begged the French" to renounce colonialism in Indochina. But to no avail.[2]

Eisenhower best expressed his anti-colonial bent in a long letter to Prime Minister Winston Churchill the day after the Indochinese settlement at Geneva in July 1954. Churchill had talked of retirement on a recent visit with Eisenhower and the president suggested that he "must have a very deep and understandable desire to do something special and additional in your remaining period of active service that will be forever recognized as a milestone in the world's tortuous progress toward a just and lasting peace." Eisenhower then outlined his proposal:

> Colonialism is on the way out as a relationship among peoples. The sole question is one of time and method. I think we should handle it so as to win the adherents to Western aims.

97

> We know that there is abroad in the world a fierce and growing spirit of nationalism. Should we try to dam it up completely, it would, like a mighty river, burst through the barriers and could create havoc. But again, like a river, if we are intelligent enough to make constructive use of this force, then the result, far from being disastrous, could redound greatly to our advantage, particularly in our struggle against the Kremlin's power.[3]

The president admitted that not all colonial people were ready for self rule, but that the Western powers could offer education and economic development to the colonies. Eisenhower argued: "If you could say that twenty-five years from now, every last one of the colonies (excepting military bases) should have been *offered a right to self-government and determination,* you would electrify the world." More than that, Eisenhower believed that if educated and assisted, the colonial countries would not want independence but "would cling more tightly to the mother country and be a more valuable part thereof." This would become a great Cold War weapon as the world could compare the West's policies to the "evil" use of Soviet power in Eastern Europe. Later, when writing of his proposal to Churchill, Eisenhower said: "My steel struck no spark from his flint."[4]

John Foster Dulles, who as secretary of state became Eisenhower's most influential cabinet member, wrote in 1950 that Indochina was one of the "most difficult of all" foreign policy problems. While not approving of French colonialism, Dulles decided that it was necessary to support France, writing: "It seems that, as is often the case, it is necessary as a practical matter to choose the lesser of two evils because the theoretically ideal solution is not possible for many reasons."[5]

President Eisenhower inherited a Truman administration policy of escalating United States commitment to the French effort to defeat Ho Chi Minh's Vietminh forces. On 18 November 1952, President-elect Eisenhower met with President Harry S. Truman and several cabinet members to discuss issues the new administration would face. President Truman emphasized the need for continuity in foreign policy. Secretary of State Dean Acheson reviewed the problems the French were facing in Indochina and impressed upon the Eisenhower party the importance of keeping that area out of Communist hands, saying: "This is an urgent matter upon which the new administration must be prepared to act." William Conrad Gibbons writes that "Eisenhower soon made it clear that his administration not only would continue but would strengthen the Truman administration's opposition to communism in Indochina."[6]

When Dwight D. Eisenhower assumed office, the Republican administration continued the financial support for the French colonialists. During the height of the McCarthy era, the new administration did not want to be accused of being soft on communism, particularly since Republicans had effectively blamed Democrats for the loss of China in the 1952 elections. However, Eisenhower had run for office as a peace candidate, which added a constraint to his actions. Eisenhower would find it difficult to engage in a new land war on the Asian continent since he had campaigned to end the war in Korea.

Eisenhower and Dulles deepened an involvement in an area our nation did not understand; there were no American books on Indochina in 1954, and one estimate put the number of American scholars who were expert on the area at less than five. Dulles became the cabinet member closest to the president,[7] and at the beginning of his presidency Eisenhower relied heavily on Dulles's expertise in foreign policy.[8] Like the rest of the country, neither Eisenhower nor Dulles understood the part of the world where the United States would fight its most tragic war.[9]

## 1953—EISENHOWER'S EARLY INDOCHINA RHETORIC

In 1953 the emerging issue of Indochina received little attention from the president; he mentioned it in public about ten times. In his February 1953 State of the Union message, Eisenhower linked Indochina to Korea and Formosa, the two areas that would dominate Eisenhower's policy considerations in the Far East. The president said of the Korean conflict:

> It is clearly a part of the same calculated assault that the aggressor is simultaneously pressing in Indochina and in Malaya, and of the strategic situation that manifestly embraces the island of Formosa and the Chinese Nationalist forces there. The working out of any military solution to the Korean war will inevitably affect all these areas.[10]

Eisenhower had breakfast with Dulles, Secretary of the Treasury George Humphrey, Secretary of Defense Charles Wilson, and Director of Mutual Security Harold Stassen on 24 March 1953. This was one of two meetings held prior to consultations with the French. The official minutes read:

> There was discussion of the Indochina situation and recognition that it had probably the top priority in foreign policy, being in some ways more important than Korea because the consequences of loss there could not be localized, but would spread throughout Asia and Europe.

> It was agreed that we would probably have to step up considerably our aid to the French in Indochina if there was a plan that promised real success.

> There was further discussion as to deterrence against the Chinese Communists so they would not send their forces openly into Vietnam as they had done in Korea after the North Koreans were defeated.[11]

After the meeting with the French, administration officials were pessimistic about France's willingness to grant autonomy to the Indochinese. Eisenhower believed that French Foreign Minister Georges M. Bidault "evaded, refusing to commit himself to an out-and-out renunciation of any French colonial purpose."[12] The French intransigence to give up colonial aims continued to place a constraint on the Eisenhower administration's ability to support the French effort.

At a news conference two days later, the president linked France's problems in Indochina with "its relationship to its capabilities in Europe." That concern led both the Truman and Eisenhower administrations to support their World War II and NATO ally in Indochina. Said Eisenhower:

> France, let us not forget, was bled white in World War I, had a long and difficult political and economic re-adjustment, and then was plunged into World War II and was overrun, its pride was trampled in the dust. It was a long time coming back. France has had a very hard time. I still think, though, that America has not forgotten the very great sentimental ties that bind us to a nation which even as far back as 1776 and 1777 was coming and helping us out.[13]

The president's position on France continued to be different in his private communication. At a National Security Council (NSC) meeting on 6 May, Eisenhower indicated that unless France made clear its intention to grant independence to the Associated States (Vietnam, Cambodia, and Laos) and to appoint effective military leadership, "nothing could possibly save Indochina, and that continued United States assistance would amount to pouring our money down a rathole." He added, "The great question was how we can make the French see the wisdom of such a course of action." Eisenhower was disturbed by a successful Vietminh sweep into Laos that caused him to demand that the French replace General Raoul Salan with a "forceful and inspirational leader, empowered with the means and authority to win victory." The following day, Eisenhower told Canadian Prime Minister Lester Pearson that "the only chance of preserving South East Asia lay in making sure of the support of the native peoples." Eisenhower returned to a Revolutionary War analogy, arguing that regular troops cannot win against guerrillas who have the support of the local population, adding that fact was proved in the case of British General Bradock.[14]

The Korean armistice was reached in late July 1953. By reaching a separate settlement over Korea, Eisenhower broke an agreement between France and the Truman administration which had been based on the premise that a unilateral settlement would increase the pressures on the nation still fighting. France had ended discussions with the Vietminh because of their agreement with Truman. The rationale behind the French/U.S. agreement proved valid inasmuch as the Korean armistice enabled China to vastly increase its support for Ho's forces, thereby weakening the French military position.[15] Eisenhower's unilateral peace accord with Korea, therefore, made it more difficult to turn down French requests for additional aid to Indochina.

Eisenhower's difficulties with Congress started in summer 1953 with a coalition of conservative Republicans and liberal Democrats. In late July, debate on aid for Indochina was highlighted by a Barry M. Goldwater (R-Ariz.) amendment, and a John F. Kennedy (D-Mass.) substitute amendment, which sought to reduce aid by twenty-five percent, and tied the aid package to a French announcement of a date for independence of the Indochinese states. Goldwater predicted that if France didn't grant freedom, "as surely as day follows night our boys will follow this $400 million." Dulles was concerned enough to have Eisenhower intervene personally with members of Congress. Goldwater received considerable support, but his amendment was defeated and Eisenhower's full amount of aid reinstated.[16] It became apparent after this debate that congressional opinion would constrain Eisenhower's policy options in Indochina.

In an August speech to the Governor's Conference, Eisenhower justified his $400 million in foreign aid to Indochina, noting the governors "have a confused idea of where it is located—Laos, or Cambodia, or Siam" (Siam became Thailand in 1939). The president described the critical role Indochina played in this early public statement of the domino theory:

> Now, first of all, the last great population remaining in Asia that has not become dominated by the Kremlin, of course, is the sub-continent of India, including the Pakistan government. Here are 350 million people still free. Now let us assume that we lose Indochina. If Indochina goes, several things happen right away. The Malayan peninsula, the last little bit of the end hanging on down there, would be scarcely defensible—and tin and tungsten that we so greatly value from that area would cease coming. But all India would be outflanked. Burma would certainly, in its weakened condition, be no defense. Now, India is surrounded on that side by the Communist empire. Iran on its left is in a weakened condition. . . . All of that weakening position around there is very ominous for the United States, because finally if we lost all that, how would the free world hold the rich empire of Indonesia? So you see, somewhere along the line, this must be blocked. It must be blocked now. That is what the French are doing.[17]

At an NSC meeting on 9 September 1953, Dulles said that Eisenhower had indicated "that the solution of the Indochina problem was the first priority. . . . The president had stated his belief that the loss of Indochina could not be insulated, and that that loss would, shortly after, cost us the rest of Southeast Asia. Korea on the other hand, might be an insulated loss."[18]

## THE DECISION NOT TO INTERVENE AT DIEN BIEN PHU

President Eisenhower's dilemma continued in 1954; he was willing neither to support French colonialism, nor to lose Indochina to Ho's Communists. Eisenhower knew little about Indochina when 1954 began, but learned a great deal during the first months of the year. Early that year, the president still referred to Thailand as Siam. On 17 March, he could not remember the name "Dien Bien Phu" at a news conference and said that he could "never pronounce" the name anyway. Thailand, Dien Bien Phu and many names central to the emerging drama in Indochina became common terms for the president by April. In that month, Eisenhower said: "The words 'Dien Bien Phu' are no longer just a funny sounding name, to be dismissed from the breakfast conversation because we don't know where it is, or what it means."[19] The president started the year considering U.S. military involvement in Indochina. His instinct told him not to make that commitment. Eisenhower's public rhetorical stance early in 1954 was soothing; he assured the American people that the United States would not become militarily involved and promised congressional consultation for any steps the U.S. would take. So soon after American involvement in Korea, public opinion constrained Eisenhower's rhetorical choices. In April, when it became likely that the U.S. would not involve the military to save Dien Bien Phu, Eisenhower's rhetorical stance became militant; his strategy was to help achieve a successful settlement at Geneva.[20]

Eisenhower's management style was conducive to quality decision making. The president expected his aides to debate issues and not to be yes-men. The options leading to the April decision not to intervene at Dien Bien Phu were thoroughly explored. Eisenhower said in a 1967 interview:

> I know of only one way in which you can be sure you've done your best to make a wise decision. That is to get all of the people who have partial and definable responsibility in this particular field, whatever it may be. Get them with their different viewpoints in front of you, and listen to them debate. I do not believe in bringing them in one at a time, and therefore being more impressed by the most recent one you hear than the earlier ones. You must get courageous men, men of strong views, and let them debate and argue with each other. You listen, and you see if there's anything been (sic) brought up, an idea that changes your own view or enriches your view or adds to it. . . . Sometimes the case becomes so simple that you can make a decision right then. Or you may go back and wait two or three days, if time isn't of the essence. But you make it.[21]

In his memoirs, Eisenhower wrote that the head of state "must give the final word on every major question—and that word must be respected."[22]

Eisenhower's style enabled Dulles to do all the legwork, but when the ultimate decision was made, the president made it.[23] This was the case with Dien Bien Phu.

On 8 January 1954, Eisenhower held a crucial NSC meeting that illustrates his management style.[24] It was at this meeting that the administration's attention shifted to the emerging drama at Dien Bien Phu, where three Vietminh divisions surrounded ten battalions of French Union forces. The French had deliberately set up the confrontation at Dien Bien Phu; French General Henri Navarre wanted a major battle with Vietminh General Vo Nguyen Giap.

Several extreme options were discussed on 8 January, including the commitment of American military forces. After the briefing, the president took charge of the meeting by asking several questions. First, he wondered why France was still unwilling to take the issue to the United Nations. Dulles explained that the French feared that the U.N. would want to consider the issue of North Africa as well. The record from the meeting documented Eisenhower's view

> that this seemed to be yet another case where the French don't know what to do—whether to go it alone or to get assistance from other nations clandestinely. They want to involve us secretly and yet are unwilling to go out openly to get allies in their struggle. For himself, said the President with great force, he simply could not imagine the United States putting ground forces anywhere in Southeast Asia, except possibly in Malaya, which we would have to defend as a bulwark to our off-shore island chain. But to do this anywhere else was simply beyond his contemplation. Indeed, the key to winning this war was to get the Vietnamese to fight. There was just no sense in even talking about United States forces replacing the French in Indochina. If we did so, the Vietnamese could be expected to transfer their hatred of the French to us. I cannot tell you, said the President with vehemence, how bitterly opposed I am to such a course of action. This war in Indochina would absorb our troops by divisions![25]

The president asked whether the French would allow the United States to aid in the training of native troops, and was told that the French were resisting such efforts and wanted to keep the Indochinese dependent on French troops. Eisenhower expressed the view "that one of the outstanding failures of the Western world in Asia was its inability to produce good fighting material in the Asian countries for which Western powers were responsible. The communists were more effective. They got hold of the most unlikely people and turned them into great fighters."

When Secretary Humphrey asked if the United States would replace the French if they were to pull out, Eisenhower said: "we would not intervene, but we had better go to full mobilization." The president softened the remark by adding an analogy: "What you've got here is a leaky dike, and with leaky dikes it's sometimes better to put a finger in than to let the whole structure be washed away."

When the possibility of sending pilots was raised, Eisenhower said "that even if we did not send pilots we could certainly send planes and men to take over the maintenance of the planes." When Admiral Arthur Radford, Chairman of the Joint Chiefs of Staff, suggested the use of a squadron of U.S. planes at Dien Bien Phu for one afternoon, the report of the meeting noted:

> The President thought . . . [of] a little group of fine and adventurous pilots. . . . Then, continued the President, we should give these pilots U.S. planes without insignia and let them go. That, said the President, was the right way to use the planes from the aircraft carrier, and this all could be done without involving us directly in the war, which he admitted would be a very dangerous thing.[26]

The meeting adjourned with Eisenhower ordering further study to determine how to better aid the French. At the beginning of 1954, Eisenhower was at least considering U.S. military involvement in Indochina. At the 21 January NSC meeting, Eisenhower cautioned that "Above all, Indochina . . . must not be allowed to go by default."[27]

Eisenhower appointed a Special Committee on Indochina to make policy recommendations. The committee was headed by long-time Eisenhower associate W. Bedell Smith, the under secretary of state, and was convened because the president was unhappy with the advice he had been receiving on Indochina. Eisenhower instructed the committee to submit an "area plan" for Southeast Asia. Gibbons points out the importance of this seemingly minor Eisenhower directive, because it allowed for a wider framework and accepted the possibility of a loss of Indochina. When the Special Committee reported on 29 January, Radford was unhappy because the report "was too restrictive in that it was premised on U.S. action short of the contribution of U.S. combat forces." Radford insisted on a new report that included the possibility of using U.S. forces. At the meeting on the 29th, they debated the French requests for aircraft and four hundred U.S. technicians. The group concluded that sending technicians would not lead to providing combat troops. Eisenhower agreed to send aircraft and two hundred technicians to Indochina immediately.[28]

Some members of Congress instantly protested the provision of technicians. John Stennis (D-Miss.) said: "First we send them planes, then we send them men . . . . We are going to war, inch by inch."[29] In private, Republican leaders expressed the same concern, leading Eisenhower to respond: "But we can't get anywhere in Asia by just sitting here in Washington and doing nothing—My God, we must not lose Asia—we've got to look the thing right in the face."[30]

But Eisenhower understood the constraints placed on him by Congress and his own party. The president started to sound cautious in his public pronouncements, distancing himself from the need to use military force to save Indochina. When asked on 10 February if sending technicians would lead to

U.S. involvement in a "hot" war, the president replied: "no one could be more bitterly opposed to ever getting the United States involved in a hot war in that region than I am; consequently, every move that I authorize is calculated, so far as humans can do it, to make certain that that does not happen." The president was sensitive to criticism from Congress that it had not been consulted when the decision was made to send U.S. technicians. He responded to a question on 10 March by saying "there is going to be no involvement of America in war unless it is a result of the constitutional process that is placed upon Congress." One week later, Eisenhower reiterated his stand on congressional involvement, implying that Truman was wrong in not getting a congressional declaration of war over the Korean conflict.[31]

In private, Bedell Smith "signaled" the administration's shift against the commitment of U.S. forces when he testified in executive session to the Foreign Relations Committee on 16 February, rejecting the domino theory and saying: "I think that, even at the worst, part of Indochina might be lost without losing the rest of Southeast Asia." It was clear that there was little concern on the committee for manipulation of Vietnamese politics. Smith reacted to a question by William Fulbright (D-Ark.) about Emperor Bao Dai's leadership by saying: "if you handle it properly you can make a *synthetic* strong man out of almost anyone who is not a coward." Fulbright, who became a vocal anti-war Senator during the Johnson administration, talked of the need for a strong native leader for Vietnam, a Kemal Ataturk, and added: "But if he (Bao Dai) is not any good, *we* ought to get another one." Smith suggested that a change in leadership had been considered and alluded to "providing certain religious leadership," which may have been a code phrase for Ngo Dinh Diem.[32]

By mid-March 1954, the military situation at Dien Bien Phu was deteriorating and pressure was building to aid the French effort. At the NSC meeting on 18 March, Central Intelligence Agency (CIA) Director Allen Dulles estimated "that the French had about a 50-50 chance of holding out." On the 23rd, John Foster Dulles sent Eisenhower a memorandum describing a meeting with Radford and French General Paul Ely, chief of staff of the French Joint Chiefs of Staff. The French wanted additional U.S. bombers with American pilots. Ely asked if the United States would use its own air force if the Chinese sent jet fighters into Indochina. The secretary of state could not answer, but said: "if the United States sent its flag and its own military establishment—land, sea or air—into the Indochina war, then the prestige of the United States would be engaged to a point where we would want to have a success." Eisenhower shared that sentiment. The next day, Eisenhower directed Dulles in a phone conversation:

> The President said that he agreed basically that we should not get involved in fighting in Indochina unless there were the political pre-conditions necessary for a successful outcome. He did not, however, wholly exclude the possibility

of a single strike, if it were almost certain this would produce decisive result . . . .
He did not, however, want anything said that would be an explicit promise that
we might not be able to live up to.[33]

When Radford and Ely met one last time, Ely left with the impression that if
the French government requested a U.S. air strike, Admiral Radford would recommend the action to Eisenhower in expectation of the president's support.
Radford's interpretation of the meeting was quite different, but the French
request for a U.S. air strike before the fall of Dien Bien Phu was based on this
miscommunication.[34]

Discussion at the NSC meeting on 25 March centered on the inability of the
French to prevent a Vietminh division from returning to Dien Bien Phu.
Eisenhower commented that the French inability to move in Indochina, except
by air, "seemed sufficient indication that the population of Vietnam did not
wish to be free from Communist domination." Eisenhower didn't respond
directly to a question whether further study should consider U.S. intervention;
instead, he turned the conversation to the possibility of multilateral intervention, through either the United Nations or Vietnam's invitation to specific
nations to come to its aid. The latter approach had the advantage of avoiding
"solely Occidental assistance to Vietnam." The president also emphasized that
Congress would have to be involved in any intervention in Indochina; "it was
simply academic to imagine otherwise." Eisenhower said it was time "to
explore with the Congress what support could be anticipated in the event that
it seemed desirable to intervene in Indochina."[35] The dual approach of seeking
united action and working to obtain congressional approval became
Eisenhower's approach to managing rhetorically the crisis at Dien Bien Phu.

Eisenhower and Dulles were struggling with the possibility of intervention.
At a Cabinet meeting on 26 March, Dulles said that the U.S. would have to take
"fairly strong action" in Indochina, "but these risks will be less if we take them
now rather than waiting for several years." Three days later, Eisenhower and
Vice-President Richard Nixon met with Republican congressional leaders.
Nixon recalled:

> Eisenhower said that if the military situation at Dien Bien Phu became des-
> perate he would consider the use of diversionary tactics, possibly a landing by
> Chiang Kai-shek's Nationalist forces on China's Hainan Island or a naval
> blockade of the Chinese mainland. Very simply, but dramatically, he said, "I
> am bringing this up at this time because at any time within the space of forty-
> eight hours, it might be necessary to move into the battle of Dien Bien Phu in
> order to keep it from going against us, and in that case I will be calling in the
> Democrats as well as our Republican leaders to inform them of the actions
> we're taking."[36]

Eisenhower's discussions with the NSC had focused on air strikes at Dien Bien Phu. The scenario he painted to the Republican congressional leadership made an air strike look like a moderate response and seems an effort to manage Congress to win approval for the air strike.

At the NSC meeting on 1 April, Eisenhower said that he understood that the JCS, with the exception of Radford, opposed an air strike using U.S. planes and pilots; and while there were "very terrible risks, there was no reason for the Council to avoid considering the intervention issue." On that same day, Eisenhower told two visitors that the "U.S. might have to make decision to send in squadrons from two aircraft carriers off coast to bomb Reds at Dien Bien Phu—'of course, if we did, we'd have to deny it forever.'"[37]

The following day, Eisenhower, Dulles, Wilson, and Radford met to discuss the draft of a possible congressional resolution on the Indochinese situation. Dulles suggested that he and Radford might view the resolution differently; the secretary of state saw it as a "deterrent" to help develop united action while the admiral viewed it "as something to be immediately used in some 'strike.'" Even Radford believed that it was too late for a strike at Dien Bien Phu, saying, "the outcome there would be determined within a matter of hours." Without the need for a bombing mission to save the French, the resolution was a "predated declaration of war" like the Formosa Resolution of 1955 and the Gulf of Tonkin Resolution of 1964. It gave Eisenhower the authority to commit air and sea forces to prevent the "extension and expansion" of communism in Southeast Asia. The resolution was to expire on 30 June, 1955.

The record of the 2 April meeting indicates that Eisenhower thought the draft of the proposed congressional resolution "reflected" what "was desirable." Eisenhower directed Dulles and Radford "to develop first the thinking of congressional leaders without actually submitting in the first instance a resolution drafted by ourselves."[38]

Dulles and Radford followed the president's directive and met with congressional leaders on 3 April in an attempt to gain their acquiescence on the resolution. Congress was sensitive to its lack of involvement in the Korean War, which was waged under executive action. A congressional resolution approving Truman's response in Korea had been discussed but never was acted upon. Majority Leader William Knowland (R-Calif.) initially agreed with Dulles on the need for a resolution over Indochina, but further discussion made it clear that Congress would not pass such a resolution without British and other allied support. Dulles recorded: "The feeling was unanimous that 'we want no more Koreas with the United States furnishing 90 percent of the manpower.'" Radford argued that the administration had no intention of committing land forces, but the congressmen responded, "once the flag was committed the use of land forces would inevitably follow." Minority Leader Lyndon Johnson (D-

Texas) was present and shared that opinion, stating that he "pounded the President's desk in the Oval Office to emphasize his opposition."[39] Johnson would change his mind by 1964. Dulles left the meeting with the impression that if he could get British and other nations to join the United States, a congressional resolution could be passed.

There is evidence that Eisenhower could have obtained the congressional resolution had he intervened personally. Eisenhower did not choose that route; he did not even attend the meeting on 3 April. Instead, he allowed Congress and the British to make the decision for him. Eisenhower's judgment was not to intervene at Dien Bien Phu anyway. So, when the French requested an air strike on 5 April, the congressional leader's opposition gave the president a convenient excuse. Leslie H. Gelb and Richard K. Betts argue that Eisenhower's strategy at the 3 April meeting accomplished three things: "First, he isolated Radford, Nixon, and other advocates of unilateral intervention." Even though they continued to discuss a unilateral air strike, the idea "was effectively buried." "Second," argue Gelb and Betts, "the President co-opted the congressional leadership. In rejecting the go-it-alone approach, they had been cornered, thus achieving Eisenhower's third purpose of building domestic support for multilateral intervention, or united action."

Eisenhower successfully managed the impending crisis over possible intervention.[40] That success was not repeated. Richard Immerman claims: "At Dienbienphu Eisenhower avoided a tragedy; at Geneva he laid the groundwork for one." Eisenhower was more interested in the military situation at Dien Bien Phu than the negotiations taking place in Geneva. The president actively managed American policy in regards to Dien Bien Phu, but remained aloof from the proceedings at Geneva.[41]

## UNITED ACTION, GENEVA, AND THE FORMATION OF SEATO

The idea of a defensive alliance in Asia had been discussed as early as 1948. At Dulles's urging, Eisenhower called for such a treaty in Southeast Asia in 1953. The president's decision to seek united action specifically for Indochina can be traced to 21 March 1954. Eisenhower made the rhetorical choice of having Dulles deliver the speech announcing united action on 29 March, before the Overseas Press Club. Dulles went "over every word of it beforehand" with the president. Indeed, the speeches that Dulles was so noted for were always read by Eisenhower, who edited them, sometimes rewriting entire sections.[42]

In the Overseas Press Club speech, Dulles used words that an aide said were "deliberately picked" to sound "menacing without committing anybody to anything." John Burke and Fred Greenstein describe Dulles's language as "forceful-sounding but unspecific." Dulles said that a Communist take-over of Southeast

Asia "should not be passively accepted but should be met by United Action." This "vague" language led to rumors of U.S. intervention that Eisenhower and Dulles chose not to deny. George Herring and Immerman call united action "part bluff," but point out that it also involved the willingness to commit U.S. military forces under the right circumstances. Eisenhower's rhetorical strategy was to use Dulles to continue this militant rhetoric until the settlement at Geneva.

The lack of clarity in Dulles's speech caused anxiety in those opposed to American intervention. On 6 April, John Kennedy delivered a Senate speech on Indochina. The future president was harsh on France for not granting independence and believed that increasing nationalist support was the crucial element to a successful outcome. In 1954 Kennedy understood that without nationalist support, the U.S. could no more succeed in Indochina than the French had. At the end of Kennedy's speech, Mike Mansfield (D-Mont.) asked Kennedy a prearranged question about what Dulles had meant when he called for "united action" in Indochina. Kennedy replied: "There is every indication that what he meant was that the United States will take the ultimate step." "And what is that,?" asked Mansfield. "It is war," replied Kennedy. Knowland was one of many who praised Kennedy's speech, demonstrating the constraint placed on Eisenhower by conservatives in his own party.[43]

The administration opposed a political settlement to the Indochina conflict, but both Britain and France were insistent that negotiations take place. Eisenhower concluded that a threatening U.S. posture might lead to a more palatable result at Geneva.[44] Dulles spent the next several months trying to hammer out Eisenhower's united action concept and SEATO was the result.

Minutes from the 6 April NSC meeting quote Eisenhower as saying "with great emphasis, 'there was no possibility whatever of U.S. unilateral intervention in Indochina, and we had best face that fact. Even if we tried such a course, we would have to take it to Congress and fight for it like dogs, with very little hope of success.'" Dulles then discussed the "feelers" he had put out to other nations with interests in the region. Eisenhower was in favor of such a "political organization which would have for its purpose the defense of Southeast Asia even if Indochina should be lost." Such a grouping, the president believed, "would be better than emergency military action." When Nixon asked Dulles if such an organization would deal "with local communist subversion," Dulles answered that it would. Eisenhower made it clear that the United States would not become a colonial power replacing France, but could only intervene in Indochina with other Asian nations. Dulles argued "that we can no longer accept further Communist take-overs, whether accomplished by external or internal measures. We could no longer afford to put too fine a point on the methods." Humphrey feared the implications of Dulles's position and "could see no terminal approach in such a process." When

Eisenhower asked Humphrey for an alternative, the president reportedly argued that

Indochina was the first in a row of dominoes. If it fell its neighbors would shortly thereafter fall with it, and where did the process end? If he was correct, said the President, it would end with the United States directly behind the 8-ball. "George," said the President, "you exaggerate the case. Nevertheless in certain areas at least we cannot afford to let Moscow gain another bit of territory. Dien Bien Phu itself may be just such a critical point." That's the hard thing to decide. We are not prepared now to take action with respect to Dien Bien Phu in and by itself, but the coalition program for Southeast Asia must go forward as a matter of the greatest urgency. If we can secure this regional grouping for the defense of Indochina, the battle is two-thirds won. This grouping would give us the needed popular support of domestic opinion and of allied governments, and we might thereafter not be required to contemplate a unilateral American intervention in Indochina.[45]

Nixon wrote in his diary:

From the conversation, however, it was quite apparent that the President had backed down considerably from the strong position he had taken on Indochina the latter part of the previous week. He seemed resigned to doing nothing at all unless we could get the allies and the country to go along with whatever was suggested and he did not seem inclined to put much pressure on to get them to come along.[46]

At his press conference the day after the NSC meeting, Eisenhower reiterated that the U.S. would not act alone in Indochina. When asked about the strategic importance of Indochina, he made his best known comment on the domino theory:

. . . you have broader considerations that might follow what you would call the "falling domino" principle. You have a row of dominoes set up, you knock over the first one, and what will happen to the last one is the certainty that it will go over very quickly. So you have the beginning of a disintegration that would have the most profound influences. . . .

So, the possible consequences of the loss are just incalculable to the free world.[47]

The president was asked if Dulles did "clear his statements on Indochina with you" since many members of Congress believed that while Eisenhower "allayed their fears, that Secretary Dulles was making them fear more." Eisenhower responded that Dulles not only conferred and cleared statements with him, but they sat down and studied "practically word by word what he is to say." But the question made a point; their different rhetorical styles often made Eisenhower and Dulles appear to play "good cop, bad cop" in their public pronouncements. At a May press conference, Eisenhower said:

> . . . some have assumed that there has been a difference of opinion between the Secretary of State and myself as to exactly what we meant. I think I have assured this group several times that I know of no important announcement made by either one of us in this regard [united action] that isn't the result of long and serious conferences. *If there are any differences ever detectable in our utterances, it must be because of language and not because of any intent.*[48] (emphasis added)

Dulles recognized his inability to predict how his rhetoric would affect the press. In a 1953 diary entry, Eisenhower commented on this aspect of Dulles's style: "But he [Dulles] is not particularly persuasive in presentation and, at times, seems to have a curious lack of understanding as to how his words and manner may affect another personality." The president believed that Dulles had a "lawyer's mind," effective at condemning Communist actions but unable to stress the positive attributes of U.S. policy. Eisenhower understood this weakness in Dulles's rhetoric and chose more positive language to express similar views, creating the "good cop, bad cop" perception. The president was a master at utilizing an aide's strengths while minimizing weaknesses, and Dulles's style sometimes proved useful to Eisenhower, as in the days leading to Geneva. As Greenstein argues:

> Eisenhower and Dulles practiced a division of labor resembling that of a client with his attorney—a client who has firm overall purposes and an attorney who is expected to help him devise ways to accomplish those purposes and to argue his case. The public impression that emanated from the quite different personal styles of these men—Dulles the austere cold warrior, Eisenhower the warm champion of peace—contributed to a further division of labor. Dulles was assigned the "get tough" side of foreign-policy enunciation, thus placating the fervently anti-Communist wing of the Republican party. Meanwhile, amiable Ike made gestures toward peace and international humanitarianism—for example, Atoms for Peace, Open Skies, and summitry at Geneva.[49]

Nixon concluded that it was important for Eisenhower to appear "the nice guy."[50] But, Eisenhower took advantage of Dulles's naturally militant rhetoric in the days leading to the settlement at Geneva.

On 10 April 1954, Dulles left for three weeks of shuttle diplomacy to push the united action concept. The British presented one major constraint to united action; they did not accept the domino theory and were not willing to fight for French colonies after giving up most of their own. While the United States wanted the French to continue the battle in Indochina, Britain hoped for a cease-fire agreement at Geneva. Britain agreed to discussions of a collective defense organization for Southeast Asia if a settlement for the Indochina crisis were found at Geneva. Dulles thus could not obtain British agreement for collective defense in Southeast Asia until after the Geneva Conference.

France presented the other international constraint because she would agree neither to complete independence for the Associated States nor to internationalize the war. From a French perspective, granting total independence could not be considered; keeping Indochina in the French Union was the object for which France was fighting. The Eisenhower administration was anxious to gain French membership in the European Defense Community (EDC), a concept that involved a rearmed West Germany. France was able to dangle that possibility in effectively resisting American demands in Indochina.

Dulles's mission was further complicated when Nixon responded to a hypothetical question on how the U.S. would react to a French collapse by saying, "we must take the risk by putting our boys in." Nixon's comment was viewed as an administration trial balloon but was more likely an attempt by the vice-president to force Eisenhower to intervene at Dien Bien Phu. The White House quickly announced that Nixon's comment did not reflect administration policy. Nixon assumed personal responsibility for his comment but later said that Dulles was in agreement. The secretary of state even suggested that Nixon's statement might prove "beneficial" to the discussions about to begin in Geneva. Eisenhower did not discourage the militant rhetoric of Nixon, and administration threats proved a useful prelude to the Geneva Conference.

The situation at Dien Bien Phu deteriorated throughout April; French Foreign Minister Bidault once again asked for an American air strike. Dulles continued to use Congress as an excuse for administration failure to aid the French. The secretary of state argued that the fall of Dien Bien Phu would not alter the military situation in Indochina and urged patience until the concept of collective defense could aid the French cause. Bidault claims that Dulles offered him the loan of two atomic weapons, but that claim seems unlikely. In his memoirs, Bidault called Dulles's Indochina policy one "of many tough words but little action."[51]

Some interesting insights into Eisenhower's views are found in a letter of 26 April to his friend, General Alfred Gruenther, NATO supreme commander. The president said that Gruenther's "adverse opinion" to unilateral American intervention in Indochina "exactly parallels mine." Eisenhower bemoaned the lack of French leadership, and in a scathing attack on Charles de Gaulle, wrote: "The only hope is to produce a new and inspirational leader—and I do *not* mean one that is 6 feet 5 and who considers himself to be, by some miraculous biological and transmigrative process, the offspring of Clemenceau and Jeanne d'Arc."[52]

The final decision not to intervene at Dien Bien Phu was never made but was overtaken by events. At the NSC meeting on 29 April, Eisenhower was given ample opportunity to defend his position on unilateral intervention as earlier expressed to Gruenther. After Radford briefed the group on the approaching fall of Dien Bien Phu, there was a heated discussion; Stassen recommended unilateral U.S. intervention in the southern areas of Indochina, anticipating congressional acquiescence. Eisenhower disagreed sharply about congressional reaction and believed that unilateral action would lead to charges of "imperialistic ambitions." He added, "without allies and associates the leader is just an adventurer like Genghis Khan." The president was "frightened to death at the prospect of American divisions scattered all over the world" and believed that such a move would lead to war with China and might involve the Soviets. Eisenhower wanted a phased French withdrawal and feared a rapid departure occurring in "such a way so as to prevent the United States from taking over the French responsibilities." Both Smith and Nixon entered the debate with hawkish positions. The meeting lasted three hours and the notes indicate that this debate must have taken up more than a third of that time. The decision on an air strike was delayed until the next week when Dulles would return, even though Dulles had cabled Eisenhower on 25 April, recommending against unilateral intervention. By the time Dulles had returned, Dien Bien Phu was about to fall and an air strike was a moot point.[53]

After the French defeat, Eisenhower and Dulles adopted a policy of opposing a cease fire in Indochina until a political agreement had been reached. If a cease fire did occur, the U.S. planned to cut off military aid to the French Union forces. The carrot of U.S. intervention was still held out to the French if they would meet U.S. conditions—genuine independence for the Associated States, U.S. shared responsibility in training and planning military operations, and a French agreement to stay and fight in Indochina. Dulles and Eisenhower did not object to the French using the possibility of U.S. intervention as a bargaining chip at Geneva; indeed, Dulles considered Communist fear of U.S. intervention to have offered the best chance for a favorable peace agreement. The administration openly considered the option of intervention until mid-June, when Pierre Mendes-France was elected France's Prime Minister on a peace platform, pledging to reach agreement on Indochina by 20 July.[54]

Eisenhower edited Dulles's 7 May 1954 television speech to the nation on the fall of Dien Bien Phu. The president wanted Dulles to sound moderate and inserted the words, "The United States will never start a war" in Dulles's text. Eisenhower, Dulles, and Radford all revised their public versions of the domino theory after the French defeat. When asked if Indochina were "still indispensable to the defense of southeast Asia," the president replied:

Well, it is very important, and the great idea of setting up an organism is so as to defeat the domino result. When, each standing alone, one falls, it has the effect on the next, and finally the whole row is down. You are trying, through a unifying influence, to build that row of dominoes so they can stand the fall of one, if necessary.[55]

For the most part, the administration considered any U.S. intervention to be limited to the navy and air force. At a meeting between Dulles and the president on 19 May, however, Eisenhower expressed the possibility of sending in "some Marines" if the United States intervened, but Dulles wrote he was "very emphatic that we must adhere to the position of not going in alone." Both men were incensed with British refusal to deal with the proposed SEATO grouping until after Geneva; Eisenhower considered writing a note to Churchill suggesting that his government "was really promoting a second Munich." The two men then turned hawkish[56] and also discussed a new effort to obtain a congressional resolution. According to Dulles's notes:

I expressed the thought that it might well be that the situation in Indochina itself would soon have deteriorated to a point where nothing effectual could be done to stop the tide of Chinese Communists overrunning Southeast Asia except perhaps diversionary activities along the China coast, which would be conducted primarily by the Nationalist forces, but would require sea and air support from the United States. The President agreed that this matter might very well prove to be the case. I mentioned, however, that we were hamstrung by the constitutional situation and the apparent reluctance of Congress to give the President discretionary authority. I showed the President a copy of a rough draft of a Congressional resolution which I had discussed with Knowland on Monday, and against which Senator Knowland had reacted strongly in opposition, saying it would amount to giving the President a blank check to commit the country to war.[57]

Public opinion always had constrained Eisenhower's choices. Gallup asked about U.S. intervention in Indochina only once during this period. On 17 May, only 22 percent of the public answered affirmatively when asked: "Would you approve or disapprove of sending United States' soldiers to take part in the fighting there?" When it was asked if U.S. involvement were limited to only naval and air, and no ground forces, 36 percent favored U.S. action. The State Department commissioned its own poll that showed 69 percent of the public would approve of committing American forces in a collective action.[58]

Dulles and Eisenhower continued to work closely on public pronouncements. The president delivered a major address at Columbia University on 31 May 1954, that included changes suggested by Dulles; changes that were a diatribe against communism. Eisenhower wrote to Dulles, "Thanks for your criticism on the draft of my talk. I shall incorporate your narrative—somewhat condensed—as one example of the kind of truth that all the world *must* know about us and the Soviets." But the president still watered down Dulles's rhetoric and sounded more the "good cop" than his secretary of state.[59]

By late June, the president was distancing himself from the settlement being reached at Geneva, responding to a question by James Reston by saying, "I won't be a party to a treaty that makes anybody a slave." The U.S. had decided not to be an active participant at Geneva and was only in attendance because of French insistence. Eisenhower and Dulles were not in total agreement on the representation issue. The president was ambivalent, fearing both that dissociation from the conference made America look like a spoiled child and that joining the meetings could lead to "splitting publicly with France and probably with the U.K."

Once again, Eisenhower was constrained by his party's right wing; Knowland called the Geneva meetings a potential "Far East Munich." Dulles and Eisenhower made a strong rhetorical statement by their choice of a leader for the U.S. delegation. Dulles attended the Korean phase of the conference for one week in late April and early May, during which he refused to shake hands with Chinese Foreign Minister Chou En-lai and shunned the Chinese delegation "lest a smile be interpreted as formal recognition." Bedell Smith returned to the U.S. in June, leaving the U.S. delegation with the third in command, U. Alexis Johnson.[60] Dulles recalled Smith both because he feared that Smith's presence put pressure on France to reach agreement too rapidly, and he wanted to focus attention on the need for united action. Johnson remained in charge of the American delegation from 20 June to 17 July. In early July, Mendes-France urged Dulles or Smith to return, but the administration was reluctant. Dulles wrote, "we cannot agree to associate ourselves in advance with an end result which we cannot see." Johnson called his instructions a "holding pattern," trying to walk the fine line between observer and participant while agreeing to nothing. These instructions were frustrating to U.S. allies and Johnson found them difficult to follow.

When the agreements were almost complete, Eisenhower overruled Dulles and sent Smith back to Geneva. Rather than being associated with Geneva's Final Declaration, the United States issued a separate statement. The settlement was reached on 21 July and Eisenhower issued a statement that has been called a "calculated ambiguity." Eisenhower said that the United States

has not itself been party to or bound by the decisions taken by the conference. . . . *The United States will not use force to disturb the settlement. We also say that any renewal of Communist aggression would be viewed by us as a matter of grave concern.* . . . The United States is actively pursuing discussions with other free nations with a view to the rapid organization of a collective defense in Southeast Asia in order to prevent further direct or indirect Communist aggression in that general area.[61] (emphasis added)

The administration and many members of Congress were publicly hostile to the agreements reached at Geneva. Privately, the administration admitted that the West had done well at Geneva. France received a much better agreement than could have been expected. Ho had opposed a divided Vietnam, a proposition that emerged from secret talks between the French and Chinese. Mendes-France may have made a secret deal with the Soviets: in return for the Soviet Union's forcing a settlement favorable to France on the Vietminh, the French would not join the European Defense Community. Based on political control and the position of the military, the 13th parallel would have been a more realistic demarcation line than the agreed upon 17th parallel (France sought the 18th parallel, Ho the 13th). At Geneva, the Vietminh were forced to cede about one-quarter of the land they controlled. The Pathet Lao and Khmer Issarak (Communist/nationalist groups in Laos and Cambodia respectively) were not seated at Geneva even though they controlled considerable territory and represented significant portions of the population.

Eisenhower's strategy of militant rhetoric contributed to the favorable agreement. The Soviet Union and China forced Ho to make concessions that were not militarily justified. China was anxious to avoid American bases in Indochina and a continued French presence seemed the best way of achieving that.

The promised 1956 elections were the reason the Vietminh accepted the final agreement; they fully expected the elections to be held and had good reason to be confident of winning. Bedell Smith had predicted that Ho would win 80 percent of the vote. Dulles testified before the Senate Foreign Relations Committee and confessed that unlike Germany and Korea, the United States did not view elections in Vietnam as urgent because Ho would receive a "very large vote." Eisenhower's pledge to "not use force to disturb the settlement" was insincere, for the administration had no intention of following the Geneva agreement if that meant allowing South Vietnam to fall to the Communist camp.[62]

In early September, the president appointed Senators Mike Mansfield (D-Mont.) and H. Alexander Smith (R-N.J.) to attend the Manila conference with Dulles as representatives of the United States to sign the Manila Pact, which created SEATO. With the exception of the United Nations Treaty, this was the first and only time that members of Congress have been treaty signatories. It was unique because Mansfield, a Democrat, was invited by a Republican administration.[63] Dulles and Eisenhower were taking no chances with Senate ratification; they wanted the Senate involved in united action, and they wanted support from both sides of the aisle.

Eisenhower's strategy worked when the Senate acted on SEATO in early 1955. The Senate Foreign Relations Committee met twice in January to discuss the Manila Pact. During Dulles's 13 January testimony, H. Alexander Smith asked him: "And you used the words 'constitutional processes,' having in mind that the

President undoubtedly would come to Congress in case of any threat of danger in the area, unless we had some sudden emergency?" Dulles replied: "Unless the emergency were so great that there had to be some prompt action to save a vital interest of the United States, then the normal process would of course be to act through Congress if it is in session, and if not in session, to call Congress." At the 21 January committee meeting, Mansfield was asked: "In other words, there is no possibility then for the President under this treaty to go to war on the scale, let us say, of the Korean war, without getting a declaration of war by Congress?" Mansfield replied: "That is my understanding." Interestingly, Wayne Morse (Ind-Ore.),[64] favored the Manila Pact and asked for the "pleasure" of making the motion that the committee ratify the treaty and send it to the full Senate. Morse would later regret his 1954 position on SEATO. William Langer (R-N.D.) cast the one vote against SEATO in the committee, where it passed 14-1. There was little debate on the treaty in the Senate and it passed 82-1; Langer again was the lone dissenter. The members of SEATO were the U.S., Britain, France, Australia, New Zealand, the Philippines, Thailand, and Pakistan. At Manila, Dulles pushed to include Laos, Cambodia, and South Vietnam, even though their inclusion would have directly violated the Geneva agreements. With strong opposition from France, a protocol was added that included the three Indochinese states in the area to be protected by the agreement. While not a direct violation of Geneva, it showed a lack of respect for the principles of that agreement. Cambodia rejected its inclusion in SEATO in 1955, and Laos was excluded by international agreement in 1962.[65]

Roger Dingman writes that "the fathers of SEATO resorted to diplomacy to conceal the inadequacy of their defenses. They wanted to do with words what they could not do with arms. Like parents, they produced a child whose life and character would be shaped as much by developments yet unseen as by the events of the past."[66] Dulles would not have disagreed; he expressed concern to Eisenhower at the time of the Manila Conference that SEATO "involved committing the prestige of the United States in an area where we had little control and where the situation was by no means promising." The secretary of state was willing to gamble because of his mistrust and misunderstanding of the Chinese. In 1955, Dulles referred to Chinese "arrogance" and said that the Chinese "with their hatred for the West, aimed to take over Southeast Asia and would prefer to die in the effort than fail to accomplish it." Rusk believed that Chinese expansion would not be stopped until the U.S. met China with force. The SEATO agreement and the Vietnam involvement it brought virtually guaranteed that the U.S. and China could not even begin to approach their differences. China correctly viewed SEATO as a U.S. attempt to circumvent the Geneva settlement. David L. Anderson concludes that while SEATO neutralized congressional concerns over unilateral involvement, thus increasing U.S. options, Eisenhower "created the legal rationale for America's next war."[67]

## THE DECISION TO BACK NGO DINH DIEM

Several weeks before the settlement at Geneva, Eisenhower accomplished his second goal following the fall of Dien Bien Phu—the selection of a nationalist leader to preserve a non-Communist South Vietnam. Ngo Dinh Diem arrived in Vietnam on 26 June 1954, as Prime Minister under Bao Dai. This was an important rhetorical step for the Eisenhower administration. It would have been difficult to sell Congress and the public on continued support for a French colonial puppet government. Diem gave Eisenhower a genuine nationalist/anti-Communist behind whom American public opinion could rally.

The origins of Diem's appointment remain an intriguing mystery. Many argue that a Vietnam lobby comprised of prominent Catholics, including Joseph Kennedy, Francis Cardinal Spellman of New York, and Senator Mansfield worked through Dulles and the CIA to bring Diem to power to squeeze out France. Supreme Court Justice William O. Douglas had visited Vietnam and written a book that claimed Diem was "revered" by his countrymen. Douglas campaigned for Diem and helped draw attention to him, introducing the Vietnamese nationalist to Senators Mansfield and Kennedy. From 1951 to 1953, Diem spent time in Maryknoll seminaries in New Jersey and New York where he performed menial tasks while speaking out on the need for an independent Vietnam. Douglas and Spellman were among the influential friends that Diem made. They viewed Diem as a "third force," a true nationalist because he opposed both communism and French colonialism.

One of Dulles's confidants claims that Diem was "discovered" by the CIA and "rammed" through the objections of the French and British by Dulles. The written record from the White House, State Department, and U.S. embassy in Saigon provides no hint that Diem was the American candidate. Any CIA involvement remains impossible to assess as their records from the period remain classified.[68] In a confidential 1955 letter to General J. Lawton Collins, Dulles claimed that "Diem was picked not by us but by the French." Dulles had no apparent reason to lie in that letter. Bidault was "supportive" of Diem; future French governments were not. France wanted Diem in mid-1954 because they needed an untainted nationalist at that moment. The appointment backfired as Diem's hatred for Vietnam's colonial masters would cause the French much future consternation.

While the specifics of Diem's advent to power remain unclear, it seems certain that Eisenhower was not directly involved in the decision to choose Diem as an American-backed nationalist to preserve an independent South Vietnam. Indeed, Eisenhower likely was unfamiliar with the name until Bao Dai appointed him prime minister. A possible scenario is that Colonel Edward Lansdale of the CIA persuaded his boss, Allen Dulles, that the U.S. should support Diem sometime after Diem's appointment as prime minister (Lansdale did not meet Diem until Diem's arrival in Saigon to assume his new post on 26 June). Allen Dulles, in turn, convinced his brother that Diem offered the best chance for success. John Foster Dulles and members of the Vietnam lobby eventually prevailed on Eisenhower to support the new prime minister.[69]

A hint at why the administration came to favor a Catholic leader in Vietnam emerges from the National Security Council meeting of 4 February 1954. Allen Dulles said what was "disheartening . . . was the evidence that the majority of people in Vietnam supported the Vietminh rebels. . . . There was no dynamism in the leadership of the Franco-Vietnamese forces. What was really needed was a leader with some of the characteristics of a (Syngman) Rhee." Eisenhower inquired if it would be possible to take advantage of the religious issue. Understanding that a majority of the population in Vietnam were Buddhists, "the President asked whether it was possible to find a good Buddhist leader to whip up some real fervor," using the example of Islam's spread into North Africa and Southern Europe in the Middle Ages. Someone "pointed out to the President that, unhappily, Buddha was a pacifist rather than a fighter," which led to laughter all around.

Prior to Diem's appointment, U.S. officials definitely were involved in "checking out" the nationalist candidate. In May, Diem's name headed an American list of sixteen Vietnamese who were considered both anti-Communist and pro-American. The report described Diem as "perhaps the most popular personality in the country after Ho Chi Minh." C. Douglas Dillon, the U.S. Ambassador to France, wrote Dulles in May 1954 after a meeting with Diem in Paris:

> He impresses one as a mystic who has just emerged from a religious retreat into the cold world which is, in fact, almost what he has done. He appears too unworldly and unsophisticated to be able to cope with the grave problems and unscrupulous people he will find in Saigon. Yet his apparent sincerity, patriotic fervor and honesty are refreshing by comparison and we are led to think that these qualities may outweigh his other deficiencies.
>
> On balance we were favorably impressed but only in the realization that we are prepared to accept the seemingly ridiculous prospect that this Yogi-like mystic could assume the charge he is apparently about to undertake only because the standard set by his predecessors is so low.[70]

After Geneva and the Manila Conference there was little public discussion of the Indochinese situation. It no longer dominated NSC meetings. Most of the communication about Indochina were cables between Saigon, Paris, and the Department of State. Cambodia was relatively stable and Laos was temporarily quiet, leaving the focus on Diem's fledgling government. While the administration hoped to create a permanent anti-Communist state in South Vietnam, everyone thought it a decided long-shot in the autumn of 1954. The difficulties America's candidate faced in creating a government in Saigon seemed insurmountable.

Diem disliked the French, and they quickly concluded that the new prime minister was not capable of leading. The American position became one of supporting Diem until a better candidate emerged. One problem Diem faced was the lack of experienced officials because the French had held all responsible positions in previous governments. Diem's government was dominated by people from the north and central parts of Vietnam, many of whom were Catholic; their selection created animosity among the native southerners and Buddhists, a religious group that made up 80 percent of the entire population. The new prime minister already relied too heavily on family members in key positions, leading to charges of a family oligarchy. The Diem government also faced the problem of settling more than eight-hundred-thousand northerners who had migrated south with the help of an effective CIA propaganda campaign. Rumors of coup plots were rampant in Saigon.

The most likely coup leader was General Nguyen Van Hinh, chief of staff of the army. Hinh had dual French citizenship, including a commission in the French military. French elements opposed to Diem prodded the chief of staff to lead a coup. Diem lacked a strong enough mandate from Bao Dai to remove Hinh. When Diem ultimately tried to fire him, Hinh refused to leave.

Diem also faced continuing coup threats from the sects: the Cao Dai—an exotic mixture of Confucianism, Buddhism, spiritualism, and Catholicism, with its own Pope and saints, including Victor Hugo, Jesus Christ, Buddha, Joan of Arc, and Sun-Yat-Sen; Hoa Hao—a fundamentalist Buddhist group; and Binh Xuyen—not religious, and originally river pirates who dominated gambling, prostitution, and opium in the Saigon area and ran the police through payments to Bao Dai. The three sects combined controlled 10 percent of the population and their three armies totaled forty to fifty thousand. The sects could not be ignored: the Cao Dai dominated the region north and northwest of Saigon, the Hoa Hao held authority over the area to the southwest, and the Binh Xuyen was a powerful force in and near the city of Saigon.

Lacking control over the military, police, the judiciary, and finances—all still under French authorities—Diem held his government together through sheer will and stubbornness. A 15 September 1954, CIA intelligence estimate said: "Trends in South Vietnam since the end of the Geneva Conference have enhanced the prospects of an eventual extension of Communist control over the area by means short of large-scale military attacks."[71]

Notes from a 22 October NSC meeting indicate the president wondered why the U.S. didn't "'get rough with the French.' If we didn't do something very quickly, Diem would be down the drain with no replacement in sight." Eisenhower followed up by making two historic rhetorical decisions about South Vietnam. First, he released a letter to Diem on 25 October pledging U.S. aid.[72] The letter had been drafted in early September. The interval between drafting the letter and the decision to follow through and send it indicates Eisenhower's hesitancy to support the new government. Eisenhower released his letter after a well-publicized report from Senator Mansfield following a visit to Vietnam. Mansfield apparently had gained credibility with Dulles on their earlier trip to Manila; his report recommended: "In the event that the Diem government falls, therefore, I believe that the United States should consider an immediate suspension of all aid to Vietnam and the French Union forces there, except that of a humanitarian nature." Anderson claims that Mansfield's report "immediately became the cornerstone of the pro-Diem position." According to Chester Cooper:

> Mansfield's report had an important influence on the Administration's decision to move forward with an aid program for the struggling Saigon Government. . . . President Eisenhower sent a letter to Premier Diem, and it was that letter that was cited by the members of the Kennedy Administration and even more often by officials in the Johnson Administration to relate the origin and continuity of U.S. policy in support of Diem.[73]

At the NSC meeting the day after the letter to Diem was released, Secretary of Defense Wilson suggested that "the only sensible course of action was for the U.S. to get out of Indochina completely and as soon as possible." The situation was completely hopeless, and the French "should be left to stew in their own juice." Eisenhower responded that "if we continued to retreat in this area the process would lead to a grave situation from the point of view of our national security." Instead, the president suggested "that we should try to get the French out of the Indochina area."

Eisenhower's second consequential decision was made on 30 October at a meeting with Dulles and other members of the State Department. The president announced that he wanted to send a high-ranking official to Vietnam "to get it straightened out." Dulles suggested that it be an army officer and offered three names. Eisenhower had his own man in mind, General J. Lawton (Lightning Joe) Collins, then with NATO. As army chief of staff during the Truman administration, Collins was cautious about U.S. commitment to Indochina. General Collins had considerable experience in Asia, including a visit to Vietnam in 1951. Collins was sent to Vietnam with the rank of ambassador for what was assumed to be several weeks, but stretched to almost seven months. The secretary of state told the new ambassador that Mendes-France was "aghast" when Dulles told him that aid would likely be cut off if Diem fell from power, and that Mansfield's report "deserves serious consideration." Dulles further told Collins that there "was a 10 percent chance of saving Vietnam from communism," and so Dulles "did not believe the prestige of the President should be too closely associated with the mission."[74]

Collins aided in removing the first of Diem's problems by helping to persuade Hinh to return to France where the Vietnamese general resumed his commission in the French military. However, Collins quickly came to agree with the French and Hinh that Diem was not capable of leading. Collins's greatest frustration with Diem was his inability to convince the South Vietnamese leader to appoint talented men to the cabinet, particularly Dr. Phan Huy Quat as Minister of Defense. On 6 December, Collins cabled the State Department that Diem must be replaced if he did not change in the next several weeks.

For the next five months, Dulles, the State Department, and Mansfield waged a polemic with Collins over the retention of Diem. Eisenhower was the final arbiter.[75] Collins's telegrams were shared with Mansfield whose dictated views were sent to Collins in Saigon. Gibbons refers to "the *pas de deux* between the State Department and Senator Mansfield."[76]

Mansfield, when later asked about his dealings with Dulles, replied:

> Very close and fairly intimate dealings. . . . He called on me many times for advice and counsel as to what should be done in Diem's early days. For a while I was quite free with my information and advice. . . .
>
> Kenneth Young [Assistant Secretary of State for the Far East] . . . was coming down to see me all the time. And I was told by Young that he was coming down at the direction of Mr. Dulles. . . .
>
> And I think it was a new area for Dulles—and for Mr. Young, too. . . . I suppose they were looking around for advice from people who may have been there in order to get some guidance until they got their feet firmly on the ground and made up their minds definitely. . . .
>
> I think he (Dulles) leaned a little bit too heavily on me in the matter of Diem and some of the moves he made after taking over South Vietnam—to such an extent that I felt it had to be broken off, because it was outside the ken of my responsibility and entirely within the purview of the Executive branch under the Constitution.[77]

Because they both backed Diem, the record does not distinguish the degree to which Dulles was influenced by Mansfield or whether the secretary of state used Mansfield.

Dulles reaffirmed U.S. support for Diem at a meeting with French General Paul Ely and Mendes-France on 19 December 1954, adding that "Mansfield believes in Diem." If it was decided that Diem must be replaced, the administration would have to consult the two congressional foreign affairs committees and decide how much more to invest in Vietnam. Dulles cabled Saigon on 24 December: "Under present circumstances and unless situation in Free Viet-Nam clearly appears hopeless and rapidly disintegrating, we have no choice but [to] continue our aid [to] Viet-Nam and support of Diem. There [is] no other suitable leader known to us." So, at the end of 1954, Dulles reaffirmed U.S. support for Diem—support that was tenuous and influenced by Mansfield. For his part, Diem continued to block attempts by France and the U.S. to force him to share power with Quat or other strong leaders.[78]

General Hinh's departure in 1954 ended the immediate threat of a military coup, but Diem's situation looked hopeless early in 1955 because of the continuing crisis with the sects. With the help of American bribes, Diem managed to keep the sects under control. In January, Diem closed down the gambling casinos in Cholon, which deprived the Binh Xuyen of their major source of income. With the aid of Lansdale and the CIA, Diem paid members of the Cao Dai and Hoa Hao to join his government. Alarmed by the defections, the three sects united. In the third week of March, Diem refused a sect demand that he reorganize his government and the six Cao Dai and Hoa Hao ministers left Diem's cabinet. The three sects then formed the United Front of Nationalist Forces. On 29 March, fighting broke out between Diem's forces and the Binh Xuyen. Collins cabled Washington that he did not think Diem could survive the crisis, and the French quickly arranged a truce.

On 1 April, Dulles called Eisenhower and suggested that they meet to talk about Diem's crisis in Vietnam. The president saw no reason for a meeting since they were in agreement on the situation. Dulles had told Collins that any decision on Diem could not be made in Washington, but the U.S. had invested much in the South Vietnamese leader and needed to be cautious about any decision to replace him. Then, the conversation turned to Mansfield:

> The Sec. said Mansfield is devoted to Diem. He thinks we ought to talk with him about it to see what line he will take. The Pres. said he does not know that we should. The Sec. might tell Collins that he is on the spot and will have to play it by ear. His telegram comes as a surprise because we bet pretty heavily on him (Diem). Let us know if we can do anything. The Sec. said he still thinks we should talk with Mansfield, and the Pres. indicated assent. The Sec. said though we should not be controlled by his (Mansfield's) judgment.[79]

Eisenhower admitted that he did "not know what we should do." The president ended the conversation by telling Dulles to warn Collins not to be "hasty," that it was important to move "slowly." Eisenhower was concerned about the position of General Paul Ely and the French. Dulles and Mansfield met later that day.[80]

On 4 April, Dulles wrote Collins that "I have just been talking with the President and his mind runs along with mine" in the following respects: 1) It was "deplorable" that the French did not allow Diem to fight the Binh Xuyen and the U.S. position should be to convince France to allow Diem to assert his authority; and 2) Collins was right about Diem's weaknesses but "the decision to back Diem had gone to the point of no return and that either he had to succeed or else the whole business would be a failure." Dulles added that he and Eisenhower "are far away and we both have great confidence in your judgment."[81]

Ely decided that he could not support Diem any longer and Collins cabled Washington on 7 April that Diem would have to be replaced. On 9 April, Collins and the American Embassy in Saigon sent a number of telegrams to

Dulles pushing for Diem's removal. Dulles replied to Collins the same day, saying that he and Eisenhower were "disposed to back" Collins's decision but the secretary of state was more cautious, questioning why nationalist leaders who were unacceptable several months ago now looked like better alternatives than Diem. Quat, for example, was less acceptable to the sects than Diem. Since Diem was perceived to be the American candidate reluctantly accepted by France, Dulles feared loss of U.S. prestige: "We will be merely paying the bill and the French will be calling the tune." Finally, Dulles warned Collins of congressional opposition, adding: "Mansfield who is looked upon with great respect by his colleagues with reference to this matter, is adamantly opposed to abandonment of Diem under present circumstances."[82] Collins responded on 10 April:

> I have no way of judging Mansfield's position *under present conditions.* These conditions are rather different than those existing when he visited Vietnam in September, 1954 when he feared military dictatorship as only alternative to Diem. . . . As practical politicians, I would think that Mansfield and his colleagues on Senate committees would give considerable weight to the arguments I have advanced.[83]

While the paper trail in the entire Diem episode points to Dulles, Eisenhower seems to have had his hands on the controls. On 11 April, Dulles spoke to his brother, Allen:

> The Sec. said it looks like the rug is coming out from under the fellow in Southeast Asia (Diem). . . . The Sec. said he talked with the boss on Saturday and he said you can't send this fellow (Collins) down here and have him work on it if his judgment is the way it is. We have to go along with it. The Sec. said he has sent 2-3 strong messages urging the other viewpoint but these have not shaken him [Collins]. . . .[84]

Both of the brothers wanted to retain Diem. Clearly, Eisenhower was leaning toward supporting Collins's judgment—his commander in the field. In 1942, after taking command of Allied forces in Europe, Eisenhower told his aides they were "free to solve their own problems wherever possible and not to get in the habit of passing the buck up."[85] This was a management strategy Eisenhower continued with Collins in 1955.

Later on 11 April, Dulles cabled Collins and agreed that Diem needed to be replaced. Dulles's draft of that telegram was edited in Eisenhower's own hand. Each of the president's comments were incorporated into the final draft. Eisenhower added wording to emphasize the need for a suitable replacement for Diem and had Dulles add a paragraph emphasizing the importance of an understanding with the French that the central government must remove the police from Binh Xuyen control.[86]

Collins was recalled to Washington on 17 April. When he arrived in Washington on the twenty-second, he spent the day meeting with the Vietnam Working Group (headed by Young) and a group comprised of members of the State Department, Defense Department, and CIA. In the middle of the meetings with Young's group, Collins went to the White House for lunch with the president. Eisenhower was surprised at Collins's belief that Diem's weaknesses as a leader doomed him, rather than French efforts to undermine Diem. Over lunch, Collins got Eisenhower to promise to support him in whatever he recommended. Collins then returned to the meeting with Young. The members of the Working Group proposed a number of alternatives, but Collins was adamant—Diem must be replaced. Young recalled that "We seemed to be confronted with a *fait accompli*, . . . it appeared to be a Presidential decision that Diem had to go."[87] The Working Group reluctantly accepted the need for a change in government and decided on a provisional government with Quat as president and Diem as chairman of a consultative council until a national assembly could create a permanent government structure. The next day Dulles met with Collins and reluctantly accepted the compromise.

At his 27 April press conference, Eisenhower was asked if "there may be the necessity to change the policy of recognition of Premier Diem?" The president responded, "I can't give you any final answer because, as you know, it is still under discussion."[88] The day Eisenhower made those remarks, Dulles sent three cables to the embassy in Paris "outlining ways and means of replacing Diem and his government."[89] While the decision to replace Diem was being made in Washington, Diem dismissed the Binh Xuyen head of police and fighting broke out between Binh Xuyen forces and the national army.

Collins met with the NSC on the twenty-eighth and told them that "Diem's number was up." Dulles said that Saigon had been instructed to "hold up action on our plan for replacing Diem." The battle "could either lead to Diem's utter overthrow or to his emergence from the disorder as a major hero." Eisenhower sided with his secretary of state, saying "that it was an absolute sine qua non of success that the Vietnamese National Army destroy the power of the Binh Xuyen."[90]

Again, with assistance from Lansdale and the CIA, Diem's forces were victorious, which postponed the U.S. decision to depose him.[91] A number of members of Congress joined a pro-Diem chorus. On 30 April, Young wrote:

> Senator Mansfield issued a long statement in support of Diem on April 29. If Diem is forced out, Mansfield would have us stop all aid to Viet-Nam except of a humanitarian nature. Senators Knowland and (Hubert) Humphrey (D-Minn.) have also backed Diem. A large number of members of the House Foreign Affairs Committee after hearing Collins have informed the Department . . . that they would not favor the State Department withdrawing support from Diem. Collins met with the Far East Subcommittee of the Senate Foreign Relations Committee, separately with Senator Mansfield and

with about a dozen of the House Committee. . . . In fact there are going to be real difficulties on the Hill if Diem is forced out by what appears to be French-Bao Dai action.[92]

Collins later wrote that after Diem's bold action and success "whatever influence I might have had either with the congressional committees I had briefed, or the State Department was quickly dissipated." On 1 May, the administration reversed itself and returned to its earlier support for Diem. Diem's victory over the sects led to the American press and government celebrating this "miracle."[93]

Diem understood Mansfield's role in continued U.S. support, writing a warm letter to Mansfield on 4 May, saying: "If I am permitted to quote Confucius, the sage said: 'Only in winter do we know which trees are evergreen.' Figuratively speaking, you are the evergreen, as luxuriant as always; not only have you been the stark fighter for democracy and human rights but also the true friend of the Vietnamese people."[94]

A number of people writing about the period credit Mansfield with saving Diem in late 1954 and 1955. Townsend Hoopes says that Mansfield caused a "national self-imprisonment" with Diem because of his influence in the Senate and his threat to terminate aid. Thus, Dulles was forced to back Diem to keep Mansfield's support. Columnist Joseph Alsop called Mansfield the "deciding factor" in the Eisenhower administration's decision to keep Diem. Mansfield recently wrote, "I hope I had some part in preventing the Eisenhower Administration from ending its support for Diem in 1955 but I do not know."[95]

Diem quickly consolidated his power after his victory over the sects. He refused Bao Dai's orders to report to France and to change the chief of staff of the army. Bao Dai sent General Hinh to South Vietnam as his personal mediator, but Diem would not allow Hinh in the country. With Eisenhower administration approval, Diem announced that he would not abide by the Geneva Conference, which called for unification elections with the North in 1956. Next, he scheduled October elections in the South where voters could choose between Bao Dai's monarchy or a Republic that Diem would head, again with U.S. concurrence. In an election filled with fraud, Diem was proclaimed the winner with 98.2 percent of the vote, winning 605,000 votes in Saigon where there were only 405,000 registered voters. The dishonesty in the election was largely ignored in the United States.[96]

With ample help from Congress, the Eisenhower administration found a nationalist leader and attempted to build an anti-Communist state in South Vietnam. In 1955 Diem seemed the best choice if the U.S. had to make a choice. Dulles was never able to find an alternative to Diem. In truth, the U.S. never found a better candidate. Quat was the name that usually emerged as a replacement for Diem in 1954-55, but when Quat finally gained power in 1965, he was quickly deposed. Joseph Buttinger said that Diem, "could have been replaced only by a regime of former collaborators with Colonialism" and such a regime would have forced more people into the Communist camp. Years after the event, Young and Mansfield continued to share that view.[97]

The question remains, should the United States have made the choice at all? In attempting artificially to create a nationalist leader to compete with Ho, the administration showed a lack of understanding of Third World nationalism that had devastating results. Had the administration not felt compelled to create a nationalist leader, the second Indochina war might have been avoided.[98]

## SUMMARY AND CONCLUSIONS

James R. Arnold writes: "Having set the course, he [Eisenhower] did not meddle in the actual sailing of the ship." After Diem's "miracle," other issues dominated the attention of the Eisenhower administration, and the belief continued that Vietnam was progressing reasonably well. While many argue that Eisenhower successfully managed South Vietnam in 1954-1955, he failed to do so for the rest of his administration. Unqualified support for Diem became the cornerstone of administration policy toward South Vietnam. After Eisenhower's September 1955 heart attack, he did not give South Vietnam the personal attention he had earlier. Beginning in fall 1956, Dulles's deteriorating health limited the time he could devote to the issue. Eisenhower effectively became his own secretary of state with the death of Dulles in 1959. Dulles's replacement, Christian Herter, assumed office without background in Southeast Asian affairs and rarely became directly involved in decision making concerning South Vietnam. The professional foreign service bureaucracy was left to implement the administration policy of supporting Diem, and the policy became one that Homer Bigart aptly labeled "sink or swim with Ngo Dinh Diem." The administration followed a rhetorical strategy of emphasizing Diem's successes while ignoring the many signs of failure. When Diem visited the United States in 1957, Eisenhower met him at the airport and called him the "miracle man" of Asia. Congress and the press were willing accomplices of the administration. During Diem's 1957 visit, Mansfield said: "President Diem is not only the savior of his own country, but in my opinion he is the savior of all Southeast Asia," while the *New York Times* wrote that "Thomas Jefferson would have no quarrel" with Diem's comments to Congress.

A 1960 Senate report predicted the U.S. Military Aid Advisory Group could be phased out in the foreseeable future. In that year, Secretary of State Herter reported the situation "as relatively quiet" in South Vietnam. The United States simply was not paying attention. Diem's failures led to renewed rebellion and the second Indochina War. While Eisenhower had violated the political elements of the Geneva settlement, he had largely followed the military ones, including limiting American military advisers to 685.[99] The Kennedy administration changed all of that.[100]

Eisenhower's thwarting of the promised 1956 elections made a Communist reaction inevitable. By rhetorically proclaiming the "miracle" of Diem and asserting a degree of freedom never achieved in South Vietnam, the Eisenhower administration trapped itself and future administrations into a commitment to prove the veracity of that rhetoric. By rhetorically overstating the importance of South Vietnam to U.S. security, Eisenhower helped lay the trap that would engulf the nation in the quagmire of the 1960s and 1970s.

## NOTES

1. As quoted in Robert H. Ferrell, *The Eisenhower Diaries* (New York: W.W. Norton and Co., 1981), 190.
2. Conversation with Malcolm Muir on/about Colonialism, 25 May 1955, Whitman File, Dwight D. Eisenhower Diary Series, Box 5, Folder 2, Eisenhower Library, Abilene, Kansas (hereafter cited as DDE Library).
3. Eisenhower to Churchill, 22 July 1954, Whitman File, DDE Diary Series, Box 4, Folder 1, DDE Library.
4. Ibid. See also, Eisenhower to Gruenther, 30 November 1954, Whitman File, DDE Diary Series, Box 8, Folder 1, DDE Library.
5. As quoted in James R. Arnold, *The First Domino: Eisenhower, the Military, and America's Intervention in Vietnam* (New York: William Morrow & Co., 1991), 83.
6. As quoted in *Harry S. Truman, Years of Trial and Hope*, vol. 2 (Garden City, N.Y.: Doubleday, 1956), 514, 519. See also, William Conrad Gibbons, *The U.S. Government and the Vietnam War*, pt. 1 (Princeton, N.J.: Princeton University Press, 1986), 88, 120.
7. Most consider Dulles and Eisenhower to have become close. Columnist Joseph Alsop argues that was not the case. See, Alsop, interview with Richard D. Challener, Washington D.C., 4 March 1966, The John Foster Dulles Oral History Project, Princeton University Library, 4-5.
8. Eisenhower said: "Foster has been in training for this job all his life" and delegated to Dulles "the responsibility of developing the specific policy, including the decision where the administration would stand and what course of action would be followed in each international crisis." See, Arnold, 93.
9. George McT. Kahin, *Intervention* (New York: Alfred A. Knopf, 1986), 38. See also, Gibbons, pt. 1, 264, 313; Richard M. Saunders, "The 1954 Indochina Crisis," *Military Review* 58 (1978): 71; David L. Anderson, "Eisenhower, Dienbienphu, and the Origins of United States Military Intervention in Vietnam," *Mid-America* 71 (1989): 102-3 and Andrew J. Goodpaster, interview with Richard D. Challener, Washington D.C., 11 Jan. 1966, 14-24, 32-33, 42-43 and Richard Nixon, interview with Challener, N.Y., 5 March 1965, The John Foster Dulles Oral History Project, Princeton University Library, 5-9, 22, 25.
10. "Annual Message to the Congress on the State of the Union. February 2, 1953," *Public Papers of the Presidents of the United States: Dwight D. Eisenhower, 1953* (Washington D.C.: Government Printing Office, 1960, 16 (hereafter cited as *Public Papers*). See also, Arnold, 128.
11. Breakfast at White House, 24 March 1953, John Foster Dulles, White House Memoranda, Box #1, DDE Library.
12. Dwight D. Eisenhower, *The White House Years: Mandate for Change, 1953-1956* (Garden City, N.Y.: Doubleday, 1963), 168. See also, Gibbons, pt. 1, 123-24.
13. "The President's News Conference of March 26, 1953," *Public Papers, 1953*, 135.

14. John P. Glennon, ed., *Foreign Relations of the United States, 1952-1954, Indochina*, vol. 13, pt. 1 (Washington D.C.: Government Printing Office, 1982), 547-49, 552 (hereafter cited as *FRUS*). See also, George C. Herring, "Franco-American Conflict in Indochina, 1950-1954," in *Dien Bien Phu and the Crisis of Franco-American Relations, 1954-1955*, ed. Lawrence S. Kaplan, Denise Artaud and Mark R. Rubin (Wilmington, Del.: SR Books, 1990), 38.

15. Arnold, 101.

16. *Cong. Rec.*, 29 July 1953, 10234-35. See also, Memorandum for the Secretary and Memorandum of Conversation with the President, 27 July 1953, John Foster Dulles, White House Memoranda, DDE Library and Gibbons, pt. 1, 129-35.

17. "Remarks at the Governors' Conference, Seattle, Washington. August 4, 1953," *Public Papers, 1953*, 540-41.

18. *FRUS*, 782.

19. "The President's News Conference of March 17, 1954," *Public Papers, 1954*, 327. See also, Arnold, 191 and Anna Kasten Nelson, "The 'Top of Policy Hill': President Eisenhower and the National Security Council," *Diplomatic History* 7 (1983): 315.

20. Melanie Billings-Yun, "Ike and Vietnam," *History Today* 38 (1988): 18.

21. As quoted in John P. Burke and Fred I. Greenstein, *How Presidents Test Reality* (New York: Russell Sage Foundation, 1989), 54-55.

22. Dwight D. Eisenhower, *The White House Years: Waging Peace, 1957-1961* (New York: Doubleday, 1965), 632-33. See also, Burke and Greenstein, 256-74 and Nixon, Dulles Oral History Project, 19-22, 30.

23. Other writers have reached similar conclusions over issues other than Indochina. See for example, Douglas Kinnard, "President Eisenhower and the Defense Budget," *The Journal of Politics* 39 (1977): 623 and Bennett C. Rushkoff, "Eisenhower, Dulles and the Quemoy-Matsu Crisis, 1954-1955," *Political Science Quarterly* 96 (1981): 466, 469, 471, 477, 479-80.

24. One study of Eisenhower and his NSC concludes that "the president actively participated in the meetings and often turned the discussion toward those questions that personally interested him," using the 8 January meeting as an example. When the NSC discussed Indochina and Eisenhower was absent, Dulles and Admiral Arthur Radford dominated the discussion. See, Nelson, 310-11, 313-14.

25. As quoted in *FRUS*, 947-49.

26. Ibid., 949-53.

27. Ibid., 953-54, 988. See also, Burke and Greenstein, *How Presidents Test Reality*, 31-35.

28. Ibid., 981-82, 1002-6, 1038, 1116. See also, Gibbons, pt. 1, 155-58 and Burke and Greenstein, *How Presidents Test Reality*, 37-40.

29. As quoted in William Bragg Ewald, Jr., *Eisenhower the President: Crucial Days, 1951-1960* (Englewood Cliffs, N.J.: Prentice-Hall, 1981), 107. See also, Arnold, 142-43; Burke and Greenstein, *How Presidents Test Reality*, 38 and Gibbons, pt. 1, 158-59.

30. As quoted in Arnold, 143.

31. As quoted in "The President's News Conference of February 10, 1954," 250, 253 and "The President's News Conference of March 10, 1954," 306, *Public Papers, 1954*. See also, "The President's News Conference of February 3, 1954," 226, "The President's News Conference of February 17, 1954, 277," "The President's News Conference of March 17, 1954," 321-23, 332, *Public Papers, 1954*; Burke and Greenstein, *How Presidents Test Reality*, 39 and Arnold, 143.

32. *Executive Sessions of the Senate Foreign Relations Committee*, vol. 6, 1954 (Washington D.C.: Government Printing Office, 1977), 115, 141-45, 153-84 (hereafter cited as *ESSFRC*). See also, Gibbons, pt. 1, 156-57.

33. *FRUS*, pp. 1132, 1141, 1143-44. See also, Memorandum of Conversation with the President, 24 March 1954, John Foster Dulles, White House Memoranda, Box 1, Folder 4, DDE Library;

Herring and Richard H. Immerman, "Eisenhower, Dulles, and Dienbienphu: 'The Day We Didn't Go to War' Revisited," *Journal of American History* 71 (1984): 346-47; Burke and Greenstein, *How Presidents Test Reality*, 42-44; Gibbons, pt. 1, 170-72 and Immerman, "Prologue: Perceptions by the United States of Its Interests in Indochina," Kaplan, et. al., eds., 15.

34. Arthur Radford, *From Pearl Harbor to Vietnam* (Stanford, Calif.: Hoover Institution Press, 1980), 400-401. See also, Burke and Greenstein, *How Presidents Test Reality*, 43-46; Herring and Immerman, 347-48 and Gibbons, pt. 1, 172-73.

35. *FRUS*, 1163-68.

36. Richard Nixon, *Memoirs* (New York: Grosset & Dunlap, 1978), 151. See also, *FRUS*, 1173.

37. *FRUS*, 1201-2, 1204.

38. Memorandum of Conversation with the President, 2 April 1954, John Foster Dulles, White House Memoranda, Box 1, Folder 4, DDE Library. See also, Herring and Immerman, 352.

39. This account comes from a 1978 interview with Senator Albert A. Gore (D-Tenn.) based on a discussion with Johnson and the democratic leaders immediately after their meeting with Dulles. Since the Dulles meeting took place at the State Department, the desk Johnson pounded must have been Dulles's. See Gibbons, pt. 1, 191.

40. Even after Eisenhower revisionism, there are still those who give most of the credit to Dulles. See for example, Frederick W. Marks III, "The Real Hawk at Dienbienphu: Dulles or Eisenhower?" *Pacific Historical Review* 59 (1990): 297-322.

41. Memorandum for the Secretary's File, 5 April 1954, John Foster Dulles, Subject Series, Box 9, Folder 2. See also, *FRUS*, 1230, 136-38; Leslie H. Gelb with Richard K. Betts, *The Irony of Vietnam: The System Worked* (Washington D.C.: Brookings Institution, 1979), 57; Billings-Yun, "Ike and Vietnam," 17-18; Gibbons, pt. 1, 73-78, 187-97, 208-9; Melvin Gurtov, *The First Vietnam Crisis* (New York: Columbia University Press, 1967), 145; Herring and Immerman, 354 and Immerman, "The United States and the Geneva Conference of 1954: A New Look," *Diplomatic History* 14 (1990): 46, 65.

42. Eisenhower wrote that Dulles "would not deliver an important speech or statement until after I had read, edited, and approved it; he guarded constantly against the possibility that any misunderstanding could arise between us." The president also took an activist role in the speeches written for him. Stassen writes of Eisenhower going over a Stassen draft of a speech "paragraph by paragraph," and concludes that the president "always did make changes" until the speech reflected Eisenhower's "own personal style and emphasis." *U.S. News & World Report* concluded that it sometimes took speech writers a dozen drafts before Eisenhower accepted a speech, adding: "Mr. Eisenhower directs the job from start to finish. He offers ideas, works over rough drafts, suggests changes, inserts phrases or thoughts of his own. The speech must reflect his beliefs." See, Eisenhower, *Waging Peace*, 365; Stassen and Marshall Houts, *Eisenhower: Turning the World Toward Peace* (St. Paul: Merril/Magnus, 1990), 122-24 and "How Ike and His Aides Work Out a Speech," *U.S. News & World Report*, 5 October 1956, 84-86. For another example of Eisenhower working directly with Dulles on a speech, see, Memorandum of conference with President Eisenhower, Augusta, GA, 19 April 1954, John Foster Dulles, White House Memoranda, Box 1, File 3, DDE Library, and Kinnard, 602. For an amusing incident that shows how involved Eisenhower was in writing his own speeches, see, G. Frederick Reinhardt, interview with Philip A. Crowl, Washington D.C., 30 October 1965, The John Foster Dulles Oral History Project, Princeton University Library, 39-40.

43. Eisenhower was less than enthused with Knowland as the new majority leader. The president wrote in early February: "Knowland means to be helpful and loyal, but he is cumbersome. He does not have the sharp mind and the great experience that [Robert] Taft did." See, "DDE handwritten notes, week of Feb. 7th, 1954," Whitman File, DDE Diary Series, Box 4, File 2, 6, DDE Library.

44. Gibbons, pt. 1, 29, 176. See also, Herring and Immerman, 351, 363; Burke and Greenstein, *How Presidents Test Reality*, 47, 58; Immerman, "Eisenhower and Dulles: Who Made the Decisions?," *Political Psychology* 1 (1979): 24; Billings-Yun, *Decision Against War* (New York: Columbia University Press, 1988), 66; Robert F. Randle, *Geneva 1954: The Settlement of the Indochinese War* (Princeton, N.J.: Princeton University Press, 1969), 77; Eisenhower, *Waging Peace*, 364; *Cong. Rec.*, 6 April 1954, 4676-77; Memorandum of Conversation with the President, 24 March 1954, John Foster Dulles, White House Memoranda, Box 1, File 4; Cabinet Record of Action, 20 October. 1954, Whitman File, Cabinet Series, Box 4, DDE Library; Arnold, 175 and "Dulles Warns Communists They Can't Have Indochina," *U.S. News & World Report*, 9 April 1954, 70-73.

45. *FRUS*, 1253-64.

46. Nixon, *Memoirs*, 151.

47. "The President's News Conference of April 7, 1954," *Public Papers, 1954*, 382-85.

48. Ibid., 387. See also, "The President's News Conference of May 12, 1954," *Public Papers, 1954*, 471.

49. Greenstein, "Eisenhower as an Activist President: A Look at New Evidence," *Political Science Quarterly* 94 (1979-80): 581-82, 584. See also, Immerman, "Eisenhower and Dulles: Who Made the Decisions?" 31-36.

50. Nixon, *Memoirs*, 198.

51. Marianna P. Sullivan, *France's Vietnam Policy: A Study in French-American Relations* (Westport, Conn.: Greenwood Press, 1978), 47, 60; Dulles to Bidault, 24 April 1954, John Foster Dulles Papers, Subject Series, Box 8, Folder 4, DDE Library. See also, "Joint Action in Southeast Asia," 12 April 1954, John Foster Dulles, White House Memoranda, Box 1, Folder 4, DDE Library; Memorandum of Conversation, 26 April 1954, John Foster Dulles Papers, Subject Series, Box 9, Folder 2; Whitman File, DDE Diary Series, 27 April 1954, DDE Library; Nixon, Dulles Oral History Project, 44-45; Stephen Ambrose, *Nixon*, vol. 1 (New York: Simon & Schuster, 1987), 345; Kahin, *Intervention*, 55; David L. Anderson, *Trapped By Success: The Eisenhower Administration and Vietnam, 1953-1961* (New York: Columbia University Press, 1991), 35; Arnold, 184-85 and Herring and Immerman, 355-62.

52. Eisenhower to Gruenther, 26 April 1954, Whitman File, DDE Diary Series, Box 4, Folder 2, DDE Library.

53. *FRUS*, vol. 13, pt. 2, 1431-45. See also, Nixon, *Memoirs*, 153-54 and Arnold, 193, 197.

54. Ibid., 1485, 1488, 1506-9, 1576, 1590. See also, Memorandum of Luncheon Conversation with the President, 11 May 1954, John Foster Dulles, White House Memoranda, Box 1, Folder 3, DDE Library and U. Alexis Johnson with Jef Olivarius McAllister, *The Right Hand of Power* (Englewood Cliffs, N.J.: Prentice-Hall, 1984), 217.

55. "The President's News Conference of May 12, 1954," *Public Papers, 1954*, 473. See also, Sullivan, 48 and Arnold, 202, 215, 234-35.

56. Nixon wrote: "With people he knew well and trusted, Eisenhower liked to think out loud. . . . He could be very enthusiastic about half-baked ideas in the discussion stage, but when it came to making a final decision, he was the coldest, most unemotional and analytical man in the world." See, Nixon, *Six Crises* (New York: Doubleday, 1962), 158-59 and Nixon, Dulles Oral History Project, 19-22, 30.

57. Memorandum of Conversation with the President, 19 May 1954, John Foster Dulles, White House Memoranda, Box 1, Folder 3, DDE Library.

58. Fred I. Greenstein and John P. Burke, "The Dynamics of Presidential Reality Testing: Evidence from Two Vietnam Decisions," *Political Science Quarterly* 104 (1989-90): 578.

59. Notes between Dulles and Eisenhower on the Columbia speech, 17 and 18 May 1954, John Foster Dulles, White House Memoranda, Box 1, Folder 3, DDE Library. See also, "Address at

the Columbia University National Bicentennial Dinner, New York City. May 31, 1954," *Public Papers, 1954*, 520.

60. In his memoirs, Johnson writes that he was surprised to be selected for the Indochina phase of the Geneva Conference since he "knew comparatively little about Indochina, I discovered when I returned to Washington that this did not automatically disqualify me, since none of my State Department colleagues seemed to have any clear notion of what we could hope to get out of the conference, and I did not hear of anyone competing for my job." See, Johnson, 202.

61. Statement by the President, 21 July 1954, John Foster Dulles Papers, Subject Series, Box 9, Folder 3, DDE Library. See also, "The President's News Conference of July 21, 1954," *Public Papers, 1954*, 642; Gary R. Hess, "Redefining the American Position in Southeast Asia: The United States and the Geneva and Manila Conferences," Kaplan et. al., eds., 137-39; Gibbons, pt. 1, 250-56; Arnold, 208-17; Stanley Karnow, *Vietnam* (New York: Penguin, 1984), 198-205; Kahin, *Intervention*, 52-61; Johnson, 204, 216-20, 224 and *FRUS*, 1795. The Eisenhower administration and future administrations conveniently violated the pledge on force. Eisenhower's warning on Communist aggression was cited by President Kennedy in justifying U.S. escalation.

62. *ESSFRC*, 622, 632, 642. See also, *FRUS*, 1732; Gibbons, pt. 1, 245, 253; Lloyd C. Gardner, *Approaching Vietnam* (New York: W.W. Norton and Co., 1988), 309; Ben Kiernan, *How Pol Pot Came to Power* (London: Verso, 1985), 142; Karnow, *Vietnam*, revised, (New York: Viking, 1991), 215-21; Johnson, 215, 218, 225; Lawrence S. Kaplan, "The United States, NATO, and French Indochina," Kaplan et. al., eds., 244; Sullivan, 49, 52; Kahin, *Intervention*, 52-65 and Hess, 140.

63. Marvin Kalb and Elie Abel, *Roots of Involvement* (New York: W.W. Norton and Co., 1971), 92-93. See also, "Dulles Taking Mansfield as Advisor," *Great Falls Tribune*, 21 August 1954, Mansfield scrapbooks, #12, Mansfield Papers, Maureen and Mike Mansfield Library, University of Montana (hereafter cited as Mansfield Papers); Mansfield, interview with Richard D. Challener, Washington D.C., 10 May 1966, The John Foster Dulles Oral History Project, Princeton University Library, 2 and Gibbons, pt. 1, 273.

64. Morse was a Senate Republican from 1945-1952 when he became an Independent. On 17 February 1955, Morse joined the Democrats, see, *Congressional Quarterly Almanac*, 84th Cong. 1st sess., 1955, vol. 11 (Washington D.C.: Congressional Quarterly News Features), 19.

65. *ESSFRC*, vol. 7, 1955 (Washington D.C.: United States Government Printing Office, 1978), 5, 12-13, 15-16, 18, 52. See also, "Senate, 82-1, Votes Pact For Defense of Southeast Asia," *New York Times*, 2 Feb. 1955, 1; Gibbons, pt. 1, 272, 275; Dean Rusk as told to Richard Rusk, Daniel S. Papp, ed. *As I Saw It* (New York: W.W. Norton and Co., 1990), 549; Sullivan, 52 and *FRUS, 1952-1954, East Asia and the Pacific*, vol. 12, pt. 1 (Washington, D.C.: United States Government Printing Office, 1984), 787-89, 806-8, 847.

66. Dean Rusk, secretary of state for both Kennedy and Johnson, and who would be at the center of Vietnam escalation decisions in the 1960s, considers the SEATO Treaty a mistake because it "became the law of the land" linking South Vietnam to the U.S. structure of collective security. When asked why the U.S. fought the second Indochina war, Rusk replied: "There was the pledge (SEATO). We had given our word." Rusk and the Johnson administration chose to interpret SEATO in that manner. Dulles himself "repeatedly denied" that the treaty committed the U.S. to military action in Vietnam to deal with revolution or subversion. Gibbons points out that the delegates to Manila were given "four uncompromisable preconditions" ignored by Johnson: a) "The U.S. would refuse to commit any U.S. forces unilaterally; b) Were military action to be required, one or more of the European signatories

would have to participate; c) The U.S. intended to contribute only sea and air power, expecting that other signatories would provide ground forces; d) The U.S. would act only against communist aggression." Rusk was deputy under secretary of state during the Truman administration and was a hawk even then. In 1951, Rusk did not believe that the Indochina war was a civil war because of Communist aid and that the Vietminh were "strongly directed from Moscow." See, Rusk, 420, 427, 549; Gibbons, pt. 1, 66, 96-98, 272-73 and Roger Dingman, "John Foster Dulles and the Creation of the South-East Asia Treaty Organization in 1954," *International History Review* 11 (1989): 475.

67. Dingman, 477. See also, David L. Anderson, "'No More Koreas:' Eisenhower and Vietnam," in *Dwight D. Eisenhower: Soldier, President, Statesman*, ed. Joann P. Krieg (Westport, Conn.: Greenwood Press, 1987), 278; Memorandum of Conversation with the President, 17 August 1954, John Foster Dulles, White House Memoranda, Box 1, Folder 1; Minutes of Cabinet Meeting, 11 March 1955, Whitman File, Cabinet Series, Box 4; Bipartisan Congressional Luncheon Meeting, 31 March 1955, Whitman File, Papers as President, Legislative Meetings Series, Box 1, DDE Library; Hess, 144; Rushkoff, 475 and Geoffrey Warner, "From Geneva to Manila: British Policy toward Indochina and SEATO, May-September 1954," Kaplan et. al., eds., 163-64.

68. The records of the CIA's predecessor, the Office of Strategic Services, remain closed regarding American involvement in Indochina during and after World War II, see Karnow, 1991, 728.

69. Dulles to Collins, 20 April 1955, John Foster Dulles Papers, Subject Series, Box 9, Container 1, DDE Library. See also, William O. Douglas, *North from Malaya* (New York: Doubleday, 1952), 180-81, 185-87; Anderson, *Trapped By Success*, 52; Neil Sheehan, *A Bright Shining Lie* (New York: Random House, 1988), 134; Gibbons, pt. 1, 232, 260-62; George C. Herring, *America's Longest War: The United States and Vietnam, 1950-1975* (New York: John Wiley & Sons, 1979), 49; Herbert Parmet, *Eisenhower and the American Crusades* (New York: Macmillan, 1972), 394; Kahin and John W. Lewis, *The United States in Vietnam* (New York: Dial Press, 1967), 67; Thomas D. Boettcher, *Vietnam: The Valor and the Sorrow* (Boston: Little, Brown and Co., 1985), 107-9; David Halberstam, *The Best and the Brightest* (New York: Random House, 1972), 147, 208; Karnow, 1984, 217; Marvin E. Gettleman et. al., eds. *Vietnam and America* (New York: Grove Press, 1985), 119; Townsend Hoopes, *The Devil and John Foster Dulles* (Boston: Atlantic, Little, Brown and Co., 1973), 251; James William Gibson, *The Perfect War* (Boston: The Atlantic Monthly Press, 1986), 69; Chester L. Cooper, *The Lost Crusade* (New York: Dodd, Mead and Co., 1970), 125; Ellen J. Hammer, *A Death in November* (New York: E.P. Dutton, 1987), 47, 49; Frances Fitzgerald, *Fire in the Lake* (Boston: Little, Brown and Co., 1972), 3; Sullivan, 55; Robert Scheer and Warren Hinckle, "The 'Vietnam Lobby,'" *Ramparts*, July 1965, 20; Cecil B. Currey, *Edward Lansdale: The Unquiet American* (Boston: Houghton Mifflin, 1988), 149 and Denis Warner, *Certain Victory: How Hanoi Won the War* (Kansas City: Sheed Andrews and McMeel, Inc., 1978), 101.

70. *FRUS, Indochina, 1952-1954*, vol. 13, pt. 1, 1014, pt. 2, 1608-9. See also, Anderson, *Trapped By Success*, 51-52.

71. Ibid., 1977-80, 1985-91, 1999-2003, 2007-10 2012-16, 2018-21, 2028-30. See also, Anderson, *Trapped By Success*, 48-49.

72. This letter violated the Geneva agreement by placing south Vietnam in an alliance and by elevating Diem's government from a temporarily divided nation to a sovereign one. See, Arnold, 241.

73. Mansfield, Report on Indochina, U.S. 83d Cong., 2d sess., S. Rept. (Washington D.C.: Government Printing Office, 15 Oct. 1954). See also, "Letter to the President of the Council

of Ministers of Viet-Nam Regarding Assistance for That Country. October 25, 1954," *Public Papers, 1954*, 948-49; *FRUS*, 2157; Anderson, *Trapped By Success*, 83 and Cooper, 134 (When asked if he agreed with Cooper's claim, Mansfield wrote, "I do not know whether Mr. Cooper was correct or not," see, Letter to the author, 1 Feb. 1990, 1).

74. *FRUS*, 2185, 2194-95, 2198-99, 2205-7. See also, J. Lawton Collins, *Lightning Joe* (Baton Rouge: Louisiana State University Press, 1979), 378-82, 411 and Arnold, 57-58, 249.

75. A recent book characterizes the president's role as that of a "referee" between Collins and Dulles. David L. Anderson suggests that Eisenhower trusted both men and "avoided an active role in the decision" while waiting for Collins and Dulles to "reconcile their differences." Anderson compares Eisenhower's management of this crisis as "similar to the pre-revisionist image of Eisenhower." See, *Trapped By Success*, 107, 109, 118.

76. Gibbons, pt. 1, 285.

77. Mansfield, The John Foster Dulles Oral History Project, 1-2, 4-5, 9-11, 15-17.

78. *United States-Vietnam Relations 1945-1967*, vol. 10 (Washington D.C.: Government Printing Office, 1971), 806-8, 811-13, 824-25, 826-29, 853-55; *FRUS*, 2198-99, 2330-34, 2378-79, 2386, 2393-94, 2398, 2400-3 and 1955-57, vol. 1 (Washington D.C.: Government Printing Office, 1985), 2; Collins papers, Box 24, # 3, 8 and 9 and Box 25, Daily Activities Book, 31 October-22 November, 23 November-31 December, and Monthly Papers, November 1954 (2), DDE Library.

79. Papers of John Foster Dulles: Telephone Calls Series, Box 10, Telephone Conversation-White House, March 7, 1955 to Aug. 29, 1955 (3), DDE Library.

80. Ibid. See also, Mansfield, 1 April 1955 memo, Mansfield Papers, Series XXII, Container 107, #11 and *FRUS*, 175-77.

81. *FRUS*, 196-97.

82. Ibid., 218-31.

83. Ibid., 234.

84. Ibid., 235.

85. Greenstein, 581.

86. John Foster Dulles, Meetings with the President, 1955, 11 April, Box 3, Folder 5, DDE Library. See also, *FRUS*, 236-38.

87. As quoted in Robert Shaplen, The Lost Revolution, revised (New York: Harper and Row, 1976), 122.

88. "The President's News Conference of April 27, 1955," *Public Papers, 1955*, 436.

89. It apparently never occurred to Eisenhower and Dulles that they were now acting as the colonial power they so detested. Ely and Collins rarely consulted South Vietnamese officials, only each other. Certainly from a Communist perspective, the U.S. merely replaced France as a colonial master. When Diem proved intractable, the Kennedy administration replaced him. See, Arnold, 258-59, 272, 351, 387.

90. *FRUS*, 294-300, 307-11.

91. Collins later said that Lansdale was "completely independent" with a separate communication channel to Washington: "The big mistake made frankly with respect to Lansdale and me, was that there were two people supposedly representing the United States government. I [was] getting instructions from the president of the United States, and this guy Lansdale, who had no authority so far as I was concerned, [was] getting instructions from the CIA. It was a mistake. That's all there was to it." Lansdale's direct channel was to CIA Director Allen Dulles and thus, to John Foster Dulles. The role of the CIA and Lansdale is difficult to assess because government documents that might provide the answer remain classified. What is clear is that the Dulles brothers had a pro-Diem source in Saigon to counter Collins. See, Anderson, *Trapped by Success*, 111-12 and Currey, 141.

92. *FRUS*, 338. See also, Mansfield, Summary of Remarks of General Lawton Collins, 27 April 1955, Mansfield Papers, Series XXII, Container 107, #11.

93. Collins, *Lightning Joe*, 397-407. For other accounts of Diem's victory over the sects, see Edward G. Lansdale, *In the Midst of Wars* (New York: Harper & Row, 1972), 282-91; Gibbons, pt. 1, 293-99; Anderson, *Trapped By Success*, 102-19; Arnold, 264-81; Hammer, 71-74; Joseph Buttinger, *Vietnam: A Dragon Embattled*, vol. II (New York: Praeger, 1967), 865-85; Cooper, 139-43; Shaplen, 119-28; Karnow, 1984, 222-23; Herring, *America's Longest War*, 51-54 and Gardner, 349-51.

94. Diem, Letter to Mansfield, 4 May 1955, Mansfield Papers, Series XXII, Container 95, #5.

95. Mansfield, Letter to the author, 1 Feb. 1990, 1. See also, Hoopes, 253-57; Joseph and Stewart Alsop, *The Reporter's Trade* (New York: Reynal and Co., 1958), 240; Joseph Alsop, interview, 11; Herring, Hess, and Immerman, "Passage of Empire: The United States, France, and South Vietnam, 1954-55," Kaplan et. al., eds., 193; Gardner, 349-50; Wesley R. Fishel, *Vietnam: Anatomy of a Conflict* (Itasca, Ill.: F.E. Peacock, 1968), 125 and Thomas Boettcher, *Vietnam: The Valor and the Sorrow* (Boston: Little, Brown and Co., 1985), 107.

96. Gibbons, pt. 1, 299-300. See also, Collins, *Lightning Joe*, 406 and Herring, *America's Longest War*, 54-55. A letter to Mansfield from Assistant Secretary of State Thruston B. Morton indicates that the U.S. still expected the Vietnam unification elections to take place as late as 18 March 1955. Dulles wired the American Embassy in Saigon as early as 6 April discussing ways to circumvent the elections. See Morton, Letter to Mansfield, 18 March 1955, Mansfield Papers, Series XIII, Container 8, #1 and *United States-Vietnam Relations 1945-1967*, Book 10, 892-93.

97. Gibbons, pt. 1, 301. See also, Moya Ball, "A Case Study of the Kennedy Administration's Decision-making Concerning the Diem Coup of November, 1963," *Western Journal of Speech Communication* 54 (1990): 561; Anderson, *Trapped By Success*, 117; Karnow, 1984, 422 and Buttinger, Letter to Mansfield, 21 Feb. 1975, 1, Mansfield Papers, Series XXII, Container 55, #1.

98. For discussion of Eisenhower's lack of understanding of Third World nationalism in Asia, see, Robert J. McMahon, "Eisenhower and Third World Nationalism: A Critique of the Revisionists," *Political Science Quarterly* 101 (1986): 457-62.

99. The Eisenhower administration actually increased the number from the Geneva-imposed limit of 342 by bringing in advisors who were ostensibly in Vietnam to recover American equipment left by the French. Arnold writes that Eisenhower's "instinctive aversion to military ground commitment in Asia led him to authorize 'little things' instead of giving final approval." By the end of his administration, Eisenhower escalated the U.S. role by allowing advisors to accompany their units into the field. On 8 July 1959, two American advisors were killed by a Vietcong unit in their billet at Bien-hoa. So, while avoiding another Asian war, Eisenhower introduced American advisors and allowed them "to edge toward active combat." See, Arnold, 297, 308-15, 340-41, 345, 377 and *FRUS, 1958-1960, Vietnam*, vol. 1 (Washington D.C.: Government Printing Office, 1986), 467-71.

100. John M. Newman, *JFK and Vietnam* (New York: Warner Books, 1992), 452. See also, Cooper, 164; Gibbons, pt. 1, 307, 332-33; Anderson, *Trapped By Success*, 151-52, 160-64, 193-209; Arnold, 240, 289, 299, 360-61, 371; John W. Sloan, "The Management and Decision-Making Style of President Eisenhower," *Presidential Studies Quarterly* 20 (1990): 309; *Cong. Rec.*, 13 May 1957, 6759-64 and Kahin, *Intervention*, 94.

Dulles and Eisenhower confer with Chip Bohlen at the Geneva Conference

J. Michael
Hogan

# Eisenhower and Open Skies
## A Case Study in "Psychological Warfare"

"He [Eisenhower] was a far more complex and devious
man than most people realized, and in the best sense of these words."[1]

Richard Nixon

With this statement, John W. Sloan has observed, Richard Nixon qualifies as
the first Eisenhower revisionist. Saddled for many years with James David
Barber's "passive-negative" label, Eisenhower ranked but twenty-second
among presidents in a 1962 poll of historians—just above the only president
ever impeached, Andrew Johnson. Now, however, we have a new portrait of
Eisenhower—one that has him doing more than passing "an inordinate
amount of time on the greens of the Augusta National."[2] The passive and unas-
suming Eisenhower has given way to an "intelligent, decisive, and perceptive"
Ike, "a strong leader who guided his administration with a deft hand and a
president who led his nation peacefully through eight tortuous years of Cold
War."[3]

Still, there remains an undercurrent of skepticism—even criticism—about
Eisenhower's leadership in foreign affairs. One recent study criticizes
Eisenhower for his "weak leadership" in national security matters and pro-
claims his policies "muddled."[4] Another study, published in 1991, takes
Eisenhower to task for his blind anti-communism and his multiple foreign
policy "failures."[5] Many still treat John Foster Dulles as the real architect of
Eisenhower's foreign policies,[6] and even sympathetic revisionists still write of
"contradictions" in those policies. As Robert A. Strong writes: "The administration that gave us 'massive retaliation' also gave us Atoms for Peace; and the
presidency that began by promising 'more bang for the buck,' ended with a
solemn warning about the 'military-industrial complex.'"[7]

Some revisionists sympathetically attribute the "contradictions" in
Eisenhower's foreign policies to the "adolescence" of strategic thinking in the
early Cold War. Others portray Eisenhower as the "hidden hand" behind John
Foster Dulles—an equally stern cold warrior who used Dulles as a lightning
rod to deflect criticism.[8] Meanwhile, Eisenhower's peace initiatives are rarely

137

taken seriously. Eisenhower, it seems, must have known that the "conflict" in his policies sabotaged any real "chances of obtaining an arms agreement."[9]

Perhaps the time has come for revising the revisionists. While the revisionist portrait of Eisenhower clearly has merit, it generally fails to account adequately for the president's disarmament initiatives. Indeed, the revisionists themselves have created something of a contradiction—a forceful, activist president who repeatedly espoused utopian arms control schemes. Yet Eisenhower himself clearly took his peace initiatives seriously, and he listed one of them—Atoms for Peace—among his greatest accomplishments in foreign affairs.[10] So why do even the revisionists give short shrift to Eisenhower's disarmament initiatives? Why do they continue to treat them, at best, as meaningless gestures? The answer lies in a failure to appreciate Eisenhower's concern with psychological strategy—the extent to which he viewed the Cold War as a "war of words."[11]

Eisenhower did not deal with the Russians out of confusion or naiveté. He pursued an astute—and perfectly consistent—rhetorical strategy premised upon the notion that the Cold War would be won, not with bombs and bullets, but through persuasion: by persuading unaligned nations to side with the West, allies to cooperate in both security and economic policies, and the U.S. Congress to fund an array of mutual security programs. Eisenhower indeed may have shared Dulles's view of the Soviet threat, as some revisionists have suggested. But he frequently differed with the secretary of state over the best way to counter that threat. While Dulles "methodically prosecuted the Soviets for their actions," Eisenhower believed that his secretary of state "neglected to emphasize sufficiently the constructive aspects of U.S. policy."[12] Thus, Eisenhower repeatedly overruled Dulles's objections to his peace initiatives, opting instead to heed the advice of his psychological strategists.

This essay begins by elucidating the significance of psychological warfare in the Eisenhower administration's Cold War strategy. Demonstrating an unprecedented concern with integrating propaganda initiatives into the policy-making process, the Eisenhower administration's Cold War policy rested upon a psychological strategy emphasizing "positive" or "constructive" overtures designed to cultivate world opinion. A classic expression of that strategy was Eisenhower's Open Skies proposal at the 1955 Geneva Conference.

Producing no new agreements, the Geneva Conference was "largely a cere-monial affair" according to textbook accounts, and Eisenhower's Open Skies initiative—his proposal for mutual aerial inspections of military installa-tions—was just a "propaganda ploy."[13] While not denying that Open Skies had propaganda purposes, this essay disputes the assumption that it therefore was of little consequence. Elucidating the strategic thinking behind Open Skies *as* propaganda, I will show that the initiative was designed to recapture the pro-paganda offensive from the Soviet Union by dramatically demonstrating the insincerity of their own disarmament initiatives.

## EISENHOWER'S "RHETORICAL PRESIDENCY"

When one thinks of "the rhetorical presidency," as David Zarefsky observes, "one thinks immediately of Wilson, both Roosevelts, Kennedy, Johnson, and even Reagan."[14] Eisenhower, with his garbled syntax and pedestrian style, would seem the very antithesis of the notion. Indeed, Eisenhower apparently disdained public speaking and television appearances. When once pressed to give a speech, as James David Barber has recounted, the president responded with typical irritation: "What is it that needs to be said? I am not going out there just to listen to my tongue clatter!"[15]

Yet Eisenhower *did* give speeches, and even Barber concedes his "great rhetorical success."[16] Furthermore, he often spoke for precisely the purpose associated with the Wilsonian concept of the rhetorical presidency: "to create an active public opinion that, if necessary, will pressure the Congress into accepting his program."[17] As R. Gordon Hoxie points out, Eisenhower did not hesitate to go on the rhetorical offensive, asking "the American people for support when a recalcitrant Congress refused to pass legislation to his satisfaction."[18] Eisenhower may not have been the most eloquent orator in American history, but contrary to Richard Neustadt's assessment, he did recognize that presidential power is the "power to persuade."[19]

Indeed, Eisenhower had, in many ways, a sophisticated view of the rhetorical presidency. Reflecting a broader conception of the persuasive aspects of his office than many of his predecessors, Eisenhower cultivated an awareness of the psychological dimensions of policy making throughout the executive branch, particularly in foreign affairs. In reorganizing the executive branch, he integrated psychological strategy more fully into the foreign policy decision-making process, and he transformed America's overseas information program into his own personal mouthpiece. Most importantly, he personally presided over an unprecedented peacetime propaganda war against the Soviets. Dictating the themes and setting the tone of that effort, he largely divested the State Department of its propaganda functions and balanced Dulles's confrontative approach with more conciliatory gestures toward the Soviets.

As Fitzhugh Green has observed, "Eisenhower had revealed an interest, unusual among army officers, in psychological operations" during World War II, and he brought his psychological warfare chief, C.D. Jackson, into the White House as a speech writer and close advisor.[20] In his peculiarly Cold War post of Special Assistant to the President for Psychological Warfare, Jackson urged "bold action to support America's promise that it was the agent of peace."[21] As Martin Medhurst has shown, it was Jackson who persuaded the president, over Dulles's objections, to launch a peace offensive against the Soviet Union in the spring of 1953,[22] and it was Jackson who, along with Walt W. Rostow, planned the opening shot of that offensive: Eisenhower's Chance for Peace speech before the American Society of Newspaper Editors on 16 April 1953.[23] Later, Jackson also served as a primary author of the Atoms for Peace speech, again overcoming "fierce disagreement" from the State Department "over the advisability of making any speech at all." Dulles, according to Jackson's recollections, "didn't like anything" about the proposed speech. But again the president overruled the secretary of state.[24]

These two well-known speeches, however, were only the tip of the propaganda iceberg. During the 1952 presidential campaign, Eisenhower had pledged to improve America's overseas information programs, and he appointed a special President's Committee on International Information Activities soon after the election. Charged with investigating and recommending improvements in America's overseas information programs, the so-called Jackson Committee was named for its chair, William Jackson. But, again, it was C.D. Jackson who, as a member of the committee, became the driving force behind its plan for "a considered policy of the entire Government to win World War III without having to fight it."[25]

Declassified in 1986, the top-secret Jackson Committee report differed little from administration hard-liners in its basic view of Soviet motivations. "The policies of the United States," began the 125-page report, "are based upon the assumption that the purpose of the Soviet rulers is world domination."[26] Yet the Jackson Committee actually downplayed the Soviet military threat, emphasizing instead the psychological dimensions of the Cold War: "It is our belief that the Soviet rulers will strive to avoid general war, primarily because of fear that their regime could not be maintained in power after a devastating atomic attack and because the opportunities for expansion by political warfare still seem good." The real threat, the committee argued, lay not so much in the Soviet's military capabilities as in their propaganda advantages:

> For the last 30 years the Soviet propaganda program has been large and centrally directed. From the time they seized power, the Bolsheviks have given high priority to propaganda, both internal and external. As a result of this long experience, the Soviet Union possesses a large group of propagandists which is continually replenished by new and well-trained recruits. They are inhibited neither by the need to tell the truth nor by public opinion at home.

Criticizing the "confusion" surrounding America's own propaganda "mission," the Jackson Committee suggested that it was not enough to criticize the Communists or to boast about America's achievements. Urging a more positive and "spiritual" approach, the committee argued that the "primary and overriding purpose" of American propaganda should be to "persuade foreign peoples that it lies in their own interests to take action consistent with the national objectives of the United States." American propagandists needed to "find out what other peoples want, to relate their wants to those of this country and to explain these common goals in ways that will cause others to join with the United States in their achievement." Above all, American propaganda needed to present a vision of a better world—a vision that would "arouse . . . an understanding and a sympathy for the kind of world order which the United States and other free nations seek to achieve."

The Jackson Committee thus called for a whole new attitude toward psychological strategy—a new emphasis on "the deeper spiritual values uniting this nation with the rest of the world." In addition, the committee complained that "opportunities have been missed to take the offensive in global propaganda campaigns." "Too often," the committee complained, "the program has been merely defensive." Furthermore, the committee recommended that psychological concerns be better coordinated and integrated more fully into the policy-making process. "Too often," the committee argued, "the United States speaks with a multitude of voices," and this lack of coordination resulted in "the haphazard projection of too many and too diffuse propaganda themes." The committee complained that previous propaganda efforts had been founded upon "a basic misconception" that psychological concerns could be separated from policy. In fact, according to the committee, there was a psychological dimension "inherent in every diplomatic, economic or military action," and there were "no 'national psychological objectives' separate and distinct from national objectives." As a White House press release summarized the point, "every significant act of virtually every department and agency of Government has its effect, either positively or negatively, in the global struggle for freedom." Thus, the committee urged the president to build "awareness throughout the entire Government of the impact of day-to-day governmental actions and to coordinate and time such actions so as to derive from them the maximum advantage."[27]

On 30 June 1953, the Jackson Committee presented its unanimous report to the president, and the National Security Council discussed psychological strategy at its meeting on 2 July. According to the top-secret report of that meeting, the president wanted to "make sure that the psychological factor in important Government actions was not overlooked"—that "someone was going to keep track of the psychological side as of major importance"—and his advisors assured him of their "continuing attention to the psychological impact of significant government action."[28]

Meanwhile, Eisenhower already had begun revamping America's international information program, ordering a "significant reorganization of the executive branch for the conduct of foreign affairs."[29] While reaffirming "the historic responsibility of the Department of State as the agency responsible under the President for the development and control of foreign policy," this reorganization plan, submitted to Congress on 1 June 1953, actually removed information activities from the State Department and created a new agency—the United States Information Agency (USIA)—with sole responsibility for "the conduct of our information programs." In view of the "direct relation" of information activities "to the conduct of foreign affairs and national security policy," the plan authorized the secretary of state to "control the content" of American information programs. At the same time, however, it ordered the head of the USIA to "report to the President through the National Security Council or as the President may otherwise direct."[30]

As a practical matter, this made the USIA—and hence all American information activities—a virtual mouthpiece of the president. In fact, a blueprint for the USIA's first year of operation—known simply as "the Plan" among insiders—proposed that all American propaganda be focused directly upon the positive aspects of "The Chance for Peace" speech. "It is the purpose of this instruction," the Plan began, "to translate the broad principles of our foreign policy, as laid down by the President in his speech of 16 April, into terms meaningful for the information program and to establish a world-wide plan of action." Explicitly invoking the Jackson Committee report, the Plan emphasized the need to stress those "goals and desires" we held "in common" with other peoples, and it identified two such themes in the president's speech: "the Faith" and "the Vision." Quoting at length from the president's call for disarmament and constructive world aid, the Plan concluded: "This is the promise, the call to action, the *vision* of 'A Golden Age of Freedom and Peace.'"[31]

Thus the USIA proposed "a modest plan" containing "the seeds of a much larger and more dynamic program in which all the agencies of the Government, as well as the American people, could actively participate."[32] Rooted in the Jackson Committee report, the Plan envisioned a multimedia assault on world opinion stressing "mutuality of interests" and presenting "the free world as the champions of peace." "We must now employ proven techniques of mass communication to carry our message of the Faith and the Vision to the farthest corners of the globe," the Plan concluded. "This message must be expressed in a few simple concepts appropriately presented in every medium and repeated, repeated, repeated."[33]

Repeated it was, not just by the USIA, but by the president himself. As his first term unfolded, Eisenhower continued to speak positively of the possibilities for world peace, and even Dulles began to "move appreciably toward the coexistence position," becoming "a good deal less impatient and bellicose" in his speeches.[34] In January 1954, of course, Dulles gave his "Massive Retaliation" speech, which still stands as the classic expression of the administration's "brinkmanship."[35] For the most part, however, the Eisenhower administration spoke a language of peace, and the consummate expression of the peace offensive was yet to come: Eisenhower's Open Skies initiative of 1955.

## THE "FAILED" GENEVA SUMMIT

In July of 1955, Dwight D. Eisenhower traveled to Geneva for a summit conference with the leaders of the other Big Four powers: Premier Edgar Faure of France, British Prime Minister Anthony Eden, and Nikolai Bulganin, the ostensible leader of Khrushchev's Soviet Union. It was the first meeting of Soviet and Western leaders since the Potsdam Conference of 1945, and it promised to be "the most spectacular event of the postwar era."[36] For three days, the president and his counterparts smiled for the photographers, disguising serious disagreements over German reunification and other matters.[37] So pleasant was the atmosphere, so amiable were the leaders, that reporters began writing about a new "Spirit of Geneva."

Yet even though Geneva "marked an end to the unlimited violence of language" in East-West relations, Louis Halle still labels it an "abortive" peace conference. Other historians have observed that it "produced no solid results"; some have even described its results as "entirely negative."[38] Realists have been particularly disparaging of the conference, presenting it as a classic case of the "disarmament game"—the pursuit of negotiations "strictly for propaganda purposes."[39] Norman Graebner, for example, complains that Eisenhower and Khrushchev "reduced peacemaking to pure symbolism,"[40] and even revisionist Charles Alexander agrees that "the spirit of Geneva produced absolutely no concrete progress on the fundamental issues dividing the two superpowers."[41]

Yet Eisenhower never went to Geneva in search of new agreements. He had no intention of negotiating with the Soviets, and he initially did not plan to propose new initiatives. Urged by Dulles to approach the conference cautiously, Eisenhower apparently left for Geneva with no firm agenda. But vigorous lobbying by Nelson Rockefeller, C.D. Jackson's successor as the president's expert on psychological warfare,[42] ultimately persuaded Eisenhower to offer his Open Skies initiative. The Soviets, of course, rejected the proposal. But precisely because they rejected it, Open Skies proved perhaps the most successful maneuver in the administration's two-year-old peace offensive.

Open Skies originated out of a series of meetings Rockefeller convened at the Quantico Marine Base in Virginia between 5 June and 10 June 1955. Although no longer officially a presidential advisor, C.D. Jackson participated in the Quantico conference, as did a number of other experts on national security from the government and the academy.[43] The task of the panel, as Rostow has recalled, "was defined somewhere in the ambiguous area of 'psychological warfare,'"[44] and an early inside account described its general purpose as considering "how the United States could retain its nuclear power but still make it clear for all to see that its purpose was peace."[45] Specifically, however, the panel had its eye on the upcoming Geneva summit. While the panel addressed many general and long-range questions about U.S.-Soviet relations, its most immediate task was to consider how the U.S. might recapture the propaganda offensive in the wake of a disarmament and inspection proposal made by the Soviets on 10 May 1955.[46]

Not surprisingly, the State Department viewed the whole Quantico affair with skepticism. As Jackson recalled in the only contemporary account of the meetings: "The State Dept. boys had ganged up against the Quantico idea as no business of outsiders, . . . Official Washington at the Indian and one-feather-chief level was not pleased."[47] Once the Quantico panel completed its work, Jackson wrote to both Dulles and Eisenhower urging them to consider the report,[48] and the president reportedly "read it with enthusiasm."[49] As Geneva approached, however, Dulles vigorously opposed any effort by Rockefeller's group to determine policy at Geneva, and he advocated a much different role for the president at the conference. As Rostow has summarized Dulles's position: "He believed the president should offer no new initiatives but should confine himself to helping generate a spirit in which later detailed negotiations . . . might succeed."[50] Indeed, Dulles apparently feared that the president might be hoodwinked by smiling Russians, as revealed in Jackson's account of a conversation with the secretary of state. According to Jackson, Dulles said:

> But what I am most worried about is the President. . . . I have nothing but admiration and respect for him, both as a person and as a man aware of foreign policy and conference pitfalls. Yet he is so inclined to be humanly generous, to accept a superficial tactical smile as evidence of inner warmth, that he might in a personal moment with the Russians accept a promise or a proposition at face value and upset the apple cart. . . .
>
> We have come such a long way by being firm, occasionally disagreeably firm, that I would hate to see the whole edifice undermined in response to a smile.[51]

Rockefeller, however, continued to push for Open Skies, arguing that Dulles's approach—the president doing nothing while the Russians proposed all sorts of initiatives—would put the U.S. in "an impossible position psychologically."[52] On 11 July he elaborated his views in a secret, forty-two-page memorandum to the president, entitled "Psychological Strategy at Geneva." The Soviets, Rockefeller predicted in his memo, would seek "psychological and propaganda advantage" at Geneva rather than "serious diplomatic negotiations." Since it was "the Soviet practice to take the offensive at conferences," one could "only assume" that they would have "bold propositions in hand," and there would be "grave dangers" in allowing them to continue their propaganda offensive. "We need our own positive approach at Geneva," Rockefeller argued, and this meant offering "specific American proposals" designed both "to capture the political and psychological imagination of the world" and "to expose . . . the falseness of the Soviet [peace] campaign."[53]

In ten separate tabs appended to "Psychological Strategy at Geneva," Rockefeller proposed a variety of specific proposals that Eisenhower might use to recapture the propaganda offensive. "Of outstanding importance," however, was his first recommendation: "That the U.S. propose international agreement for mutual inspection of military installations, forces and armaments without provisions, initially, for limitations or reduction of armaments." The Soviets were "almost certain to press discussion" on disarmament, Rockefeller explained, and they had "the initiative in this field by virtue of their May 10, 1955, proposals which represent, for them, great concessions." Moreover, disarmament, "more than any other world problem," had "universal appeal and decided psychological aspects." A proposal for mutual inspection would regain for the U.S. "the initiative in disarmament negotiation" and pose "a difficult decision for the Soviets." As Rockefeller explained: "If the Soviets agree to establish such an inspection system, *which is highly doubtful,* it appears that we can afford to implement the agreement without risk to our security." More likely, however, they would reject such an initiative, thereby exposing the "phoniness" of their own inspection and disarmament proposals of 10 May 1955.[54]

In a meeting on the eve of the summit, Eisenhower appeared to side with Dulles, reportedly exploding in anger at Rockefeller's continued advocacy of Open Skies: "Nelson you have heard Foster. . . . We are going to do what Foster recommends."[55] Eisenhower also rejected Rockefeller's draft for his departure speech to the American people—a speech deliberately designed, in Rostow's words, "to foreshadow and, if possible, to commit the president to making concrete proposals, as opposed to Dulles's notion of his merely identifying areas for later negotiation by the foreign ministers."[56] Following Dulles's advice to eschew "quick solutions,"[57] Eisenhower told the American people that he sought only "to change the spirit that has characterized the intergovernmental relationships of the world within the past ten years." Previous postwar conferences, he explained, had been "characterized too much by attention to details," while too little attention had been paid to "spirit and attitude."[58]

Yet Eisenhower kept his options open. While Dulles accompanied the president to Geneva, Eisenhower ordered Rockefeller and his staff to set up shop in Paris—just in case. And although he rejected yet another speech drafted by Rostow and submitted by Rockefeller,[59] his opening statement at Geneva on 18 July at least hinted at the Open Skies initiative. Early in the speech, the president echoed Dulles's theme that "we cannot expect here, in the few hours of a few days, to solve all the problems" in the world, and he again called for a "new spirit" that might make "future solutions" possible. Yet toward the end of the speech, Rockefeller won at least a limited victory as the president broached the subject of mutual inspection:

> Surprise attack has a capacity for destruction far beyond anything which man has yet known. So each of us deems it vital that there should be means to deter such attack. Perhaps, therefore, we should consider whether the problem of limitation of armament may not best be approached by seeking—as a first step—dependable ways to supervise and inspect military establishments, so that there can be no frightful surprises, . . . In this field nothing is more important than that we explore together the challenging and central problem of effective mutual inspection. Such a system is the foundation for real disarmament.[60]

As the conference progressed, Rockefeller continued to rally support among Eisenhower's top advisors, including Admiral Arthur Radford, chairman of the Joint Chiefs of Staff. On 19 July Rockefeller and his staff were ordered to Geneva. On 20 July, the day before the summit meeting focusing upon disarmament, Eisenhower met with his national security staff and decided to go with the inspection initiative. Apparently persuaded by the senior military officials—and by Eisenhower's own strong interest in the proposal—even Dulles finally gave in, proclaiming the idea "very promising," both from the standpoint of "drama" and of "substance."[61]

On 21 July, the fourth day in Geneva, Eisenhower dropped his propaganda bombshell. Two-thirds through his prepared remarks, the president put down his text, removed his glasses, and spoke directly to the Russian delegation:

> Gentlemen, since I have been working on this memorandum to present to this conference, I have been searching my heart and mind for something that I could say here that could convince everyone of the great sincerity of the United States in approaching this problem of disarmament.
>
> I should address myself for a moment principally to the delegates from the Soviet Union, because our two great countries admittedly possess new and terrible weapons in quantities which do give rise in other parts of the world, or reciprocally, to the fears and dangers of surprise attack.
>
> I propose, therefore, that we take a practical step, that we begin an arrangement, very quickly, as between ourselves—immediately. These steps would include:
>
> To give each other a complete blueprint of our military establishments, from beginning to end, from one end of our countries to the other; . . .
>
> Next, to provide within our countries facilities for aerial photography to the other country—we provide you . . . ample facilities for aerial reconnaissance, . . . ; you to provide exactly the same facilities for us . . . , and by this step to convince the world that we are providing as between ourselves against the possibility of great surprise attack, thus lessening danger and relaxing tensions.[62]

The story of what happened next is the stuff of political folklore. According to the version Eisenhower himself promoted in his memoirs, even the gods seemed to thunder their approval of the president's dramatic gesture:

> As I finished, a most extraordinary natural phenomenon took place. Without warning, and simultaneous with my closing words, the loudest clap of thunder I have ever heard roared into the room, and the conference was plunged into Stygian darkness. Our astonishment was all the greater because in our air-conditioned and well-lighted room there had been no inkling of an approaching storm.

> For a moment there was stunned silence. Then I remarked that I had not dreamed I was so eloquent as to put the lights out. This was rewarded with laughter, only because it was an obvious break in the tension, and in a few moments the lights came back on.[63]

Spanier and Nogee have argued that Russian acceptance of Open Skies "was, of course, precluded by the fact that this would mean conceding far more than could be gained."[64] Revisionist Charles Alexander agrees, explaining that "Open Skies would have given the Pentagon most of the closely guarded information it needed about Soviet capabilities, while the Russians would have learned relatively little they did not already know."[65] These assessments, however, entirely miss the point of the Open Skies initiative. As Eisenhower himself later conceded: "We knew the Soviets wouldn't accept it. We were sure of that, but we took a look and thought it was a good move."[66] From Khrushchev's perspective, as Eisenhower recalled, Open Skies was "nothing more than a bald espionage plot against the U.S.S.R."[67] But from the American perspective, it accomplished precisely what it had been *designed* to do: it recaptured the propaganda offensive from the Soviet Union and brought Eisenhower worldwide acclaim as a champion of peace.

As Chalmers Roberts has written, Open Skies proved "an immensely popular conception in many parts of the world."[68] It strongly reinforced Eisenhower's "image as a statesman trying to lead the world toward peace,"[69] while it "dimmed the Soviet image as the virtuous advocate of disarmament."[70] As Nelson Rockefeller reported to the president on 25 July 1955, European press reactions were "preponderantly favorable,"[71] and on 3 August Rockefeller sent the president results from USIA public opinion surveys in four Western European nations. As Rockefeller summarized the findings, a "substantial majority" (from 60 to 67 percent) of Europeans approved of Open Skies, while less than 15 percent, on average, disapproved. "There is little doubt," Rockefeller concluded, "that the conference increased hope in Western Europe that world problems might be solved."[72]

Perhaps more importantly, Open Skies led to at least a tacit understanding that the superpower conflict "was to be kept within such limits as would obviate any extreme risk of a great nuclear war."[73] As Roberts recently summarized the psychological effects of Open Skies, "it was a proposal so fraught with hope for a war-weary world that it propelled both sides forward in the search for arms control agreements."[74] Open Skies may have produced no agreements, but for a time it got the two sides talking. It opened, as Eisenhower hoped it would, at least "a tiny gate in the disarmament fence."[75]

The crises in Hungary and the Middle East would subsequently bring an end to the "Spirit of Geneva." Yet the Eisenhower administration continued to milk Open Skies for all it was worth, repeatedly reminding the world of the Soviets' rejection of this "chance for peace." In the fall of 1955, the United States pushed for Open Skies both at the Foreign Ministers Conference in Geneva and in the United Nations. Yet as U.N. Representative Henry Cabot Lodge, Jr., suggested in a letter to Harold Stassen, the U.S. was more concerned with keeping the issue alive than with Soviet acceptance: "I am afraid that the Soviet Union may try to . . . delay and confuse the issue and thus cause us to lose the position of unprecedented advantage that the President's aerial photography proposal at Geneva has won for us. . . . The advantage . . . must be maintained. This means in essence a strategy of keeping constantly focused on his proposal, . . . In one way or another we must 'worry' the aerial photography proposal like a dog with a bone."[76] On 1 February 1956, Premier Bulganin criticized the proposal in a letter to Eisenhower,[77] and again Lodge sensed a propaganda opening: "Now he has provided us with an ideal opportunity to wrap the 'Open Sky' plan right around his neck, in full view of the public."[78] Over the next two years, Eisenhower himself corresponded publicly with Bulganin and Khrushchev, repeatedly reminding them—and the whole world—that the Soviet Union surely would have agreed to Open Skies if it were "as peace-loving as it professes."[79] And when the Soviets shot down a U.S. spy plane in May of 1960, Open Skies came to the rescue, blunting the Soviets' propaganda advantage by making the U-2 flights at least somewhat easier to justify.[80]

Upon his return from the Geneva conference of 1955, Eisenhower told the American people that the "Spirit of Geneva" consisted of a "growing realization by all that nuclear warfare, pursued to the ultimate, could be practically race suicide." He also expressed his confidence that negotiations could now be "conducted without propaganda and threats and invective." Yet while the "Spirit of Geneva" at least temporarily ended the threats and invective, it hardly stopped the propaganda. As Eisenhower himself acknowledged, "the principal purpose" of Open Skies had been "to convince every one of Western sincerity in seeking peace."[81] And that, of course, was the whole idea behind his peace offensive.

## CONCLUSION

As Franck and Weisband have observed: "it is fashionable for 'hard headed realists,' a category of intellect much prized in government, to discount words and principles." Distinguishing between words and deeds, the rhetorical and the real, many Americans, both in and outside of government, "regard verbal strategy as very much on the fringes of national policy." This "scorn for verbal conceptualization in international politics," however, "is a persistent and widely shared folly." Verbal weapons may be as real in "their strategic potential as missiles and submarines," and the failure to recognize this can allow the U.S. to "be maneuvered into strategic positions . . . which are not in its national interest."[82]

Dwight D. Eisenhower often spoke the language of a hard-headed realist, challenging the Soviets to demonstrate their good-will, not with words but with deeds. "We care nothing for mere rhetoric," he declared in his speech "The Chance for Peace,"[83] and many historians have taken him at his word. Revisionists have begun to reassess Eisenhower's communicative skills, discovering evidence of "a skilled, sophisticated use of language on Eisenhower's part."[84] As yet, however, we have failed to appreciate fully the importance of psychological warfare in the Eisenhower administration's Cold War strategy. Redefining propaganda in more "positive" terms, the Eisenhower administration pursued a coordinated psychological strategy and integrated propaganda concerns more fully into the policy-making process. Reorganizing America's overseas information program, Eisenhower personally articulated the themes and set the tone of a major peace offensive against the Soviets. Recognizing that there is more to rhetoric than speech making and more to the presidency than the chief executive himself, Eisenhower brought new meaning to the notion of a rhetorical presidency.

Open Skies may indeed have been a propaganda ploy. But contrary to conventional historical wisdom, it did not therefore accomplish nothing. As an important element in the administration's peace offensive, it did precisely what it was designed to do: it recaptured the propaganda offensive from the Soviet Union and cultivated favorable world opinion. But beyond these immediate effects, Open Skies also had positive long-term effects—perhaps unintended and unforeseen—on U.S.-Soviet relations. As Rostow has suggested, Open Skies may well have played a major role "in the decision finally made by the Soviet Union to accept as common law mutual satellite photography."[85] Subsequently, mutual inspection became an integral component in all arms control talks, from SALT I to the Reagan administration's INF treaty. Historically, as Chalmers Roberts has argued, Open Skies may be seen as "the ancestor" of virtually all "of today's many arms control and reduction measures." Indeed, Open Skies "broke the mold of the Cold War" by establishing the premise that "nuclear war had now become unthinkable" and by charting one of the key "paths to meaningful peace."[86]

In 1989, President Bush attempted to revive the idea of Open Skies in a major foreign policy address at Texas A&M University. Quoting Eisenhower on the need to "convince the world that we are lessening danger and relaxing tension," Bush proposed that the superpowers again explore the possibility of allowing "unarmed aircraft from the United States and the Soviet Union to fly over the territory of the other country."[87] As national security advisor Brent Scowcroft admitted, Bush's proposal for a new Open Skies was mostly of symbolic significance in the age of satellite surveillance.[88] But so, too, it had mostly symbolic purposes when Eisenhower first proposed it. Like Eisenhower, President Bush hoped to test the Soviet Union's "commitment to change."[89] Unlike Eisenhower, however, Bush lived to witness the demise of the Soviet Empire. With nuclear arsenals on both sides now being reduced, one might say that the test has finally been met.

## NOTES

1. Richard M. Nixon, *Six Crises* (Garden City: Doubleday, 1962), 172.
2. John W. Sloan, "The Management and Decision-Making Style of President Eisenhower," *Presidential Studies Quarterly* 20 (Spring 1990): 305; James David Barber, *The Presidential Character: Predicting Performance in the White House*, 3rd ed. (Englewood Cliffs: Prentice-Hall, 1972), 134-48; Arthur M. Schlesinger, Jr., "Our Presidents: A Rating of 75 Historians," *New York Times Magazine*, 29 July 1962, 12, 40-41; Richard A. Melanson and David Mayers, preface to *Reevaluating Eisenhower: American Foreign Policy in the 1950s* (Urbana: University of Illinois Press, 1987), 1.
3. Mary S. McAuliffe, "Commentary: Eisenhower, the President," *Journal of American History* 68 (December 1981): 625.
4. H.W. Brands, "The Age of Vulnerability: Eisenhower and the National Insecurity State," *American Historical Review* 94 (October 1989): 975, 984.
5. Chester J. Pach, Jr. and Elmo Richardson, *The Presidency of Dwight D. Eisenhower*, rev. ed. (Lawrence: University Press of Kansas, 1991), esp. 75-104, 187-210.
6. As Richard Immerman has observed, scholars disagree in their assessments of Dulles's character and performance, yet "virtually all agree that Eisenhower's diplomacy from 1953-1959 was in fact designed by Dulles." Richard H. Immerman, "Eisenhower and Dulles: Who Made the Decisions?" *Political Psychology* 1 (Autumn 1979): 22.
7. Robert A. Strong, "Eisenhower and Arms Control," in *Reevaluating Eisenhower*, ed. Melanson and Mayers, 241.
8. Strong, 241; Fred I. Greenstein, *The Hidden Hand Presidency: Eisenhower as Leader* (New York: Basic Books, 1982), 89-91.
9. Thomas F. Soapes, "A Cold Warrior Seeks Peace: Eisenhower's Strategy for Nuclear Disarmament," *Diplomatic History* 4 (Winter 1980): 70.
10. R. Gordon Hoxie, "Dwight David Eisenhower: Bicentennial Considerations," *Presidential Studies Quarterly* 20 (Spring 1990): 260-61.
11. Although revisionists such as Charles Alexander have acknowledged that the Eisenhower administration "had made much of the need for a psychological-warfare offensive"

against the Soviets, few have treated psychological strategy as an integral part of the administration's foreign policy. In one recent study, for example, David Rosenberg explores "the reality of nuclear policy that underlay the public rhetoric," ignoring the psychological strategy behind many of those very policies. See Charles C. Alexander, *Holding the Line: The Eisenhower Era, 1952-1961* (Bloomington: Indiana University Press, 1975), 96; David Alan Rosenberg, "The Origins of Overkill: Nuclear Weapons and American Strategy, 1945-1960," *International Security* 7 (Spring 1983): 3.

12. Immerman, 36.

13. Thomas G. Paterson, J. Garry Clifford, and Kenneth Hagan, *American Foreign Policy: A History* (Lexington, MA: D.C. Heath, 1977), 490.

14. David Zarefsky, *President Johnson's War on Poverty: Rhetoric and History* (University, Al: University of Alabama Press, 1986), 7.

15. Eisenhower quoted in Barber, 135.

16. Attempting to resolve this apparent contradiction in his assessment of Eisenhower, Barber suggests that Eisenhower's rhetorical success was somehow accidental; it just "happened" despite neither "great skill" nor "great energy" on Eisenhower's part. Barber, 138.

17. James W. Ceaser, Glen E. Thurow, Jeffrey Tulis, and Joseph M. Bessette, "The Rise of the Rhetorical Presidency," *Presidential Studies Quarterly* 11 (Spring 1981): 163.

18. Hoxie, 260.

19. Arguing that presidential leadership involves helping "to shape the meaning of events, the terms of discourse, the attention paid, and the noise level," Neustadt renders a harsh judgment of Eisenhower: "Eisenhower's years were marked by a pervasive fog of self-congratulation, muffling noise. The fog machine was centered in the White House." Richard E. Neustadt, *Presidential Power: The Politics of Leadership* (New York: John Wiley and Sons, 1960), 210.

20. Fitzhugh Green, *American Propaganda Abroad: From Benjamin Franklin to Ronald Reagan* (New York: Hippocrene Books, 1988), 28-29.

21. Soapes, 59.

22. Martin J. Medhurst, "Eisenhower's 'Atoms for Peace' Speech: A Case Study in the Strategic Use of Language," *Communication Monographs* 54 (June 1987): 206.

23. Dwight D. Eisenhower, "Address 'The Chance for Peace' Delivered Before the American Society of Newspaper Editors, April 16, 1953," in *Public Papers of the Presidents of the United States: Dwight D. Eisenhower, 1953* (Washington: Government Printing Office, 1960), 179-88 (hereafter cited as *Public Papers*).

24. Medhurst, 217.

25. C.D. Jackson, Memorandum to General Eisenhower, 17 December 1952, Psychological Warfare, Box 29, Administration Series, Whitman File, Eisenhower Library, Abilene, Kansas (hereafter cited as DDE Library).

26. "The President's Committee on International Information Activities: Report to the President, June 30, 1953," Report to the President, Box 14, Alphabetical Subject Series, U.S. President's Committee on International Information Activities (Jackson Committee), DDE Library, 1. All subsequent quotations from the Jackson Committee report come from this document, pp. 4, 55-56, 58-60, 90, 120.

27. James C. Hagerty, White House press release, 8 July 1953, Time Inc./Jackson Committee, Box 52, C.D. Jackson Papers, DDE Library, 3.

28. National Security Council, 2 July 1953, 152nd Meeting of NSC, Box 4, National Security Council Series, Whitman File, DDE Library, 16-17.

29. Memorandum to the Heads of All Executive Departments, June 1, 1953, Official File 103-A, May-June 1953, Box 461, White House Central Files, DDE Library, 1.

30. Message to Congress, 1 June 1953, Official File 103-A, May-June 1953, Box 461, White House Central Files, DDE Library, 1, 3.

31. "The USIA Program for 1954," 15 July 1953, Official File 247, Box 909, White House Central Files, DDE Library, 1-4. "The Plan" explained that "the Faith" went beyond "crude materialism"; it existed "independently of ownership of the means of production," and it rose "triumphantly above the squirrel-cage of the dialectical process." It consisted of "belief in the omnipotence of the spirit," and since this was a "faith which all men share," it made for "good propaganda." "The Faith" expressed not "what *we* believe but what *we and they believe in common*," and those common beliefs constituted "the springboard for effective communication." Similarly, "the Vision" referred to themes that were not only "deeply imbedded in the American mind and character," but also evoked aspirations shared by other nations.

32. John Read Burr to Abbott Washburn, 15 July 1953, Official File 247, Box 909, White House Central Files, DDE Library.

33. "The USIA Program for 1954," 4-5.

34. Eric F. Goldman, *The Crucial Decade—and After: America, 1945-1960* (New York: Vintage Books, 1960), 284-85.

35. John Foster Dulles, "The Evolution of Foreign Policy," address before the Council on Foreign Relations, New York, NY, 12 January 1954, in U.S. Department of State *Bulletin* 30 (25 January 1954): 107-10. Historians have disagreed over whether Eisenhower approved of Dulles's speech. According to Louis Halle, "Massive Retaliation" was one of the few speeches Dulles wrote without input from either the White House or his own State Department advisors. Halle has argued that historians generally ignore the fact that Eisenhower denied that Dulles's speech announced any new decisions about American foreign policy at a press conference the very next day, and Dulles himself immediately began working on an article for *Foreign Affairs* that "expounded the strategy of the United States in terms that reduced the more extreme implications of what he had seemed to be saying in his 'massive retaliation' speech." Peter Lyon, on the other hand, has argued that Eisenhower "should have shared any blame" for the speech, "for almost certainly he submitted a draft of Dulles's speech to careful study and revision." Lyon also has pointed out that the President had "five days earlier used similar language," and he argues that the President did not "alter any of the emphases of Dulles's speech" during his press conference. See Louis J. Halle, *The Cold War as History* (1967; New York: Harper Colophon Books, 1971), 280-83; Peter Lyon, *Eisenhower: Portrait of the Hero* (Boston: Little, Brown, 1974), 624. See also "The President's News Conference of January 13, 1954," in *Public Papers, 1954*, 58; John Foster Dulles, "Policy for Security and Peace," *Foreign Affairs* 32 (April 1954): 364.

36. Alexander, 95.

37. As Eisenhower later recalled, the American delegation "seriously discussed the wisdom of leaving the meeting abruptly as a protest against obvious Soviet resistance to any logical solution to the problem" of German reunification. See Dwight D. Eisenhower, *Mandate for Change, 1953-1956* (Garden City: Doubleday and Co., 1963), 524.

38. Halle, 332; Goldman, 328; Joseph P. Morray, *From Yalta to Disarmament: Cold War Debate* (New York: MR Press, 1961), 232.

39. John W. Spanier and Joseph L. Nogee, *The Politics of Disarmament: A Study in Soviet-American Gamesmanship* (New York: Frederick A. Praeger, 1962), 5, 48-49, 91-92.

40. Norman A. Graebner, *Cold War Diplomacy: American Foreign Policy, 1945-1960* (Princeton: D. Van Nostrand Co., 1962), 128.

41. Alexander, 98.
42. Jackson, who frequently interrupted his publishing career with Time, Inc. for government service, resigned his White House post on 31 March 1954. But "by no means did his official and unofficial connections with the Administration end at that time." In the fall of 1954, he served with the American delegation to the ninth General Assembly of the United Nations, and in the summer of 1958 he returned to the White House to assist in preparing a major presidential address on the Lebanon crisis. All the while he continued to advise the president informally. See David Haight, "The Papers of C.D. Jackson: A Glimpse at President Eisenhower's Psychological Warfare Expert," *Manuscripts* 28 (Winter 1976): 27-37. See also H.W. Brands, Jr., *Cold Warriors* (New York: Columbia University Press, 1988), 117-37.
43. Among those participating, in addition to Rockefeller and Jackson, were presidential speech writer Walt W. Rostow, Max Millikan of MIT's Center for International Studies, Frederick Dunn of Princeton's Center of International Studies, Ellis A. Johnson of the Operations Research Office, Philip Mosely of Columbia University's Russian Institute, and Stefan Possony, air intelligence specialist for the Department of the Air Force. The group presented its conclusions on the last night of the conference to a group of administration officials, including CIA director Allen Dulles and Harold E. Stassen, special assistant to the president on disarmament. The only major State Department official to participate was Walworth Barbour, who attended the opening session of the conference. See Walt W. Rostow, *Open Skies: Eisenhower's Proposal of July 21, 1955* (Austin: University of Texas Press, 1982), 26-27.
44. Rostow, 37.
45. Robert J. Donovan, *Eisenhower: The Inside Story* (New York: Harper and Brothers, 1956), 345-46.
46. The Soviet proposal called for phased disarmament, including a provision for international inspection teams stationed at ports, railway junctions, highways, and airfields "to ensure that no dangerous concentration of military land forces or of air or naval forces takes place." The inspection proposal apparently constituted a major concession on the part of the Soviets, and hence it gave them a significant advantage on the propaganda front. For the text of the Soviet inspection proposal see Rostow, 114-18.
47. "Jackson's Account of the Evolution of the Open Skies Proposal," reprinted from Log-1955 folder, Box 56, C.D. Jackson Papers, DDE Library, in Rostow, 120.
48. "Jackson's Letters to Eisenhower and Dulles on the Quantico Report," reprinted from Eisenhower Correspondence through 1956 (1), Box 41, and John Foster Dulles, Box 40, C.D. Jackson Papers, DDE Library, in Rostow, 165-66.
49. Donovan, 346.
50. Rostow, 38, 47.
51. "Jackson's Account of Dinner with Dulles on the Eve of His Departure for Geneva and Dulles' Response," reprinted from Log-1955, Box 56, C.D. Jackson Papers, DDE Library, in Rostow, 160.
52. Hugh Morrow, oral history interview with Nelson Rockefeller, 14 July 1977, quoted in Rostow, 49.
53. Nelson A. Rockefeller, "Psychological Strategy at Geneva," 11 July 1955, Geneva Conference, June 18-23, 1955 (1), Box 2, International Meetings Series, Whitman File, DDE Library.
54. Rockefeller, "Psychological Strategy at Geneva," tab 1, 1-4. Emphasis added.
55. Morrow interview, quoted in Rostow, 50.
56. Rostow, 51.

57. "Dulles' Suggestions for Eisenhower's Presummit Talk to the American People," reprinted from President's Opening Statement at Geneva (1), Box 3, Presidential Speech Series, John Foster Dulles Papers, DDE Library, in Rostow, 167.

58. "Radio and Television Address to the American People Prior to Departure for the Big Four Conference at Geneva, July 15, 1955," in *Public Paper, 1955*, 702-3.

59. See "Two Presummit Speech Drafts Submitted to Eisenhower by Rockefeller," reprinted from President's Opening Statement at Geneva, Box 1, Presidential Speech Series, John Foster Dulles Papers, DDE Library, in Rostow, 177-83.

60. "Opening Statement at the Geneva Conference, July 18, 1955," in *Public Papers, 1955*, 708, 710.

61. See "Documents Bearing on the 6:00 P.M. July 20, 1955, Meeting," reprinted from Geneva Conference, July 18-23, 1955 (3), Box 1, International Meetings Series, Whitman File, DDE Library, in Rostow, 104-11.

62. "Statement on Disarmament Presented at the Geneva Conference, 21 July 1955," in *Public Papers, 1955*, 715.

63. Eisenhower, *Mandate for Change*, 521.

64. Spanier and Nogee, 91.

65. Alexander, 97.

66. Eisenhower quoted in Herbert S. Parmet, *Eisenhower and the American Crusades* (New York: Macmillan, 1972), 406.

67. Eisenhower, *Mandate for Change*, 521.

68. Chalmers M. Roberts, *The Nuclear Years: The Arms Race and Arms Control, 1945-1970* (New York: Praeger, 1970), 34.

69. Rostow, 9.

70. Spanier and Nogee, 92.

71. Nelson A. Rockefeller, Memorandum for the President, 25 July 1955, "Rockefeller, Nelson, 1952-55," Box 30, Administration Series, Whitman File, DDE Library.

72. "Opinion Reactions in Western Europe to the Four-Power Conference," 3 August 1955, "Rockefeller, Nelson, 1952-55," Box 30, Administration Series, Whitman File, DDE Library, 11-12.

73. Halle, 335.

74. Chalmers M. Roberts, "Ike and the Cold War Thaw," *Washington Post*, 7 October 1990, D2.

75. From John Foster Dulles's account of a telephone conversation with the President, 6 July 1955, reprinted from White House Telephone Conversations, March-August 1955, Box 10, Telephone Conversation Series, John Foster Dulles Papers, DDE Library, in Rostow, 46.

76. Letter From the Representative at the United Nations (Lodge) to the Deputy Representative on the United Nations Disarmament Commission (Stassen), 11 August 1955, in *Foreign Relations of the United States, 1955-1957*, vol. 20: *Regulation of Armaments; Atomic Energy*, ed. David S. Patterson (Washington: GPO, 1990), 169.

77. See "Correspondence of President Eisenhower and Premier Bulganin on Disarmament and U.S.-Soviet Relations," in U.S. Department of State *Bulletin* 34 (26 March 1956): 517.

78. "Letter from the Representative at the United Nations (Lodge) to the Secretary of State," 3 February 1956, in *Foreign Relations of the United States, 1955-1957*, vol. 20, 314.

79. "President Eisenhower to Premier Nikita Khrushchev, April 8, 1958," in Robert L. Branyan and Lawrence H. Larsen, *The Eisenhower Administration, 1953-1961: A Documentary History* (New York: Random House, 1971), 658. See also "President Eisenhower to Premier Nikolai Bulganin, 2 January 1957," in Branyan and Larsen, 648-49.

80. As Stephen Ambrose has suggested, Eisenhower's decision to propose Open Skies in the first place may have been based, at least in part, on foreknowledge of the U-2 flights; once

they were exposed the Americans were quick to remind the world of their proposal for mutual inspections. After first claiming that the U-2 was a NASA research plane engaged in "high-altitude weather studies," the State Department finally admitted the truth: that such flights had been going on ever since the Open Skies proposal was "rejected out of hand by the Soviet Union." On 9 May, Secretary of State Christian Herter criticized the Soviets for "their continual rejection of our repeated proposals for effective measures against surprise attack and for effective inspection of disarmament measures," and he accused the Soviets of seeking "to exploit the present incident as a propaganda battle in the cold war." Two days later, the president himself reminded the world of Open Skies and also complained about "propaganda exploitation" of the incident. "We prefer and work for a different kind of world," the president declared, but the Soviet "fetish of secrecy and concealment" made spying "a distasteful but vital necessity." See Stephen E. Ambrose, *Ike's Spies: Eisenhower and the Espionage Establishment* (Garden City: Doubleday, 1981), 270; "Statements by National Aeronautics and Space Administration," in U.S. Department of State *Bulletin* 42 (23 May 1960): 817; "Department Statement, May 7," in U.S. Department of State *Bulletin* 42 (23 May 1960): 818-19; "Statement by Secretary Herter, May 9," U.S. Department of State *Bulletin* 42 (23 May 1960): 816-17; "U.S. States Position on U-2 Incident: Statement by President Eisenhower," U.S. Department of State *Bulletin* 42 (30 May 1960): 851-52.

81. "Radio and Television Address to the American People on the Geneva Conference, July 25, 1955," in *Public Papers, 1955,* 728-29.
82. Thomas M. Franck and Edward Weisband, *Word Politics: Verbal Strategy Among the Superpowers* (New York: Oxford University Press, 1981), 117-18.
83. Eisenhower, "The Chance for Peace," 184.
84. Fred I. Greenstein, "Eisenhower as an Activist President: A Look at New Evidence," *Political Science Quarterly* 94 (Winter 1979-80): 587.
85. Rostow, 83.
86. Roberts, "Ike and the Cold War Thaw," D2.
87. "Transcript of Bush's Remarks on Transforming Soviet-American Relations," *New York Times,* 13 May 1989, 6.
88. Maureen Dowd, "Bush Voices Hope on Soviet Change, But With Caution," *New York Times,* 13 May 1989, 6.
89. "Transcript of Bush's Remarks on Transforming Soviet-American Relations," 6.

Eisenhower campaigns in 1956 while Suez and Hungary heat up

Richard B.
Gregg

# The Rhetoric of Distancing
## Eisenhower's Suez Crisis Speech, 31 October 1956

On Wednesday afternoon, 31 October 1956, Emmet John Hughes, one of President Dwight Eisenhower's speech writers, sat in the White House facing a formidable and frantic task. In the span of a few hours, he must write a speech for the president to deliver to the nation and the world. Nineteen fifty-six was a presidential election year, and while campaign rhetoric filled the newspapers and airwaves, two intrusive events demanded that Eisenhower speak.

On 22 October a rebellion against Soviet authority broke out in Hungary as the faculty and students of three universities marched in the streets of Budapest, calling for the return of Imre Nagy as premier. In response to the provocation, secret police forces fired on the demonstrators, and violence continued for a week. Suddenly, Khrushchev announced that mistakes had been made, that the Soviet Union supported more equality in a commonwealth of socialist nations, and that Soviet troops would be removed from Budapest. Hungarian revolutionaries proclaimed victory. The announcement proved to be premature, as Russian troops began to move back into Budapest on the twenty-ninth. But the full extent of the bloody repression to come was not foreseen on the afternoon of the thirty-first as Hughes hurriedly drafted the presidential address scheduled for 7:00 p.m. that evening.

At the White House, the more immediate concern was centered on the Middle East, where, two days earlier following a series of tortuous events and diplomatic exchanges, the American government learned that Israeli paratroopers had been dropped into the Sinai Desert only thirty miles from Suez. While to some this military action might have seemed an intense reprisal by Israel against Egypt, just another of the intermittent bloody skirmishes conducted between Arabs and Israelis over the recent years, Eisenhower knew better. U-2 overflight photos revealed the surreptitious gathering of French military forces at Tolon and Marseilles, and of British forces at Malta and Cyprus. While in the hospital on 27 October for a physical exam—an election-inspired maneuver to demonstrate the robustness of Ike's health—the president sent a message to Israeli Prime Minister David Ben Gurion urging that he

157

do nothing to upset the fragile Middle East peace. His urging was to no avail. On the twenty-ninth, Eisenhower informed Israel, Britain, and the people of the United States that he would go to the United Nations to prevent aggression. On the thirtieth, Ambassador Henry Cabot Lodge introduced a cease-fire resolution that was vetoed in the Security Council by Britain and France. On the thirty-first, the same two nations vetoed a similar Russian resolution. Eisenhower, caught in a touchy international situation, decided to move matters to the U.N.'s General Assembly. In the White House, the decision was made to have the president address the nation. The rhetorical context within which the speech of 31 October would become embedded can be seen by reviewing the days immediately preceding Ike's speech.

On Monday, 29 October, Eisenhower was on a campaign swing in the South. Just before departure from Jacksonville to Richmond where he was scheduled to deliver his final speech of the day, he learned of Israeli troop movements into Egypt. He decided to deliver the Richmond speech as scheduled, then return to Washington for a meeting with his aides. Prior to his arrival back at the White House, a campaign strategy session took place. At that meeting, Republican National Chairman Leonard Hall was urging the president to include a strong plea for the election of a GOP majority in Congress in the last campaign speech he would deliver in Philadelphia. The reply of Sherman Adams, Ike's chief of staff, reflected both Eisenhower's own feeling about his reelection, and the change of focus demanded by the Middle East crisis: "'Look the most use and help the boss can be to all those fellows is to pile up his own majority as high as possible. Hell, with this war on our hands, he may not even get away from his desk to give any speech. If he does, it's fine with me if he talks to a political rally so seriously he doesn't get a single burst of applause.'"[1]

Upon Eisenhower's arrival at the White House, discussion centered on what the response of the United States should be. At first, Hughes believed no public statement would be made that evening, but at 9:00 p.m. Jim Hagerty, press secretary to the president, gave him a brief text to be released to the press. The president's statement revealed that the United States was committed to coming to the aid of any victim of aggression in the Middle East, and that the commitment would be honored. It was a nice moralistic stand, Hughes later recalled, but its meaning regarding how the enforcement was to be employed wasn't clear.

Early the next morning, 30 October, a scheduled campaign trip to Texas was canceled, and Adams suggested that Eisenhower might present a televised report to the nation on this day or the next. But as Hughes later recalled, Eisenhower put off this idea, saying "'No, I'd rather avoid that. Under this damn FCC principle, the other fellows would right away be claiming equal time, and then we'd be in just the sort of public discussion we least need at this time.'"[2]

At the White House there seemed to be general agreement on several issues: that the United States must uphold the Tripartite Agreement in which France,

Britain, and the United States jointly pledged to prevent aggressive actions among countries in the Middle East; that the United States should go to the United Nations to secure passage of a resolution ordering an immediate cease fire, despite the apparent opposition of Britain and France who claimed that Nasser's nationalization of the Suez Canal the previous July rendered the Tripartite agreement moot; and that a special session of Congress might be needed. Around noon, Prime Minister Anthony Eden presented the British House of Commons with an ultimatum for delivery to Israel and Egypt both to withdraw to a distance ten miles from the Suez Canal, and to allow Anglo-French troops into the canal zone ostensibly to maintain the peace. In his continuing effort to determine what was meant by the statement issued the night before, Hughes talked with Eisenhower late in the afternoon, finding him both anxious and overly optimistic. He hoped, noted Hughes, that the British ultimatum might halt the Israeli offensive. If not, the president exclaimed, "'Hell, I don't know where we'll be at.'"[3] A bit after 6:00 p.m. Hughes was called into Sherman Adams's office where a proposal was discussed to have Eisenhower speak to the United Nations in opposition to the actions of Israel, France, and Britain. Hughes believed this approach would not display firm leadership, and suggested a breakfast meeting the next morning to discuss further the specifics of a speech.

Growing strain and consternation revealed itself at breakfast on the thirty-first with the proposal of one staffer that the United States fly an airplane loaded with an atom bomb over the Middle East, threatening to drop it if all sides refused to desist. The meeting ended with Sherman Adams agreeing to ask Secretary of State John Foster Dulles to draft a speech for possible delivery by the president that very night. At this point, Hughes went to Eisenhower to review comments for the campaign speech to be given in Philadelphia the following evening. He found Ike still upset about the actions of America's allies, but responding favorably to Hughes's lines about the need for adherence to international law to prevent aggression.

By midafternoon, plans were set for the delivery of a presidential speech to the nation at 7:00 p.m., and the Oval Office was being prepared for the event. The speech draft itself, however, was not yet written. Dulles's draft did not get to Hughes until 3:15 p.m., and a reading convinced Hughes that it was impossible, reciting and rambling "with no force of argument." Eisenhower was equally disappointed. According to Hughes, the two of them decided "(1) to junk Dulles' draft and start anew; (2) to divide speech equally between events in Hungary and in Egypt; (3) to tone down Dulles' reference to 'irresistible' forces of 'liberation' unleashed in Eastern Europe; (4) to affirm American intent to appeal to UN on Middle East strife; and (5) to relate U.S. position to concept of 'law' in international community."[4] The president then went outside to hit golf balls.

The next several hours were extremely tense for Hughes, as he dictated the speech text to two secretaries typing in relays. Because of time constraints,

Dulles was asked to come to the White House, rather than trying to get the text to him. Hughes describes the scene to the moment of delivery as follows:

> We go past 6:00 still dictating, typing, pencil-editing, with Dulles reviewing text as it comes back from typewriter. He is ashen gray, heavy-lidded, strained. His shoulders seem to sag as he murmurs: "I'm just sick about the bombings . . . the idea of planes over Cairo right now!" He suggests only most trivial word-changes—except for characteristically deleting a temperate phrase about hopes in Hungary ("There seems to appear the dawn of hope") to read confidently: "There is the dawning . . ." Rush to President's bedroom just after 6:15 so he can read text aloud while he dresses. He has just one sub-stantive enjoinder as he starts reading: "I want to be sure we show clearly in here how vital we think our alliances are. Those British—they're still my right arm!" He approves text with scarcely any change and I race back to Cabinet room to start underlining, for speech-emphasis, his large-type reading copy. He enters at 6:45 and sits across from me, as I underscore text with grease pencil and unceremoniously push it across to him page by page. It's four minutes before seven as I hand him last page. He clutches them, jesting: "Boy, this is taking it right off the stove, isn't it?"[5]

One might draw several conclusions from this account. While there was general agreement that the United States was bound by the Tripartite Agreement to prevent aggression in the Middle East, the administration was not sure who the aggrieved party or parties would turn out to be, and thus could not determine on the thirty-first which aggressors might appropriately be the target for pressure. The picture was confounded by the fact that Israel, attempting to draw attention away from Suez so that the French and British could intervene militarily, initiated a substantial military raid against Jordan. On the night of 10 October, Israeli forces had moved against the village of Qalqilya, where fierce fighting ensued. Should such raiding continue, Jordan might call upon Egypt and Britain to come to her aid. The French, who enjoyed a close liaison with Israel, could be drawn in on the opposing side. It was an uncomfortable and ambiguous position for America to be in. Further, as Hughes indicates, while enforcing peace and stability through the United Nations appeared to be appropriate action to take, no one seemed to know quite how enforcement might be practically employed. In light of the felt need for the immediate delivery of a presidential address, the speech text could not undergo the usual procedures for its composition. There was no time for the kind of drafting and redrafting that normally would occur as a result of garnering suggestions from all of the governmental bureaus and agencies that could be effected. Hughes had to rely upon the past experiences he had had with Eisenhower, conversations between the two of them, statements the president had made, and an intimate understanding of Ike's typical ways of behaving. The speech reveals the constraints of the moment. It is brief, reflecting the president's desire to avoid lengthy addresses. The language tends to be simple and direct.

The message gathers its force and form from the abstract principles it employs, typical of Eisenhower's public statements. The speech contains no eloquence friendly to the memory of history. It works within its moment, evokes themes already firmly established, and omits far more than it reveals of the situation at hand. It succeeds in distancing a multitude of ancient and contemporaneous exigencies, and in so doing, achieves its objective.

The context for Eisenhower's speech was complex and variegated. A number of historic events came together in the fall of 1956 to ignite the Suez affair. Space does not allow me to provide a complete accounting of all of those events. But some background is necessary if we are to understand the workings of the speech, its nuances of the past, its portents of the future, its resonances of the moment, and its reflections, selections, and omissions throughout all of them. The thrust of four select historic constraints that converged over time help set the scene.

## HISTORICAL CONSTRAINTS

### Establishment of Israel

On 14 May 1948, with the British mandate in Palestine ending, the Jewish provisional government in Tel Aviv announced by proclamation the establishment of the State of Israel. Eleven minutes after the proclamation, President Harry Truman's press secretary, Charlie Ross, released a statement to the press declaring de facto recognition of the new state.

Even before Israel proclaimed independence, the Egyptian government, on behalf of the countries of the Arab League, announced that force would be used to prevent the imposition of a Jewish state on Palestinian soil. On the day of the Israeli announcement of statehood, Arab League nations were preparing to invade from three directions. In a short time, despite United Nations intervention, armed conflict in the first Arab-Israeli war was underway. In a way, the official response of the United States was a harbinger of things to come in 1956. Americans did not perceive their country's vital interests to be directly involved in the Middle East. The United States was not dependent on the area either for oil or for shipping access, as the countries of Europe were. Responsibility for the area was perceived to be a British, not an American burden. Mideast tension and violence, military thrust and counterthrust, commando raid and counter-raid continued beyond the Truman years into the first term of President Dwight Eisenhower.

### The Need for Oil

A second historical constraint involved British dependence on Middle Eastern oil. By 1912, First Lord of the Admiralty Winston Churchill had become convinced that the British fleet must adopt oil as its source of fuel, replacing coal. During 1913, Churchill waged an intensive campaign to convince the British Parliament of the need to obtain a secure source of oil in the Middle East. After hard argument, Churchill convinced the Parliament to pass a bill allowing the British government to buy controlling shares in the Anglo-Persian oil company. Steady access to oil, argued Churchill, was needed not only for military purposes, but also for the shipment of oil, corn, and the multitude of other commodities to maintain Great Britain's economy.[6] Churchill also championed an idea birthed by Ernest Swinton, a British colonel, who conceived the need for an armored vehicle, moving on land by a traction system, immune to small arms fire, powered by an internal combustion engine. Supported by naval funds provided by Churchill, the experimental vehicle developed under the code names "cistern" and "reservoir" to finally become known by a third code name, "tank."[7]

Increasing mechanization and modernization following World War I assured that Britain, and indeed all of Europe, would quickly come to appreciate Churchill's stand on behalf of the importance of oil. The Suez Canal proved to be a valuable pipeline as Western powers became more and more dependent on oil from the Mideast. By 1955, two-thirds of the shipping through the canal was involved with the transport of petroleum, and two-thirds of that oil found its way to Europe. Thus, it was not surprising that there was growing concern in Britain in the early 1950s as anticolonial feelings festered in the Middle East, encouraged by Egypt's flamboyant new leader, Gamal Abdel Nasser. The concern of British government leaders reached a fever pitch when, in July 1956, Nasser nationalized the Suez Canal, thus assuming the power to close off the canal to international traffic if he chose. Prime Minister Anthony Eden was informed of Nasser's action while attending a royal dinner at 10 Downing Street. The tone of the planned social evening changed. Eden called a cabinet meeting around midnight and began by announcing that "the Egyptian has his thumb on our windpipe."[8] Eden was experiencing a growing desire to retaliate. A few weeks later, Eisenhower, following his political instincts and purposes, warned Eden that it was a mistake to make Nasser seem more important than he really was, but Eden's own view was further bolstered by his foreign office undersecretary, Sir Ivone Kirkpatrick:

> I wish the President were right. But I am convinced that he is wrong. . . . If we sit back while Nasser consolidates his position and gradually acquired control of the oil-bearing countries, he can, and is, according to our information, resolved to wreck us. If Middle East oil is denied to us for a year or two our gold reserves will disappear. If our gold reserves disappear the sterling area disintegrates. If the sterling area disintegrates and we have no reserves we shall not be able to maintain a force in Germany or, indeed, anywhere else. I doubt whether we shall be able to pay for the bare minimum necessary for our defense. And a country that cannot provide for its defense is finished.[9]

As Eden saw it, the welfare of England demanded that Nasser be removed from power; if force was called for, then he was willing to resort to force.

## Cold War Ideology

The third constraint that enveloped the Suez crisis in 1956 was driven by ideology. Broadly speaking, an ideology is a way of viewing events in the world. It is a perspective, a mind set, built upon definitions, concepts, and values that place past phenomena in historical context, provide definition for events of the moment, and project goals and objectives for future attitude and action. An ideology is thoroughly rhetorical in character and pragmatic force. The predominant ideology alive in 1956 was the mind set of the Cold War.

The Cold War was birthed from the debris of World War II, when the United States and the Soviet Union emerged as the world's dominant powers. By purpose and by default, both nations found themselves jockeying for advantageous position by establishing global spheres of influence. The Soviet Union, continuing to occupy Eastern European countries and establishing governments amenable to her purposes, sought to secure a buffer zone beyond Soviet borders. The United States found herself moving into a leadership role on the European continent, partly to fill a power void created by the seriously weakened economies of countries affected by the war and the continued waning of the colonialist control of Britain and France in the face of a burgeoning nationalistic spirit. Immediately after the war, there came an intense focus on the Middle East, where the Soviet Union might gain access to a warm water port, where the United States might protect the economic supply line of the Suez Canal for her Western allies, and where both powers might have access to the petroleum resources of the area. Iran, Greece, and Turkey were the immediate areas of concern.

Fearing the nation might return to an isolationist mood following the war, President Truman delivered a speech to the Congress, broadcast by radio to the nation, in which he placed the plan for strategic containment of the Soviets into a larger ideological conflict. Early in the speech, Truman declared that the foreign policy and the national security of the United States were involved in a grave situation. Truman described Greece as a country devastated by war, where a militant minority, "led by Communists," was threatening Greece's survival as a free and democratic country. The situation in Turkey, said the president, while not as desperate, was extremely serious, for Turkey needed additional aid to modernize in order to maintain its national integrity. "That integrity," said Truman, "is essential to the preservation of order in the Middle East."[10]

Congress voted in favor of the aid package, and the public granted immediate support, beginning an extended debate about how much American commitment Truman was proposing. However, it is clear that the president's speech played a major role in structuring the ideology that would prevail for years to come, an ideology that would justify American involvement around the world. The proximate enemy was Russia, from which the threat of international communism would spread. Communism was portrayed as a sinister threat to freedom around the world in general and to the well-being of the American way of life in particular. The expansion of American influence to the international scene, the actions taken to preserve other governments to create the stability which protected America's welfare, and the regional defense pacts—NATO, SEATO, and the Bagdad Pact—all were included in the policy of containment. The ideological context was one of war; the enemy was granted the status of transcendent importance; the struggle for preeminence became one of survival or death for a whole style of life.[11] Although Eisenhower was elected to be the first Republican president in twenty years, he inherited a firm foreign policy, which enjoyed bipartisan political support and was bolstered by a public concerned with dangers both within and beyond its borders.

### Eisenhower's Persona

The public persona of Dwight Eisenhower must be the fourth major factor in the context of Suez, because his fellow citizens assigned him a unique degree of authority. The door of fame opened to him when at 4:15 a.m., 5 June 1944, in Southwick House near Portsmouth, England, he gave the final order for the great Allied invasion of Europe to commence on the beaches of France. As commander-in-chief, Eisenhower's stature grew as the Allied victories led to the end of the war in the West. His popularity continued throughout a postwar tenure as Army Chief of Staff and NATO commander. By 1948 both major parties in the United States wanted Ike as their candidate. When at last Eisenhower broke his silence about his party affiliation and declared himself to be a Republican, leaders of the GOP's moderate wing won his nomination, culminating in his election to the presidency in 1952.

Throughout his public life Eisenhower gave little impression of having strong political ambition, constantly claiming to dislike the nuts and bolts of practical politics. Yet there can be no doubt that he negotiated his military career with the kind of political acumen and adeptness required for advancement in that area. An important component of his public ethos consisted of his perceived ability to secure cooperation from disparate and disagreeing parties. As Ward Just noted, "His image of affability camouflaged other abilities that he possessed; Eisenhower is often cited as the quintessential bland harmonizer, but that is to misread Eisenhower's career as well as underestimate his considerable energy and strong intelligence."[12] Eisenhower emerged from the war with a hero's status. He was perceived to be confident but modest, cheerful but able to be appropriately stern, direct and candid in speech, paternalistically caring and honest. Throughout all that he did to engender such positive qualities, he revealed little of himself. There was another side. While disavowing politics, he often acted with astute political savvy. Appearing to care greatly for others, he always kept his own credibility clearly in mind. Imbued with candor by others, he tended to reveal only what he believed to be necessary and of rightful interest to others.[13] He took these qualities with him into the White House.

As the end of his first term approached, Eisenhower found himself in an interesting and enviable position. His popularity ratings remained at unprecedented heights. The ending of the Korean War redounded to his credit, and the world seemed essentially at peace. He had managed to place himself above the dangerous machinations of McCarthyism and watched as Senator Joseph McCarthy faded from influence. He had kept heated civil rights issues at a distance and refused to become entangled in the maneuvering to remove Vice-President Richard Nixon from the ticket as his running mate. The general state of the economy was the strongest it had been since World War II. Most importantly, he was successfully convincing the American public that he had fully recovered from his heart attack in 1955 and an operation for ileitis shortly before his renomination. There was little question that he would win reelection.

A facet of historical interest did appear to present a problem to Eisenhower and his aides. By constitutional amendment the president could not hold office for a third term. He therefore felt he needed to win the election by the largest possible margin to be able to wield power and influence in his second, and final, term. The question was not whether Ike would win, but by how much. The problem, as Emmet Hughes saw it, was to avoid losing the campaign while winning the election.[14] Although Eisenhower's carefully controlled campaign went well, his aides remained alert to the attacks being made by his opponent, Adlai Stevenson. The final scare came only shortly before election day. During the fall, Stevenson had accused the Eisenhower administration of being diplomatically inept at ending the growing tension resulting from Nasser's nationalization of the Suez Canal. At a news conference on 12 October 1956, Eisenhower expressed a very optimistic hope that forthcoming negotiations would avert a crisis in the Middle East. But the next day, the Soviet Union used a Security Council veto to block a U.S. resolution proposing an international organization—the Suez Canal Users Association—to assure operation of the Canal. Stevenson's charges appeared on target.

These historical constraints converged with contemporary contextual factors to create the Suez crisis of 1956. Space does not allow a complete recounting of the ambiguous and synergistic events, actions, motives, and outcomes, but a brief recounting of the contemporary context is necessary.

## CONTEMPORARY CONTEXTUAL FACTORS

On the night of 28 February 1955, Israeli paratroopers moved into the Gaza Strip and attacked an Egyptian army camp. It was the most violent and deadly conflict since 1948. The attack put pressure on Nasser to prepare the Egyptian military, humiliated in the war of 1948, for retaliation and defense. In order to upgrade his forces, Nasser decided to turn to the West for arms. One of his first acts was to urge Eisenhower to fulfill a pledge made earlier to provide Egypt with military aid. At the time, America was not heavily involved in or dependent on the Middle East. The Eisenhower administration did not intend to become involved in large shipments of arms to any of the countries in that area. But Eisenhower did not consider Nasser's request to be a major one. Still, out of his deep respect for the British, he delayed shipment of the arms at Churchill's written request. Irritated at the delay, Nasser decided to explore the possibility of getting arms from Russia, and he informed the United States in May that he was exploring such a possibility. The State Department thought that Nasser was applying pressure and decided not to respond to an act of blackmail. Nasser, still hoping to get arms from the West, did not hurry to engage Soviet help, but continued to request aid from the U.S. However, when no positive response came, by end of summer Nasser finally decided to consummate an arms deal with Russia. He first informed the American ambassador of his decision on 23 September 1955, then announced it to his own people on 27 September. Tension immediately grew in the Middle East as Israeli citizens began to donate jewelry to their government to purchase arms in response to Egyptian action.

Nasser initiated another request for aid from the West in 1955, a far more important one than his quest to purchase weapons. His greatest desire was to provide irrigation for new Egyptian farmland and electrical power to stimulate Egypt's industrialization. Word circulated that Russia was willing to finance and build the proposed dam, but Nasser informed the U.S. that he would rather receive aid from the West. Soon thereafter, Eugene Black, an American banker who was president of the International Bank for Reconstruction and Finance of the United Nations, sent engineers to Cairo to investigate possibilities for the project. Despite concern that Nasser might be playing East against West, an Anglo-American offer of aid was announced on 16 December 1955. At approximately the same time, Secretary of State John Foster Dulles convinced the administration of the need for a new, secret attempt to budge Israel and Egypt into a peace treaty by securing permanent boundaries in the Middle East. Eisenhower dispatched an old friend, Robert P. Anderson, to make the attempt. Anderson left on his mission on 9 January 1956. The attempt failed; Ben Gurion insisted on negotiating with Nasser in a public face-to-face meeting, but internal politics forced Nasser to refuse such conditions. The Eisenhower administration did not know that at the same time Ben Gurion was urging the Israeli government to approve a military takeover of the eastern Sinai Peninsula.[15]

During the spring, the Soviet Union suggested an arms embargo of the Middle East under the auspices of the United Nations. Fearful that his arms suppliers might suddenly refrain from helping him, Nasser recognized the government of

Communist China as legitimate. This move added force to an already waning interest on the part of the United States to carry through with its offer to help finance the Aswan Dam. The possibility that Nasser might turn to Russia for aid was irritating to Dulles and others, a feeling exacerbated by the Egyptian recognition of China. In addition, a growing pro-Israeli sentiment against any aid to Arab states was building in the country. Fearing the threat of Egypt's potential ability to produce cheap cotton, agricultural interests from southern states added their voices to those opposing the creation of the dam. Dulles and Eisenhower were coming to the decision that Nasser's influence had to be reduced in the face of growing anti-Western sentiment; they believed that refusing to give Nasser aid was a way to achieve that goal. When the administration was informed that Congress was willing only to appropriate aid to either Tito of Yugoslavia or Nasser, Eisenhower and Dulles chose Tito. On 19 July 1956, the United States informed Nasser that aid for the dam would not be provided. A similar announcement was made by Britain on the following day.[16] On 26 July Nasser nationalized the Suez Canal, and events moved swiftly to armed conflict.

On 27 July Eisenhower learned that Eden might be contemplating military action to retain access to the Canal. Ike believed the matter might be nothing more than contingency planning, but began indicating to Eden that the United States would not allow itself to be drawn into armed conflict. On 28 July, French and British military planners began to confer about the possibility for a joint operation. Israel would soon be invited to join the mix.

France became involved in the Suez affair for her own reasons. There was strong support in French quarters for Israeli objectives following World War II, and France had begun to provide arms to the Israelis. In 1954, as the French attempted to counter the Arab threat, the Algerian uprising against the French led to an increase in the flow of arms to Israel. Stung by defeat in Indochina, France was determined not to lose its remaining important colony. In the midst of these events, the French came to believe that Nasser was aiding the Algerian rebels, both militarily and rhetorically. In the winter of 1956, the French and the Israelis formed a secret pact against Nasser.

Both Eden and Premier Guy Mollet of France came to project Nasser as a fiendish enemy. Both disliked the severe anti-communist attitudes of John Foster Dulles. Both were more willing and interested in exploring openings for accord with the Russians. Meeting together in March, the two leaders discovered they had common cause in the Middle East. On 27 July Britain and France froze all Egyptian assets in retaliation for Nasser's nationalizing the Canal and began to plan a joint military action to retake it. On 1 September, the French invited the Israelis to join the venture. On 14 September Eden and Mollet ordered all non-Egyptian canal personnel to leave their jobs, believing the Egyptians could not operate the canal on their own. This pretext for moving into the canal zone vanished when Egyptian operators proved entirely capable of running a smooth and economical operation.

The period from 1 September to 30 October saw various diplomatic activities that appeared to be attempts to ease tension and avoid war, while behind the scene Britain, France, and Israel continued surreptitious planning for the conflict they each wanted. Dulles proposed a Western power Suez Canal Users Association that was too ambiguous ever to be effective. On 2 October 1956, Dulles announced that the United States would remain aloof from Mideast involvement as the area moved from colonialism to independence. On 5 October, during United Nations debate on Suez, the British and French suggested a new plan for canal operation involving principles they believed Egypt would not accept. To everyone's surprise, Egypt agreed, another pretext for military operations vanished, and the invasion date had to be postponed again. Then, unknown to others, the French proposed to the British that Israel undertake an incursion in the direction of the canal to provide a pretext for British and French intervention. Though surprised at the extent of French collaboration with the Israelis, Eden eagerly agreed. On 14 October Britain placed a blackout on all information to the United States. On 22 October Israel, France, and Britain finalized plans for the start of action on 29 October. During this period, overflights of the new United States U-2 spy plane brought Eisenhower evidence of Israel's military buildup with French arms, and he realized his allies had deceived him. Before starting on a final campaign swing, Eisenhower instructed Dulles to tell Ben Gurion in no uncertain terms that the United States would not support any Israeli military action, and that he would not budge just because a presidential election vote was about to be held. Israeli parachute drops began in the Sinai on 29 October, as planned. Within the confines of this context, historic and immediate, Hughes wrote in an intensely short period of time, and Eisenhower spoke with assurance.

## The Speech of 31 October 1956

The speech as delivered reflected Hughes's understanding of Eisenhower's thought and manner, his conversation with Ike only hours before the presentation, and his notes based on Ike's dictation of the moment. The text is brief, consisting of 39 paragraphs, not counting the salutation and the closing. The length of the paragraphs is brief; 14 of the 39 consist of one sentence only, with 7 occurring in the section dealing with Eastern Europe and 7 pertaining to the Middle East. The first 19 paragraphs are centered on events in Poland and Hungary; the last 29 treat matters in the Middle East.

Brief notes taken as Eisenhower dictated thoughts late on the afternoon of the speech reveal the intent and spirit of some of his ideas. One full paragraph of dictation is concerned with what Ike wanted to say in his introduction. He wanted to emphasize that his comments were not to be taken as campaign rhetoric: "I realize that all of us are now caught up in the throes of a political campaign, but the situations and developments I want to place before you this evening have nothing whatever to do with partisanship." In keeping with such intention, the president will give "a completely factual presentation" so that all voters, regardless of party, can "give personal thought and consideration" to international events.[17] Hughes will modify, tighten, and rearrange the language for the official draft, but the spirit will remain the same. As we shall see, the introduction importantly frames the remainder of the speech.

Eisenhower's dictation then turns to Eastern Europe, specifically to Poland and Hungary; he clearly wants to identify happenings there with ideals firmly nested in American political ideology, such as "love of liberty" and "respect for the dignity of man." These ideals oppose their opposites, "regimentation" and "tyranny." Soviet reaction, continues Eisenhower, could indicate significant change for these peoples. He notes that the United States entertains no ambitions with regard to these countries, but only hopes they may have the opportunity to chart their own independent course of action.

Eisenhower then turns his attention to what he terms "ominous developments in the Mid East." He suggests that "We should think of this situation in terms of concern, but not of hysteria." Then, in vague and rambling fashion, he refers to the many "races, tongues, religions and political nationalities" that are present around the world, each concerned for itself and carrying with it "animosities" that are too often "directed toward their own neighbors," thus threatening the peace. He states that all of these factors are present in the Mideast "on a vast and intensive scale" with antagonisms that were "lost in legend." At this point, the dictated notes end. Eisenhower's comments about the Middle East situation seem to reflect the ambiguities and uncertainties that the administration perceived to be present and that were, in fact, existing. They may also give some evidence of the uncertainty regarding a course of action to be taken to end the conflict just begun and to ease tensions in the area.

Our focus now turns to a close examination of the speech addressed to the nation at 7:00 p.m., 31 October 1956. A presidential speech dealing with matters of substance and importance can serve several functions at once. It can provide information that may help give definition to the situation at hand. It can present justification for actions to be proposed or announced. By articulating such actions, it serves as a statement of policy. Eisenhower's speech does all of these. But inevitably, it will do more. All public addresses constitute a form of symbolic inducement, a factor that functions rhetorically in all symbolic acts. That is, it will invite members of the audience to perceive phenomena in a particular way, to adopt attitudes toward them, to evaluate and value them, and to situate them in a larger symbolic context. In so doing, it will necessarily be selective, emphasizing some options while closing off others, and ignoring some possibilities altogether. Eisenhower's speech on this occasion must be explicated on several different levels.

## ANALYSIS OF THE TEXT

The president begins his remarks with a direct and simple statement: "Tonight I report to you as your President."[18] The statement is one of obvious fact, hardly needing mention. Even as an obvious fact, however, it begins to function in a directive fashion, for it shifts emphasis away from Eisenhower, the person, to Eisenhower the president. While it is difficult to separate persona from office, the presidency is an institution that can evoke historic, mythic nuances of national inclusiveness. It is an institution that represents all the diversity of the peoples of the nation, standing somehow above and apart from partisan, sectarian differences. In his study of the presidency, Thomas Cronin points out that Americans hold paradoxical expectations of the office and those elected to hold it. To be sure, we expect presidents to be practically and pragmatically effective, to know how to initiate and guide policy, to be programmatically adept. Such achievements obviously require tough political skills. But we also want a president who will express the national purpose and gain public commitment to it, uphold the laws of the country, and establish an agenda that arouses our highest aspirations.[19] As Cronin points out, "The Presidency necessarily changes with the incumbent, the crisis, and the season, but the constants are greater than is usually appreciated."[20]

We should note that the mythic separation of the office of the presidency from the everyday world of politics was more easily held in the 1950s than it is now after the disillusioning experiences of Vietnam, Watergate, and the Iran-Contra affair. We should also note that the public persona of Eisenhower was that of a person who only reluctantly entered the world of politics and who responded to duty much more than to political advantage. It was an image he encouraged and, to a large extent, was what he honestly felt. He was not loath to take advantage of the image, however, to enhance his credibility. On this occasion, Ike's reference to the office not only reflected his credibility, it served to separate and to demarcate his comments from the ongoing presidential campaign. His following remarks emphasized the separation:

> We all realize that the full and free debate of a political campaign surrounds us. But the events and issues I wish to place before you this evening have no connection whatsoever with matters of partisanship. They are concerns of every American—his present and his future.

The term "partisanship" has the potential to evoke more than just the thought that the issues and events Eisenhower will place before the public are not to be considered political matters. Considered in such a manner, they would be rendered neutral. To consider them in a bipartisan fashion, however, would be to cast a more positive light on their character, for starting in 1947 the term "bipartisan" became an integral part of American thinking about foreign policy. The Truman administration, in fashioning the policy of containment, sought to gain the support of influential Republican party leaders to help secure congressional and public backing. It was successful in the attempt, and though there was constant need to reinforce and maintain the concept of "bipartisanship" the idea that political divisions stopped at the water's edge became an essential ingredient of the Eisenhower administration as well. A bipartisan approach would tend to dull the edges of potential debate, an objective Eisenhower clearly had in mind. It seems likely that he wished to evoke connotations of bipartisanship in this paragraph.

The next paragraph continues the process of symbolically distancing Eisenhower from the political affairs of the moment. The audience will be given "a report of essential facts so that you—whether belonging to either one of our two great parties, or to neither—may give thoughtful and informed consideration to this swiftly changing world scene." Instead of talking of "issues," which are often framed within the context of differing views, Eisenhower will present "facts." Rather than calling for debate, the president encourages "thoughtful consideration."

These two paragraphs of introduction operate as an attempt to frame the major content of the speech, to place boundaries around it, to bracket it out from the rhetoric of a campaign and place it on a more elevated plane of statesmanship. With this directive prologue delivered, Eisenhower turns to his major topics of the evening. He will talk first about Eastern Europe and then about the Mideast. We shall first consider his comments in light of his intention to present "essential facts."

Though events in Eastern Europe would not seem to be our major concern, Eisenhower's comments about them are worth our brief attention. Eastern Europe is the first subject taken up by Eisenhower following the introduction and illustrates the way the tone established in the introduction is further developed. In this sense, the first section of the speech influences response to the second. Further, the manner or style in which the "essential facts" of the speech are presented is maintained throughout the speech. Once again, any authoritativeness established in the first part easily extends into the second. Finally, though the two topics discussed are structured and presented in a way that encourages one to perceive their separateness, in reality they are of a piece both substantively and strategically.

Because the statements of fact presented by Eisenhower are imbedded in the usual linguistic units of articles, prepositions, modifiers, and amplifiers, one must abstract and restate them in order to arrive at those that are essential. They are as follows:

> Following World War II, the Soviet Union used military force to impose puppet governments on the countries of Eastern Europe.

The United States helped keep alive the hope of freedom for these countries, though force could not be used to do so.

A few days ago, the people of Poland took action to secure a peaceful transition to a new government.

More recently, Hungary is struggling to achieve free nationhood.

Yesterday the Soviet Union issued a statement indicating a need to modify policy to meet the demands of the people.

The fervor of these peoples brings hope for freedom.

Favorable Soviet reaction will advance justice, trust, and understanding among nations.

Following the paragraphs in which these essentials are presented and elaborated, Eisenhower declares: "These are the facts." In the final two paragraphs of this section, he outlines American policy, indicating that the United States is ready to assist these countries who are trying to achieve independence and will place no demands on them nor entertain any ulterior motives. Though Eisenhower was addressing policy matters at this point, his presentation continued in a factual manner.

Linguistic terms surrounding the essential facts almost inevitably provide partisan interpretation of those facts. In addition, statements of attitude, judgment, opinion, and bias can take on the flavor of factuality when mingled with facts in a statement emphatically billed as factual. So it was in this speech. Eisenhower begins the section by declaring, "In Eastern Europe there is the dawning of a new day." He ends his factual segment by saying, "We have rejoiced in all these historic events." These are bracketing statements, strongly implying finality to changes announced within. In actuality, of course, they expressed hopes soon to be dashed, especially those pertaining to Hungary. The spirit of bipartisanship, which the president hoped to pervade his message, is stated again in the third paragraph of this section, as he refers to events in Eastern Europe: "It has been consistent United States policy—without regard to political party—to seek to end this situation." Thus, the tone of the introduction is maintained. When explaining the policy further, he places the approach of the United States in the larger, idealistic context of the United Nations: "We could not, of course, carry out this policy by resort to force. Such force would have been contrary both to the best interests of the Eastern European peoples and to the abiding principles of the United Nations." This is the first time the United Nations is mentioned. It will be referred to ten other times directly, and there are several other indirect but clear references to it, all of them in the section dealing with the Middle East. As we shall see, this number of references to the international organization in such a short address signals its symbolic importance.

In this portion of the speech, facts nestle among elements of situational fixing, and elements of situational fixing body forth facts. The essential facts, then, become these: nations in Eastern Europe, especially Poland and Hungary, are attempting to gain their independence from Soviet domination. The Soviet Union has indicated a willingness to be more amenable to such a goal. The United States is willing to support those countries that gain independence with economic aid. Adhering to the principles of the United Nations, the United States has not used force in the past and will not use force now or in the future.

Eisenhower then turns to the longest portion of his speech dealing with the Middle East, where he acknowledges the existence of a somber situation. He quickly moves to proscribe boundaries around the extent and intensity of affairs in that region: "It is not a situation that calls for extravagant fear or hysteria. But it invites our most serious concern." This is an important defining statement, based not upon the facts per se, but upon facts as they are placed in interpretation. As we observe Eisenhower's discursive development of "the facts," we shall be alert to matters of interpretation that slip in.

He begins once again with historical description, pointing out that after World War II all countries in the Middle East won independence, and that the state of Israel was mandated from Palestinian territory. While legally true, the emotional reality was that the spirit of colonialism continued as a presence, especially in the minds of British leaders who were loath to lose the military base they had occupied for years on the Suez Canal. The psychological urge that Nasser symbolized was the felt Egyptian need to be free of British physical presence in Egypt. In his next paragraph, the president acknowledges the continuing irritation of colonialism, tensions springing from the establishing of Israel as a state, and the long-standing struggles among Arabs themselves.

> These historic changes could not, however, instantly banish animosities born of the ages. Israel and her Arab neighbors soon found themselves at war with one another. And the Arab nations showed continuing anger toward their former colonial rulers, notably France and Great Britain.

Through all of the conflict in the postwar period, Eisenhower stated, the United States worked to bring peace and stability in the area, but passion continually threatened peace and the Middle East suffered from "almost continuous fighting." In a statement immediately preceding this one, he restated America's approach to the area as he had done consistently in public statements: "We have considered it a basic matter of United States policy to support the new State of Israel and—at the same time—to strengthen our bonds both with Israel and with the Arab countries."

These are indeed statements of fact, but it is often the case that the full meaning of facts is shorn from them when interpretation and explanation is missing. For instance, what form did the efforts to establish peace and stability take? A bit later in the speech, Eisenhower provides some explanation of his administration's action in the immediate situation. Noting responses to Nasser's nationalizing of the canal, the president says:

> Now there were some among our allies who urged an immediate reaction to this event by use of force. We insistently urged otherwise, and our wish prevailed—through a long succession of conferences and negotiations for weeks—even months—with participation by the United Nations. And there, in the United Nations, only a short while ago, on the basis of agreed principles, it seemed that an acceptable accord was within our reach.

But he quickly explains that worsening relations between Egypt and Israel, France, and Great Britain led the latter powers to conclude they must protect their vital interests with force.

As he had earlier emphasized America's forswearing of force in the affairs of Eastern Europe, so he remains consistent by rejecting the use of force in the Middle East. He believes our allies are mistaken in their decision to do so, and pledges that this nation will refrain from military action in the current situation: "In the circumstances I have described, there will be no United States involvement in these present hostilities." He had stated earlier that use of force in Eastern Europe would not have been in keeping with the principles of the United Nations. Now he observes that the allied use of force could "scarcely be reconciled with the principles and purposes of the United Nations to which we have all subscribed." The president's explanation of America's working for peace and stability, then, features negotiation among the parties and points toward moving the negotiations to the level of the United Nations should they fail at the "local" level. The continuing efforts of the United States are placed under the canopy of the idealistic goals of the established international organization created to promote peace throughout the world. The direction of involvement here is not only away from force, but also away from unilateral involvement. The realities of past unilateral involvement and the possibility of such future involvement are never mentioned; the Suez Crisis will not sit on the doorway of American concern and therefore need not arouse unreasonable anxiety. As we shall see, this is a highly selective presentation of the facts.

Eisenhower's explanation of the concrete events culminating in the immediate crisis is direct, forceful, and helpful to the perspective he is attempting to establish. In a situation already tense, Egypt "aggravated" matters by rearming itself with communist weapons. On 26 July, it "seized" the canal. Believing that force was necessary, on the previous Sunday, Israel mobilized and on Monday "penetrated" into Egypt, closing down the canal. On Tuesday, the British and French governments delivered a twelve hour "ultimatum" to Israel and Egypt to call a truce, and attacked Egypt when it was ignored. Then comes a final descriptive statement of absolute fact, presented in a manner that reveals none of the anger the president felt: "The United States was not consulted in any way about any phase of these actions. Nor were we informed of them in advance."

There are two observations that must be made about Eisenhower's characterization of these events. First, while Egypt is pictured as triggering immediate events by purchasing communist arms and "seizing" the canal, the allies made a mistake to respond by force. Thus, America's intention to maintain a balanced approach to Mideast affairs is maintained; all parties share blame in the imbroglio. Further, the allies error is the more egregious because they did not share their plans with the United States, a fact of great service to the strategy of the speech. The United States is not to blame for what has happened. Events are removed from our intentions and policies; we could not intervene to head off trouble through negotiations. At the same time, we are not obligated to join our long-standing allies in their cause, especially with use of force. Eisenhower announces that "as it is the manifest right of any of these nations to take such decisions and actions, it is likewise our right—if our judgment so dictates—to dissent." Such action, he insists, does not lessen our friendship with these nations whom we know to have been subjected to repeated provocations. Their action, he declares, is not only inconsistent with the purposes and principles of the United Nations, but on a practical level, "We are forced to doubt that resort to force and war will for long serve the permanent interest of the attacking nations."

What then shall the administration's policy be? Eisenhower's reply is reassuring. While alert to all possibilities, it will remain "the dedicated purpose of your government to do all in its power to localize the fighting and to end the conflict." Plans to achieve the objective are presented. The American resolution calling for an end to the conflict will be offered in the United Nations General Assembly, thus avoiding rejection by veto. Then, in a summary of factual hope, Eisenhower concludes the policy portion of his address: "In the past the United Nations has proved able to find a way to end bloodshed. We believe it can and that it will do so again."

The essential facts as Eisenhower outlines them are seen as follows: The Middle East had long experienced tension. Tension increased when Egypt purchased communist arms and nationalized the Suez Canal. To protect what they perceived to be their vital interests, Israel, France, and Britain tried to retake the canal by use of force. In an attempt to end the conflict, the United States would move the conflict to the United Nations.

The facts presented in this speech are foregrounded against the ideology of the Cold War, an ideology publicly articulated in 1946 by Winston Churchill and Americanized by President Harry Truman in his famous speech to the Congress and the people on 12 March 1947, urging support for an aid program for Greece and Turkey. The Truman Doctrine speech structured a justification for American aid within a framework of good and evil, wherein the United States would provide support for democratic peoples who desired to thwart the imposition of alien forms of government inimical to freedom and independence. Truman's justification seemed to suggest that the United States should be willing to aid any nation that appeared to be so threatened. With his election in 1952, Eisenhower appeared to pick up the gauntlet which Truman had cast. In his inaugural address Ike said, "The world and we have passed the midway point of a century of continuing challenge. We sense with all our faculties that forces of good and evil are massed and armed and opposed as rarely before in history."[21] And later in the speech he said, "Freedom is pitted against slavery; lightness against dark."[22]

In Eisenhower's speech of 31 October 1956, the terminology of the first section on Eastern Europe evokes the imagery of the Cold War. After World War II, it was the Soviet Union that "used military force to impose on the nations of Eastern Europe, governments of Soviet choice—servants of Moscow." The peoples of Eastern Europe, particularly Poland and Hungary, were the victims "over-run by wartime armies." But the Poles possessed a "proud and deathless devotion to freedom," and the brave Hungarians "have offered their very lives for independence from foreign masters." Poland strives for "national independence" and Hungary for "full and free nationhood." It is the United States that has kept alive the goal of freedom and who is ready now to provide economic aid to those moving toward democracy and independence. These descriptions resonate with the spirit of the Cold War. But in the section dealing with the Mideast, there is only a fleeting reference to communism and none to the adversarial relationship of Russia and the United States. However, as we shall see, Russia very much figured in the internal thinking of the administration.

I turn now to examine Eisenhower's speech as strategy. Despite a long-standing myth in our society that our presidents are representative of all the people and despite the fact that in the inaugural addresses that symbolically begin their first term in office newly elected presidents like to claim their victory elevates them suddenly above the politics of party, few presidential statements transcend partisan impact. Eisenhower may have come closer to being perceived in a nonpartisan role than other presidents of this century. There are several reasons for any success he may have had in that regard. He remained aloof from politics throughout his military career and seemed a reluctant politician when he finally declared. He often revealed that he did not like campaigning or the grit of everyday party politics. And he seemed to be honestly motivated by his perceived need to elevate the presidency above the barnyard clatter of partisan wrangling. The speech we are focusing on here, however, can clearly be understood as a piece of political strategy.

As strategy, the speech operated to distance the events, to which Eisenhower refers, from the United States and thus from any major concern of the American public. This was accomplished by bracketing events and by placing boundaries around them in such a way that the arena of action was not allowed to impinge upon vital concerns of the country.

The president's attempt to place the issues and events he wants to discuss beyond the range of partisanship is itself a partisan strategy. We saw earlier that he expressed his preference for not delivering a speech at all. He did not want to give the Democrats an opportunity to respond to him or call attention to issues that might be embarrassing so late in his campaign for reelection. But matters pressed upon him and upon public attention, and he had to make a statement. He tried to remove his speech from the context of the presidential campaign by announcing that it was so removed. Therefore he would deal only with "essential facts" so that citizens need not be aroused to do more than thoughtfully consider the world scene. He places the entire address off limits, politically speaking.

The chances that his introductory remarks might be accepted at face value were rather good. Eisenhower's aides were often surprised at how accepting the American public was of him, no matter what he said or did. As Bryce Harlow put it:

> Eisenhower liked people so people liked Eisenhower, . . . Eisenhower trusted people; therefore they trusted Eisenhower. Eisenhower could fall flat on his tokhus out in public, do something very wrong or very stupid, make a big goof, and the American people would rush forward as one and grab him and pick him up and dust him off and say, "Don't bother at all about that. We like Ike." And on he'd go.[23]

In this instance, Eisenhower's positive persona would act to make his distancing strategy acceptable as nonstrategy.

We turn now to the bracketing and placing of events as they are described in the body of the speech. In order to gain a sense for the strategy of distancing that occurs, I shall be concerned with how Eisenhower characterizes problems, the actions that he deems appropriate in light of conditions, and the role he announces for the United States to play. I shall also indicate that what was ignored, not stated, bracketed out by silence, helps us understand how very different the distancing might have been and how much closer to American shores the events discussed could have been perceived.

Eisenhower was able to portray the postwar status of Hungary and Poland quickly. He assigned blame for their subjugation equally quickly; the Soviets were placed easily in the devil role assigned to them in America's Cold War ideology. During the years when they were occupied, the purpose of the United States, said the president, was to keep alive the hope for freedom. As Eisenhower describes the scene, Poland appeared to have succeeded in effecting change to a more representative form of government. The Hungarian situation was more dangerous as "this brave people, as so often in the past, have offered their very lives for independence from foreign masters." But the president intimated that success was in the offing, with "a new Hungary . . . rising from this struggle, a Hungary which we know from our hearts will know full and free nationhood." In response to these pressures, the Soviet Union was indicating a willingness to loosen control.

Up to this point, America's role, as explained by Eisenhower, could be likened to that of providing support by example and serving as interested spectator. The United States joined the rest of the world in watching the struggle and "rejoicing in all these historic events." Should the promise of liberty be realized, then the United States was ready to assist these new governments with economic aid without strings, making clear to the Soviet Union that we did not wish to convert them to military allies.

Eisenhower could have pictured the action in Eastern Europe to be much closer to certain American interests and efforts. In May 1952, *Life* magazine carried an article by Dulles in which he proposed new directions in foreign policy. He had sent the piece to Eisenhower earlier, both to influence Ike who seemed likely to win the Republican party's nomination for the presidency and to enhance his own prospects for being chosen secretary of state. In the essay, Dulles began by disagreeing with the Truman Doctrine and the policy of containment. He argued that the policy was essentially passive, aimed toward living with communism rather than actively defeating it around the world.

To alter the course, the first step to be undertaken, wrote Dulles, was for the free world to organize militarily so that it could retaliate instantly against communist aggression anywhere it might occur and by any means at its disposal. The expressed philosophy here was one that fully included the possibility of nuclear war. Once this perspective was established, argued Dulles, a political offensive could be launched, based on the belief that moral superiority was the great spiritual weapon of the free world that could be used to encourage the overthrow of communist dictatorships around the world.

To help achieve such an objective, Dulles proposed that the United States announce publicly that it expected such liberation to occur, an act which, of itself, would mobilize occupied countries to action. Then, more specifically, the United States would make no deals confirming Moscow's domination and would end diplomatic relations with puppet governments if that would promote peace. On the positive side, America would welcome task forces in other countries to develop peace programs, encourage democratic leaders to escape from behind the Iron Curtain, coordinate the Voice of America and private committees to aid freedom activities, and coordinate economic aid programs with such efforts. The result would be the proclaiming of a whole new international Declaration of Independence. Dulles ended by asserting that the United States wanted no uprisings or reprisals as a consequence of any of this.[24]

An examination of Dulles's proposed new doctrine reveals troublesome ambiguities and a glaring lack of concrete practical measures to be taken. Emmet John Hughes, at the time working as foreign affairs editor of *Life*, kept trying to get Dulles to be more specific but with no results, as Townsend Hoopes reports:

"'What are you proposing that U.S. policy should do?' Hughes kept asking. But Dulles, leaning against the mantelpiece in his library on Ninety-first Street, remained entirely vague concerning the operational implications."[25]

While Dulles wanted to emphasize a new boldness in his approach, the fact is some of Dulles's guidelines had been articulated earlier in a Draft Report, National Security Council Staff, 30 March 1949, for President Harry Truman. Pertinent items, listed under the heading "Foreign Information Program," are these:

> The United States should strengthen, maintain and intensify for as long as necessary, a vigorous coordinated foreign information program directed primarily toward the USSR and its armies, Soviet satellites, countries where there is a serious communist threat, and countries not sufficiently aware of real Soviet objectives.
>
> a. Stress the fact that the Western way of life increasingly offers greatest and most enduring benefits to the individual, and is therefore destined to prevail over the communist ideology with its inevitable police state methods.
>
> b. Endeavor to strain the relationships between Moscow and satellite governments by encouraging the latter to take independent action within the United Nations and elsewhere.[26]

Evidence shows that in 1950 Eisenhower promoted the efforts of Radio Free Europe, and that from then on RFE had bombarded Eastern Europe with exhortations to shed the evil of communism and strive for freedom. Evidence also shows that the Hungarian revolutionaries were spurred by what they understood to be the promise of American aid that was never forthcoming, and that they felt betrayed when their pleas for help went unanswered. Finally, evidence shows that RFE played a role in so antagonizing the Russians that the Kremlin ordered fresh troops back into Hungary to quell the rebellion in the days following Eisenhower's speech of 31 October, resulting in the deaths of over thirty thousand Hungarians. The emptiness of Dulles's bold proposals proved fatal.[27]

In his speech of 31 October, Eisenhower does not mention Dulles's doctrine nor does he draw any connections between it and America's involvement in Eastern European affairs via psychological provocation. America observes. America supports from afar. America will not get involved at the moment of decision. America will remain at peace.

In the section of his address dealing with the Middle East, Eisenhower also distanced problems in that region but in a different way. His explanation of factors leading to the military confrontation between Egypt and Britain, France, and Israel are explained in a cursory fashion. Though the countries of the Middle East gained their independence from colonial powers following World War II, old enmities and tensions remained. The establishment of Israel as a state further compounded the problems. Through all the difficulties, the United States remained evenhanded in its support. Tension did not ease, however, and the Egyptians triggered the immediate conflict by purchasing arms from communist powers and "seizing" the Suez Canal. In response to Egyptian action, Britain, France, and Israel collaborated to use military force to regain control of the canal.

The United States was not informed of the allies' military plans nor was such action supported at any time. The United States was thus no factor in the cause of the problem. But unlike Eastern Europe, we would attempt to play a role in solving the matter and restoring peace to the area. We would do so by attempting to localize the problem. We would thus place it away from us in a way that would not require us to intervene militarily. We would attempt to force the problem to a transcendent state, above nations, so to speak, by moving it to the level of the United Nations and put our faith in that organization to find a way to achieve peace. In support of its effort, we would constantly uphold and support the principles of the U.N.

The ending paragraphs of Eisenhower's speech constitute an encomium to the United Nations in which idealism and pragmatism run together. The president announces his belief that "the processes of the United Nations represent the soundest hope for peace in the world," and therefore those processes must be "further developed and strengthened," particularly the U.N.'s "ability to secure justice under international law." War, says Eisenhower, is not the solution to present difficulties in the Mideast, and the code of international conduct must be applied evenly to all:

> The peace we seek and need means much more than the mere absence of war. It means the acceptance of law, and the fostering of justice in all the world.

> To our principles guiding us in this quest we must stand fast. In so doing we can honor the hopes of all men for a world in which peace will truly and justly reign.

Submitting the Mideast conflict to the United Nations was an act of ultimate distancing, placing the bracketed, thus localized, region of difficulty above the United States to the level of international concern in the United Nations General Assembly. There, we might conclude, the ideals of the United States would be subsumed under the principles of peace and justice for all. At the same time, we might also conclude that the interests of the United States would be psychologically removed from the status of a national concern. The symbolic inducement of shifting concern to the level of the United Nations should be appreciated for its potential to evoke positive response. As J. Fred McDonald points out in his study of the development and impact of television on this country, "early coverage of the proceedings of the U.N. General Assembly helped to popularize that international organization and reverse traditional isolationist American foreign policy."[28] We must also remember that Eisenhower's appointment of Henry Cabot Lodge, Jr. to be the United States Ambassador to the U.N. was an indication of the importance of that post at the time the appointment was made.

Once again, the nature of the problem and its placement in relation to the United States could have been radically different. Two significant topics were not mentioned in the Mideast section of the speech either of which could have drastically altered perception. The first has to do with the involvement of Russia in the whole affair and the second with the importance of the major international commodity of the Middle East, oil.

Though Russia was not directly mentioned in the portion of the speech dealing with the Mideast, there can be no doubt that possible Russian intrusion into the affair was of primary concern to the Eisenhower administration. At the time of the speech there was a special agony. Just as the West appeared to be in a position to savor a "victory" over communism in Eastern Europe, the Mideast posed a dilemma and a possible no-win situation for the United States. America could come to the aid of Egypt and risk alienating allies of long standing, or she could come to the aid of Britain, France, and Israel and alienate the Arab nations at a time when Arab nationalism seemed sure to prevail over colonial influence. In either case, the Russians might gain advantage from the outcome.

In private correspondence to his boyhood friend, Swede Hazlett, Eisenhower expressed his personal concern:

> The existence of this problem does not make sleeping any easier—not merely because of the things I recite above, but because of the opportunities that we have handed to the Russians. I don't know what the final action of the United Nations on this matter will be. We are struggling to get a simple cease-fire and, with it, compulsion on both sides to start negotiations regarding the Canal, withdrawal of troops, and even proper reparations. But the possibility that both sides will accept some compromise solution does not look very bright, and every day the hostilities continue the Soviets have an additional chance to embarrass the Western world beyond measure.[29]

The possibility of Russian intrusion was a primary justification that Eisenhower used early in the fall with Eden to try to keep affairs with Nasser low-key in an attempt to defuse rather than increase tension. While Russia sent signals that she might provide military support to Egypt, Eisenhower never believed the possibility was real. Nor did the president ever really believe that material support should be provided by the United States to Britain, France, or Israel. He emphatically believed that the influence of Britain and France would continue to wane around the world and that the United States must therefore avoid being identified too closely with these former colonial powers lest important leverage be lost with the Arab nations. Israel he considered to be a clear aggressor in the affair, and he believed America must not be seen to support aggression.

But the fear persisted that Russia might enlarge her influence in the Middle East, primarily by forcing the United States to become publicly identified with Britain and France. One of the ways this might be achieved would be for the Soviet Union to move first with a resolution in the United Nations calling for a cease-fire. If that happened, the administration felt sure that the Soviet proposal would take a form that would condemn Britain and France as aggressors and force the United States to take sides. Thus, the conflict in the Middle East would not be just a localized affair, but a part of the worldwide Cold War. The evidence revealing this perspective can be found in the official summaries of meetings that occurred in the days following Eisenhower's speech.

On 1 November 1956, at a regularly scheduled meeting of the National Security Council, the subject of Russia was of central concern. Eisenhower made it clear that except for a briefing by the director of central intelligence on the situation in Hungary, he wanted the discussion to center on the Middle East. Following the briefing, he asked John Foster Dulles to bring the NSC up to date on Mideast diplomatic developments. Following a brief summary of the military activities of Britain, France, and Israel, Dulles turned to activities at the U.N. Since Britain and France had vetoed the United States peace resolution in the Security Council, a meeting of the General Assembly was called for 5:00 p.m., when the position of the United States would be considered. Dulles warned that we must be prepared to exercise our leadership in this matter because if we did not, leadership would be seized by the Russians. Dulles went on to warn, however, that asserting our leadership would cause a problem because for years the United States had been walking a tightrope between our allies, Britain and France, and newly independent countries around the world trying to shed colonialism. In view of pressures coming from independent countries, Dulles stated he did not believe we could walk the tightrope any longer. Unless the United States asserted leadership, the independent countries would turn to Russia, and we would be looked upon forever as being tied to colonialism. Dulles asserted his strong belief that Britain and France could not win.

Secretary of Defense Charles Wilson argued for more time and Secretary of the Treasury George Humphrey said the United States should defer action until an aggressor was defined. Dulles said that to follow this course would allow the Russians to introduce their resolution first, that they would declare Britain and France to be aggressors, and that the Soviet resolution would win by acclamation. Thus, we would lose our leadership. Further, if we did not support the Russian resolution, the United Nations would not survive a failure to act on the great issues in the Near Middle East. After further discussion, the president closed the meeting by saying he agreed with Dulles, and he believed the United States must do something with vigor to assert leadership or the Soviets would take over leadership from us.[30]

A week later, the National Security Council met again. During this meeting, Russia's Middle East activities, apparently directed toward keeping the Arab countries stirred up, were noted. On the morning following the NSC meeting, the administration was scheduled to brief the leadership of the Congress. Briefing strategies were discussed. Eisenhower emphasized that, above all, everyone involved in the briefing should bear in mind that the real enemy of the United States was Russia, not Cairo or Tel Aviv.[31] The summary of the leadership meeting shows that Eisenhower reminded everyone that Moscow remained the big enemy and that, despite a family fight, America's alliance with Western Europe remained strong.[32]

The possibility of Russia somehow gaining a Cold War victory in the Middle East was a recurrent theme in the administration's thinking during the crisis. But the speech delivered to the nation on 31 October 1956, made no mention of the concern. As noted earlier, Russia's role in Eastern Europe, discussed in the first section of the speech, was clearly described. But there was no direct reference to Russia in the second section dealing with the Middle East and only one brief mention of communism. The very separation of the discussion of Eastern European affairs from problems in the Mideast served to diminish the immediacy of Russia and the Cold War.

In hindsight, it may seem strange that the major commodity of the Middle East—oil—was never mentioned. Space does not allow me to recount the history of the development of oil in that region. To fully understand how Eisenhower avoided the subject entirely would require a lengthy explanation. At the time of the Suez Canal crisis, the United States was not particularly dependent on the Middle East for oil. America was in possession of a huge oil surplus and had access to other areas of the world for more should the need arise. However, the opposite was true for Great Britain. She was highly dependent on Middle East oil, and other member nations of the Western Allies would suffer as well. This situation could have an impact on NATO's ability to respond firmly to a military threat from communism should such a threat occur. When Nasser sank ships to totally block the Suez Canal shortly after hostilities began, Britain's outlook was bleak. As the crisis unfolded during the fall, Eisenhower established a Middle East Emergency Committee to consider plans for providing alternate oil supplies. And at various meetings of the administration, the problems of oil shortage in Western Europe often were discussed. While the severity of the shortages over time were fully realized, Eisenhower steadily made it clear that the United States would not facilitate the sending of emergency supplies until a truce was reached, hostile troops withdrawn, and a U.N. peace force in place in the areas of conflict. "I'm inclined to think," he told aides, "that those who began this operation should be left to work out their own oil problems—to boil in their own oil, so to speak."[33] And he informed the congressional leaders at the meeting cited earlier that any considerations about oil were being withheld from public discussion so that focus would remain on the need to stop the fighting.

It was not surprising when Britain announced the beginning of fuel rationing on 7 November; if American aid was not forthcoming, there would have to be rationing throughout Western Europe in the winter months ahead. In addition, the English faced fundamental economic difficulties across the board. Early in the fall, a run began on Britain's financial reserves. With the beginning of the attack on Suez, the run increased dramatically. There was a suspicion in London that the drain had been at least aided and abetted by the United States if not instigated by the Eisenhower administration. Whether true or not, responding to pressure from the United States, the International Monetary Fund refused to provide aid when Britain appealed for help. When the threat of an American embargo on oil to Britain and France surfaced, Anthony Eden knew the game was up. At the end of November, Britain and France pledged to remove their troops from Egypt. Eisenhower then began to ease restrictions on emergency aid to Western Europe. Oil, the primary coin of exchange in the Middle East and a commodity to become increasingly important to the United States, although never mentioned in Eisenhower's speech, was a potent weapon in his hands during the crisis.

Israel proved more difficult to deal with. While agreeing to a cease fire and a withdrawal of troops, the Israeli government claimed that Gaza did not belong to Egypt, and therefore the occupation would become permanent in that area. Despite growing Jewish pressure within the United States, Eisenhower refused to budge on a series of economic embargo measures he was ready to enforce through the United Nations. Finally, when other countries supported the American position, the Israelis began total withdrawal on 16 March 1957.

## CONCLUSION

What emerges from beneath Eisenhower's speech of 31 October 1956, a speech of idealism, upholding principle, law, and international commitment, all in the name of securing peace, is a world of realpolitik. The realm of idealism professed by Eisenhower served to distance two areas of conflict in the world from the shores of this country and thus from the immediate concerns of the American public. With the presidential election only a few days away, the bipartisan, nonpolitical discussion announced by Eisenhower, serves an important partisan objective. It mutes potentially volatile issues; it lends whatever stature it can to the United Nations; it is another piece of evidence in support of the words that adorn the base of the statue at the Eisenhower Library in Abilene, Kansas, "Champion of Peace."

There were outcomes in the realpolitik sense as well. Nasser emerged with the highest level of popularity he would ever enjoy in the Arab world. Despite

Eisenhower's attempt to lay the crisis at Egypt's doorstep, his policies tilted against Britain, France and Israel. Years later, when asked what had saved him in the Suez crisis, Nasser coolly replied, "Eisenhower."[34] America emerged as the prominent power in the Middle East, though Russia enlarged her foothold a bit. In the United States, the Jewish lobby learned a lesson and strengthened itself to become what some have called the strongest lobby in this country.[35] No subsequent president would apply the pressure again to Israel as Eisenhower did, and stubbornly stay the course. Though Eisenhower's speech treated Eastern Europe and the Middle East as two separate incidents, thus distancing them from each other, they were in reality closely knit. If Russia lost control of Eastern Europe, she might make a rash move that could lead to all-out war. Eisenhower made clear he would not enter the area with force, and the Soviets put rebellion down in a bloody fashion. By moving quickly with a U.N. resolution, the administration assumed a leadership role in achieving peace in the Middle East. By patiently applying sanctions against the allies and refusing to bow to contrary pressure, the administration avoided antagonizing Arab nations and other newly independent countries around the world. The Cold War remained in place, a hot war was avoided, and the international balance of power was not significantly altered. Eisenhower's speech "informed" the average American citizen that these events could be considered at a distance removed.

Sherman Adams, who was Eisenhower's Chief of Staff until 1958, later summed up Ike's presidency in the following manner: "A lot of our most important accomplishments were negative—things we avoided. We maintained a peaceful front and adjudicated a lot of issues that seem ominous and threatening at the time."[36] The Suez Crisis is a case in point, and Eisenhower's speech of 31 October 1956 was a crucial part of that case.

## NOTES

1. Adams cited in Emmet John Hughes, *The Ordeal of Power* (New York: Dell Publishing Company, 1964), 186. Because of the continuing popularity of Eisenhower with the American public, the outcome of the 1956 election was a foregone conclusion. The problem, as Ike and his advisors saw it, was to win with a large majority. Hughes recalls Eisenhower discussing the matter with him:

> Next term, I'll be the first President to try to run things under the two-term limitation—with everybody knowing I'm politically on my way out. So the size of my majority will be the most important weapon I'll have for the next four years—especially with the Republicans. They have got to be made to understand what kind of principles and policies can win elections, and I'm going to need all the power I can show to get those monkeys to do the thing I want for a change. (172-73).

For a discussion of the factors that provided Eisenhower with a substantial margin in public opinion throughout the 1956 campaign, see Herbert S. Parmet, *Eisenhower and the*

*American Crusades* (New York: Macmillan, 1972), esp. 460-69.

2. Eisenhower cited in Hughes, *Ordeal*, 187.
3. Ibid., 187-88.
4. Ibid., 191.
5. Ibid., 192.
6. Daniel Yergen, *The Prize* (New York: Simon and Schuster, 1991), 154-64.
7. Ibid., 170-71.
8. Eden quoted in Donald Neff, *Warriors At Suez* (New York: Simon and Schuster, 1981), 276.
9. Kirkpatrick quoted in Yergen, *Prize*, 488.
10. For a complete text of Truman's speech, see *Public Papers of the Presidents of the United States: Harry S. Truman, 1947* (Washington D.C.: Government Printing Office, 1953), 176-80.
11. A detailed analysis of the Truman speech can be found in Wayne Brockriede and Robert L. Scott, *Moments in the Rhetoric of the Cold War* (New York: Random House, Inc. 1970), 10-43.
12. Ward Just, *Military Men* (New York: Alfred A. Knopf, 1970), 102-3.
13. Peter Lyon, *Eisenhower: Portrait of a Hero* (Boston: Little, Brown and Company, 1974), 345-48. With regard to personal credibility, see esp. Richard E. Neustadt, *Presidential Power and the Modern Presidents* (New York: The Free Press, 1990), 190-91. It is of particular interest that Eisenhower often expressed a dislike for campaigning, for mingling with or addressing crowds of people, or engaging in speech making. He often argued against appearing on television, feeling the people had more important things to do than listen to him speak. When cajoled to speak, he wanted to be assured that something needed to be said, saying he didn't want to just listen to himself talk. He constantly demanded that speaking time be kept brief. See James David Barber, *The Presidential Character* (Englewood Cliffs, N.J., 1972), 156-60.
14. Hughes, *Ordeal*, 153.
15. For the chronology of events I rely upon Lyon, Neff, Parmet, and Townsend Hoopes, *The Devil and John Foster Dulles* (Boston: Little, Brown and Company, 1973).
16. It is interesting that in his diary, Eisenhower refers to aid to Nasser in an offhand manner, little reflecting the more complete consideration of events and motives that actually took place. He wrote:

> When we made our first offer, I think more than a year ago, to help build the Aswan Dam, it was conceived of as a joint venture of ourselves and the British, which, once accomplished, would enable the World Bank to go in and help Nasser to completion of the work. It was felt that under this basis, the project would be feasible but would require all the resources that Egypt could donate to public affairs.
>
> Egypt at once did two things: (1) They sent back to us a whole list of conditions that would have to be met before they would go along with this plan, and some of these conditions were unacceptable. (2) They began to build up their military forces by taking over equipment provided by the Soviets, and they went to such an extent that we did not believe they would have a sufficient balance of resources left to do their part in building the dam.
>
> We lost interest and said nothing more about the matter.
>
> Suddenly, about a month ago, Nasser sent us a message to the effect that he had withdrawn all of the conditions that he had laid down and was ready to proceed under our original offer. Since conditions had changed markedly and we had thought the whole

project dead, we merely replied we were no longer interested. *The Eisenhower Diaries,* ed. by Robert H. Ferrell (New York: W. W. Norton and Company, 1981), 330.

17. The President's dictated suggestion for tonight's TV talk—unfinished. 31 October 1956, Whitman File, Speech Series, B 19, Eisenhower Library, Abilene, Kansas (hereafter cited as DDE Library). All references to dictated comments are from this source.

18. All quotations from the speech are taken from the official White House release: "Text of the President's Report to the People of the Nation on Developments in Eastern Europe and the Middle East, Delivered from the White House Wednesday Evening, 7:00 P.M. EST, 31 October 1956 (As Actually Delivered). Whitman File, Speech Series, B 19, DDE Library.

19. For a thorough discussion of the presidency, see Thomas E. Cronin, *The State of the Presidency* (Boston: Little, Brown and Company, 1980).

20. Cronin, *Presidency,* vi.

21. "Inaugural Address," *Public Papers of the Presidents of the United States: Dwight D. Eisenhower, 1953* (Washington D.C.: Government Printing Office, 1960), 1 (hereafter cited as *Public Papers*).

22. Ibid., 4.

23. Harlow cited in Hedrick Smith, *The Power Game* (New York: Random House, 1988), 55.

24. John Foster Dulles, "A Policy of Boldness," *Life* (19 May 1952): 146-57.

25. Hughes cited in Hoopes, *Dulles,* 128.

26. Abstracts of the Draft Report may be found in *The Truman Presidency: The Origins of the Imperial Presidency and the National Security State,* ed. by Athan Theoharis (Stanfordville, New York: Earl M. Coleman Enterprises, Inc., 1979), 165-67.

27. These events are recounted in Lyons, *Eisenhower,* 707-10.

28. J. Fred MacDonald, *One Nation Under Television* (New York: Pantheon Books, 1990), 71.

29. Letter to Swede Hazlett, Whitman File , DDE Diary Series, Box 20, Misc. (4), 2 November 1956, DDE Library. The scope and content note in the finding aids for the Eisenhower papers offers the following comment:

> In regard to the philosophical dimension of Eisenhower, the President's correspondence with Swede Hazlett should be singled out for special mention. The President wrote exceedingly long letters to his Abilene boyhood friend, a retired naval officer living in Chapel Hill, North Carolina.—Hazlett correspondence touches upon most of the prominent public-policy issues and perhaps most fully reveals Eisenhower's attitudes, beliefs, and values. Whitman File, Name Series, 2.

30. "Discussion at the 302nd Meeting of the National Security Council, Thursday, 1 November 1956." Whitman File , NSC Series, Box 8, DDE Library.

31. "Discussion at the 303rd Meeting of the National Security Council, Thursday, 8 November 1956." Whitman File, NSC Series, Box 8, DDE Library.

32. "Bipartisan Legislative Meeting, 9 November 1956." Whitman File , Legislative Meetings Series, Box 2, DDE Library.

33. Eisenhower cited in Yergin, *Prize,* 491.

34. Nasser cited in Jean Lacouture, *Nasser* (New York: Alfred A. Knopf, Inc., 1973), 181.

35. See Isaac Alteras, "Eisenhower, American Jewry, and Israel," *America Jewish Archives* 37 (2) (1985): 257-74, and George W. Ball, "The Coming Crisis in Israeli-American Relations," *Foreign Affairs* 58 (1979-1980), 231-56.

36. Adams cited in Steve Neal, "Why We Were Right to Like Ike," *American Heritage* (December 1985): 54.

Ike and Orval Faubus meet at Newport, Rhode Island

Steven R.
Goldzwig and
George N.
Dionisopoulos

# Crisis at Little Rock
## Eisenhower, History, and Mediated Political Realities

Presidential rhetoric attending U.S. foreign policy crises has received a good deal of scholarly attention. Fewer studies have focused on domestic policy crisis.[1] There is little doubt that domestic division over civil rights has given the contemporary presidency one of its most thorny, if not recalcitrant domestic concerns. Presidential discourse intended to resolve crisis in the civil rights arena is never without rhetorical constraints; these limitations remind us of the tendency of public presidential address to reverberate in various sectors of the nation with differing consequences for each.

In the age of televised and print-mediated reality, the echoes of presidential discourse resound in sometimes unexpected and usually wholly fragmented tidbits, creating afterimages and impressions capable of overpowering any clear description of original intent. A study of domestic presidential crisis rhetoric in the age of mass-mediated reality invites a focus on the responses of mass opinion leaders that create the "crisis" label and establish its "resolution." The fundamental negotiation of a civil rights "crisis," then, also invites an investigation into mediated responses.

A recent critique argues, however, that merely examining the interpretive processes of audience members in the act of decoding mediated texts is not enough. As Kevin Carragee observes, "[i]nterpretive mass communication research has failed to place media texts and media audiences within meaningful historical, social, and cultural contexts."[2] This essay adopts a strategy to correct this oversight. We believe a focus on media coverage alone will yield a truncated view of history and, simultaneously, that a pure focus on the historical "record" cannot fully reflect history as experienced through the mediated coverage that is also part of the ongoing cultural milieu.

Kathleen J. Turner argues that the study and the processes of history are essentially rhetorical in nature and function. Accordingly, Turner believes "we need both rhetorical criticism's message-centered focus and rhetorical history's contextual construction." Moreover, "the melding of historical and rhetorical methodologies can contribute to an understanding of the complex latitudinal and longitudinal processes of symbolic influence."[3] In this essay, we adopt both historical and critical methods in an effort to demonstrate how the history and mediated coverage of a contemporary domestic crisis can be mutually informative. By outlining the rhetorical norms, strategies, and constraints involved in a print-mediated crisis and by supplementing it with historical investigation, we hope to create a richer understanding of the rhetorical dimensions of the mass media, as well as highlight the historical and cultural legacy of that experience. In Turner's phraseology, both the latitudinal and longitudinal aspects of rhetorical history will constitute our primary subject matter. In particular we focus on mediated coverage of President Eisenhower's handling of the Little Rock, Arkansas, school desegregation crisis of 1957.

## HISTORICAL CONTEXT

The desegregation crisis at Little Rock's Central High School, precipitated by the 1954 *Brown v. Topeka Board of Education* decision, provided President Eisenhower "with the most persistent and critical domestic challenge of his eight-year presidency."[4] The civil rights issue was particularly vexing to Eisenhower because of a number of factors including the president's: (1) personal philosophy and temperament; (2) view of the role, powers, and function of the executive, judicial, and legislative branches of government; (3) fear that the implementation of the *Brown* decision would precipitate federal-state rancor and division, creating a constitutional crisis; (4) own regard for and political relationship with the South.

### Personal Philosophy and Temperament

According to Robert Fredrick Burk, Eisenhower was ill at ease about racial matters. He preferred a moderate approach rather than the "bully pulpit." His belief in "free enterprise" caused "revulsion at any form of 'coercive' federal regulation."[5] By temperament, Eisenhower's philosophy of government was to find a "middle way"; he made an effort to avoid and discount extremes "on both sides." Moreover, "Eisenhower was utterly convinced of the superiority of this approach."[6] In a cabinet meeting of March 1956, in response to a cabinet paper circulated by Attorney General Herbert Brownell that outlined suggestions on civil rights legislation, the president observed:

> I believe that Herb Brownell should put forward what he has got here, but with a statement that many Americans understandably are separated by deep emotions on this subject. One of the prime reasons for this is that, after all, another system was upheld by the Supreme Court for 60 years. These people in the South were not breaking the law for the past 60 years, but, ever since

the "separate but equal" decision, they have been obeying the Constitution of the United States. Now we cannot erase the emotions of three generations just overnight. . . . People have a right to disagree with the Supreme Court decision—since the Supreme Court has disagreed with its own decision of 60 years standing—but, of course, the new decision should now be carried out.[7]

Eisenhower adopted a narrow definition of how constitutional law should be enforced and, as a result, critics felt that he was somewhat ambivalent, if not opposed, to a vigorous fight for black civil rights.[8]

### Attitudes Toward the Coordinate Branches

Eisenhower believed in limited government. He felt that law was not the ultimate solution to moral turpitude. When faced with any crisis, he had developed a "personal habit of caution" and, not surprisingly, this led him to "moderation in the exercise of presidential powers."[9] He preferred to address racial issues at a cabinet or subcabinet level. When he talked of racial equality it was through the "occasional assertion of democratic principles. At the same time the [p]resident carefully circumscribed his subordinates' activities to areas of clear federal jurisdiction, greatest international propaganda value, and minimum risk of political fallout or domestic unrest."[10] His ideology actually was translated into careful, jurisdictionally controlled federal efforts such as desegregating the military and schools on army posts.

Eisenhower opposed an active judiciary in areas such as public school desegregation because he believed that in the South, in particular, such activism threatened state support for public schools.[11] He felt that the *Brown* decisions of 1954 and 1955 had made the executive's job more burdensome. In a private letter to his friend "Swede" Hazlett, Eisenhower lamented: "I think that no single event has so disturbed the domestic scene in many years as did the Supreme Court's decision in 1954 in the school desegregation case. That decision and similar ones earlier and later in point of time have interpreted the Constitution in such a fashion as to put heavier responsibilities than before on the Federal government in the matter of assuring each citizen his guaranteed constitutional rights." Yet Eisenhower would also adamantly maintain: "There must be respect for the Constitution—which means the Supreme Court's interpretation of the Constitution—or we shall have chaos. . . . This I believe with all my heart—and shall always act accordingly."[12]

Eisenhower was especially uneasy with post-*Brown* implementation decisions on behalf of desegregation, fearing that forced efforts would result in the complete federal assumption of public education, a prospect the president reportedly abhorred.[13] In a letter to Governor James F. Byrnes of South Carolina, Eisenhower described his concerns regarding executive action pertaining to *Brown*: "It was my purpose . . . to provide a moderate approach to a difficult problem and to make haste slowly in seeking to meet it. I believe that in the question under discussion there are moral values as well as legal requirements to be considered; moreover, I am aware that emotions are deeply stirred on both sides."[14] In a personal letter to George Landes dated 12 September 1957, Eisenhower also wrote: "The fact is that many states are stoutly opposed to any entry of the Federal Government into school affairs, maintaining that the final result would be Federal control of education. This, of course, would be a calamity. . . . [I]t is clear that primary responsibility for the schools in our country properly devolves upon local and state authorities."[15] Thus Eisenhower championed local, gradual efforts at desegregating the schools and this gradualism was of some comfort to Southern segregationists. It also caused much discomfiture for civil rights advocates.

### Federal-State Relations and Constitutional Crisis

Eisenhower once privately told Governor Byrnes of South Carolina that

> improvement in race relations . . . will be healthy and sound only if it starts locally. I do not believe prejudice . . . will succumb to compulsion. Consequently, I believe that federal law imposed upon our states in such a way as to bring about a conflict of the police power of the states and the nation, would set back the cause of progress in race relations for a long, long time.[16]

This fear was in part responsible for increasing tension between the executive and judicial branches regarding "appropriate" action in response to *Brown* and subsequent implementation of desegregation plans for public schools. When Attorney General Herbert Brownell was asked by the Supreme Court to file an *amicus curiae* brief regarding the *Brown* case, Eisenhower questioned the Justice Department's authority to "speak out on state-enforced segregation." Moreover, Eisenhower's belief in the separation of powers among the three branches of government continuously led him to refuse comment on any Supreme Court ruling. The president believed that commentary on any case would be an open invitation to comment on each one—something he wanted to avoid. His consistent position in this regard was that of "executive neutrality."[17]

Eisenhower was equally cautious regarding implementation of the *Brown* decision.[18] In a brief filed 11 April 1955, the Eisenhower administration advocated a "middle-of-the-road concept of moderation with a degree of fairness" that left implementation of desegregation plans to the federal district courts who were to be given power to approve or deny local desegregation plans.[19] The Supreme Court followed this approach in its implementation decision of 24 May 1955. Such plans were to be accomplished with "all deliberate speed." But it was questionable as to how federal district judges in the South would interpret that particular directive.

In addition, the president was quite concerned that local police powers be given every opportunity to restore law and order in the event that violence attended attempted enforcement. The idea of federal troops occupying Southern states evoked grim images of Reconstruction, the negative history and outcome of which Eisenhower adamantly preferred to avoid during his administration. It remained unclear, however, as to how the administration would respond to violent segregationist obstruction. Mob violence in Texarkana and Mansfield, Texas, as well as in Clinton, Tennessee in 1956 did little to reassure civil rights advocates that both their rights and their safety would be protected by federal intervention. In response to such incidents, the president would take the position that "Under the law the federal government cannot . . . move into a state until the state is not able to handle the matter."[20] Exactly when and under what circumstances federal intervention would occur remained decidedly vague. At the 1956 Republican National Convention in San Francisco, Eisenhower personally squelched efforts to strengthen the party's desegregation plan and complained privately that the Supreme Court was moving too fast and excoriated it for its "stupidity."[21] The furor refused to abate. Circumstances were afoot that would throw the president headlong into a cauldron of constitutional crisis at Little Rock.

For a time, Eisenhower also seemed reticent to introduce legislation in the civil rights arena, preferring voluntary to compulsory efforts. Because of his moderate stance, legislative proposals were left to "languish in the Congress."[22] An "emasculated version" of a civil rights bill actually was passed by Congress in 1957; less than one month later, the Little Rock crisis began.[23]

## Political Relations with the South

It was of no little consequence that many of the positions outlined above were also based on Eisenhower's belief that a strong anti-segregationist stance would ultimately "defeat forever the possibility of developing a viable Republican Party in the South."[24] This belief no doubt provided a rather striking rationale for Eisenhower's cautious approach to the question of school desegregation. Moreover, Eisenhower had spent a good deal of time in the South and was sensitive to southern history and sensibilities. The moderate position seemed principled and reasonable to Eisenhower, but it also, at times, played into the hands of segregationists who were intent upon obstructing any form of integration. Eisenhower continued to view "extremists" with suspicion, whether they were from the White Citizen's Councils or the NAACP. J. Edgar Hoover's ongoing updates on both groups increasingly gave the president little comfort. Events in Little Rock, Arkansas, during September 1957, could not help but add to the president's discomfiture. A true political media extravaganza was in the offing.

## Mediated Political Realities

According to Murray Edelman, "Political leaders become signs of competence, evil, nationalism, future promise, and other virtues and vices and so help introduce meaning to a confusing political world."[25]It was just such a world that the average American encountered in the morning newspaper on 25 September 1957. The day before, Dwight David Eisenhower federalized the Arkansas National Guard and brought in paratroopers from the 101st Airborne Division to enforce the court-ordered desegregation of Little Rock's Central High School. President Eisenhower and Governor Orval Eugene Faubus became key political antagonists in a dramatic exchange. Tension was symbolically created not only in the authorization of federal troops to quell unrest in the state of Arkansas, evoking negative images of Reconstruction with its attendant federal-state clashes, but also in the mediated clash of wills between the president and the chief executive of the state. That mediated reality, in turn, presents a unique opportunity to examine a modern political spectacle.

"Mediated, secondhand reality is our politics," according to Dan Nimmo and James Combs, "and there is little we can do about it."[26] Edelman maintains that

> News . . . is not so much a description of events as a catalyst of political support and opposition in the light of the spectator's sensitivities, areas of ignorance, and ideological stance. The acceptance of a story plot that defines the background of a reported development and its future consequences is crucial. The scenarios for the future that news accounts evoke are rarely acted out according to their scripts. They are aborted or replaced by alternative scenarios implicit in later news accounts, but before that happens they influence political support and action. In this light, politics consists of a panoply of overlapping and conflicting spectacles that fade from the scene as they give birth to their successors.[27]

Moreover, "News of controversial issues keeps tensions between groups alive or intensifies or broadens them."[28] Exposure to the ambiguities and controversies of the news not only defines our images of the political world but also our self-images. Audiences interpret news interpretations against their own background, experience, and ideology and what plays itself out in newspaper or magazine accounts is a dramaturgical dance of both self and political society.

We will maintain that print-mediated accounts of the crisis at Little Rock unfolded in three acts. The changing scenarios within each act were crucial to audience interpretation and provide a centerpiece for our analysis of mediated responses. In particular, we will argue that these mediated responses helped shape the short-term political, historical, and cultural consciousness. As the characteristic themes of each scene burned brightly and then, in turn, faded out, we find an interesting, if not provocative, political spectacle. For Edelman, then, "[t]he political spectacle. . . evokes a drama that objectifies hopes and fears" but probably resolves very few of them.[29]

Nimmo and Combs also note that mediated political realities have a "melodramatic imperative." The key to melodrama is to mount a series of scenic environments wherein moral justice is on trial. More than merely identifying heroes and villains, melodramatic imperatives require suspense to maintain audience interest and, as such, evoke both quiescence and arousal in audiences. Danger, threat, narrow escapes, heroic and villainous action, and reward and punishment for good and evil are staples of the genre; news narratives are often constrained to both create and follow these imperatives. While happy endings may be useful, they are not essential; sometimes full resolution is simply not a realistic option. The content and structure of mediated political reality is a joint product of audience expectations and media attempts to fulfill them.[30] We believe that the news sources' and audiences' sense of melodrama is particularly heightened when events, personages, and mediated behaviors are also saddled with the label, "crisis."

## CRISIS AT LITTLE ROCK

Following the Supreme Court's integration rulings of 1954 and 1955, the Little Rock School Board, at the direction of Superintendent Virgil T. Blossom, drew up plans for the gradual integration of the public school system in Little Rock. This was a three-phase plan in which the high schools would be integrated by 3 September 1957, at the start of the school year. According to Daisy Bates, a member of the NAACP in Little Rock, the city "had apparently accepted the board's plans; and there seemed little reason to expect serious opposition, much less what followed."[31] What followed was perceived by some as the most serious challenge to federal authority since the Civil War. Enacted on a daily basis in a mediated environment, the rhetorical characteristics of this particular drama unfolded in three acts.

### *Act One*

Act One of the mediated narrative began on 2 September when the engaged public was informed that tensions of high national interest were percolating precariously in Arkansas. The audience was given a brief précis of the plot, the location, and the cast of characters crucial to unfolding events.

### The Plot Unfolds

The "action line" of the plot was presented in a direct, straightforward manner. Under the Little Rock School Board desegregation plan, the first school to be integrated was Central High School. A series of legal challenges by various groups such as the segregationist Capital Citizens Council resulted in a ruling by a Federal District Court that the integration of Little Rock's public educa-tion facilities had to begin with the start of the 1957 school year.

On 2 September 1957, Arkansas Governor Orval E. Faubus activated the state's National Guard and placed it at Little Rock's Central High School. The "270 armed Arkansas militia and fifty members of the state police patrolled the school grounds and stood guard at all the entrances," charged by the governor to prevent any outbreak of violence that might accompany the integration of Little Rock's public schools.[32]

That night, at 10:05 p.m., Faubus addressed the people of Arkansas from the studios of station KTHV. According to the governor, since "a federal court has ruled that no further litigation is possible before the forcible integration of Negroes and whites in Central High School tomorrow, the evidence of discord, anger and resentment has come to me from so many sources as to become a deluge." As the governor described it, Little Rock was a city "on the brink of a riot [while] outraged white mothers . . . prepared to march on the school at 6 a.m.; caravans of indignant white citizens . . . converg[ed] on Little Rock from all over Arkansas. And Little Rock stores . . . were selling out of knives."[33]

Given these circumstances, the governor argued, "it [was] necessary to sum-mon the Guard in advance of the school's opening to forestall violence."[34] Faubus explained that the mobilized National Guard at Central High School would serve neither as "segregationists nor integrationists, but as soldiers. . . carry[ing] out their assigned tasks:"[35] to "maintain or restore the peace and good order of this community."[36] Faubus refused to say "whether the troops were called out to prevent Negroes from entering the school," but he warned that "if any Negro tried to enter [Central High] violence would break out . . . and he was against violence."[37]

On 3 September, the opening day of school, "peace" was maintained when the Little Rock Board of Education urged the nine black students selected to integrate Central High School to stay home, and nineteen hundred white stu-dents entered the school "through a cordon of several hundred Guardsmen armed with carbines and billy clubs."[38] The Board of Education went to the U.S. District Court to ask Judge Ronald Davies to clarify the issue. After a four-minute hearing, Judge Davies ruled that integration at Central High School must "begin forthwith."[39] Worried about the safety of the nine black students, members of the Little Rock NAACP arranged a police escort for the next morning. But Daisy Bates was told by a police officer that city police could not escort the students up to Central High because the "school is off limits to the city police while it's 'occupied' by the Arkansas National Guardsmen"[40]

Eight of the nine black students were told to meet the escort of police and ministers from the Interracial Ministerial Alliance at 8:30 on the morning of 4

September. The ninth student, fifteen-year-old Elizabeth Eckford, was not contacted and the next morning she attempted to enter Central High School alone. When she approached the entrance "she found a youth, barely older than she, in the uniform of the National Guard, barring her way,"[41] and the drama was underway.

Thus, during act one the basic facts of the plot line were presented in a fairly concise, straightforward manner. The sitting governor of a state had issued an order to the National Guard to "keep the peace" in Little Rock. The order prevented the court-ordered integration of Central High School. As the *Arkansas Gazette* observed, when the Arkansas National Guard carried out the orders of Governor Faubus and blocked the entrance of Elizabeth Eckford to Central High School, the issue was "no longer segregation vs. integration. The question has now become the supremacy of the United States Government in all matters of law."[42] As Attorney General Herbert Brownell put the matter in a summary statement to the president, "no effort whatever had been made by the Governor of Arkansas to use his powers to uphold the jurisdiction of the federal court and to aid, rather than subvert, the execution of its orders. On the contrary, his purpose seemed clearly directed toward a nullification of the court's mandate."[43]

### Momentous, Historic Conflict, or Potential Crisis

The opening act of the mediated drama of Little Rock suggested that the events being played out in Arkansas were part of a much larger issue, an issue of possible historic significance. As *Time* observed, "Through the U.S. South ran the sight and sound, the pain and glory of historic sociological change. . . . As is often the case in such moments of history, the worst and the best in man—hate and human charity, stupidity and wisdom—came out before the world."[44] Events in Little Rock, reportedly "the first time that the issue of Federal versus state authority has been reached on the integration problem," now "set the stage for the first major test of the United State Supreme Court's decision of May 1954, that racial segregation in schools is unconstitutional."[45]

Early on then, the news media pegged the issue in Arkansas as an important "constitutional question"[46] that had "agitated constitutional lawyers since the earliest days of the Republic. . . . Where does the Federal authority end, and where do states' rights begin?"[47] The *Arkansas Gazette* observed:

> Until last Thursday the matter of gradual limited integration in the Little Rock schools was a local problem which had been well and wisely handled by responsible local officials who have had—and we believe still have—the support of a majority of the people of this city. On that day Mr. Faubus appeared in Chancery Court on behalf of a small but militant minority and chose to

make it a state problem. On Monday night he called out the National Guard
and made it a national problem."[48]

News coverage seemed to underscore a feeling of unexpectedness—that
somehow this historic drama should not have taken place at this location involving these characters. The stage for mediated melodrama was set. Arkansas was
not really a part of the Deep South but was, instead, "on the periphery of the
die-hard states" with their strategy of "all-out resistance to school desegregation."[49] The Arkansas State Board of Education had already integrated the seven
state colleges and the University of Arkansas had admitted blacks into the grad-
uate school as early as 1948.[50] The state did "not have a record of racial violence;" in fact, during the "very week that Little Rock was supposed to explode,
three other Arkansas communities—Ozark, Fort Smith and Van Buren—integrated without a murmur. . . . [B]us integration [wa]s a statewide fact, and Little
Rock's white and Negro citizens ha[d] become accustomed to their Negro
policemen."[51] In Little Rock itself the "consensus among responsible citizens was
that while integration of public schools was not popular, it was nonetheless
inevitable." Most "civic, religious, educational and business leaders supported
the Little Rock Board of Education's decision to carry out the integration
order."[52] Yet, the Supreme Court's decision mandating school integration was
"unexpectedly getting its first major test" in Little Rock, Arkansas.[53]


## Vivid Characterization and Lengthy Rationales for Mysterious Action

That same element of surprise also seemed to permeate the mediated development of the most interesting character in this phase of the drama—Arkansas
Governor Orval Eugene Faubus. As constructed in the media, his contradictory persona mysteriously lacked a history of deep ideological conviction to
motivate his action in Little Rock.

Both *Time* and *Newsweek* ran profiles of the governor. While each differed
regarding Faubus's exact place of birth, they did agree on his bucolic origins.
Under the title "Hillbilly, Slightly Sophisticated," *Time* noted that in his first
term Faubus had been an "Arkansas-style progressive." He was a "product of
the hill country;" born "so far back in the Ozarks of Northwest Arkansas that
the first paved road to the outside world was not completed until 1949." This
article highlighted the fact that there were few blacks in this area of Arkansas
and Faubus had "no background of race prejudice."[54] *Newsweek* crafted
Faubus's characterization by noting that "Of all the South's governors, Orval
Eugene Faubus of Arkansas might seem the least likely to set himself against
the power of President Eisenhower and the Federal government over the issue
of school integration." He was born "so deep in the Ozark hills that a man
might pass a lifetime there without ever seeing a Negro."[55] Similarly, the *New*

*York Times* said that Faubus appeared "from his record to be the least likely of all the Southern Governors to volunteer for a leading role in the school integration showdown."[56] In background stories about the crisis, the *Times* referred to the Governor as "a Democrat with a liberal background."[57] The Faubus "turnabout" was described as being "so abrupt that no one had anticipated it. For weeks, Gov. Orval Faubus . . . had been silent on the integration attempts that would be made this fall in the schools of several cities in his state. His public stand had always been that integration was strictly a problem for local school boards to decide."[58] Thus, although in the past Faubus had exhibited "a moderate stand in favor of segregation,"[59] there was no indication of a professed ideological basis for his opposition to the federal government. Such inscrutability made him all the more mysterious. Crackpot, opportunist, or southern savior were different labels audiences could apply to fill in the mediated mosaic of ideological ambiguity.

However, as the opening day of school drew closer, "Faubus began to sound very much like an entirely different man." He "issued a statement bitterly accusing the Federal government of trying to cram integration down Arkansas' throat;"[60] appeared in a state court hearing where he won an injunction against the integration order by arguing that "a great majority of the people of Little Rock are opposed to integration;" and publicly warned that "bloodshed and mob violence would result."[61] When U.S. federal district Judge Ronald Davies threw out the injunction, Faubus "went on television and radio to drop a bombshell: He was calling out the Arkansas National Guard to preserve the peace at Little Rock's Central High School."[62] Along with the contradictions in Governor Faubus's persona, the media also designated him as the responsible character in the unfolding Little Rock melodrama. He was labeled as the specific agent who had set the drama in motion by ordering the National Guard into action. The "troops acted under direct orders of Gov. Orval E. Faubus,"[63] who had "create[d] the crisis."[64]

Portrayed as a fanatic who had lost touch with the reality of the very situation for which he was responsible, the Faubus character took on almost comic proportions. All during the Little Rock drama, Faubus maintained that he had done nothing to frustrate the order to integrate. He maintained, instead, that he had acted within his rights as governor to "preserve peace and to prevent bloodshed."[65] Faubus insisted that he was "not violating the order issued by a Federal District Court," but rather, was "using the Guardsmen to prevent violence."[66]

The Governor's persistence in this position was contrasted with print-mediated reports suggesting that regardless of Faubus's stated reasons, he was indeed frustrating the order to integrate and defying the authority of the United States federal government. For example, a headline in the *New York Times* announced, "Faubus Bids U.S. Recede on Order For Integration." The article quoted the governor as saying that the only way to prevent bloodshed was "that the United States would have to recede from its demand for immediate school integration" in Little Rock—Faubus saw "no alternative."[67]

Thus, as mediated, Faubus was portrayed as a man "face to face with the power of the U.S. Government, and that Government could not possibly ignore or withdraw in the face of Faubus's challenge to its courts, to law and simple decency."[68] While this image might engender support among some of the more fanatic states' rights advocates, for most it probably conveyed the image of an unrealistic obstructionist. This perception was heightened by mediated reports that Faubus had retreated "behind the guarded gates of his executive mansion."[69] As *Time* noted, "To ward off all invaders, Orval Faubus deployed his militia around his pillared executive mansion, disappeared from public view like a feudal baron under siege."[70] By implication, mysterious machinations inside the mansion were purposefully denied public scrutiny.

From the Governor's mansion—"still guarded by the state police"[71]— Faubus had "fired off a wild-eyed message to the President of the U.S."[72] The telegram was widely reported as asking for Eisenhower's help in stopping the "unwarranted interference of Federal agents in this area," declaring that Faubus would "not cooperate with the Federal agents now investigating his use of troops to block integration,"[73] complaining that "his telephone lines were being tapped," and saying he feared that "Federal authorities [were] . . . plotting to arrest him."[74]

Faubus's persona was developed further as the media tried to capture his motivation. Described as an "opportunist" who did not represent the people in whose name he had undertaken this action, the Governor provided "no reasonable explanation for [his] highhanded action, except that he hoped to make political capital for himself."[75] Moreover, engaged audiences learned that Faubus recently had begun "talking about running for a third term in a state that traditionally frowns on three terms for a governor. He needed a dramatic issue, and he needed the red-neck votes of segregationist eastern Arkansas."[76] Thus, he may have decided "that a strong stand for segregation now would be politically popular in 1958, when he [could] bid for a third term."[77]

The media found "indications that Faubus was being used by segregationist politicians in the South,"[78] who planned to issue the first challenge to federally ordered integration outside of their own region. As noted in the *New York Times*, "What has taken shape [since the Supreme Court's 1954 decision] is an unremitting war for the border states which are divided on racial policies because of their mixed population ratios. Deep South political leaders, seeing the encirclement threat, have regularly sent emissaries to the border states to bolster their position."[79]

The media coverage did portray some support for the governor's action; however, most of it was localized in the South. For example, the *Memphis Commercial Appeal* maintained that although the "successful refusal by anyone to obey the orders of the court would lead to confusion that would eventually amount to chaos," the issue in Arkansas was a "clash between unrealistic laws and rulings . . . and the responsibility of a state's chief executive to preserve order. Governor Faubus has raised a national issue intimately concerned with how a theory not accepted by a people can be hastily translated into action."[80]

However, the media also indicated that Faubus was not speaking for the community of Little Rock. Indeed, it maintained Little Rock did not ask for help, and high-profile citizens were quoted as saying that the governor's aid was unnecessary. Thus, while the majority of citizens in Little Rock may not have welcomed the order to desegregate, there was also a "growing body of Southern white opinion that segregation must yield to the times."[81] The *Arkansas Gazette*—"the state's leading newspaper"—maintained that the "matter of gradual limited integration in Little Rock schools was a local problem which had been well and wisely handled by responsible local officials who had—and we believe still have—the support of a majority of the people of this city."[82]

Probably the most vocal and widely covered critic of Governor Faubus's action was the Mayor of Little Rock, Woodrow Wilson Mann. Mann was adamant that no one in Little Rock had asked Faubus to send troops to the city, and the mayor and the Board of Education had insisted that the local police force could handle any potential mayhem.[83] Mann "vehemently attacked Faubus's intervention as a 'political hoax,'"[84] and demanded that the Governor "give the people of this state evidence of possible racial violence instead of running off and hiding" behind the guarded walls of the mansion.[85] According to Mann, the Governor made a "wholly unwarranted interference with the internal affairs of this city." He acted "without request from those of us who are directly responsible for the preservation of peace and order. The only effect of his action is to create tensions where none existed. If any racial trouble does develop the blame rests squarely on the doorstep of the Governor's mansion."[86]

Mann's criticism of Faubus was not limited to the governor's thwarting of the agreed-upon integration plan. The mayor also expressed the concern of many: The governor had placed himself and the state on a collision course with the United States government. Mann, quoted on the front page of the *New York Times*, charged that Faubus's "words spell sedition, his defiance rebellion. . . . His word and action echo another period of our history when irresponsible men plunged this nation into a tragic civil war."[87] The mayor also made public appeals to the other main character of this drama—President Eisenhower. Maintaining that Faubus's calling out the National Guard to prevent integration had created a "state of anarchy,"[88] Mann called upon Eisenhower for action: "The President of the United States can no longer ignore the gravity of the situation. Time for realistic action is long-since delayed. The issue of integration has become secondary—the security and prestige of the United States of America is paramount."[89]

Eisenhower's character in this mediated narrative is intriguing. His role is analogous to Beckett's *Godot*: While he is an integral part of the plot narrative, he always seems to be just offstage during act one. One explanation for this is that Eisenhower had physically removed himself from the nation's capital. On 4 September, the president and Mamie went to Newport, Rhode Island, for a vacation that Eisenhower predicted would be "the time of our lives."[90] At a press conference before leaving Washington, Eisenhower was asked about the developing situation in Little Rock. He observed that there "seems to have been a road block thrown in the way [of integration] and the next step will have to be by the lawyers and the jurists."[91] This remark signaled what was to be the underlying tone of Eisenhower's "go slow" approach for most of act one.

The media assured Americans the administration was "keeping on top of the situation." Almost as soon as the events in Arkansas became national news, Eisenhower ordered the Justice Department to keep in "close touch" with "the school integration dispute in Little Rock." However, spokespersons for the administration were always careful to add that there were "no plans for Federal intervention. Officials took the position that it was neither legally possible nor politically desirable for the Executive branch of the Government to step in at this stage. They said the next move was up to the Federal district judge sitting in the case."[92]

Part of the reason for the perceived dearth in presidential leadership during what we are calling act one no doubt also stems from Eisenhower's own beliefs, especially those regarding the Supreme Court's rulings on desegregation. As Eisenhower biographer Stephen E. Ambrose notes: "Eisenhower had great sympathy for the white South . . . and Faubus counted on it to keep the President inactive while he battled the federal court."[93]

Eisenhower was described as taking "a moderate stand on the integration question. While recommending a go-slow policy, he has often spoken of its inevitability."[94] At a press conference on the morning the news of Little Rock broke, Eisenhower responded to a question about the events in Arkansas with a "call for restraint on the racial issue." He added "You cannot change people's hearts merely by laws. Laws . . . presumably express the conscience of a nation and its determination or will to do something. But the laws here are to be executed gradually." The president said that while he remained cognizant of the "emotional difficulties" encountered by blacks who attend separate schools, he also recognized that "there [we]re very strong emotions on the other side, people that see a picture of the mongrelization of the race, they call it."[95]

The president felt that Americans would "whip this thing in the long run" by "being true to themselves and not merely by law."[96] Eisenhower had earlier stated he could "conceive of no situation in which he would use Federal troops to enforce school integration or other civil rights matters in the South."[97] The positions advocated publicly by the president were not incompatible with Faubus's. At times, Faubus even cited President Eisenhower to support a traditional states' rights philosophy. Faubus maintained Eisenhower had described the federal government as "a creature of the states," warning that it should not become "a Frankenstein that would engulf and destroy the separate state governments."[98]

Although the president made it clear that he had "no desire to get the Administration involved in the controversy," he did telegram Governor Faubus saying, "The only assurance I can give you is that the Federal Constitution will be upheld by me by every legal means at my command."[99] This message was described in the *New York Times* as "the strongest stand the President has yet taken in support of the United States Supreme Court decision declaring unconstitutional segregation of Negro and white students in the public schools."[100]

As the curtain drew down on act one, the media directed attention to the impasse in Arkansas, President Eisenhower's desire not to involve the federal government, his professed hope that good sense would prevail, and the complex and dangerous legal options that loomed if the situation did not resolve itself. In closing our description of act one, we conclude that emergent rhetorical characteristics associated with this print-mediated narrative included dramatic staging with potential for historic or widespread conflict, vivid characterization, and lengthy, sometimes tortuous, mediated rationales to impute motives for inexplicable or mysterious actions. Moreover, disputants and disputes were located in several areas simultaneously; in this instance, local, regional, and national arenas.

### Act Two

Act one ended with a fully developed problem and no real sense of future direction. Act two was to provide a hope for resolution, but as with most three-act dramas, that hope would prove to be false. A peaks and valleys scenic environment of raised hopes and dashed expectations would dominate act two as an increasingly complex dramatic narrative continued to unfold.

#### Protagonist and Antagonist Meet

Heroes and villains eventually face each other. The White House strategy was to let Faubus play out his hand with the hope that he would eventually realize how untenable his situation was. Faubus, in turn, seemed to be looking for a quick exit from his present dilemma. As *Newsweek* noted: "It was at the height of the pressures against him, when seemingly he couldn't escape from his own trap, that the way was opened to him."[101] That "way out" was to have a meeting with the president. Attorney General Herbert Brownell was strongly against the meeting because Faubus had "soiled" himself. Brownell also pointed out that Arkansas Congressman Brooks Hays, "two senators, a Little Rock newspaper publisher, and Winthrop Rockefeller had all tried, and 'all came to the conclusion it was hopeless.' 'Well,' Eisenhower replied, 'Perhaps the time is now ripe.'" And he told the attorney general to get together with Sherman Adams to compose a telegram "for Faubus to send to Newport, requesting a meeting."[102]

The media held that the meeting was at Faubus's request. The *New York Times* reported that Governor Faubus "asked President Eisenhower today to confer with him on racial integration of Central High School in Little Rock. The President promptly suggested a meeting [at Newport] Friday afternoon or Saturday morning." The *Times* also seemed skeptical, observing that the day before Faubus had "seemed reluctant to talk to the President about the Arkansas situation," but, the *Times* reasoned, it would be "unseemly" to "refuse a meeting with the President. . . . That language hardly suggested he would ask for a conference and include in his request a statement of willingness to comply with Federal Court decrees." However, the administration's spokespersons were adamant in their claim that the governor's telegram "had reached the White House without advance notice," and that no "White House staff members including Sherman Adams, the President's principal deputy, had been in touch with Governor Faubus by telephone in advance of the Governor's message."[103]

The meeting at Newport—"a momentous confrontation, set before a backdrop of high feeling and history"[104]—yielded some hope that the drama in Little Rock could be resolved. The print-mediated environment implied that because of the titanic stakes involved, reason would prevail. No longer was the president "off stage," playing golf and delegating aides to keep him informed about events. He was, instead, "taking charge" and acting in a manner suitable to a chief executive facing a constitutional crisis.

Historically, we know that at the Newport meeting Eisenhower suggested that instead of withdrawing the militia, Faubus simply "change the orders, directing the Guard to maintain the peace while admitting the Negro pupils. . . . Eisenhower said it was not beneficial to anybody 'to have a trial of strength between the President and a governor because there could only be one outcome—that is, the state would lose, and I did not want to see any governor humiliated.' Faubus seemed to seize the offer." Eisenhower and Faubus were then joined by Adams, Hays, and Brownell. "To that group," according to Ambrose, "Faubus reiterated his intention to change the Guard's orders."[105]

What actually transpired at the meeting between the two was not revealed publicly. Our reading of notes dictated by the president covering the events at Newport confirmed that by the end of the meeting, the president believed the governor was "very appreciative" of *his* stance and it was Eisenhower's "understanding that he was going back to Arkansas to act within a matter of hours to revoke his orders to the Guard to prevent re-entry of the Negro children into the school."[106] The media explained: "Full details of the agreement between the Governor and the President cannot be made public until Governor Faubus returns to Arkansas and again assumes the powers of Governor that lapse when he leaves the state."[107] Although the media could not "reveal the details" of the meeting, the engaged public was assured that Faubus had agreed to "respect and carry out Federal court orders for racial integration of the Little Rock high schools."[108]

The coverage carried an additional message: The president had been firm with the governor. Faubus reportedly received "a 'Dutch Uncle' talk from the man under whom he served [in the Second World War]. The President could, of course, appreciate the governor's responsibility to preserve law and order in his state. . . . But when it came to flouting the authority of the courts there could be no compromise, no other answer. The courts must be obeyed."[109] "[T]he result," according to *Time* magazine, "was clear: the President of the United States had flatly insisted that the governor of Arkansas must bow to the law and withdraw from his position of rebellion."[110]

Thus, immediately following the Newport conference, there was a collective sense that the crisis of Little Rock may be over—resolved by the president. However, when Faubus returned to Little Rock he neither withdrew the Guard nor changed their orders. Now the narrative shifted and "an air of pessimism crept into the situation" as reliable sources indicated that Faubus had "hardened . . . his attitude."[111]

Faced with the stark realization that Faubus was not going to honor the agreement reached in Newport, Eisenhower immediately "wanted to issue a statement denouncing Faubus for his duplicity," but was talked out of it by Brownell and Adams.[112] Instead, two separate messages seemed to come out of the White House. Publicly, press secretary James Hagerty "would not concede that the [Newport] conference . . . between the President and Governor Faubus had been a failure. Nor would he say whether the President felt the Governor had failed to keep promises made to him." Instead the administration adopted a "wait and see" public stance.[113]

The White House also leaked a statement Eisenhower reportedly made to staffers indicating he was "'deeply disappointed'" voluntary efforts had failed to settle the school integration controversy at Little Rock. This pronouncement was interpreted as "an official admission that the conference with Governor Orval E. Faubus here last Saturday had failed to produce the results the President had expected."[114]

Act two moved toward a conclusion with a hearing held in Judge Ronald N. Davies' federal court on 20 September. Faubus did not appear in person, but his lawyers "read a statement questioning the federal court's authority," and then left. Judge Davies "promptly enjoined Faubus and the Guard from interfering with the progress of integration at Central High."[115] *Newsweek* magazine wrote that a "legal point of some importance in the problem of integration was settled last week in Little Rock, Ark.: The National Guard cannot be used to enforce segregation."[116] The Justice Department greeted that ruling with "relief and satisfaction." Engaged publics were told that in the "view of officials . . . the integrity of the judicial process and the principle of Federal supremacy had been victorious. . . . [T]he first officially backed physical resistance to the policy had ended in failure."[117]

The governor issued a statement that although he had instructed his attorneys "to exhaust every legal remedy to appeal," he would comply with the order as long as it was in effect.[118] The legal pathway was cleared for the nine black students to enter Central High School. After issuing the orders to withdraw the Guard, Faubus promptly left for Georgia to attend a conference of southern governors.

### A Touchstone Incident: Violence at Central High School

On 23 September, a "howling racist mob gathered around Central High, screaming protests against integration.[119] While the mob busied itself beating four black reporters, eight black students slipped into Central through a side door. Urged on by screams of "The niggers are in our school," the mob rushed police lines. Shouts of "lynch the niggers" were reported. The black students in the school were not physically harmed, but alarmed school officials sent them home at noon. As Ambrose noted wryly, "Integration at Central High had lasted three hours."[120] In a private letter dated 24 September 1957, the president defended being away from the White House while the trouble ensued and indicated that he did "not want to exaggerate the significance of the admittedly serious situation in Arkansas." Calling Faubus "misguided" and "motivated entirely by what he believes to be political advantage in a particular locality," the president maintained that the United States had "ample resources . . . to cope with this kind of thing." "The great need," he said, was "to act calmly, deliberately," and give "every offender opportunity to cease his defiance of Federal law and to peaceably obey the proper orders of the Federal court." Then, "even if it becomes necessary to employ considerable force," it can be "understood by all, and the individuals who have offended are not falsely transformed into martyrs."[121]

Such moderate claims aside, the governor's prophetic warnings of violence had been fulfilled. "But there was growing belief that the governor and his entourage had taken steps to make his own predictions come true."[122] As reports from Arkansas "clearly indicated the inability—and in some instances the unwillingness—of the Little Rock police to cope with the mob,"[123]

Attorney General Brownell said that "the President had to act. Eisenhower agreed,"[124] and prepared "his first step" toward "intervention."[125]

At the close of act two, we find an explanation for how the narrative drama had expanded. Symbolic influence occurs as protagonist and antagonist meet; there is seeming agreement and hopes are raised for resolution. Then there is a time of seeming betrayal and confusion followed by a touchstone incident that dashes hope for a peaceful denouement. The violence occurring as the curtain closes on act two demands resolution. The stage is now set for the dramatic confrontation and conclusion contained in act three.

### Act Three

Events in act three unfold quickly, dramatically and in rapid-fire, but not unexpected, ritual sequence. The essence of the melodrama is highlighted in act three; it is here that the crisis gets its most decisive definition and enactment.

#### Coercive Persuasion

The mediated description of "Eisenhower in action" was impressive. The president was described as "angry" and threatening to use force to "prevent obstruction of law and enforce court-ordered school integration" in Little Rock. Calling the mob actions in Little Rock "disgraceful occurrences," Eisenhower declared: "I will use the full power of the United States including whatever force may be necessary, to prevent any obstruction of the law and to carry out the orders of the Federal Court."[126]The New York Times observed that this was "by far the strongest statement the President yet had made on any civil rights matter. It marked a reversal of his 17 July news conference statement that he could not think of a situation in which he would want to use or where it would be wise to use Federal troops to enforce decrees affecting civil rights controversies."[127]

#### Truly "Administrative" Rhetoric

On the evening of 23 September Eisenhower signed "an emergency proclamation commanding all persons obstructing justice to cease and desist and to disperse." This was labeled by the White House as a "necessary legal prerequisite to the calling out of Federal troops if the enforcement of law in Little Rock continues to be impeded."[128] The next day it became obvious that "his legally correct order went unheeded and a mob ringed Central High a second day."[129] The president took action, which Time magazine headlined as "Quick, Hard and Decisive." "The weeks of patient working toward peaceful solution were over. . . . Two aides and a secretary watched silently as President Eisenhower, his decision made, picked up a pen and signed a historic document" ordering the secretary of defense "to use the armed forces of the U.S. to uphold the law of the land in Little Rock."[130]

### An Appeal to Law and Order and Presidential Duty

On 24 September 1957, flanked by the portraits "of the four leaders whom the President had stated he regards as the greatest American heroes—Benjamin Franklin, George Washington, Abraham Lincoln, and Robert E. Lee"— Eisenhower delivered from the White House a thirteen minute address to the nation concerning the situation in Little Rock. It was "a firm address, with some language unusually strong for President Eisenhower."[131]

The president provided background on a "sequence of events" leading to the Little Rock school case. Eisenhower stated that the Little Rock School Board had approved a "moderate plan for the gradual desegregation of the public schools in that city."[132] The United States court in Little Rock "which has supervisory responsibility under the law for the plan of desegregation in the public schools," approved the plan, finding it a "gradual rather than an abrupt change from the existing system." The Court issued three separate orders directing that the approved desegregation plan be carried out. "Proper and sensible observance of the law then demanded the respectful obedience which the nation has a right to expect from all its people. This, unfortunately, has not been the case at Little Rock." Although never mentioning the governor by name, the president blamed "demagogic extremists" and "certain misguided persons, many of them imported into Little Rock by agitators," for creating the present difficulties.

Eisenhower said that it had been his "hope this localized situation" would be resolved on a local level. However, "[l]ocal authorities have not eliminated that violent opposition and, under the law, I yesterday issued a Proclamation calling upon the mob to disperse." The main thrust of Eisenhower's address to the nation was that, as president, he was bound to act to uphold the federal law when it was violated. "Whenever normal agencies prove inadequate to the task and it becomes necessary for the Executive Branch of the Federal Government to use its powers and authority to uphold Federal Courts, the President's responsibility is inescapable."

The president said that the use of the powers of the executive branch is "limited to extraordinary and compelling circumstances. Manifestly, such an extreme situation has been created in Little Rock." While acknowledging that the Court's integration decision "affects the South more seriously than it does other sections of the country," Eisenhower was conciliatory, telling the nation that he knew from his "intimate personal knowledge," that the "overwhelming majority of the people of the South—including those of Arkansas and of Little Rock—are of good will, united in their efforts to preserve and respect the law even when they disagree with it." As Ambrose observes, "In his statement to the nation, the President emphasized that he was not sending U.S. troops into the South to integrate the schools, but only to maintain the law."[133]

The media coverage of the president's address was correct in its portrayal of the president's concern for the maintenance of federal authority as well as in its depiction of his conciliatory tone toward the South. In particular, our analysis of the president's address reveals that Eisenhower added the following words extemporaneously as he delivered his speech: "The running of our school system and the maintenance of peace and order in each of our States are strictly local affairs and the Federal Government does not interfere except in very special cases and when requested by one of the several States." The only other significant passage added to the delivery copy of the address included the following extemporaneous observation: "[I]n a number of communities in Arkansas integration in the schools has already started and without violence of any kind."[134]

The international implications of the Little Rock situation were also put into studied relief by the president. Those states that complied with the *Brown* decisions "demonstrated to the world that we are a nation in which laws, not men, are supreme." Where noncompliance occurs, "a tremendous disservice . . . has been done to the nation in the eyes of the world." Moreover, "it would be difficult to exaggerate the harm that is being done to the prestige and influence, and indeed to the safety of our nation and the world." America's "enemies are gloating over this incident," and, all the while, the U.S. is "portrayed as a violator" of human rights. Troops will be removed, said Eisenhower, when the "City of Little Rock . . . return[s] to its normal habits of peace and order and [then] a blot upon the fair name and high honor of our nation in the world will be removed. Thus will be restored the image of America."[135]

There was clear indication that international embarrassment had as much to do with Eisenhower's motivation to resolve the Little Rock crisis as any concern over the morality of the cause or the consistency of his ideology. By implication, Little Rock constituted a loss in the propaganda battle with the Soviets.[136] Moreover, the legal arguments advanced in the speech and portrayed by the press coverage seemed to overshadow Eisenhower's stated international image concerns. The address conspicuously avoided the ethical questions raised by resistance to desegregation. As will become even more apparent, Eisenhower's focus on legal rather than moral issues, consistent with his belief that it was inadvisable, if not impossible to legislate morality, enacted an important rhetorical template with significant implications for the country and future presidents.

Federal Troops in Little Rock

As if reconnected to the coverage in act one, the mediated coverage in act three reemphasized the observation that—as stated in *Newsweek,* "what happened at Little Rock went far beyond Central High."[137] Eisenhower's "history-making" decision was "based on a formal finding that his 'cease and desist' proclamation issued last night, had not been obeyed" and "was one of historic importance politically, socially, constitutionally."[138] This immediate judgment on U.S. cultural history was reified in the images surrounding the federal "occupation."

Once in Little Rock, the soldiers of the 101st Airborne Division, some thousand strong, "cowed racist agitators." "With bayonets fixed on their M-1 rifles, troops in battle dress broke up small, sullen knots of civilians as soon as they formed" around the school. As the *New York Times* put it: "Integration at bayonet point was effected at 9:25 a.m., forty minutes after the opening bell."[139]

Then the commanding officer, General Edwin Walker, delivered a "lecture on civics" to the white students assembled in the auditorium of Central High School. As *Life* magazine portentously explained, "He assured the students they had nothing to fear from the troops. But in solemn voice and with steely deliberation he warned that any students who interfered with the integration plans would be removed by officers and handed over to the local police. Most of the students applauded." *Life* readers were also told: "No citizen, including the President, thought that this settled anything except that the federal government is supreme. This is all the troops were supposed to prove."[140] Thus, there was a mediated reality that suggested that the federal intervention in Little Rock did not end the dispute.

Another piece of evidence supporting this view is Governor Faubus's reconstruction of "the battle of Little Rock" two days after the "occupation" of the city by the 101st Airborne. The governor's stories of abuse at federal hands abounded. But few, including other Southern governors, took him seriously, and these recriminations probably should be considered a mere epilogue.

We do believe, however, that the rhetorical contours of act three deserve a bit more scrutiny. The use of coercive persuasion, administrative rhetoric, a major national presidential address stressing law and order, duty, and national unity, and the commitment and ongoing presence of troops all gave engaged publics a mediated perception of crisis. Each of these characteristics was also crucial in reifying the crisis atmosphere established in acts one and two. The final act, of course, was pivotal in completing the dramatic narrative.

## IMPLICATIONS AND CONCLUSION

According to Edelman, "The dissemination of contradictory messages and the alternation of threat and reassurance . . . serve both to keep people anxious and to keep them docile." Villains, victims, and heroes are crucial to the political news story; and it is the dynamism of this interactive spectacle that is critical, not necessarily the substance of the story itself. Thus news reports tend to focus upon "constructed reality" rather than the dynamics of immediate experience and its situated import.[141] The mediated images help construct our joint sense of contemporary political reality; however, in the heat of the symbolic battle, we may be unable to conduct a close examination of structural relations accounting for the actual meaning of unfolding events and to find the immediate curative historical narratives that help explain that experience.

Revisionist historians and recent presidential scholars have gradually reassessed Eisenhower's leadership abilities as well as his actions on civil rights.[142] R. Gordon Hoxie, for example, argues that Eisenhower has been "[q]uite unfairly . . . portrayed as dragging his feet in the civil rights area." At the time, regarding Little Rock, however, Eisenhower "had [the] overwhelming support of the press."[143] While this may be true, Eisenhower's actions were not unanimously praised by historians.

By constructing intensive narrative plots, story lines, villains, heroes, themes, images, and contexts which helped audiences define and interpret a political crisis, mediated narrative requires careful analysis and circumspection. In this essay we have tried to indicate that part of such scholarly care ought to include a context developed by historical investigation which helps the scholar interpret more richly the mediated environment of the time. Both the mediated environment and the history are rhetorical constructions. We have merely tried to give both text and context clearer theoretical and methodological underpinnings.

We tentatively suggest that mediated crisis narratives may negatively impact our immediate collective sense of history. Early historians judged Eisenhower deficient in his handling of Little Rock. Revisionist historians were less harsh. One explanation, beyond the new archival evidence open to Eisenhower scholars, might be that the revisionists were a bit more removed from the mediated coverage than earlier historians. Such speculation must remain merely that at this writing. Other issues are a bit clearer.

After *Brown vs. Board of Education*, writes Elmo Richardson, "a great bull lurched into [Ike's] orderly schoolroom." Richardson maintains further that Ike misjudged the intransigence of southern extremists and overestimated the public's understanding of the issues—what Ike referred to as the "common sense" of the American people. Eisenhower waited for events to cool and they merely heated. Other negative evaluations were mounted by the critics. For example, it was argued that the international shame of Little Rock did little for the "nation's image abroad" and many felt Eisenhower's interest in civil rights was chiefly a result of that fact. According to Richardson, such an "image" demeaned the administration's actual record.[144]

Early historians also charged Eisenhower with weakness, citing his slow response to the crisis and his seeming insensitivity to the morality of the situation. The mere fact that he was vacationing while human rights were being trampled gave cause for political sniping.[145] Arthur Larson, however, maintains that the charge is misleading. He insists that Eisenhower was no different than other presidents when denounced for inaction in their presumed role as chief moral educators for the nation. While one may fault "[b]ackground, environment, age, limited exposure to the problem . . . or [even] an excessively constricted conception of the presidency," Larson argues, one must not attribute Little Rock to "indecision, weakness or lack of initiative."[146]

We believe the president's so-called detachment was a matter of both principled substance and rhetorical style. Such a view comports with what Fred I. Greenstein has labeled Eisenhower's "hidden-hand" presidency.[147]Certainly Eisenhower's principled position to avoid, if at all possible, federal intrusion into the lives of U.S. citizens was a tack that was easily demonstrable early in the first campaign and consistently held throughout his presidency. As Eisenhower indicated by night letter to Senator Richard B. Russell on 27 September 1957, "Few times in my life have I felt as saddened as when the obligations of my office required me to order the use of force within a state to carry out the decisions of a Federal Court." Yet the president lamented: "Failure to act. . . would [have] be[en] tantamount to acquiescence in anarchy and the dissolution of the union."[148]

We believe Eisenhower's public style was in opposition to mediated melodramatics of any sizeable dimension. Ike's moderation, or, for some, extreme restraint could have been (and perhaps properly was) perceived as especially unseemly in the context of a mediated crisis. The president paid a price north and south for trying to walk the tightrope between what he termed, the "extremists" on either side.[149]The president's style was especially in relief during Little Rock and we believe it was incommensurate with the mediated imperatives. Even if there is an element of truth to perceptions of Eisenhower as reactionary rather than initiator—as one who left details to others and subsequently paid the price—such negative evaluations can hardly explain the social, moral, and political complexities that Little Rock would come to symbolize.

If unforeseen circumstances forced Eisenhower to intervene at Little Rock, positive and negative judgments on the propriety, intensity, and consistency of his actions would engage audiences no matter what he did or when he did it, nor would it please all participants vis-a-vis how it was accomplished. Such evaluation is the natural outcome of testy and intractable domestic conundrums faced by all presidents. Such judgments are necessary if not sufficient conditions for mass-mediated politics. While we still might censure Eisenhower for narrow vision, narrow construction of the powers of the presidency, a flawed understanding of the separation of powers, and a certain amount of undue restraint owing to his pro-southern sensibilities (both political and personal), given the novelty of his charge and the intensity of the political and social stakes, one might be hard pressed to find a president to do better under similar circumstances. By both photograph and printed word, an historical epoch was captured in the mediated realities. We have tried to temper part of the heady immediacy of these media-documented events with the historical record.

A comparison between Eisenhower and his successor John F. Kennedy is surely instructive in this context. Neither the first nor the last president to go slow on moral advocacy efforts, Eisenhower was the first president to confront a monumental federal-state conflict over civil rights in this century, and his hard knocks were instructive and sobering to subsequent presidents. And while it may be the case that John F. Kennedy finally did throw down the moral gauntlet and perform the expected ritual of moral educator after the Birmingham crisis in 1963, there were, arguably, two long years of inaction on his part with respect to black civil rights.[150] Kennedy's inaction was in part due to the ghosts of Little Rock and the long shadows of federal bayonets raised on southern soil. Kennedy also suffered recriminations for action too little and too late on this great moral frontier. In addition, both Eisenhower and Kennedy feared international opprobrium during their respective civil rights challenges. Both were anxious to resolve the incongruity of exporting "freedom" abroad and the increasing evidence of its absence in the United States. The Soviet Union, of course, was exploiting the inequities involved for its own purposes.[151] Little Rock and Birmingham cast a domestic shadow that ran willy-nilly into the center of the Cold War.

Finally, given the widespread public accounts of President Eisenhower's feelings about the Supreme Court's integration decision, his sympathy for the South, and his concerns for the doctrine of states' rights, we find that the president may have inadvertently given comfort to the very extremists he decried in his televised address. As Tony Fryer asserts, "Long after the end of the crisis . . . Little Rock retained a place in the nation's collective memory." Little Rock became a harbinger of future racial unrest in this nation. Fryer faults both Eisenhower and Faubus with being "unwilling to subordinate narrow electoral goals to the enforcement of moral principle." And, without necessarily questioning their motives, both men certainly "entangled desegregation in a mass of political considerations that invited confrontation." Fryer also highlights a historical trend:

> The focus on legalism, which continued until at least the 1980s, had the effect of confusing means with ends. Obedience to law itself—not the substantive value of equal educational opportunity—became the basis for both compliance and resistance. In short, many government leaders expected first Southerners, then all Americans, to accept minority rights as a matter of compulsion rather than consent.[152]

Ironically, then, if Fryer is correct, Eisenhower's discourse on civil rights, with its focus on law and order, served to reinforce the very thing Eisenhower most feared, legal compulsion on a contested moral issue. For while it was the case that Eisenhower fully believed that the issue indeed was a moral question, he railed against legal sanctions as remedies, especially remedies that would put the federal government at loggerheads with the states.

In turn, "focus on the rule-of-law led inevitably to controversy over the nature of judicial power in a representative democracy." Thus the polarized camps between local and federal authority and between judicial activism versus restraint were allowed to set up their tents in a valley rent by conflict. The result of this debate over federal versus state authority and the nature and scope of "proper" exercise of judicial power "was that questions of moral principle" were submerged and subordinated to a "conservative moderation."[153] Thus did the nation veer from its traditional ideals of justice, encapsulated in notions of equity and fairness embodied in a representative democracy for all.

Michael R. Belknap highlights a different lesson but a related legacy:

> In leaving the job of combating these troublemakers to unreliable state authorities, the Eisenhower administration evaded an obligation. It also courted disaster. Little Rock was the price the nation paid for the failure of the President and the Justice Department to assume responsibility for controlling disorder ignited by the Federal government itself.[154]

Because "the violent bigots of the Eisenhower era made explosives their weapon of choice," Belknap argues, Eisenhower's emphasis on states' rights merely allowed local officials in the South "to exploit [their power] to keep blacks from exercising their constitutional rights."[155]

Perhaps Eisenhower did not take up the moral gauntlet because of his abiding trust in the common sense and morality of the majority of the American people, who, he seemed to feel, would eventually overcome the injustices of racism. Certainly Eisenhower sent in federal troops to prevent mob rule and to protect his and the nation's constitutional authority, as he had stated in his address to the nation. E. Frederic Morrow, an Eisenhower appointee and the "first black person in history to have served a United States President in an executive capacity," ascribes Eisenhower's insertion of troops to more narrow motives: Faubus had ridiculed the president and the troops were sent in as a direct response to personal insult.[156]

We believe the mediated drama at Little Rock was inevitable. In that narrative, there was a rich source of conflict and deep emotional and legal tensions. We find an intriguing ally for this stance in the words of Presbyterian minister Dunbar H. Ogden, the president of the Greater Little Rock Ministerial Association:

> This had to happen someplace in the South. It was inevitable that there was going to be a plan, worked out, approved and accepted, for gradual integration. It was inevitable that somewhere a governor, under pressure of extreme segregationists, was going to stop integration by calling out the National Guard. This may be looked back upon by future historians as the turning point—for good—of race relations in this country. If the Supreme Court's interpretation of the Constitution can be made good in Little Rock, then it can be made good in Arkansas, then eventually it can be made good throughout the South.[157]

We would merely observe here that the good minister's assessment that Little Rock would be regarded by future historians as a "turning point" for "good" "race relations" was perhaps a bit too optimistic.

Despite the mixed evaluations documented here, we would be remiss if we did not end on one positive note. Eisenhower was the first president in the twentieth century who faced a domestic crisis that had provoked images of the Reconstruction era. It was a difficult and profoundly vexing problem, with long roots and deep divisions. Events and subsequent mediated narratives emanating from Little Rock, however, did much to force his hand. Thus we would observe that media creates as well as reflects history and history can at times serve as a corrective to mediated realities. Taking an even longer view of history, we believe that by sending federal troops to Little Rock to protect the equal rights of children to attend school, Eisenhower became a key participant in helping restore a political, historical, and cultural vision of a nation and a republicanism represented by one of his most esteemed predecessors, Abraham Lincoln.

## NOTES

1. See Richard A. Cherwitz and Kenneth S. Zagacki, "Consummatory Versus Justificatory Crisis Rhetoric," *Western Journal of Speech Communication* 50 (1986): 307-24; D. Ray Heisey, "Reagan and Mitterrand Respond to International Crisis: Creating Versus Transcending Appearances," *Western Journal of Speech Communication* 50 (1986): 325-35; David C. Klope, "Defusing a Foreign Policy Crisis: Myth and Victimage in Reagan's 1983 Lebanon/Grenada Address," *Western Journal of Speech Communication* 50 (1986): 336-49; Ralph E. Dowling and Gabrielle Marraro, "Grenada and the Great

Communicator: A Study in Democratic Ethics," *Western Journal of Speech Communication* 50 (1986): 350-67; Thomas A. Hollihan, "The Public Controversy Over the Panama Canal Treaties: An Analysis of American Foreign Policy Rhetoric," *Western Journal of Speech Communication* 50 (1986): 368-87. Two examinations of domestic civil rights crisis can be found in Steven R. Goldzwig and George N. Dionisopoulos, "John F. Kennedy's Civil Rights Discourse: The Evolution from 'Principled Bystander' to Public Advocate," *Communication Monographs* 56 (1989): 179-98; Martin J. Medhurst, "Eisenhower, Little Rock, and the Rhetoric of Crisis," in *The Modern Presidency and Crisis Rhetoric,* ed. Amos Kiewe (New York: Praeger, 1993), 19-46..

2. Kevin M. Carragee, "Interpretive Media Study and Interpretive Social Science," *Critical Studies in Mass Communication* 7 (1990): 87.

3. Kathleen J. Turner, "Rhetorical History as Social Construction." Paper delivered at the annual meeting of the Southern Communication Association convention, Tampa, Florida, April 1991; quotations, 2.

4. James C. Duram, *A Moderate Among Extremists: Dwight D. Eisenhower and the School Desegregation Crisis* (Chicago: Nelson-Hall, 1981), 52. The decision was handed down 17 May 1954.

5. Robert Fredrick Burk, *The Eisenhower Administration and Black Civil Rights* (Knoxville: University of Tennessee Press, 1984), 23, 109.

6. Duram, 54.

7. President's Response to Statement of Attorney General Herbert Brownell, Whitman Files, Cabinet Series, Box 6, Cabinet Meeting of 9 March 1956. Eisenhower Library (hereafter cited as DDE Library).

8. Burk, 132.

9. Duram, 55.

10. Burk, 23-24.

11. Duram, 60-61.

12. Personal letter from the President to Captain E.E. "Swede" Hazlett, Whitman File, DDE Diary Series, Box 25, July 1957, DDE Dictation, 22 July 1957, DDE Library.

13. Duram, 64.

14. Letter from the President to the Honorable James F. Byrnes, Whitman File, DDE Diary Series, Box 25, July 1957, DDE Dictation, 23 July 1957, DDE Library.

15. Letter from President Eisenhower to Mr. George Landes, Whitman Files, DDE Diary Series, Box 26, September 1957, DDE Dictation (2), 12 September 1957, DDE Library.

16. Duram, 61.

17. Ibid., 62-63.

18. The plan was actually handed down on 24 May 1955, one year after the *Brown* desegregation decision. The original *Brown* decision, of course, struck down the "separate but equal" doctrine established in *Plessy v. Ferguson.*

19. Burk, 150.

20. Ibid., 167,

21. Ibid., 165, 171.

22. Hugh Davis Graham, *The Civil Rights Era: Origins and Development of National Policy, 1960-1972* (New York: Oxford, 1990), 16-17; Burk, 163.

23. Duram, 143.

24. Ibid., 60-61.

25. Murray Edelman, *Constructing the Political Spectacle* (Chicago and London: University of Chicago Press, 1988), 37.

26. Dan Nimmo and James E. Combs, *Mediated Political Realities*, 2nd ed. (White Plains: Longman, 1990), 18.
27. Edelman, 93-94.
28. Ibid., 94.
29. Ibid., 96.
30. Nimmo and Combs, esp., 16-17.
31. Daisy Bates, *The Long Shadow of Little Rock: A Memoir* (New York: David McKay Company, 1962), 3.
32. Benjamin Fine, "Little Rock Told to Integrate Now Despite Militia," *New York Times*, 4 September 1957, A1.
33. "The South: Making a Crisis in Arkansas," *Time* (16 September 1957): 23.
34. William A. Emerson, "The South Gives Ground," *Newsweek* (9 September 1957): 34.
35. "The Great Issue," *Newsweek* (16 September 1957): 34.
36. "The South: Making a Crisis in Arkansas," 23.
37. Fine, A37.
38. "The Great Issue," 34.
39. Fine, A1, A37.
40. Bates, 65.
41. "The Great Issue," 33.
42. "Editorial Comments from the South," *New York Times*, 6 September 1957, A9.
43. Brownell to President, Whitman File, Administration Series, Box 8, 7 November 1957, 11-12, DDE Library.
44. "The Nation: Pains of History," *Time* (16 September 1957): 23.
45. Benjamin Fine, "Arkansas Troops Bar Negro Pupils; Governor Defiant," *New York Times*, 5 September 1957, A1, A20.
46. Benjamin Fine, "Little Rock Faces Showdown Today Over Integration," *New York Times*, 7 September 1957, A8.
47. "The Great Issue," 33.
48. Quoted in "Editorial Comments From the South," A9.
49. John N. Popham, "Strategy Test in South," *New York Times*, 9 September 1957, A18.
50. Bates, 49.
51. "The Nation: Pains of History," 24; Virgil T. Blossom, *It Has Happened Here* (New York: Harper & Brothers, 1959), 38.
52. "The News of the Week in Review: Little Rock, Arkansas," *New York Times*, 8 September 1957, E1.
53. Popham, A18.
54. "Hillbilly, Slightly Sophisticated," *Time* (16 September 1957): 24.
55. "The Governor . . . Who Put Himself Against the President and Federal Authority," *Newsweek* (16 September 1957): 34.
56. Anthony Lewis, "Washington Studies Little Rock Dispute," *New York Times*, 4 September 1957, 37.
57. "The News of the Week in Review: Up to Faubus," *New York Times*, 15 September 1957, 4, E1.
58. "The News of The Week in Review: Little Rock, Arkansas," E1; Emerson, 34; "Governor on the Spot," *New York Times*, 4 September 1957, 37.
59. "The Governor . . . Who Put Himself," 35.
60. Emerson, 34.
61. "The News of the Week in Review: Up to Faubus," E1.

62. Emerson, 34.
63. Fine, "Arkansas Troops Bar Negro Pupils," A1.
64. "The Nation: Pains of History," 25.
65. Fine, "Arkansas Troops Bar Negro Pupils," A1.
66. Fine, "Little Rock Faces Showdown Today, A1.
67. Benjamin Fine, "Faubus Bids U.S. Recede on Order For Integration," *New York Times*, 9 September 1957, 25.
68. "The Nation: Pains of History," 25.
69. "The Great Issue," 35.
70. "The Nation: Pains of History," 25.
71. Fine, "Little Rock Faces Showdown Today," A8.
72. "The Nation: Pains of History," 25.
73. Fine, "Arkansas Troops Bar Negro Showdown Today," A1.
74. Fine, "Little Rock Faces Showdown Today," A8.
75. "The Nation: Pains of History," 25.
76. Ibid., 23.
77. "The Great Issue," 35.
78. "The Nation: Pains of History," 25.
79. Popham, "Strategy Test in South," A18; Blossom, 49.
80. "Editorial Comments From the South," *New York Times*, 6 September 1957, 9; "Faubus Defended," *New York Times*, 7 September 1957, A9; "Arkansas," *The New Republic* (16 September 1957): 5.
81. "The News of the Week in Review: Little Rock, Arkansas," E1.
82. "Editorial Comments From the South," A9.
83. Fine, "Little Rock Told to Integrate Now," 37.
84. "The Great Issue," 35.
85. Fine, "Little Rock Faces Showdown Today," A8.
86. Fine, "Arkansas Troops Bar Negro Pupils," A1.
87. Fine, "Faubus Bids U.S. Recede," A1.
88. Anthony Lewis, "President Weighs Integration Move," *New York Times*, 8 September 1957, A66.
89. Fine, "Faubus Bids U.S. Recede," A1.
90. Stephen E. Ambrose, *Eisenhower: The President* (New York: Simon and Schuster, 1984), 413.
91. "Arkansas," 5.
92. Lewis, "Washington Studies Little Rock Dispute," A1.
93. Ambrose, 414.
94. "The News of the Week in Review: Little Rock, Arkansas," E1.
95. "The President's News Conference of September 3, 1957, *Public Papers, 1957*, 640, 646.
96. Lewis, "Washington Studies Little Rock Dispute," A37.
97. W. H. Lawrence, "President Sees Brownell Today," *New York Times*, 7 September 1957, A1.
98. Fine, "Faubus Bids U.S. Recede," A18.
99. Ambrose, 414.
100. W. H. Lawrence, "President Warns Governor Faubus He'll Uphold Law," *New York Times*, 6 September 1957, A1.
101. "The Governor's Broken Blade," *Newsweek* ( 23 September 1957): 30.
102. Ambrose, 415.

103. W. H. Lawrence, "President Agrees to Bid by Faubus For School Talks," *New York Times*, 12 September 1957, A1, A25.

104. "The Nation, Retreat from Newport," *Time* (23 September 1957): 11.

105. Ambrose, 416. We have adopted Ambrose's interpretation of the non-mediated private conversations and events that preceded, constituted, and followed the Newport meeting. Interpretations of the historical record, of course, may differ. For a different view see Medhurst.

106. "Notes dictated by the President on 8 October 1957 concerning the visit of Governor Orval Faubus of Arkansas to Little Rock on 14 September 1957," Whitman File, Administration Series, Box 23, 8 October 1957, DDE Library.

107. W. H. Lawrence, "Gov. Faubus Assures President He'll Obey Integration Order, But Asks For Patience By U.S." *New York Times*, 15 September 1957, A1, A56.

108. Lawrence, "Gov. Faubus Assures President," A1. According to the *New York Times* the "statements of President Eisenhower and Gov. Orval E. Faubus after their Newport meeting created confusion and uncertainty" in Little Rock. Those closest to the dispute were saying that the situation was "still in a state of confusion," and "still vague and ambiguous." John N. Popham, "Confusion Grows in Arkansas Capital After Gov. Faubus and President Hold Parley," *New York Times*, 15 September 1957, A56.

109. "The Governor's Broken Blade," 29.

110. "The Nation, Retreat from Newport," 11.

111. Benjamin Fine, "Faubus Continues Talks with Hays, Impasse Remains," *New York Times*, 19 September 1957, A1.

112. Ambrose, 416.

113. W. H. Lawrence, "Eisenhower Adopts 'Wait and See' Stand on Moves by Faubus," *New York Times*, 21 September 1957, A11.

114. W. H. Lawrence, "Eisenhower 'Disappointed' By Impasse at Little Rock," *New York Times*, 20 September 1957, A1.

115. Ambrose, 417.

116. "Segregation: Battleground," *Newsweek* (30 September 1957): 38.

117. Anthony Lewis, "Action By Faubus Cheers U.S. Aides," *New York Times*, 21 September 1957, A1.

118. Benjamin Fine, "Gov. Faubus Withdraws Troops: Obeys Federal Court Injunction on Integration, But Will Appeal," *New York Times*, 21 September 1957, A10.

119. Ambrose, 418.

120. Ibid.

121. Letter to General Alfred M. Gruenther from the President, Whitman File, Diary Series, Box 9, 24 September 1957, DDE Library. Although he gave no direct public indication, there is some reason to suspect that the president actually felt deeply betrayed by Faubus. Whether guided by personal animosity through a perceived double cross at Newport, or merely expressing his irritation at having a visit to the links postponed, approximately one month later, the president, lamenting his inability to schedule a golf game with the vice-president, dictated the following message: "Dear Dick: I had been hoping to play golf this afternoon. . . .If you already have a game, please don't think of changing your plans because mine are necessarily so uncertain because of the stupidity and duplicity of one called Faubus." Dictation by the President to the Vice-President, Whitman File, DDE Diary Series, 20 October 1957, DDE Library.

122. "A Historic Week of Civil Strife," *Life* (7 October 1957): 37.

123. Ibid., 39.

124. Ambrose, 418.

125. "A Historic Week of Civil Strife," 39.

126. W. H. Lawrence, "President Threatens to Use U.S. Troops, Orders Rioters in Little Rock to Desist; Mob Compels Nine Negroes to Leave School," *New York Times*, 24 September 1957, A1, A21.

127. Lawrence, "President Threatens to Use U.S. Troops," A21.

128. Ibid., A1.

129. "A Historic Week of Civil Strife," 40.

130. "Quick, Hard & Decisive," *Time* (7 October 1957): 21-22.

131. Anthony Lewis, "President Sends Troops to Little Rock, Federalizes Arkansas National Guard; Tells Nation He Acted to Avoid Anarchy," *New York Times*, 25 September 1957, A14.

132. Unless otherwise specified all references to this address are taken from Dwight D. Eisenhower, "Federal Court Orders Must Be Upheld: President's Responsibility Is Inescapable," *Vital Speeches of the Day* 24 (15 October 1957): 11-12. When necessary, we will refer to the delivered speech and the delivery text, indicating important similarities and differences.

133. Ambrose, 420.

134. Text of the Address by the President of the United States, Delivered from his Office at the White House, Tuesday 24 September 1957, at 9:00 p.m., EDT, *As Actually Delivered*, Whitman File, Administration Series, Box 23, Little Rock Arkansas (2), DDE Library. The actual delivery text can be located in the Whitman Speech File, Box 22, Speech Drafts, DDE Library.

135. "Text of the Address by the President," 4.

136. The human rights abuses in the Soviet Union and in recent events describing the Soviet invasion of Hungary, in particular, were common to U.S. parlance at the time. A report that crossed the president's desk noted the following: "Soviet media single out the Little Rock situation for special attention and take pains to point out that armed national guardsmen are not there to protect the Negro children from the fanatics of the Ku Klux Klan, but to prevent them from entering the school." The same report quotes Radio Moscow as saying: "'Mr. Lodge tells lies stuffed with slander and makes a great deal of fuss trying to prevent the Hungarian people from living in peace and quiet, but the cries of hundreds of Negro children, ill-treated by the whites, rise from the Southern states and drown out his voice.'" World Reaction to U.S. Racial Integration Incidents and Reaction to U.S. Integration Incidents Increases, Whitman File, DDE Diary Series, Box 27, September 1957, Toner Notes 12 and 13, September 1957, DDE Library.

137. "The President . . . The South," *Newsweek* (7 October 1957): 27.

138. Lewis, "President Sends Troops to Little Rock," A1.

139. Homer Bigart, "U.S. Troops Enforce Peace in Little Rock As Nine Negroes Return to Their Classes; President to Meet Southern Governors," *New York Times*, 26 September 1957, A1.

140. "A Historic Week of Civil Strife," 44, 43.

141. Edelman, 98; 101-2.

142. See for example, Fred I. Greenstein, *The Hidden-Hand Presidency: Eisenhower as Leader* (New York: Basic Books, 1982); Anthony James Joes, "Eisenhower Revisionism: The Tide Comes In," *Presidential Studies Quarterly* 15 (1985): 561-71; Mary S. McCauliffe, "Commentary/Eisenhower, the President," *Journal of American History* 68 (1981): 625-32; Mark Stern, "Presidential Strategies and Civil Rights: Eisenhower, The Early Years,

1952-1954," *Presidential Studies Quarterly* 19 (1989): 769-95; Michael S. Mayer, "With Much Deliberation and Some Speed: Eisenhower and the Brown Decision," *Journal of Southern History* 52 (1986): 43-76; Joann P. Krieg, ed., *Dwight D. Eisenhower: Soldier, President, Statesman* (New York: Greenwood Press, 1987); Medhurst.

143. R. Gordon Hoxie, "Eisenhower and Presidential Leadership," *Presidential Studies Quarterly* 13 (1983): 601-2.

144. Elmo Richardson, *The Presidency of Dwight D. Eisenhower* (Lawrence: The Regent's Press, 1979), 106, 125.

145. As Marquis Childs maintains: "Many northern newspapers gave him a measure of praise for having acted to end an intolerable situation. . . . But this was grudging tribute from those who felt that, if only he had acted more quickly, the worst consequences of this shameful episode might have been avoided." Marquis Childs, *Eisenhower: Captive Hero— A Critical Study of the General and the President* (London: Hammond, Hammond and Company, 1959), esp. 224-27; quotation, 226.

146. Arthur Larson, *Eisenhower: The President Nobody Knew* (New York: Charles Scribner's and Sons, 1968), 132-33.

147. Fred I. Greenstein maintains that Eisenhower exercised "hidden-hand leadership," "instrumental use of language," and "selective delegation" in enacting his role as president. Eisenhower strove to create a sense of national unity and to garner respect for the institutional office of the presidency and his role as Chief of State. (See esp. 233-41).

148. Night Letter from the President to the Honorable Richard B. Russell, Whitman File, Administration Series, Box 23, 27 September 1957, DDE Library.

149. See Duram, vi; Burk, 153; Barber, 138. Norman Thomas, a syndicated columnist for the *Los Angeles Mirror*, among others, took great exception to Eisenhower's reference to "extremists on both sides" in his depiction of violence and school desegregation. Thomas wrote the president: "Unfortunately that expression is too often understood as apportioning guilt about equally between the aggressive segregationists and the advocates of obedience to the order of the Court." Letter of Norman Thomas to the President, White House Central Files, General File, Box 916, 124-A-1, School Decision (1), DDE Library.

150. Goldzwig and Dionisopoulos.

151. For a sample of the international concerns experienced and expressed by both presidents see their respective speech texts. Eisenhower's, of course, is cited herein. Kennedy's is cited in Goldzwig and Dionisopoulos. An interesting example of Eisenhower's concern can be found in the following. At Eisenhower's request, Henry Cabot Lodge outlined his suggestions for international damage control. See Letter to the President from Henry Cabot Lodge, Whitman File, Administration Series, Box 24, Henry Cabot Lodge, 1957-1958 (3), 15 October 1957, DDE Library.

152. Tony Freyer, *The Little Rock Crisis: A Constitutional Interpretation* (Westport: Greenwood Press, 1984), 171-72; block quotation, 172.

153. Freyer, 173-74.

154. Michael R. Belknap, *Federal Law and Southern Order: Racial Violence and Constitutional Conflict in the Post-Brown South* (Athens and London: University of Georgia Press, 1987), 52.

155. Ibid., 53, 48.

156. Milton S. Katz, "E. Frederick [sic] Morrow and Civil Rights in the Eisenhower Administration," *Phylon* 42 (1981): 133-44; see esp. quotation 133 and 138-39.

157. "The Meaning of Little Rock," *Time* (7 October 1957): 21.

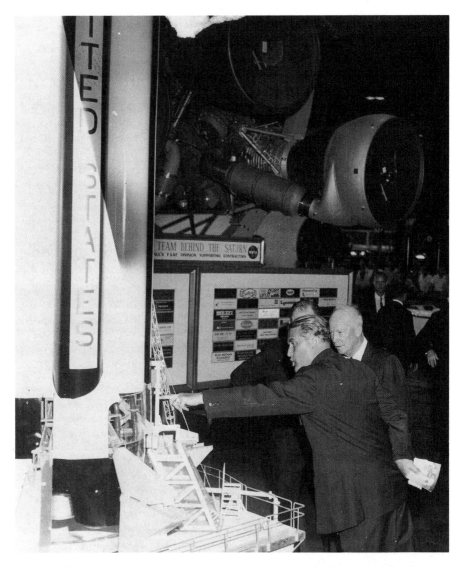

Eisenhower and Werner Von Braun examine a model of the Saturn rocket

David
Henry

# Eisenhower and Sputnik
*The Irony of Failed Leadership*

Writing to his brother Arthur in November 1957, Dwight D. Eisenhower recounted how "This past year seems to have been one of steadily mounting crises and pressures, culminating in the Little Rock situation at home and the blows to our prestige by that and by the Russian scientific achievements the past few weeks."[1] The launching of Sputnik I on 4 October 1957, and Sputnik II early in November constituted the scientific achievements to which Eisenhower referred. Combined with the domestic strife caused by the constitutional crisis in Little Rock, the Soviets' success in space contributed to one of the most crucial moments of Eisenhower's presidency.[2] At such a moment, Ike's leadership skills were severely tested.

Even though Eisenhower's own view was that the earth satellites' practical applications in defense or military planning were negligible, his reluctance to credit the importance of such satellites to the propaganda war and to move swiftly to counter the Soviets' success comprises an instructive study in failed rhetorical leadership. Irony is perhaps the most striking feature of Eisenhower's inability to recognize and counter the potential propaganda value of Soviet technological achievement. Only four years earlier, Ike himself had taken the propaganda initiative by delivering his "Atoms for Peace" speech to the United Nations General Assembly. The date was 8 December 1953. In this speech, Eisenhower invited the world to view the "Atoms for Peace" proposal as a call for nuclear arms control, while at the same time he aimed to secure a psychological victory in the Cold War.[3] In view of his success with the "Atoms for Peace" campaign, the president's failed rhetorical response to the Sputnik crisis seems ironic, and warrants careful examination.

That failure stemmed from Eisenhower's view of presidential leadership. Eisenhower articulated his conception of leadership in the fall of 1957 when he recruited Arthur Larson to the White House to help plan a public campaign on "Science and Security." Larson would draft the president's speeches for the campaign and, equally important, would aid in planning how best to use the chief executive's powers to effect the administration's goals in science and technology. Shortly after Larson's arrival from his post as Director of the

United States Information Agency (USIA), Eisenhower confided to his aide: "Leadership is deciding what needs to be done, and then getting other people to *want* to do it." Larson later lauded his commander in chief for having "made the decisions needed to set America on the right direction, and . . . hav[ing] in large measure succeeded in getting people to want to follow that direction."[4] Ike's advocacy on behalf of "Science and Security," however, raises questions about the adequacy of any leadership theory that attaches limitless power to the president. For in the case of Sputnik, that view led to severe miscalculations in developing a strategy responsive to the exigencies of the situation.

Eisenhower underestimated the importance which the American public— inundated by media coverage of Sputnik—would attach to the perception that the United States was falling behind in the space race. Once the president and his advisors finally understood the need for a sustained effort to calm the nation's anxieties, uninspired—and hence uninspiring—rhetorical choices virtually guaranteed a weak kickoff. Initially, four speeches were planned to set the campaign on track. Textual and contextual decisions alike worked to the president's disadvantage in his first rhetorical response, delivered from the Oval Office on 7 November 1957. Just six days later, on 13 November, Eisenhower hit his stride in a national radio and television address presented before a live audience in Oklahoma City's municipal auditorium. Preparing for the third speech in this ongoing campaign, a speech scheduled for presentation in Cleveland during the last week of November, the president was felled by a stroke.

Whether a completed campaign would have enabled Eisenhower to get the public to do what needed to be done in response to Sputnik is, of course, speculative and beyond the scope of this essay. What is clear, however, is that a poor initial assessment of the situation and audience led to weak strategic choices at the inception of the "Science and Security" campaign. The resulting rhetoric graphically demonstrated Eisenhower's inability to convert personal popularity to productive leadership on the question of U.S. policy in science and space.

## RHETORICAL CRISIS AND INITIAL RESPONSE

According to George Reedy, who served in the White House under Lyndon Johnson, chief among the skills essential to presidential leadership is the ability to maintain "a monopoly on authoritative answers." Reedy points to Eisenhower's miscalculations of Sputnik's importance as illustrative of how personally popular presidents are not always able to translate popularity into leadership. Noting that Eisenhower entered office "on a tidal wave of enthusiasm," Reedy attributes that enthusiasm to the president's image as "a father, a grandfather, and a kindly uncle all combined. He could do no wrong." Nonetheless, Reedy continues, "no man since Warren Gamaliel Harding permitted the powers of leadership to be taken from him on so many occasions," as demonstrated by the Sputnik case. The Soviets' success shattered the illusion of American technical superiority. Although Eisenhower knew of the probability of a launch, and had even mentioned the administration's awareness of the Russians' rapid progress in rocketry during a press conference, he had done little to prepare the American public for either the event or the propaganda campaign that followed. "To the feverish imagination of people too unskilled to realize the limitations of technology," Reedy concludes,

> [Sputnik] opened up limitless vistas of hideous nightmares. . . . Visions were created of Soviet spies with superpowerful binoculars who could ferret out the most cherished secrets of our country. Without knowing how it could be done, the "man on the street" assumed that control of space around the earth would mean control of the earth itself. And if there was one thing of which Americans were certain in the fall of 1957, it was that they did not want the earth controlled by the Soviet Union.[5]

The prominence of Eisenhower's critics and the president's initial reticence did little, however, to dispel fears of growing Soviet power.

## The Challenge

While Eisenhower moved deliberately to confer with his advisors and to plan carefully his campaign to reassure Americans that the Soviets had not attained control of the earth, three diverse sources—the Soviet Union, the American press, and American political leaders of both parties—helped to sustain public fears. The Soviet Union led the way, swiftly capitalizing on the event to gain the upper hand in Cold War persuasion. Following a lengthy technical narrative of Sputnik's operation, a press release from the Soviets' official news agency, Tass, declared: "Artificial earth satellites will pave the way for space travel, and it seems that the present generation will witness how the freed and conscious labor of the people of the new socialist society turns even the most daring of man's dreams into reality."[6] The *New York Times* both reprinted the Tass opinion verbatim, and lent credence to the press release's claims by lauding the Soviets' skill in exploiting the "opportunity to use the launching for propaganda purposes."[7]

Coverage in the *New York Times* reflected the propensity of the press, particularly the print media, to keep the Soviet Union's apparent superiority in space at the center of public attention. For weeks, newspapers and news magazines devoted front page space and cover stories to the topic, often generating fear, albeit unwittingly, about America's status in the space race. *Newsweek's* first cover after the launching of Sputnik was illustrative. A last-minute substitution for a planned lead on small cars that was already coming off the presses when word of the launch reached the magazine's editors,[8] the cover carried the heading "INTO SPACE" in oversized, bold-faced print. Three themes, in smaller but still striking graphic form, descended from the lead. *Newsweek* cast the event as "The Red Conquest," promised to explain "The Meaning to the World," and indicated an intention to explore "Why We're Lagging." An artist's drawing of an orbiting capsule brought the reader's attention to the magazine's "Special Space Section,"[9] a forerunner of what would become a regular weekly feature on "Space and the Atom." Explaining the new section several weeks later, editors placed "Space and the Atom" in the context of *Newsweek's* practice of establishing departmental status for topics of historic import. In "Space and the Atom," they concluded, "perhaps the most significant of all special departments has appeared. It recognizes that the world stands on the threshold of a new scientific era of even greater potential impact on all of us than the dawn of the atomic age in the '40s."[10]

Coverage in the *New York Times*, the nation's newspaper of record, reflected a similar sentiment. Noted for its conservative approach to journalism and an aversion to the sensationalist tactics of its competitors, the 5 October front page was devoted completely to Sputnik and related stories. A rare three-level headline covered the entire top of the issue:

> Soviet Fires Earth Satellite into Space;
> It is Circling the Globe at 18,000 M.P.H;
> Sphere Tracked in Four Crossings Over U.S.

Four front-page stories accompanied the headline, introducing readers to the satellite's course, distance from earth, weight, and powerful communication signals. Four more stories began on the second page, two others on the third.[11]

Certainly the event warranted close immediate coverage. What differentiated American reporting, however, was the continued preoccupation with the story in ensuing weeks. International journalists in such centers as London, Beirut, Hong Kong, Vienna, Rome, Madrid, Tokyo, and Cairo reported the event, averred that with Sputnik the Soviets surpassed the United States in space science, and then turned their attention to other news[12]—as did world leaders. On a state visit in late October, for example, Queen Elizabeth and Prince Philip both remarked to Eisenhower that they found curious America's continued preoccupation with the space launch. The British monarch told Eisenhower, who later repeated the conversation to speech writer Emmet John Hughes, that "people in London just gave it one day of excitement, then went on about their business."[13] But the American press treated Sputnik almost as the only business that mattered. Perhaps presaging *Newsweek's* weekly reports on "Space and the Atom," the *New York Times* had at least one front-page story on the U.S.-Soviet space race daily from 5 October through 15 October. Except for 11 October when the lone front page story occupied the paper's left-hand column, editors deemed the topic sufficiently significant to feature it in the right-hand column, traditionally the location of each day's most important news.

Finally, American political figures from both parties provided the press with stories to report, thus helping sustain the nation's focus on space. Democrats' reactions ranged from the quiet planning of a legislative strategy to exploit Eisenhower's perceived weakness on space policy to denunciations of the administration for putting budget concerns ahead of defense. Lyndon Johnson, the Senate Democratic leader who would eventually confront Eisenhower over space policy, shifted his attention from economic issues to defense soon after Sputnik.[14] In his role as a legislative leader, Johnson conferred with the president throughout the fall, vowing to work with the White House to forge legislation in the best interest of all Americans. Eisenhower recalled Johnson telling him that he had resisted pressures to convene a special session of Congress, "hop[ing] we would close ranks, forget anything about Republicans and Democrats, and do the job." But the president was realistic about Johnson's bipartisanship. The Senator "said all the right things," Eisenhower recalled, and "I think today he is being honest."[15] The president's caution proved prudent, for within three months Johnson used space policy both to challenge Eisenhower and to promote his own ambitions for increased visibility and prominence in national leadership.[16]

But while Johnson at least worked initially to cooperate with the administration, his Democratic colleagues in the Senate exercised less restraint. Missouri's Stuart Symington and Washington's Henry Jackson issued a statement the day after the Sputnik I launch, blaming the Eisenhower administration's "economy program" for the Soviet triumph. The satellite, they contended, provided further evidence of the Soviet Union's superiority in long-range missiles.[17] Shortly thereafter, Symington was among those pushing Johnson and Eisenhower to convene a special session of Congress. A special session offered the president a forum from which he could "explain to the Congress and the people the national emergency in which our lagging defense program—particularly in the ballistic missile, the anti-submarine, and the anti-ballistic missile programs—has placed us." Warned Symington, "There had better be a speed-up if the United States is to remain a free nation."[18]

Twenty members of a Democratic Advisory Committee, with former President Harry Truman in the lead, focused on the Soviet threat to that freedom. Calling for increased attention to technical research and education in science, the committee argued that the:

Russian achievement is visible proof that the administration has failed to understand the amount of effort which is needed by our country in basic research and in applied engineering if we are not to become inferior to the Russians in air atomic power.

It is proof that the Administration has been leading the people to believe that we have a national security which in fact we are rapidly losing.

We call for an all-out national effort to regain our position in the armaments field and to lead the world in a drive for peace.[19]

At the center of such an effort, Truman added in a front-page essay for the *New York Times*, should be the creation of a central organization to oversee the nation's missile program. "If we are to meet the current Russian challenge," Truman wrote, "I would urge the immediate setting up of a new Government agency headed by a strong and able bodied man, responsible only to the President, to be in absolute charge of our long-range missiles." The threat constituted by inaction, he continued, paralleled that experienced by Europe during Hitler's rise to power. In the former president's view, "unless we are strong, peace will be in jeopardy. And Russian propaganda may even now deceive some nations into misjudging our real power and potential and panic some people into surrender and compromise, as some were bullied by Hitler into doing."[20]

Even members of Eisenhower's own party called for forceful presidential leadership. Senator Clifford Case of New Jersey, for example, addressed the Young Republicans in San Francisco one week after the Sputnik launch. "This may be a healthy thing for us," he told reporters in a news conference before his speech. "We may have been going along in a fool's paradise."[21] Case defined the consequences of that course to the Young Republicans, contending that "We cannot maintain an adequate program on a piecemeal basis, carried on in starts and spurts, at one time forcing drastic reductions and then reversing field in a moment of panic." Intimating that the absence of national leadership had led to such panic, Case concluded that coordinated decision making involving both the president and the Congress could right the country's course:

Together we created in Washington an atmosphere of integrity and sound thinking. We mapped out a program and launched it with high hopes. We must revive the enthusiasm and driving desire to meet the needs of our people that inspired the original proposals. This is the time for responsive and responsible Republicanism—for imaginative thinking and effective leadership in the executive and the legislative branches of government. The challenge is before us. If we try we will succeed.[22]

In concert with the Democrats' charges, continual press coverage, and the Soviets' exploitation of Sputnik for strategic propaganda advantage, such comments from the president's own party helped maintain a public focus on the space race. The situation demanded rhetorical leadership from the president that would reassure the public about America's preeminence in world affairs and inspire confidence in the nation's scientific, technical, and military expertise.

### Initial Response: Diversion

The administration's initial strategy, however, operated to undercut confidence and create confusion. Although Eisenhower was not idle throughout the month of October, he preferred to avoid the issue when possible.[23] When public communication was unavoidable, decisions in rhetorical strategy proved insufficient to counteract the combined impact of his critics and inquisitors. The president attempted to downplay the issue by announcing the expected launching of Sputnik II, reframing the issue during his press conferences, and leaving the business of direct commentary on Soviet progress in space to surrogate administration rhetors.

Almost immediately after the first launch, Eisenhower announced the likelihood of a second Sputnik, an announcement designed to minimize the event's impact. Ironically, however, accompanying the announcement was the news that the United States had also had advanced knowledge of Sputnik I, but chose not to make it public. Rather than commending Eisenhower for his new openness, critics charged the administration with secretive policy making, a practice clearly not in the best interests of the American people.[24] The situation called for reassuring leadership, but the president asked the people not to be concerned over a second Sputnik.

Similarly, in engaging the topic at two press conferences in October, the president asked the people for patience and faith.[25] His intent, noted General Andrew J. Goodpaster, was "to allay histeria [sic] and alarm, and to bring out that the Russian action is simply proof of a thrust mechanism of a certain power, accuracy and reliability."[26] Eisenhower's initial tack was to address what was an emotionally charged issue in dry, technical terms. He opened the 9 October press conference, for instance, not with an introductory statement that might have been designed to calm public fears, but with a direct request for questions from reporters. Merriman Smith of United Press responded: "Mr. President, Russia has launched an earth satellite. They also claim to have had a successful firing of an intercontinental ballistic missile, none of which this country has done. I ask you, sir, what are we going to do about it?"

The question afforded Eisenhower an ideal opportunity to inspire public confidence. In tone and substance, Smith's "what are we going to do about it?"

invited an answer that might well have initiated America's strategic response to the psychological warfare being waged by the Soviets. Instead, Eisenhower held forth in soporific, didactic prose. Handed the opportunity to assume the role of inspirational leader, he chose instead to act the pedant. Consider the following:

> Well, let's take, first, the earth satellite, as opposed to the missile, because they are related only indirectly in the physical sense, and in our case not at all.
>
> The first mention that was made of an earth satellite that I know of, was about the spring of 1955—I mean the first mention to me—following upon a conference in Rome where plans were being laid for the working out of the things to be done in the International Geophysical Year.

Eisenhower framed his responses to reporters' other questions about Sputnik, space, and science in similar fashion.[27] The decision to emphasize the historic and the technical over the political and the psychological came to typify the president's discourse in the first month after Sputnik.

At his next press conference, on 30 October, Eisenhower sought to move the issue from center stage. He opened with a two-part statement, first condemning the bombing of the Israeli Cabinet that morning, and then announcing his likely participation at a forthcoming NATO meeting that would involve heads of state. A brief exchange about which members of Congress might accompany the president to the NATO meetings followed, wherein Eisenhower observed that such decisions entailed careful consideration of which legislators might be most likely to help the president generate public interest in foreign policy. Then the president acknowledged Douglas Cornell of the Associated Press. "In keeping with those remarks about awakening the public," Cornell began,

> I wonder if you would have any reaction to something Dr. Vannevar Bush said. He says that he isn't optimistic about our overtaking Russia in outer space developments, although it might be possible if the public is awakened and alerted. He said he can't say more for security reasons, but that the matter of alerting the public is up to the President, and that the advantage of alerting the public must be weighed against the disadvantages of possibly revealing something that would be of value to Russia.

Eisenhower's response evinced a two-part strategy for defusing the urgency of what had come to preoccupy the public as the "space race." First, he used the authority of scientists to divert public attention from space issues. Eisenhower was "astonished," he told Cornell, to discover in his meetings with experts that "their chief concern is not the relative position of ourselves today in scientific advancement with any other nation, but where we are going to be in ten years." The scientists had requested the president's support in "awakening the United States to the importance and indeed the absolute necessity of increasing our scientific output of our colleges and universities." Though he thus embraced the charge to help bring science to the center of the political dialogue, a second tack made doubtful the goal's imminent achievement. For when asked shortly thereafter by the *New York Herald's* Robert Donovan to "tell us more, sir, about your planned speeches, where they are going to be, when, how many, what they will be like?," good intentions gave way to the press of events. "Well, I must tell you," Eisenhower responded, "it is a very difficult thing to plan, but I think there will be an announcement as to the first talk at a very early date. It happens to be one of those falls where I seem to have a lot of things on my plate, and it is hard to tell which to attack first."[28] The balance of the news conference confirmed the president's claim, as the session shifted to a broad range of issues, including civil rights, perceived changes in the Soviet Union's power structure, inflation, cooperation between the U.S. and Britain, the defense budget, and the stock market.

Although the media and even his critics acknowledged the press of events, Eisenhower's pleas for patience and efforts to divert attention to scientific education constituted an inadequate rhetorical response for a public so consumed by the perceived Soviet lead in space. Thus, concurrent with the president's own appearances, surrogates started to carry the administration's message forward. But the mixed nature of the messages did little to calm public fears. Press secretary James Hagerty, for example, sought to shape reports, and hence public perceptions, the day after the Soviets' success with Sputnik I. In what was to become a frequent line of argument by administration rhetors, Hagerty discounted the image of a competition between Russia and America. Asked to explain how and why the Soviet Union had surpassed the United States in scientific and technical expertise, Hagerty retorted, "We never thought of our program as one which was in a race with the Soviets."[29] One way to ensure not losing a competition, was simply to declare the competition nonexistent.

Less than two weeks later, though, Vice-President Richard M. Nixon contended that the Soviets' success did not constitute a victory over the free world.[30] Addressing the International Industrial Development Conference, he declared that "There has been a lot of loose talk to the effect that this one event has changed the balance of military power in the world today." Nixon intended to "set the record straight." "Militarily," he maintained, "the Soviet Union is not one bit stronger today than it was before the satellite was launched."[31] Moreover, he added in a speech to the National Association of Manufacturers, Americans need not fear Sputnik, for "[t]his was not a military missile. It in no way indicates a lack of progress or failure [on the part of the United States] in the military missile field."[32] Yet only continued progress, he assured both audiences, could guarantee the ultimate success of freedom over totalitarianism. Acceptance of new taxes to fund technological advancement, he vowed, portended ultimate victory.

The public remained unmoved. Despite a range of tactics by surrogate rhetors and Eisenhower himself, the messages from the Soviets, the president's political opponents, and the press continued to dominate political discussion. One month after Sputnik, the public remained convinced that the United States *was* in a race with the Soviet Union to achieve superiority in space. Worse, America was losing. Despite Eisenhower's warnings to expect Sputnik II, the Soviets' second launch added to the country's fears about what it meant to be behind. "Can the U.S. Catch Up?," asked one lead for a *Newsweek* feature article; "Sputnik II: The Surge of Soviet Science," declared the heading of another.[33] Events demanded presidential action. On 7 November, the president acted.

## THE CAMPAIGN FOR "SCIENCE AND SECURITY"

Eisenhower's resistance to what he considered precipitate action was rooted both in his view of how research in science and space should proceed, and in his view of the balance necessary between military spending and the rest of the national economy. Whereas the Russians' rapid deployment of satellites reflected their perception of space exploration as a key to success in Cold War propaganda, Eisenhower believed the U.S. should work "simply to develop and transmit scientific knowledge." Moreover, the president resisted calls to engage the Soviets in a space race, for he "thought that to make a sudden shift in our approach would be to belie the attitude we have had all along."[34] Still, by not making that attitude clear and salient to the American public, the administration ensured continuation of the fears, doubts, and apprehension stirred by Sputnik. Ironically, both the advice he received from an array of sources and his own communication skills urged a rhetorical strategy responsive to the demands of the situation.[35] The president and his strategists recognized the wisdom of such an aggressive course only after a slow start in their campaign, a start from which they ultimately could not recover.

### Situation, Audience, Speaker

The advice Eisenhower received from both outside and inside the administration urged action. Gabriel Hauge, special assistant for economic affairs, sent a handwritten note to Arthur Larson during Larson's preparation of the 7 November speech. "More and more comments are reaching me on this Sputnik business that bear on the 11/13 speech—these are from friends." Five specifics documented the urgency of a presidential response:

1. Reaction of bewilderment is shifting to anger.

2. A scapegoat is wanted.

3. DDE's speech has to have some simply understandable idea that something has been changed—whether a Missile Czar (without calling it that), I don't know.

4. DDE's prestige in his special area is slipping.

5. Reassurance in concrete terms that this setback can be overcome and that it will not lose neutral nations to Soviets.

Hauge concluded: "I am amazed at the extent and depth of the reactions as I pick up my contacts around the country."[36] Other advisors arrived at similar judgments.

Bernard Baruch, whose opinions influenced presidents from Woodrow Wilson to Eisenhower, assessed the public attitude in light of Sputnik as "worried now and in a condition to see the needs on defense and our economy. I think they are in a frame of mind to give you the support and even the sacrifice to put both our defense and economy on a sound footing."[37] Although Baruch's self-importance and seemingly endless advice often frustrated the president, Eisenhower noted that Baruch's "standing and reputation in the public mind" made it necessary to take him seriously,[38] particularly when his views coincided with those expressed by others.

Among the others voicing sentiments in line with Baruch's was the National Planning Association, a voluntary advisory group based in Washington, D.C. On 15 October, the group forwarded to Eisenhower a nine-page, single-spaced document detailing the need for presidential leadership in the wake of Sputnik. In a letter accompanying the document, the Association's Board of Trustees made clear the urgency of action:

> It is imperative that you, Mr. President, assert that high quality of leadership in which you excel and *in a series of public statements undertake to dispel the illusion with which so many citizens have been bemused, and to breathe new vitality into the spiritual values of our Western civilization.*

> Our people trust you implicitly and if you tell us in your own way the policies you wish to pursue and the appropriations you require to implement them, the Congress will not be slow to follow an aroused public opinion.

> No matter what sacrifices you may feel obliged to call for, you can confidently rely upon the national response.[39]

Specifying in the document both the importance of the president's role and the response he might anticipate, the association contended that times of peril call for "imaginative and courageous leadership." The public, the group argued, "has not been made sufficiently conscious of the deterioration of our position." Only the president, because of his position and personality, was adequately situated to "explain to people everywhere the principles to which we stand committed." In employing that position, the association urged, Eisenhower would do well to go on the offensive. Rather than attacking the Soviets or his detractors, they suggested, the president would do well to delineate what he hoped the nation aimed to achieve in its own commitments to research in space and science. For in "spelling out in no uncertain terms the human values we seek to preserve, we would have taken an immense forward step in the psychological offensive. World attention for too long has been focused upon what we are against rather than what we are for." The wisest forum for such an offensive, the group concluded, was a televised campaign.[40]

Eisenhower did not agree with all of the association's recommendations, and even observed that some of the group's members "command[ed] something less than my complete admiration." Nevertheless, he wrote to Secretary of State John Foster Dulles, noting that with "a truly effective speech covering the points . . . the attached document makes, I would be more than delighted to find the proper platform to make such a speech—a platform that would give to it the widest possible publicity."[41] Contemplating the substance of a "truly effective" speech, the president consulted the nation's scientific leaders.

The morning of 15 October, Eisenhower met with more than a dozen research scientists, inventors, technical experts, and authorities in the military applications of scientific studies. The group included physicists I.I. Rabi, Hans Bethe, and D.W. Bronk; Edwin Land, inventor of the Polaroid camera and a Nobel prize winner in 1952; and James Killian, president of MIT. The scientists' advice aligned markedly with that which the president received from the National Planning Association. Land spoke eloquently of the country's need for an expanded emphasis on science, but argued even more passionately that such emphasis would not follow without Eisenhower's central participation in a campaign to generate public interest and support. With the president's help, Land maintained, scientists who felt isolated and alone could be brought into the mainstream of American political life. Rabi added that a logical starting point would be the addition of a scientific advisor in the White House, who in turn would head a committee of distinguished scientists on whom the president could rely for guidance in an era of rapid technological progress.

Eisenhower listened carefully, concluding that he would take the earliest opportunity to begin to speak out on the importance of the American people taking an interest in science, and not "just leav[ing] the matter to scientists." Although he intended to begin his speaking as early as the press conference scheduled two weeks later, the president's most promising comments indicated that he both understood the long-term commitment the campaign required, and recognized the importance of timing to the campaign's success. One speech would "not do the job," he said, concluding that there would "be a need for great carrythrough." But the time to start was at hand: "People are alarmed and thinking about science, and perhaps this alarm [can] be turned to a constructive result."[42]

Eisenhower's recognition of the significance of timing was more than intuitive. Despite a reputation as a speaker of modest skill, the president brought to the situation substantial rhetorical gifts. He was an experienced writer, had a keen sense of what he wanted his speeches to achieve, focused his writing and speaking on utilitarian objectives, and benefited enormously from an innate talent in promoting often complex identifications between speaker and audience. These talents often puzzled his critics.

As Theodore White lamented after misjudging Eisenhower's prowess as a communicator, "I had made the mistake so many observers did of considering Ike a simple man, a good straightforward soldier." The reality, White discovered, was that "Ike's mind was not flaccid; and gradually, reporting him as he performed, I found that . . . the tangled, rambling rhetoric of his off-the-cuff remarks could, when he wished, be disciplined by his own pencil into clean, hard prose."[43] The president took pride in his writing, as Arthur Larson noted. Eisenhower knew his critics questioned his reliance on speech writers, like Larson, who drafted initial versions of his speech texts. What those critics often did not realize, however, was that Eisenhower's pen had created the words uttered by other speakers lauded for great oratorical achievements. "Let me tell you something, Art," he said to Larson. "You know that General MacArthur got quite a reputation as a silver-tongued speaker when he was in the Philippines. Who do you think wrote those speeches? I did." Eisenhower worked with Larson in all phases of speech preparation, "content, clarity, correctness, [and] style." He insisted that his writers adhere to four rules: 1) they should focus on a single idea—a "Q.E.D."; 2) be brief; 3) use simple prose; and 4) evince a tone of dignity.[44]

A key feature of Eisenhower's rhetorical appeal, one consistent with the plain style the president charged Larson to achieve, was the president's capacity to promote identification between himself and the audience. As Richard Crable notes, few leaders in the nation's history have so successfully fulfilled apparently contradictory roles. Eisenhower appealed to the country as a warrior-pacifist, leader-common man, candidate-nonpartisan, and politician-nonpolitician. What publics might perceive as contradictory in others, they accepted in Eisenhower because of his skill in achieving complex levels of identification. Audiences believed the president because he was able at once to be *of* the people and to speak *for* the people.[45] Combined with the reading of the audience and situation provided by his advisors, Eisenhower's own communicative skills should have urged an aggressive campaign in praise of American achievement. Instead, the president chose to initiate the speech series with a recitation of U.S. military preparedness, a lesson ill-adapted to situation and audience.

### *"Science in National Security"*

In retirement, Eisenhower recalled the 7 November 1957 speech as "the first of a series of nationwide talks on science and defense. This was no exercise in positive thinking based on hopes alone. We had much about which to be confident. The talk bristled with specifics."[46] In response to increasing criticism from Congress and others who questioned the slow response to Sputnik, the president canceled a scheduled press conference and substituted the nationally televised address. Even though a second address would follow less than a week later, the president and his advisors recognized the public relations potential of a 7 November presentation, as the speech could be expected to pull attention away from the Soviets' celebration of the fortieth anniversary of the Bolshevik revolution, a revolution given new energy by the Sputnik success. In addition, advisors searching for symbols to counter Sputnik informed the White House that Eisenhower could "have [an] actual nose cone that re-entered [the] atmosphere for display" during the speech; alternatively, an Air Force plane could set speed and distance records the day of the speech, should Eisenhower so desire.[47] While the president would use the nose cone as a visual aid, he chose to cast the text as a lesson in America's defense capabilities.

This less spectacular course surely fit Eisenhower's perception of what the situation required, but it did little to inspire the American public. On an early draft of the text, Ike noted to Larson:

> Try theme of *facts*, not opinions—I am going to give you facts about where we stand, facts on what we are doing about it. I am not going to tell you to be self-satisfied, nor am I going to try to scare you to death. I am going to give you the real facts—as many as time and security allow—and you will be able to draw your own conclusions.[48]

Eisenhower made similar comments through at least four early versions of the speech, editing right up until the evening of 7 November, when he faced the television audience from his desk in the White House. In slightly over twenty-seven minutes, the president provided a talk in which he urged that the people be guided by patience rather than emotion. In content, tone, and delivery the speech embodied the president's appeal to reasoned contemplation. He spoke deliberately, evenly, and with only occasional hints of passion. "Let me tell you what I am going to do in this talk and in my next," he began.

I am going to lay the facts before you—the rough with the smooth. Some of these security facts are reassuring; others are not—they are sternly demanding. Some require that we resolutely continue lines of action now well begun. Others require new action, and still others new dimensions of effort. After putting these facts and requirements before you, I shall propose a program of action—a program that will demand the energetic support of not just the government but every American, if we are to make it successful.[49]

The first facts concerned the state of the nation's security, which the president termed "one of great strength." The war in Korea had taught the United States that reliance on superior conventional forces would no longer suffice. American ingenuity responded with a New Look defense strategy, one dependent "more upon modern science and less upon mere numbers of men." Subsequent years saw an "across-the-board program to bring all units of our defense into line with the possibilities of modern technology," culminating in a ballistic missile system second to none.

Eisenhower's framing of the argument is therefore instructive. The Soviets may have fired a rocket into orbit, he argued, yet that satellite had no known practical military or technological benefit. But in the United States, "our military forces, scientists, and engineers" had worked in concert "in recent years . . . to put current scientific discovery at the service of our defense." What followed was a recitation of those achievements: thirty-eight different types of missiles, "adapted to every kind of distance, launching, and use"; Navy combat vessels equipped with guided missiles and atomic depth bombs; aircraft in the Army and Air Force bearing air-to-air missiles; and anti-aircraft guns replaced by surface-to-air missiles.

Two tactics followed the dry recitation of data. First, in a move that became common during the nuclear-space age, the president referred to the new weapons by name, the "Matador, Honest John, and Corporal missiles." Second, Eisenhower translated the technological achievements to "give [the viewer] some idea of what this means in terms of explosive power: *Four battalions of Corporal missiles alone are equivalent in fire power to all the artillery used in World War II on all fronts.*" The second World War provided the marker for appreciating the B-52 bomber as well. Standard in the Strategic Air Command, "*One B-52 can carry as much destructive capacity as was delivered by all the bombers in all the years of World War II.*"

So progressed the first third of the speech, prepared by Larson on Eisenhower's direction to stress defense rather than scientific invention and education, topics featured in earlier drafts.[50] Only late in the speech did Eisenhower turn to the proof a worried public might interpret as evidence that Sputnik did not constitute a significant Soviet lead in space science. But even this proof was shrouded in didactic prose, as the president maintained that American research was moving apace with, if not ahead of, the Cold War enemy. "One difficult obstacle on the way to producing a useful long-range weapon," Ike explained, "is that of bringing a missile back from outer space without its burning up like a meteor, because of friction with the earth's atmosphere." As Eisenhower completed his sentence, the camera left the speaker for the first time and panned to a metal object. He continued: "Our scientists and engineers have solved the problem. This object here in my office is the nose cone of an experimental missile fired over a long distance. It has been hundreds of miles to outer space and back. Here it is, completely unharmed, intact." In a classic instance of a rhetor burying the lead argument, Eisenhower concluded the first phase of his speech:

> These illustrations—which are, of course, only a small sample of our scientists' accomplishments—I give you merely to show that our strength is not static but is constantly moving forward with technological improvement.
>
> Long range ballistic missiles, as they exist today, do *not* cancel the destructive and deterrent power of our Strategic Air Force.

Following a brief discussion of the continental defense established in cooperation with Canada, and even further into the thick of the text, the president returned to the same theme: Although "the Soviets are quite likely ahead in some missile and special areas, and are obviously ahead of us in satellite development, *as of today the over-all military strength of the free world is distinctly greater than that of the communist countries.*"

Despite a decided military advantage, however, the critical "question is: How about the future?" The facts dictated that any advantage was not necessarily permanent, for "*we could fall behind*—unless we now face up to certain pressing requirements and set out to meet them promptly." Urging all citizens to set aside partisanship, the president declared confidently that "We will close ranks as Americans, and get on with the job to be done." That job entailed both long-term and short-range goals.

Referring to his flurry of recent meetings with political and scientific advisors, Eisenhower declared that these advisors had convinced him that, for the long term, "one of our most glaring deficiencies is the failure of the United States to give high enough priority to scientific education and to the place of science in our national life." Attention now to preparing scientific educators and to increasing support for basic research were essential if science in the free world was to keep pace. In the short-range, Eisenhower pledged the United States to a new openness in the exchange of scientific information between and among allies, and charged others in government to join him in generating executive-legislative cooperation in the promotion of science and technology.

For his own part, Eisenhower articulated a six-part plan of action. The first, and by far most noteworthy, step entailed the creating of "a new office, called the office of Special Assistant to the President for Science and Technology, [whose occupant] will have the active responsibility of helping me follow through on the program of scientific improvement of our defenses." Eisenhower named Dr. James Killian, president of the Massachusetts Institute of Technology, to the office.

"I am not forgetting," the president confided in his conclusion, "that there is much more to science than its function in defense, and more to our defense than the part played by science." For science's "peaceful contributions" to healing and enriching life "are the most important products of the conquest of nature's secrets," and the "spiritual powers" of the nation "are the most important stones in any defense structure." Nevertheless, until the Soviets "align themselves with the practical and workable disarmament proposals approved yesterday by a large majority of the United Nations," the use of science in defense remained vital. "What the world needs today even more than a giant leap into outer space," Eisenhower concluded, "is a giant step toward peace."

The next morning, Frank Stanton, the head of CBS, reported to the White House that forty-five million viewers saw the president's speech.[51] Reaction in Congress, scientific circles, and the press was mixed. Republican Senator Jacob Javits of New York lauded the president as "the Eisenhower of the Crusade in Europe. The President touched all the bases. This is a crisis." Representative Daniel Reed (R—NY) agreed, saying it "was one of the best speeches the President has ever made and should have a good effect on those who have been in doubt about our position." Lyndon Johnson, head of the Senate Democrats, was predictably less enthusiastic, commenting that "I had hoped that the President would stress what we need to do as well as what we have done. But I am happy that he noted the necessity for a 'high sense of urgency.'" John McClellan, another Democrat, called the speech "not altogether convincing." And Representative Wayne Hays (D-Ohio) lamented, "It's the same old story— appoint a committee to study the problem and hope the problem will go away."[52] Press response was less pessimistic about the establishment of the office of a presidential special assistant on science and technology, and praise in the scientific community greeted James Killian's appointment to the post.[53]

There remained in the broader public, however, a keen sense of urgency. *Newsweek* correspondents reported three recurring concerns in interviews with citizens across the country:

- A dawning realization that supposedly backward Russia had somehow beaten the U.S. at its own game of science, technology, and know-how.

- A growing belief that the world is entering a new era of space exploration, and this country has failed to lead.

- A determination to catch up, and fast.[54]

Eisenhower's insistence that a recitation of the facts would curtail public fears proved errant, as did a textual structure that buried the speech's most psychologically potent proofs. The result demanded a revised rhetorical strategy, one aimed more at inspiration than instruction.

### "Our Future Security"

From the staging used to the president's demeanor to the employment of techniques better fitted for rhetorical leadership, the Oklahoma City address of 13 November 1957 differed radically from the White House speech. *Time* reported:

> Dwight Eisenhower's political fire, according to all polls, was burning low. But no one could ever have told it from his appearance in Oklahoma City last week for the second of his television series on national issues. From the moment of his arrival, he threw off the old popularity sparks. Riding in from Will Rogers Field in the presidential Lincoln, he stood like a campaigner with hands aloft before sign-carrying crowds ("We Liked Ike in '56, We Like Him Today").[55]

The staging of the speech anticipated such a reaction. Scheduled as part of a four-month long celebration marking Oklahoma's fiftieth anniversary, the setting promised a supportive and eager audience. Speaking in Oklahoma City's Municipal Auditorium, the president addressed six thousand listeners in the immediate audience, and millions more over television.[56] Television coverage opened with a visual of the presidential seal, accompanied by a CBS announcer's voice-over: "From the Municipal Auditorium in Oklahoma City, Oklahoma . . . we present an address by the President of the United States, Dwight D. Eisenhower. President Eisenhower will speak on the subject, 'Our Future Security.' He will be presented by Donald S. Kennedy, trustee of the Frontiers of Science Foundation of Oklahoma. Mr. Kennedy."[57] The camera focused on Kennedy, who said simply, "Ladies and Gentlemen, the President of the United States." The camera drew back to an open shot of the podium, with Oklahoma and American flags to either side. As Eisenhower entered, a wider shot encompassed the audience, responding with a standing ovation. As if on cue, the president raised his arms in a campaign-like victory salute to his supporters. Eisenhower moved to the podium, put on his glasses, and began.

From the outset, the performance played to the potential of rhetorical leadership in the age of a television presidency.[58] In virtually all respects, the speech revealed a rhetor with superb persuasive instincts and skills, traits not even hinted at just six days earlier in the broadcast from the White House. Gone were the dry recitation of facts and didactic tone characteristic of the first speech. In their stead, Eisenhower spoke in broad themes on the issues of military preparedness, scientific discovery, and technological progress. Moreover, this was a personalized speech, wherein Eisenhower's own life, experience, and family not only provided the points of identification between himself and the audience, but also offered evidence of the efficacy of his proposed policies. Most important, the text's themes, proofs, and presentation generated an enthusiasm in the immediate audience that played well over television, thus yielding a rhetoric appropriate for countering the negative frame of mind that Sputnik had embedded in the nation's collective psyche.

After greeting the assembled dignitaries with whom he shared the podium, Eisenhower thanked the audience for the opportunity to share in Oklahoma's anniversary celebration. He then initiated the strategy of speaker-audience identification that would recur throughout the speech: "Born in the Lone Star State just to your south, and reared in the Sunflower State just to the north. I have a fine feeling of coming home again."[59] He then deviated from the prepared manuscript, alternating between his hand-written editing and extemporaneous discourse. Removing his glasses, the president continued:

> So your generous welcome has a special significance for me tonight. Frankly, I wish I could stay until Saturday. From all my friends this afternoon, I've heard you have a pretty fair sort of football team. (Applause) And, of course, I should very much like to see it play. And I'm going to let you in on a secret. No matter how good it was before, since this afternoon when they made my grandson sort of an honorary member, it's a much better team. He is now the proud possessor of a white football signed by Bud Wilkinson and all his players, and my son [sic] is the best 90 pound tackle in the whole country.

The president put his glasses back on, and returned to his script: "Last week I spoke of science in security," he said, "this week I speak of security in a somewhat wider context."

Although he had urged all Americans in his 7 November speech to work together in the nation's best interests, the appeal was directed more at congressional-executive and Democrat-Republican cooperation than at a shared sense of history, values, and experiences. While the former traits surely served public talk in some arenas, the 13 November address demonstrated the power of history, values, and personal experiences in mediated discourse, particularly when the context calls for reassurance. Eisenhower grounded that reassurance not in the technical narrative of numbers of arms, but in the purposes to which American and Soviet achievements were directed. Placing Sputnik in the setting of the Soviet Union's fortieth anniversary celebration of the country's revolution, he acknowledged the impressiveness of their accomplishment in space. Though their system often put the government ahead of the individual, he maintained, the space launch constituted "very dramatic evidence that even under such a system it is possible to produce some remarkable material achievements." But, the president wondered, at what cost are such achievements attained? In an increasingly strident and powerful delivery, he offered his own answer:

> When such competence in things material is at the service of leaders who have so little regard for things human, and who command the power of an empire, there is danger ahead for free men everywhere. That, my friends, is the reason why the American people have been so aroused by the earth satellites.
>
> Of course, free men are meeting and will meet this challenge.

To a degree, meeting the challenge meant matching Soviet technological advances. In the end, however, no such advance could compete with the western allies, whose most important weapon consisted in a way of life incompatible with the Soviet ideology. The president maintained:

> The real strength with which the self-governing democracies have met the tests of history is something denied dictatorships.
>
> It is found in the quality of our life and the vigor of our ideals. It manifests itself in the ever-astonishing capacity of free men for voluntary heroism, sacrifice and accomplishment when the chips are down.
>
> This is the weapon which has meant eventual downfall for every dictator who has made the familiar mistake of thinking all democracies "soft."
>
> Now, once again, we hear an expansionist regime declaring "We will bury you."

With pause for effect, Eisenhower engaged the audience and uttered the line on which press reports of the speech would focus to describe its tenor and theme. "In a bit of American vernacular," Ike intoned, "Oh, Yeah?" The audience erupted in applause. Recalling Hitler, the president warned the audience not to ignore seemingly innocuous claims by Soviet propagandists. But while wisdom demanded vigilance, Americans also needed to recognize that the nation was more than prepared to meet any challenge.

Continued preparation, though, required continued research and development, and hence a substantial economic commitment. Calling for such a commitment during difficult economic times was, Eisenhower acknowledged, much to ask. Yet the evidence forced both the request and a positive response from the public. Approximately one-fourth of the way into his text, the president for the first time alluded to the particulars of weaponry and defense systems that had dominated the earlier speech. Contrary to his treatment of those topics on 7 November, however, the litany was brief, as Eisenhower focused instead on the more pressing public concern of the space race, an issue treated only tangentially the week before. "There has been much discussion lately about whether Soviet technological break-throughs in particular areas may have suddenly exposed us to immediately increased dangers in spite of the strength of our defenses," he began. "As I pointed out last week, this is not the case." The camera moved from Eisenhower to an applauding audience. And while recommendations for responding to Sputnik ranged "from acceleration of missile programs, to shooting a rocket around the moon, to an indiscriminate increase in every kind of military and scientific adventure [the script called for "expenditure"] common sense demands that we put first things first. And the *first of all firsts is our nation's security.*"

For the next one-third of the speech, the president addressed that security in terms of weapon systems, technological development, recruitment and retention of troops, and other important but potentially uninspiring details. Wisely, however, he addressed those details in terms of their inseparable link to the preservation of freedom. Military and economic assistance, he explained, "helps other countries keep free of dependence upon the Soviet help, which too often is the prelude to Soviet domination. It shows the free world's ability to develop its resources and to increase its living standards. It helps allied economies support needed military units and remain sturdy partners of ours in this world-wide struggle." Having framed the immediate issue of preparedness in terms of the overarching emphasis on freedom, Eisenhower turned his attention to the future.

The nation's, indeed the world's, future security required a prolonged commitment to scientific education and support for basic research. Without such a commitment, he warned, the defense superiority now enjoyed would be in jeopardy. To maintain the current pace, his scientific advisors told him, "we need scientists. In the 10 years ahead, they say we need them by thousands more than we're now presently planning to have." Attracting youth to science required, on the president's view, "incentives for high-aptitude students to pursue scientific or professional studies; a program to stimulate good-quality teaching of mathematics and science; provision of more laboratory facilities; and measures, including fellowships, to increase the output of qualified teachers." And who is to see that such programs are pursued? Government can do its part, but in the end, "this task is in the hands of you, as citizens. This is National Education Week. It should be National Education Year."

After addressing the need for increased attention to basic scientific research in similarly personal terms, Eisenhower returned in his peroration to the theme of freedom. While the Soviet system was destined to produce students educated in biology, physics, and engineering, he contended, it was essential that American schools not only train technicians, but educate leaders as well. For the future required "not just engineers and scientists, but . . . in every field, leaders who can meet intricate human problems with wisdom and with courage. In short, we will need not only Einsteins and Steinmetzes, but Washingtons and Emersons." Promise that such leadership would emerge, he concluded, could be found in Oklahoma City's own experience.

Closing the speech as he began, Eisenhower departed from the typed script, improvising a conclusion based on the day's experiences. Speaking extemporaneously and from handwritten notes in the margins of his text, Ike explained the impressions that his tour of the Frontiers of Science Foundation had left: "Today I had the great privilege of a few minutes visit with Dr. Harlow and with about half a dozen of his bright youngsters. I congratulate you on them, and on the institution. You have every reason to be proud of both, and I hope other states will follow your example." For not to do so, would be to risk the principles and values that defined America:

> My friends, it has always been my faith that the eventual triumph of decency and freedom in this world is inevitable.
>
> But, as a wise American once remarked, *it takes a lot of hard work and sacrifice by a lot of people to bring about the inevitable.*
>
> Thank you very much, and good night.

As the audience stood to applaud, the camera pulled back to show Eisenhower shaking hands with several people on stage. "You have just heard . . . 'Our National Security,'" said the anonymous television announcer, "the second in a series of talks to the American people. This program came to you from the municipal auditorium in Oklahoma City."

Although some educators resisted selected specifics of the proposed education program, and response in the Congress was mixed,[60] the speech's staging, text, and presentation demonstrated Eisenhower's potential power as a rhetorical leader. Speaking in value-laden themes, adapting those themes to the experiences of both the immediate and larger audiences, and promoting identification between himself and all Americans, the president performed in a manner conducive to relieving the fears of a nation concerned with the threat of losing the space race to the Soviet Union.

## CONCLUSION

Dwight Eisenhower's election to the presidency coincided with the emergence of television as a vital component of contemporary presidential leadership. His response to the perceived crisis created by Sputniks I and II in the fall of 1957 illuminate both the nature of rhetoric in an era of a mediated presidency, and the limits of a perspective on the office that wills omnipotent power to the occupant of the White House. The American public's reaction to the Soviet space launch demanded a reassuring presidential response. Instead, Eisenhower's response unfolded over the course of six weeks. He moved gradually from a posture of cautious concern, to the assumption of a role as the nation's teacher, and finally to acceptance of the need to act as a rhetorical leader.

Bolstered by the success of the Oklahoma City performance, Eisenhower prepared for the third in his series of talks, tentatively scheduled for Cleveland.[61] But on 25 November, the president was felled by a stroke.[62] Whether continued good health would have allowed Eisenhower to capitalize on the momentum provided by the speech in Oklahoma is, of course, outside the rhetorical critic's domain. What is clear, however, is that situational and audience requirements in the fall of 1957 demanded a rhetorical leader who could inspire the public and convince the citizenry that a space launch did not constitute a reason to lose faith in America. Eisenhower was well equipped to provide such leadership, but his timing and initial choice of strategies were seriously flawed. These flaws, followed by the president's untimely stroke, allowed the domestic opposition to exploit the Sputnik launches and to create a powerful issue during the 1960 presidential campaign.

## NOTES

1. Letter from Dwight Eisenhower to Arthur Eisenhower, 8 November 1957, Whitman File, DDE Diary Series, Box 28, DDE Dictation, Eisenhower Library, Abilene, Kansas (hereafter cited as DDE Library).

2. One national news magazine reported Eisenhower's popularity at "an all time low," attributing the decline to Sputnik and Little Rock: "His Standing Now," *Newsweek*, 11 November 1957, 36. Though *Newsweek* may have overstated the case, Gallup Poll data indicate two important pieces of evidence. First, though not his lowest, Eisenhower's approval ratings in six Gallup surveys from October 1957 to March 1958, ranging from 51% to 60%, were among the lowest of his tenure. Second, the 57% and 58% favorability ratings for October and November culminated a steady decline in popularity from the 73% rating with which he had inaugurated his second term in January. George C. Edwards III, with Alec M. Gallup, *Presidential Approval: A Sourcebook* (Baltimore and London: The Johns Hopkins University Press, 1990), 21-24.

3. Martin J. Medhurst, "Eisenhower's 'Atoms for Peace' Speech: A Case Study in the Strategic Use of Language," *Communication Monographs* 54 (1987): 204-20.

4. Letter from Arthur Larson to Dwight Eisenhower, 8 August 1958, White House Office, Office of the Staff Secretary: Records, Subject Series, Box 16, Arthur Larson (August 1958), DDE Library.

5. George E. Reedy, *The Twilight of the Presidency* (New York: New American Library, 1970), 55-57.

6. "Text of Satellite Report," *New York Times*, 5 October 1957, 3.

7. William J. Jorden, "560 Miles High," *New York Times*, 5 October 1957, 1.

8. "For Your Information," *Newsweek*, 21 October 1957, 21. *Time* editors, in contrast, retained the magazine's original cover focus, a story on small home appliances and repairmen in "push button America."

9. *Newsweek* cover, 14 October 1957.

10. "For Your Information," *Newsweek*, 25 November 1957, 25.

11. The *New York Times* front page stories of 5 October 1957, included Walter Sullivan, "Course Recorded," 1 and 3; Jorden, "560 Miles High," 1 and 3; Roy Silver, "Satellite Signal Broadcasts Here," 1 and 3; and a special to the *Times*, "Device is 8 Times Heavier than One Planned by U.S.," 1 and 3. In addition to Richard Witkin's "US Delay Draws Scientists' Fire," page two carried three stories without bylines: "Soviet Satellite Visible with Binoculars," "Soviet Claiming Lead in Science," and "3-Stage Rockets for US Satellites." Two stories appeared on page three: Robert K. Plumb, "Satellite Flight is Step into Space," and Theodore Shabad, "Launching Timed as if for Tribute." The tribute alluded to was the 100th anniversary of the birth of Konstantin E. Tsiolkovsky, a pioneer in Soviet space research.

12. Summaries of reports from these cities are consolidated in "World Newspapers See Soviets Taking Lead from United States in Space Science," *New York Times*, 7 October 1957, 17.

13. Reported in Emmet John Hughes, *The Ordeal of Power* (New York: Atheneum Publishers, 1963), 216.

14. "The Presidency," *Time*, 18 November 1957, 19.

15. Dwight Eisenhower, Whitman File, DDE Diary Series, Box 28, DDE Library.

16. Reedy, *The Twilight of the Presidency*, 58-65.

17. "Senators Attack Missile Fund Cut," *New York Times*, 6 October 1957, 1.

18. Cited in John W. Finney, "Missiles Speed-Up Termed Doubtful By Defense Aides," *New York Times*, 15 October 1957, 1 and 14.

19. Quoted in "President Pushes Rockets Program," *New York Times*, 12 October 1957, 1.

20. Harry S. Truman, "Truman Urges An Agency to Rule All Missile Work," *New York Times*, 31 October 1957, 1.

21. Quoted in "Case Sees Folly in Defense Cuts," *New York Times*, 13 October 1957, 1.

22. "Excerpts from an Address by Senator Case to Young Republicans on Defense Lags," *New York Times*, 13 October 1957, 37.

23. Eisenhower's first public comment after the Sputnik I launch, for example, was entitled "Filmed and Taped Statement of the President for Newsreels and TV Cameras on The Satellite Situation," 9 October 1957, Whitman File, Speech Series, Box 22, DDE Library. Access to the text was limited, as only 30 copies were made and no copies were distributed to the press.

24. "President Pushes Rockets Program," 2.

25. Carolyn Smith sketches both Eisenhower's contributions to the institution of presidential news conferences and his tactics for dealing with the press in *Presidential Press Conferences: A Critical Approach* (New York: Praeger, 1990), 37-40. Samuel Kernell discusses Eisenhower's role in using press conferences to exercise leadership in *Going Public: New Strategies of Presidential Leadership* (Washington, D.C.: Congressional Quarterly Press, 1986), 68-9 and 180-83. Roderick Hart questions the impact Eisenhower exercised in the setting, given the president's convoluted syntax, preference for abstractions, and tendency to "circumnavigate an issue." Eisenhower's press conferences, Hart concludes, "challenged reporters to find answers within answers": *The Sound of Leadership: Presidential Communication in the Modern Age* (Chicago: University of Chicago Press, 1987), 146.

26. A.J. Goodpaster, Memorandum of Conference with the President [8 October 1957, 5 PM], Whitman File, DDE Diary Series, Box 27, October 1957 Staff Notes (2), DDE Library. Though his official title on arriving at the White House in 1954 was Staff Secretary to the President, General Goodpaster "became, without question, Eisenhower's closest adviser and confidant," remaining through the president's second term. Goodpaster's presence at key meetings, combined with his habit of keeping detailed records, makes his work of inestimable value to scholars: Stephen E. Ambrose, *Eisenhower: The President* (New York: Simon and Schuster, 1984), 217.

27. "The President's News Conference," *Public Papers of the Presidents: Dwight D. Eisenhower, 1957* (Washington, D.C.: Government Printing Office, 1958), 719-22 and passim (hereafter cited as *Public Papers*).

28. "The President's News Conference of October 30, 1957," *Public Papers, 1957*, 774-778.

29. Quoted in "Senators Attack Missile Fund Cut," 1.

30. For a provocative critique of Nixon's advocacy of U.S. space policy, see: Stephen P. Depoe, "The Race for Outer Space: Terminological Transformation in Vice President Richard Nixon's Response to the Sputnik Launches of 1957." Paper presented to the annual meeting of the Speech Communication Association, 1990.

31. Richard M. Nixon, "Text of Address by Nixon in San Francisco Assessing Challenge of Soviet Satellite," *New York Times*, 16 October 1957, 14.

32. Richard M. Nixon, "Text of Speech on Foreign Policy before the National Association of Manufacturers," *New York Times*, 7 December 1957, 16.

33. "Can the U.S. Catch Up?" and "Sputnik II: The Surge of Soviet Science," both appeared in *Newsweek*, 11 November 1957, 35-36; 73-76.

34. A.J. Goodpaster, Memorandum of Conference with the President [8 October 1957], Whitman File, DDE Diary Series, Box 27, October 1957 Staff Notes (2), DDE Library.

35. For a delineation of what constitutes "strategic rhetoric" in response to situational constraints, particularly during the Cold War, see: Martin J. Medhurst, "Rhetoric and Cold War: A Strategic Approach," in Martin J. Medhurst, Robert L. Ivie, Philip Wander, and Robert L. Scott, *Cold War Rhetoric: Strategy, Metaphor, and Ideology* (Westport: Greenwood Press, 1990), 19-27.

36. Letter from Gabriel Hauge to Arthur Larson, 4 November 1957, Arthur Larson Papers, Box 3, President's Speeches: Science and Security Background Material for 7 November and 13 November, DDE Library.

37. B.M. Baruch. Memorandum, 23 October 1957, Whitman File , DDE Diary Series, Box 27, DDE Diary [October 1957], DDE Library.

38. Cited in Ambrose, *Eisenhower: The President*, 314.

39. Letter from National Planning Association to Eisenhower, 15 October 1957, Whitman File, DDE Diaries, Box 27, DDE Library.

40. Letter from National Planning Association to Eisenhower, 8 October 1957 (pp. 5, 6, 7, and 9), Whitman File, DDE Diaries, Box 27, DDE Library.

41. Letter from Dwight Eisenhower to John Foster Dulles, 14 October 1957, Whitman File, DDE Diary Series, Box 28, October 1957 DDE Dictation, DDE Library.

42. Eisenhower's comments and the narrative of the conference are provided in A.J. Goodpaster, Memorandum of Conference with the President [15 October 1957, 11 AM], 16 October 1957 (pp. 2-4), Whitman File, DDE Diary Series, Box 27, October 1957 Staff Notes (2), DDE Library.

43. Theodore H. White, *In Search of History* (New York: Harper and Row, 1978), 347.

44. Arthur Larson, *Eisenhower: The President Nobody Knew* (New York: Charles Scribner's Sons, 1968), 145-49; Letter from Arthur Larson to Saxton Bradford, 14 November

1957, Arthur Larson Papers, Box 1, Chronological: October-December 1957, DDE Library.

45. Richard E. Crable provides insight into Eisenhower's paradoxical nature and his ability to overcome paradox through three levels of identification in "Identification, Argument, and Paradoxical Appeal," *Quarterly Journal of Speech* 63 (1977): 188-95.

46. Dwight D. Eisenhower, *Waging Peace, 1956-61* (Garden City, N.Y.: Doubleday & Company, 1965), 223.

47. Robert F. Whitney, "President to Go on Air Tomorrow in Science Report," *New York Times*, 6 November 1957, 1 and 12; "Sputnik, Politics, People," *Newsweek*, 18 November 1957, 31; Murray Snyder, Memorandum for Arthur Larson, no date, Arthur Larson Papers, Box 3, Science and Security—Background Material: Defense and John Hamlin, DDE Library.

48 Dwight Eisenhower, "Science and Security" speech draft (p. 1), Arthur Larson Papers, Box 2, President's Speeches: Science in National Security—Drafts, 7 November 1957, DDE Library.

49. The text used for analysis is a copy of Eisenhower's reading manuscript of "Science in National Security," 7 November 1957, Whitman File, Speech Series, Box 23, Science in National Security 11/7/57, DDE Library. The 42-page text, typed in over-sized print, was verified against a filmed copy of the speech held by the Eisenhower Library. All quotations are from this source. Unless otherwise noted, all emphasis is in the original text.

50. Memorandum from Dwight Eisenhower to Arthur Larson, 5 November 1957, Whitman File, DDE Diary Series, Box 28, November 1957 DDE Diary, DDE Library. The president's exact words were that the "educational phase in your draft must be contracted . . . because there are so many parts of the defense problem that have *really* to be put before the American people" (p. 1).

51. Memorandum from Anne Wheaton to Ann Whitman, 8 November 1957, Whitman File, Speech Series, Box 23, Science in National Security 11/7/57, DDE Library.

52. "Democrats Back Science Speed-Up," *New York Times*, 8 November 1957, 11; James Reston, "The President's Speech," *New York Times*, 8 November 1957, 12.

53. Allen Drury, "Killian Name to Spur Science," *New York Times*, 8 November 1957, 1 and 10; Walter Sullivan, "Scientists Cheer Choice of Killian," *New York Times*, 8 November 1957, 12; John W. Finney, "U.S. Gain Depicted," *New York Times*, 8 November 1957, 1 and 10; "Words Were Plain," *Newsweek*, 18 November 1957, 38-39.

54. "The Go-Ahead Feeling," *Newsweek*, 18 November, 1957, 39.

55. "The Presidency: Answer in Oklahoma," *Time*, 25 November 1957, 26.

56. W.H. Lawrence, "President Asks Arms Rise to Match Soviet, At Cost of Other Items in Budget," *New York Times*, 14 November 1957, 1 and 14.

57. Comments on the television broadcast are based on the author's notes, taken when viewing the CBS film of "Our Future Security," a copy of which is held by the Eisenhower Library.

58. Though it is not addressed in her insightful analysis of television's impact on political discourse, Eisenhower's performance informs, and is informed by, Kathleen Hall Jamieson's *Eloquence in an Electronic Age: The Transformation of Political Speechmaking* (New York: Oxford University Press, 1988). For a recent treatment of Eisenhower as a television president see Craig Allen, *Eisenhower and the Mass Media: Peace, Property, and Prime-time TV* (Chapel Hill: University of North Carolina Press, 1993)

59. Whitman File, Speech Series, Box 23, Our Future Security, 13 November 1957, DDE Library. This 36-page manuscript is Eisenhower's reading copy, completed in large type for ease in presentation. The author verified and corrected the text against the Library's

copy of the CBS film of the speech. All quotations are from this source. Unless otherwise noted, all emphasis is in the original.

60. "Reaction is Split on Oklahoma Talk," *New York Times*, 14 November 1957, 14; "Educators Score Eisenhower Plan," *New York Times*, 15 November 1957, 8.

61. Memorandum from Arthur Larson to Governor Adams, 20 November 1957, Arthur Larson Papers, Box 1, Gov. Sherman Adams, DDE Library; Letter from Dwight Eisenhower to Arthur Larson, 23 November 1957, Arthur Larson Papers, Box 4, President's Speeches: Security and Peace 2/25/58, DDE Library.

62. Eisenhower, *Waging Peace*, 226; Larson, *Eisenhower: The President Nobody Knew*, 159-60.

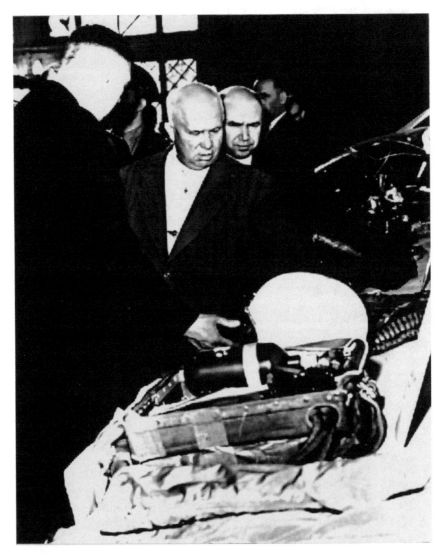

Khrushchev with equipment retrieved from the downed U-2 spyplane

Lawrence W.
Haapanen

# The Missed Opportunity
## *The U-2 and Paris*

Throughout his life, and even in the course of many trials and tribulations while president, Dwight D. Eisenhower was imbued with a steady optimism that seemed to grow stronger with time. Halfway through his first term in the White House, Eisenhower noted in his diary that he had "so often been through these periods of strain that I have become accustomed to the fact that most of these calamities we anticipate really never occur."[1] His experience in the wake of the U-2 incident would prove to be a daunting challenge to this optimistic outlook. For almost a month, Eisenhower's time and energy would be spent trying to escape from what, in the words of one biographer, was his administration's "most embarrassing predicament."[2] In the end, he found himself speaking out publicly on sensitive matters he never expected to discuss outside the confines of the Oval Office. This essay will trace the rhetorical trajectory followed by Eisenhower from the time he was informed that a U-2 spy plane had been shot down over the Soviet Union on 1 May 1960, to Eisenhower's address to the nation on 25 May 1960.

To explicate in detail each act of rhetorical discourse that followed in the wake of the U-2 incident would take a book-length study. What deserves attention in this essay is the manner in which President Eisenhower, having first tried to maintain silence on the U-2 incident and as much distance as possible from it, broke that silence, and in so doing complicated the situation and contributed to the breakup of the Paris summit conference. This, in turn, demanded of Eisenhower a carefully conceived rhetorical response that would plausibly frame the events that had occurred and deflect as much blame as possible from his administration for the handling of those events. Since these purposes were in large part accomplished by his 25 May address to the American people, the primary focus of this essay will be on that speech.

One striking characteristic of Eisenhower's 25 May address is that it not only looked backward at what had happened, but it also looked to the future, and gave a guardedly optimistic forecast of U.S.-Soviet relations. In doing so, it remained consistent with the optimistic approach to world events that was so characteristic of Eisenhower, and also gave to the events of May 1960 the

251

calming appearance of stability and continuity rather than the complexion of an abrupt and foreboding break in the tense relationship between the two countries.

Secondly, President Eisenhower went no further in his 25 May address than he had in his earlier pronouncements in taking personal responsibility for the U-2 overflights in general and the ill-fated 1 May overflight in particular.[3] Whether he had approved each of these flights individually, or only the program; whether he ever had reservations about the overflights; precisely why the 1 May overflight had been authorized—these questions went unanswered. That the public, the news media, and the Congress allowed these questions to go unanswered is a tribute to President Eisenhower's credibility at a time when the phrase "credibility gap" had yet to be coined.

Third, President Eisenhower's 25 May address was the public manifestation of a communication campaign that also was being carried on behind the scenes in the weeks following the U-2 incident. The comments made in public offered a narrower perspective on events than those made in private—to congressmen, the Cabinet, the National Security Council, and others—yet they all had to add up to a coherent whole.

## In Search of a Strategy

The program of U-2 overflights that took place between 1956 and 1960 was one of the most closely kept secrets of the Cold War. In November 1957, Eisenhower gave some thought to revealing to the world that the United States was capable of photographing the Soviet Union from very high altitudes, but this was never done.[3] With all matters of policy, he was "constantly at pains to analyze not only what policies and actions were needed, but also whether actions should be publicized at all."[4] On a matter as sensitive as the overflights, it's a small wonder he decided against publicity. The U-2 program operated under a principle common to espionage—"plausible deniability." If an act of espionage is exposed, it is useful for the guilty nation to deny any knowledge of the act, and especially for the chief of state to be portrayed as having no knowledge of it. The United States, its allies, and the Soviet Union had all employed this principle, and for the U.S. to have publicized the U-2 overflights would have violated the principle, putting both the nation and its president in a very embarrassing position. The Soviets were aware of the overflights, and twice they made secret diplomatic protests to the U.S., but as long as they could do nothing to thwart them, they kept publicly silent and waited their chance.

On 1 May 1960, when word reached Washington, D.C., that Francis Gary Powers's U-2 was missing somewhere in the Soviet Union, there was no panic. The immediate reaction was sympathy for the pilot, since the Director of

Central Intelligence, Allen Dulles, had always insisted that no U-2 pilot "would ever be taken alive."[5] While President Eisenhower remained largely uninvolved in the decision-making process, CIA and State Department officials chose to release a cover story (drawn up earlier and never revised) that a NASA weather research plane had experienced some mechanical difficulty and was missing near the Turkish-Soviet border. The situation changed dramatically on 5 May, when Soviet Premier Nikita Khrushchev announced that a U.S. spy plane had been shot down.

Eisenhower heard of the Soviet announcement while presiding over a meeting of the National Security Council at a secluded location outside Washington. Following the regular meeting, he convened a smaller group of his closest advisors and argued against immediately issuing a public statement. He allowed himself to be overruled, however, when the rest of the group unanimously agreed that a statement should be released without delay.[6] The new statement adhered to the original cover story, and simply made matters worse when, on 7 May, Khrushchev surprised the U.S. by announcing that the U-2's pilot, Francis Gary Powers, had been captured alive. Khrushchev did, however, leave the door open for Eisenhower to escape blame for the overflight by asserting that he was "quite willing to grant that the President did not know anything about the fact that a plane had been sent into the Soviet Union and had not returned."[7]

Khrushchev's 7 May announcement came while Eisenhower was beginning a day of golf at Gettysburg. He continued to spend the day relaxing while Secretary of State Christian Herter and a contingent of CIA, State Department, and White House personnel worked out a new response in Washington. When a new cover story was finally hammered out later that afternoon, Eisenhower's approval was obtained via telephone. It only added to his problems because, going beyond the admission that the U-2 lost over the Soviet Union had been on an intelligence-gathering mission, the revised story went on to say that there had been no authorization for the flight by authorities in Washington. Dulles, who had offered to resign if necessary, was told by Herter that the disclaimer of administration approval for the flight was to "get the President off the hook."[8] What it did, however, was stretch plausible deniability to the breaking point, and force Eisenhower into abandoning his hands-off posture toward the U-2 incident.

For the first week following the loss of the U-2, Eisenhower had managed to keep his distance from the matter, both publicly and behind the scenes. Now, he quickly decided to speak out publicly on the U-2 incident. There are two schools of thought on why he did so. According to one school, the 7 May cover story made it appear that the U-2 overflights had been going on without Eisenhower's knowledge, and this was untenable. Vice-President Richard Nixon expressed this sort of concern when he told Herter that "we simply can't leave the President in the posture where he says he doesn't know anything about this; to give this impression would be to imply that war could start without the President's knowledge."[9] This interpretation was also expressed in the media. Drew Pearson, writing on 10 May, noted: "In denying that it authorized the flight, the administration has entered a plea of incompetence."[10] The second school of thought is that Eisenhower, realizing that the 7 May cover story would inevitably lead to the sacrifice of some subordinate (if not Dulles, then someone farther down the line of command at the CIA), decided he could not fire someone simply to maintain plausible deniability. At the end of May, he told his national security advisor, Gordon Gray, that he had decided "he simply could not sacrifice a subordinate as some people had wanted him to do."[11] Regardless of which school of thought is correct, Eisenhower made up his mind to accept personal responsibility for the U-2 overflights, and directed Secretary Herter to issue a new statement on 9 May so stating.[12]

Returning to work at the White House on 9 May, Eisenhower presided over a meeting of the National Security Council, and "announced that he would take full responsibility for the missions. 'We're going to take a beating on this,' he said, 'And I'm the one, rightly, who is going to have to take the brunt.'"[13] Between then and 11 May, he recruited his staff secretary, General Andrew Goodpaster, to draft remarks on the U-2 for a televised presidential news conference. Also during this time, there were meetings with key congressmen—one group on 9 May, briefed by Dulles and Herter, and two more groups on 10 and 11 May, at breakfast with the president. Meanwhile, Allen Dulles began to pursue an idea of his own. Herter told Eisenhower on 9 May that Dulles had stated, apparently at the meeting with congressional leaders, "that it looked as though this [the U-2] was not shot down from high altitude."[14] And on 10 May, Herter told the president's press secretary, Jim Hagerty, that Dulles would like Eisenhower to say he doubts the U-2 was shot down from a high altitude, "which would help in the case of some of our allies who are worried about Soviet capabilities in high altitudes."[15]

Eisenhower's 11 May news conference fully followed his intention to take personal responsibility publicly for the U-2 overflights. Asserting that afterwards he would have nothing more to say on the subject, he began by defending intelligence-gathering activities on the grounds that they protected the United States against surprise attack, and he blamed the Soviets for having a "fetish of secrecy and concealment" that constituted a "major cause of international tension." While not making specific reference to the U-2 overflights, he argued that intelligence-gathering activities were "a distasteful but vital necessity," and he asked that "an incident" not cause distraction from "the real issues of the day . . . the ones we will be working on at the summit—disarmament, search for solutions affecting Germany and Berlin, and the whole range of East-West relations, including the reduction of secrecy and suspicion." Finally, he expressed hope "that we may make progress on these great issues."[16]

This optimistic note turned the eyes of his audience to the upcoming Paris summit and gave hope that the U-2 incident could somehow be set aside when he sat down with Khrushchev.

In the middle of his 11 May statement, Eisenhower claimed that "there is some reason to believe that the [U-2] plane in question was not shot down at high altitude."[17] While he mentioned this as an example of discrepancies in the Soviet Union's allegations (Khrushchev had boasted that Soviet missiles had brought down the plane), it is clear that this was included in response to Allen Dulles's earlier request to Secretary of State Herter. On 31 May, testifying before the Senate Foreign Relations Committee, Dulles admitted having made one suggestion for the president's 11 May statement, "which I think was included."[18]

President Eisenhower's 11 May statement abandoned "plausible deniability" and injected him personally into the U-2 incident in a way that had been avoided up to that point. It is difficult not to agree with Harrison Salisbury's assessment that from that point on the fate of the summit was sealed.[19] Eisenhower's acceptance of responsibility had one additional effect, however, and that was it permitted him to reduce the distance that had been previously maintained between himself and the U-2 incident. He would henceforth lead the way, and not defer to his advisors, in deciding how to handle and what to say about the whole affair.

On the afternoon of 11 May, presidential assistant and speech writer Bryce Harlow phoned Herter regarding a possible speech to be given by Eisenhower on 13 May, the eve of his departure for Paris, a draft of which was being worked on at the White House and would be sent to Herter and Dulles for comments.[20] Later, Herter called Harlow back and recommended that Eisenhower's statement be very brief, make "no mention" of the U-2 incident, and be "matter of fact, solemn, not overoptimistic or too pessimistic."[21] By early that evening, Eisenhower returned to the office after a round of golf, saw Harlow, and "decided against a telecast before leaving for the Summit."[22] Why he decided not to make a predeparture speech is not known, but it probably reflects, once again, his natural reticence about speaking out publicly without a clear and sufficient reason.[23]

On 12 and 13 May, Eisenhower took steps to make sure no additional operations of a provocative nature would occur to complicate matters, and he also privately expressed "a major question in his mind as to whether it was not a mistake to have talked so much and so quickly as a government on this [U-2] matter."[24] He pressed forward with the thought in mind that, as expressed in a staff conference on 10 May, that he intended to let Khrushchev "talk as much as he wanted about the plane, and then quietly suggest that he should come around and talk privately to the President about it."[25] Herter subsequently passed the word to the British and French governments that this would be how

Eisenhower would handle the subject if Khrushchev brought it up at the summit, and in his first staff meeting after arriving in Paris on 15 May, Eisenhower again "said he is of the view that he should see Khrushchev bilaterally early in the sessions—immediately if Khrushchev brings up the U-2 question."[26]

Eisenhower came to Paris brimming with conciliation, and hoping against hope that Khrushchev would follow suit. Only one meeting took place between the assembled heads of state, however, and Khrushchev used it as a forum for his demands that the U.S. apologize, promise never to launch spy flights against the Soviet Union again, and punish those responsible for Powers's flight. Ambassador Charles Bohlen was present, and noted that as Khrushchev spoke, "Eisenhower's bald head turned various shades of pink, a sure sign that he was using every bit of will to hold his temper."[27] Eisenhower replied by pointing out that while he had banned further U-2 overflights, he would not apologize. The meeting broke up, and at meetings over the next two-and-a-half days, Eisenhower and his advisors found themselves unable to come up with a plan that would revive the conference without apologizing, something Eisenhower refused to do. Finally, four days later, on 19 May, the president headed back to Washington, Khrushchev having already departed with angry words about Eisenhower and his treachery. Refusing to apologize to the Soviets, Eisenhower found the American public of a like mood; indeed, a high school teacher in Washington state was dismissed because his class had wired Eisenhower and urged him to apologize to the Soviets.[28]

Had the summit gone well, Eisenhower would have gladly addressed the nation upon his return. While it undoubtedly made the prospect of a speech an unpleasant one for the president, the failure of the summit made the need for a speech even more pressing. News organizations had begun to castigate the Eisenhower administration for its actions even as the president was on his way home. Walter Lippmann, for one, hit on "the series of blunders on the gravest matters in the highest quarters," and warned that the damage that had been done to U.S. prestige "would be irreparable if we all rallied around the President and pretended to think that there was nothing seriously wrong."[29] These sentiments were echoed in the editorial pages of newspapers from coast to coast, and while Khrushchev's performance in Paris was widely condemned, the Eisenhower administration was faulted for its lying, bureaucratic bungling, and alleged lack of leadership. These pronouncements of the elite press did not, of course, reflect the opinions of all Americans, and Eisenhower enjoyed widespread support that was evident in the highly supportive tone of most telegrams received by the White House in early May 1960.[30] Moreover, Khrushchev's performance in Paris was widely condemned by the American media. Given a choice, the vast majority of Americans would have been on Eisenhower's side in a dispute with the Soviets, regardless of the errors of judgment with which the media might charge the president.

Plans for a post-summit Eisenhower address to the American public were already developing on 18 May, before he left Paris, when the president's son and aide, Major John Eisenhower, sent a message to presidential speech writer Dr. Malcolm Moos regarding a "possible train of thought for a fifteen-minute tv talk the president might make soon after arrival home."[31] The president, freshly back in Washington on 20 May, conferred with several aides and "said he had in mind an address to the nation. He thought it could wait until Tuesday night [24 May], but had better not wait beyond that point."[32] At this point, drafts began to be sent over for Eisenhower's perusal, the chief contributors being Malcolm Moos and Bryce Harlow; by 22 May the president's aides were conferring at the White House to hammer out a final draft, now scheduled for delivery on 25 May.[33] On 24 May, Eisenhower met with General Goodpaster, who was working with Dr. Moos on the speech, and Secretary of State Herter. According to Goodpaster, the president wanted the speech "to be positive without being truculent, and to give an explanation of events without being defensive." Eisenhower recognized that the task would be difficult. "The President," noted Goodpaster, "said he wants to keep the door open to negotiation but added that we learned at the time of Korea that we must negotiate from strength rather than weakness."[34]

On the same day, Eisenhower presided over a meeting of the National Security Council. This was an elite audience, far more knowledgeable than the general public about the events that had occurred in Paris, but in need of guidance from Eisenhower on how best to respond to those events. The first thing on the president's mind was the prospect of congressional hearings on the U-2 incident and Paris summit, and, in order to continue the appearance of at least some distance between himself and the U-2 incident, he advised that in those hearings "the impression should not be given that the President has approved specific flights, precise missions, or the timing of specific flights."[35] He also laid the blame for the summit's collapse squarely on the Soviets, saying that "the idea that we could have done anything to save the Summit Conference was ridiculous. . . . Khrushchev deliberately decided to blow up the Summit Conference, knowing that he (the President) could not accept the demands Khrushchev made."[36] The thrust of this meeting was to get a large number of administration insiders (there were twenty-eight attendees) briefed on what hopefully would be a consistent story that could be disseminated in coming days to the Congress and the public.

The twenty-fifth of May was a day of last-minute preparations for the 8:00 p.m. nationally televised address by the president. As the final draft was being refined at the White House, Secretary of State Herter called to find out if Ambassador Bohlen could see the speech, since Bohlen "had done more research than anyone on the chronology of the U-2 business and we want to be certain the President is completely solid in his presentation." Herter then called

Bohlen to dispatch him to the White House, but Eisenhower called back a half-hour later to tell Herter that "a large group in his office . . . had just gone over his speech and so drastically revised it" that Herter was told to ignore the previous draft sent to him.[37] Whether Ambassador Bohlen saw the final draft is not clear, but it seems doubtful. Years later, when Bryce Harlow was asked why representatives of the State Department were not consulted more closely on the writing of the 25 May address, he replied that the "White House writes the speeches better."[38] This may have been true, or it may be simply that the president had decided to depend on his own White House staff for such a delicate task, given how things had gone in the first week of May when he had relied on the State Department and others outside the White House to provide guidance.

In addition to finalizing the text of the speech, thought was given on 25 May to using photographs taken by the U-2 to serve as dramatic visual evidence of the value of the U-2 overflights. Eisenhower called Herter to say that he'd been talking to Vice-President Nixon and White House Chief of Staff Wilton Persons about this idea, and asked Herter to speak to Allen Dulles about using two photos, one of the U.S. and one of the Soviet Union. Eisenhower said the only reason not to do this was that the Senate Foreign Relations Committee might demand the whole file, but Herter assured him that they could not do that. Herter then called Dulles, who recommended using photos of San Diego and Tyuratam, a Soviet ICBM test center, and said he'd get them to Persons right away.[39] However, it was subsequently decided to use only one photo of a navy base in San Diego during the address, presumably to avoid inflaming the situation by rubbing the Soviets' noses in the photographic "take" of the overflights.[40] These were the preparations that led to the president sitting down at his desk in the Oval Office at 8:00 p.m. on Wednesday, 25 May 1960, to make his nationally televised address to the American public.

## SETTING THE RECORD STRAIGHT

Ostensibly, the president's purpose in addressing the nation was to set the record straight, to provide an accurate account of what had transpired at the Paris summit conference, and to share his personal views of those events that had so unsettled U.S.-Soviet relations. The reality, of course, was that Eisenhower intended to set the record straight but do it in a way that would cast the best possible light on his administration's handling of events and, yet, not so blame or darken the image of the Soviet Union that further progress in U.S.-Soviet relations would be precluded. This was a delicate balance that, to his credit as a rhetor, would be successfully accomplished. In the process, however, the record would be revealed on a carefully selected basis.

Eisenhower chose not to reveal the reservations he had expressed privately on several occasions about the wisdom of continued U-2 overflights. As early as 1958, he told his advisors that the U-2s had already located adequate Soviet targets and that he was concerned that they had been tracked by the Soviets.[41] In 1959, Eisenhower told the National Security Council that he was "reserved on the request to continue reconnaissance flights on the basis that it is undue provocation."[42] Also in 1959, he expressed concern "over the terrible propaganda impact that would be occasioned if a reconnaissance plane were to fail."[43] Finally, and most telling, on 2 February 1960, just three months before the U-2 incident, Eisenhower met with his Board of Consultants on Foreign Intelligence Activities. According to a memorandum of that meeting: "The President said that he has one tremendous asset in a summit meeting, as regards effect in the free world. That is his reputation for honesty. If one of these aircraft were lost when we are engaged in apparently sincere deliberations, it could be put on display in Moscow and ruin the President's effectiveness."[44] Despite these misgivings about provoking the Soviets, giving them a propaganda windfall, and undermining his own effectiveness as president, in late April 1960, Eisenhower had given his approval for one additional flight, to be made before 1 May.[45] There was no mention of these misgivings in his 25 May address, for such mention would have opened Eisenhower to even more criticism of his decision to make the 1 May overflight. He did privately state, in the summer of 1960, that all of his advisors "had missed badly in their estimate regarding the U-2. They had never had an idea of what the reaction in the world to a failure would be. He did not wish to say 'I told you so' but recalled that he was the one and the only one who had put much weight on this factor, and that he had given it great emphasis."[46] But that was for private consumption only.

Another item Eisenhower was not about to include in his 25 May address was a list of intended targets of the 1 May overflight. Actually, hundreds of targets were located within the swath that the U-2 would photograph as it transversed the Soviet Union, culminating in a suspected ICBM base at Plesetsk in the far north.[47] Revelation of a suspected ICBM base, however, would have poured fuel on the fire of the so-called Missile Gap controversy. Some elements of the U.S. intelligence community believed that the Soviets were developing an ICBM capability at a much faster rate than later proved to be the case, and some members of Congress shared this fear and were highly critical of the Eisenhower administration for apparently lagging behind the Soviets. It was not until after the 1960 presidential election campaign that satellite reconnaissance of the Soviet Union proved the missile gap a myth. Divulging the targets of the 1 May overflight would have been very risky politically for Eisenhower.[48]

## Analysis of the Text

Aside from a brief opening and close, the address had five parts. The first part dealt with the background of the Paris summit; the second touched on the U-2 incident; the third summarized the events at the summit; the fourth looked to the future; and the fifth stated the direction of postsummit U.S. foreign policy. The content and evolution of each of these five parts will be examined in turn.

The theme of the first part of the speech, the background of the summit, can be found in almost all drafts, indicating the speech writers realized that the audience needed to consider the events of the summit in light of recent U.S.-Soviet relations. In the speech, Eisenhower alluded to his conversations with Khrushchev during the Soviet leader's 1959 trip to America, when "a small improvement in relations between the Soviet Union and the West seemed discernible."[49] Believing that progress might be possible on persistent problems like disarmament and Berlin, the Allies agreed to meet with the Soviets in Paris, but without abandoning their basic policies or thinking that the Soviets had abandoned theirs. At the same time, the United States had done nothing to relax its vigilance, and this meant continuing to gather information on "other powerful nations, especially those that made a fetish of secrecy."[50] This first part of the speech thus portrayed the Eisenhower administration as going to the summit cautiously, with eyes wide open, and without any intention to compromise American principles.

The second part of the speech dealt with the U-2 incident and attempted to answer questions about the timing of the flight and the first government statements after its failure. This subject was not addressed in the earliest outlines of the speech, but appeared in the 22 May draft and remained in all subsequent drafts. Eisenhower first pointed out that the Soviets were well aware that U-2 overflights had taken place during the preceding four years, yet they had said nothing until after the failure of the 1 May flight. Why, he asked, all this furor over one flight? As far as the timing was concerned, he argued that a nation never can relax its intelligence activity, even on the eve of a summit meeting, since "from Pearl Harbor we learned that even negotiation itself can be used to conceal preparations for a surprise attack."[51] This reference to Pearl Harbor, sure to strike a chord with American listeners, appeared in the last several drafts of the speech.

Eisenhower said that the government's initial cover story was issued to protect the pilot, his mission, and U.S. intelligence processes, at a time when the facts were undetermined. "For these reasons," he asserted, "what is known as a 'covering statement' was issued," but when its assumptions were exposed by the Soviets, "the factual details were set forth."[52]

Next, Eisenhower stressed two facts: first, that he had personally approved the program of aerial reconnaissance (he did not say, however, that he had specifically approved the 1 May flight); and, second, that the U.S. must keep abreast of Soviet military activities, just as the Soviets employ espionage against the U.S. and other countries. Dropped from the speech was an argument included in some earlier drafts that the impending summit actually made it more imperative to send that flight. Perhaps it was felt that if the importance of the 1 May flight were played up too much, its failure would cause concern about the intelligence that had been lost.

Toward the end of this part, Eisenhower explained that, before leaving Washington, he had decided further flights over the Soviet Union would be halted, since their usefulness had been impaired and their continuation would only further hinder America's foreign relations. He also mentioned that "new techniques, other than aircraft, are constantly being developed."[53] This highly veiled reference to reconnaissance satellites may have been intended to reassure his audience that as necessary as the U-2 flights may have been, their discontinuance would not cripple U.S. intelligence gathering.

In the third part of the speech, Eisenhower dealt with the events at the summit. He began by explaining that his decision to stop U-2 flights was not announced publicly prior to his trip to Paris because he wanted to communicate it personally to Khrushchev. But when Khrushchev demanded a public apology and punishment of those who had sent the 1 May flight, Eisenhower "would not respond to his extreme demands," and thus, in effect, "the Soviet Union was scuttling the conference."[54] A 22 May draft of the speech had noted that "Conceivably an earlier announcement [of the flights' discontinuance] could have altered the turn of events in Paris. But even in retrospect I consider this unlikely." Written next to this passage is the notation, "Defensive?"[55] Thus the barest hint of doubt about the Soviets being totally responsible for the demise of the summit was deleted. As delivered, the speech heaped blame on the Soviets, charging them with "scuttling" and "torpedoing" the summit in keeping with plans arrived at even before the Soviets had left Moscow.[56]

The final paragraphs of this mid-section of the speech injected the first dose of optimism, as Eisenhower said there was "black ink" as well as "red ink" to be shown for the summit. First, he said, the Soviets had "turned the clock back in some measure," but at least Khrushchev did not go beyond his customary invective, and, second, "The conduct of our allies was magnificent" as French President De Gaulle and British Prime Minister Macmillan stood behind the Americans.[57]

An optimistic tone continued in the fourth part, which dealt with the future. Eisenhower warned of the dangers of a nuclear war, but pointed out that Khrushchev also realized "that general nuclear war would bring catastrophe for both sides."[58] What is needed, Eisenhower said, is that the U.S. pursue three policies: keep up its strength; continue businesslike dealings with the Soviets; and move ahead with positive programs at home and abroad.

The last part of the speech was a more detailed look at each of the three policies, and an affirmation that each policy was being pursued vigorously. Eisenhower was particularly expansive on the subject of U.S.-Soviet relations, noting that some progress had been made, and that the U.S. would preserve and build on that progress. He also renewed his offer, first made in 1955, of an "Open Skies" program, and showed a photo of the North Island Naval Station in San Diego to show what could be accomplished with aerial reconnaissance.

The optimistic tone of the speech becomes more apparent when some of the language dropped from earlier drafts is examined. For example, one early outline alluded to signs of "a radical return to Stalinism in Moscow, perhaps under the influence of Peiping."[59] Even more alarmingly, "Draft #2" of the speech stated, in a handwritten addition, "The Soviet leaders scuttled the Paris conference; in desperation they could try to scuttle the world."[60] While hardly benign, the picture of the Soviet Union presented was one of a nation at odds with the U.S., one possessing military strength and a fetish for secrecy that necessitated our continued strength and vigilance. Yet it also was a nation whose citizens "have a sincere friendship for the people of America" and who want a "lasting peace and a chance for a more abundant life in place of more and more instruments of war."[61]

Eisenhower concluded the final part of his speech by calling on the U.S. to promote programs that would enhance the welfare of people everywhere, particularly those in newly developing nations who might otherwise be driven into the arms of the Soviets. In this respect, he specifically warned against cutting mutual security programs. He then quickly closed the speech with a pledge to his audience to pursue peace and work for the survival of all mankind in freedom.

## EXTERNAL REACTION

President Eisenhower had, on occasion, expressed dismay at what he perceived as an "extraordinary amount of distortion and gross error that characterizes so much of what appears in newspapers."[62] His doubts about the ability of the press to report accurately the facts of the day had led him, in January 1955, to allow the networks to film and televise his news conferences. His reasons were in keeping with a thought expressed earlier by his press secretary, Jim Hagerty: "To hell with slanted reporters. We'll go directly to the people who can hear exactly what [the] President said without reading warped and slanted stories."[63] In a televised address such as the one delivered on 25 May 1960, it is safe to assume that Eisenhower's intended audience was the American public, not the press. While it is, of course, easier to locate and interpret evidence of press reaction to a presidential address, there is ample reason to believe that the public responded favorably to Eisenhower's remarks.

On 23 May 1960, William E. Robinson, chairman of the board of the Coca Cola Company and a friend of Eisenhower's, wrote the president a remarkable letter. It's questionable whether Eisenhower saw the letter before he spoke on 25 May, but the letter is noteworthy because of how accurately it seemed to sense the mood of the American public regarding the U-2 incident and the Paris summit. The third and fourth paragraphs of the letter read as follows:

> My own notion is based on the premise that, except those who are blindly partisan and others who engage in intellectual exercise about superficialities, the great mass of the American public is solidly behind you. They are not interested in who said what to whom when the U-2 plane was caught in Russia. They know we were trying to find out all we could about the Communists in order to prevent another Pearl Harbor. And they bitterly resent the Khrushchev attack on you. They will not relish any breastbeating or excuses or explanations or apologies. And, by and large, they resent that section of the press and those political partisans who have engaged in these tactics. They don't expect you to tell them the whole story in detail and they are fully aware of the fact that you have to leave many things unsaid. In other words, I think that any semblance of an apology or even an "explanation" would be a mistake. In the present mood even the slightest inference in this direction would cause the newspapers to run headlines—"President Admits Mistakes." And if this is certain to happen in the United States, we can be sure the foreign press will double it in spades.[64]

Although we can see that Robinson's letter lacks objectivity in its estimation of Eisenhower's critics, it reflects the thoughts of someone who knew Eisenhower well, thoughts perhaps similar to those on the president's mind as the 25 May address was written. The address, as delivered, did emphasize the necessity of the U-2 overflights, did avoid being defensive or apologetic, and did leave much unsaid.

We lack precise information about the effects of the speech on public opinion, but we do have the results of a Gallup Poll conducted during a seven-day period beginning on 26 May 1960. This poll asked people if they had "heard or read about the U-2 plane being forced down by the Russians?" 96 percent of the respondents said yes. Those who said yes were then asked, "Do you think the Eisenhower Administration handled this situation well or badly?" The results were that 58 percent answered "Handled well," 29 percent "Handled badly," and 13 percent had no opinion.[65] As the president's last public pronouncement on the subject prior to the poll, the 25 May address may be assumed to have played its part in helping form the public's largely positive reaction to the president's handling of the situation that followed the loss of the U-2. From 26 May to 31 May, the Gallup Poll measured the president's approval rating and found that 65 percent approved, 22 percent disapproved, and 13 percent had no opinion. This was an actual increase from his approval rating of 62 percent measured between 26 April and 3 May, although the increase cannot be attributed solely to the effects of the U-2 incident or to any particular action taken by the president.[66] The end result was that Eisenhower managed to keep the U-2 incident and failure of the Paris summit from tarnishing his favorable public image, and his rhetorical responses to those events should not be underestimated as important contributions to that success.

The press appears to have taken little note of the 25 May address. The *Washington Post* did run a column the following day, expressing sympathy for Eisenhower "as he recounted what must have been a shattering personal experience in the national setback at Paris." His explanation of the events, however, was said to be "somewhat feeble and unsatisfying."[67] What seems to have bothered the *Post* writer the most was that Eisenhower failed to admit the various mistakes that had been pointed out in recent days by the president's critics, mistakes such as lying and bungling. It was, of course, Eisenhower's refusal to admit mistakes that pleased the president's supporters, and, judging from public opinion polls, their numbers were in the majority before, during, and after both the U-2 incident and the Paris summit. All in all, by virtue of being a "calming report to the nation," the address had the desired effect on the American public, a partisan minority and a handful of journalists excepted.[68]

## INTERNAL DEBATE

One final chapter, the congressional debate over the events of May 1960, was yet to play itself out. Hearings were set to begin before the Senate Foreign Relations Committee on 27 May. Eisenhower met the day before with congressional leaders to try to set the right tone. First, he dutifully reported that the U-2, as evidenced by bullet holes in its wings, was shot down at a relatively low altitude. (Eventually, these bullet holes proved nonexistent, but the explanation was consistent with Allen Dulles's.) He then emphasized, once again, that the responsibility for the U-2 flights was his alone. When the Foreign Relations Committee Chairman, J. William Fulbright, criticized Eisenhower for taking responsibility, the president responded that "if he didn't take responsibility someone else would have had to. He said he agreed that Khrushchev had tried to give him an out on this, but that he looked upon it as his responsibility, and he assumed it." As to whether the initial cover story had been wise, however, he admitted that "it would have been a good idea to count to ten." And anticipating the beginning of hearings the next day, he expressed fear that the Senate inquiry "would try to dig into the interior of the CIA and its covert operation," which would be harmful to national security.[69]

On the afternoon of 26 May, Eisenhower presided over a Cabinet meeting called specifically to review the Paris summit—and, incidentally, give Cabinet members who had not been previously briefed a sense, at last, of being in the know. Again, Eisenhower reported that the U-2 was not hit by a missile but was brought down from a lower altitude. As far as the summit was concerned, he repeated that the Soviets had arrived in Paris with their minds made up, and it was pointless to try to continue discussion. This view was backed up by remarks from Undersecretary of State Livingston Merchant and Ambassador Bohlen. Allen Dulles also was present to put a positive face on the U-2 over-flights, saying that they'd "been of value for much longer than ever expected." Eisenhower related Jim Hagerty's opinion that releasing the undelivered text of the planned opening statement for the summit might be helpful; and it was decided that Herter consider the wisdom of this.[70]

In the course of the two meetings on 26 May, Eisenhower had managed to bolster Dulles's version of the U-2's mishap, reiterate the scenario that the Soviets had scuttled the summit by seizing on the U-2 incident as a pretext, and, finally, warn of the dire consequences if the Foreign Relations Committee pressed too hard in its hearings. In the hearings that followed (27 May through 3 June), the administration officials who testified—Herter and Dulles, most prominently— kept a distance between Eisenhower and the 1 May flight, admitting only presidential approval on a "blanket basis." Dulles also main-tained that the U-2 "was initially forced down to a much lower altitude by some as yet undetermined mechanical malfunction" and became a "sitting duck" for Soviet air defenses.[71] They also declined to identify the specific tar-gets of the 1 May overflight.

By the end of the hearings on 3 June, some of the committee members—especially Democrats—were uneasy about the answers they had received from the administration witnesses. An examination of the ensuing discussion among the committee members indicates they often were divided along partisan lines; but all members seemed to have a sensitivity for the damage that might be done to U.S. credibility and prestige if the Eisenhower administration, rather than the Soviets, was made the villain of the U-2 incident and the Paris sum-mit. Some senators even expressed pride in the way that Eisenhower took responsibility for the overflights, viewing it as an injection of truth into the nasty business of spying and lying; as Senator Alexander Wiley put it, "We are saying the truth is more powerful than lies."[72] Beyond this, some members feared that making public any serious criticism of the Eisenhower administra-tion would be giving aid and comfort to the enemy. In the end, the sense that the U-2 flights were necessary (even without knowing any of the targets) coun-terbalanced the committee's apprehension that the 1 May flight had been ill-timed and that the summit would have gone on as planned (although not necessarily to a successful completion) if the U-2 incident had not happened.

Beyond this, it must be recognized that the committee was given, and for the most part accepted, only a very carefully proscribed picture by the administration's witnesses. That they believed what they heard, and failed to insist on hearing more than what was provided, is a testament, no doubt, to their basic faith in the honesty and good judgment of President Eisenhower himself.

## CONCLUSION

As the most important presidential pronouncement during the biggest foreign policy crisis of his second term, President Eisenhower's address of 25 May 1960, is worthy of examination for what it may tell us about presidential rhetoric in general and Eisenhower's rhetoric in particular. Concerning presidential rhetoric, the address and the 11 May statement that preceded it confirm Colin Seymour-Ure's conclusion that presidential silence in impossible. "The President," Seymour-Ure wrote, "is a person from whom 'No comment' is an opinion and whose absence fills space as well as his presence."[73] Eisenhower managed both to avoid comment on the U-2 incident for ten days and to absent himself from Washington for part of that period to further distance himself from the unfolding events; but he could not hope to remain silent indefinitely. On 11 May, he broke his silence and, in so doing, broke a tradition of silence by heads of state on such matters.

We also can see Eisenhower's rhetorical activity in May 1960 as confirmation of several of Fred Greenstein's conclusions about Eisenhower's leadership style, the first being that Eisenhower exercised "hidden-hand leadership." By this, Greenstein meant that Eisenhower's presidential activity was not transparent to his nonassociates, and that he frequently concealed his maneuvers when he felt that publicity would be detrimental to the end results.[74] Had Eisenhower publicly revealed the many times he had expressed reservations about continued U-2 flights over the Soviet Union, for example, he would have given his critics more ammunition to use against him after the U-2 incident; he could repeat those reservations only to trusted listeners behind closed doors.

Also illustrated by Eisenhower's rhetoric of May 1960. is what Greenstein calls "instrumental use of language." While sometimes Eisenhower deliberately sought ambiguity in his public statements, he was skilled in choosing language carefully and precisely to achieve a desired effect on the public.[75] With the help of his aides and speech writers—Goodpaster, Moos, Harlow—Eisenhower clearly did choose his language carefully in planning his public utterances of 11 and 25 May 1960. The discourse was straightforward, reasoned rather than emotional, calming in tone—typical Eisenhower, one might say—for a public audience that by 1960 was comfortable with, and comforted by, such discourse from their president.

Lastly, Greenstein notes, one of Eisenhower's leadership strategies was the building of public support. Eisenhower's great popularity with the American public was neither a fluke nor based solely on his status as war hero; rather, "Eisenhower prepared his speeches with an understanding of his public image and endeavored to enhance and maintain it."[76] We know from his earlier ruminations on the risks of the U-2 overflights that Eisenhower knew he was a man people trusted, and that a U-2 failure could jeopardize that trust and, indeed, his effectiveness as president. It logically followed that his public statements in the wake of the U-2 incident and Paris summit were designed to bolster his public image, and, as discussed earlier, it appears they did so. For a president to promote his own popularity did not strike Eisenhower as crass or self-serving but as necessary to remain effective. According to Greenstein, "This accounts for the great care he took in preparing speeches, planning campaigns, and working at the task of exhibiting the buoyant, optimistic side of his personality."[77]

Rhetoric has its limits. While it can allow a rhetor to frame events for an audience in a way that is in keeping with the rhetor's goals, it cannot undo those events. Regardless of how well Eisenhower succeeded in achieving the goals of his 25 May address, he could not modify all of the circumstances in which he found himself. As Martin Medhurst pointed out in his explication of the strategic approach to Cold War discourse, "It is only when one knows what possibilities for rhetorical modification exist that one can adequately judge whether those possibilities are being most fully exploited by the practitioners of Cold War rhetoric."[78]

It was beyond the reach of Eisenhower's 25 May address to reestablish any sort of productive relationship between himself and Khrushchev, and Eisenhower knew it. He therefore discarded his usual tactic of ignoring opponents, illustrated in such remarks as: "If someone's been guilty of despicable actions, especially toward me, I try to forget him."[79] Instead, he accused Khrushchev of staging a "tirade" and "torpedoing the conference."[80] This ended any semblance of a positive relationship between the two men, and placed the goal of further improvement in U.S.-Soviet relations beyond the reach of the Eisenhower administration. Nothing Eisenhower could say or do could revive the possibility of reaching this goal, and he found this terribly frustrating. George Kistiakowsky, his science advisor, saw him some weeks later at the White House, and later recalled that Eisenhower

> began to talk with much feeling about how he had concentrated his efforts the last few years on ending the cold war, how he felt that he was making big progress, and how the stupid U-2 mess had spoiled all his efforts. He ended very sadly that he saw nothing worthwhile left for him to do now until the end of his presidency.[81]

This failed Paris summit also destroyed the prospect of a postsummit trip to the Soviet Union, where Eisenhower was to have given speeches in Moscow, Leningrad, and Kiev. Andrew Berding, Eisenhower's assistant secretary of state for public affairs, felt this missed opportunity was the most tragic outcome of the U-2 incident.[82] Counting Eisenhower's never-delivered opening statement at the Paris summit, at least four foreign policy speeches were thus precluded by the U-2 incident, and, given Eisenhower's sincere desire for world peace, these four speeches might have constituted one of the most significant bodies of pro-peace discourse ever delivered by a U.S. president. Nothing Eisenhower could say in his 25 May address, no matter how positive or optimistic, could make up for this great rhetorical loss.

## NOTES

1. Robert H. Ferrell, ed., *The Eisenhower Diaries* (New York: W. W. Norton & Co., 1981), 50.
2. Peter Lyon, *Eisenhower: Portrait of the Hero* (Boston: Little, Brown and Co., 1974), 809.
3. Memorandum of Conference with the President, 7 November 1957, Meetings with the President—1957 (2), Box 5, J. F. Dulles Papers, Eisenhower Library, Abilene, Kansas (hereafter cited as DDE Library).
4. Fred I. Greenstein, "Leadership Theorist in the White House," in *Leadership in the Modern Presidency*, ed. Fred I. Greenstein (Cambridge: Harvard University Press, 1988), 94.
5. John S. D. Eisenhower, *Strictly Personal* (Garden City, N.Y.: Doubleday & Co., 1974), 270.
6. Dwight D. Eisenhower, *The White House Years: Waging Peace 1956-1961* (Garden City, N.Y.: Doubleday & Co., 1965), 549.
7. "Khrushchev's Closing Speech to Supreme Soviet on U-2," *The Current Digest of the Soviet Press*, 8 June 1960, 6.
8. Presidential Phone Calls, 7 May 1960, Herter Papers, Box 10, DDE Library.
9. CAH Telephone Calls 3/28/60-6/30/60 (2), Herter Papers, Box 12, DDE Library.
10. Drew Pearson, "The Spy Plane," *Washington Post*, 10 May 1960, reprinted in *Congressional Record*, 23 June 1960, S13942.
11. Memorandum of Conference with the President, 31 May 1960—Meetings with the President—Vol. I (3), Records of the White House Office-Office of the Special Assistant for National Security Affairs: Records 1952-61, Special Assistant Series, Presidential Subseries, DDE Library.
12. Foy Kohler, *Understanding the Russians* (New York: Harper & Row, 1970), 327.
13. John S. D. Eisenhower, *Strictly Personal*, 271.
14. Presidential Telephone Calls 1-6/60 (1), Herter Papers, DDE Library.
15. Ibid.
16. "U.S. States Position on U-2 Incident," Department of State *Bulletin*, 30 May 1960, 851-52.
17. Ibid., 851.
18. U.S. Senate Committee on Foreign Relations, Hearing Regarding Summit Conference of May 1960, and Incidents Relating Thereto, Transcript, Vol. 1A, 405.

19. Harrison Salisbury, *A Journey for Our Times* (New York: Harper and Row, 1983), 490.
20. CAH Telephone Calls 3/28/60-6/30/60 (2), Herter Papers, Box 12, DDE Library.
21. Presidential Phone Calls 1-6/60 (1), Herter Papers, Box 10, DDE Library.
22. Whitman File, Whitman Diary Series, Box 11, May 1960, DDE Library.
23. Harlow, who was present when Eisenhower scrubbed the predeparture speech, could not explain his decision. Personal communication from Bryce Harlow, 18 December 1980.
24. Memo of 5/16/60, Staff Notes May 1960 (1), DDE Diary Series, Box 32, DDE Library.
25. Memorandum of Conference with the President, 10 May 1960, Staff Notes May 1960 (2), DDE Diary Series, Box 32, DDE Library.
26. Memorandum of Conference with the President, 15 May 1960, Staff Notes May 1960 (1), DDE Diary Series, Box 32, DDE Library.
27. Charles E. Bohlen, *Witness to History 1929-1969* (New York: W. W. Norton and Co., 1973), 468.
28. *New York Times*, 21 May 1960, 24.
29. Walter Lippmann, "First of All," *Washington Post*, 19 May 1960, reprinted in *Congressional Record*, 23 June 1960, S13918.
30. For reprints of newspaper editorials and stories, see *Congressional Record*, 23 June 1960, Senate section. For letters and telegrams to the president, see Folder 225-G, White House Central Files, Official File, DDE Library.
31. Speeches of DDE, Box 35, Bryce Harlow Papers, DDE Library.
32. Memo of 5/26/60, Staff Notes, May 1960 (1), DDE Diary Series, Box 32, DDE Library.
33. See routing slips, dated 20 May and 22 May 1960, speech drafts, Speeches of DDE, Box 35, Bryce Harlow Papers, DDE Library.
34. Goodpaster memo, 5/26/60, State Department—1960 (March-May) (6), White House Office, Office of the Staff Secretary, Alphabetical Series, State Department Subseries, Box 4, DDE Library.
35. Discussion at the 445th Meeting of the National Security Council, Tuesday, 24 May 1960, 5, NSC Summaries of Discussions, Ann Whitman File, NSC Series, Box 12, DDE Library.
36. Discussion at the 445th Meeting, 8.
37. Phone Calls, 5/25/60, CAH Telephone Calls, 3/28/606/30/60 (2), and Phone Calls, 5/25/60, Presidential Phone Calls, 1-6/60 (1), Herter Papers, DDE Library.
38. Personal communication from Bryce Harlow, 18 December 1980.
39. Phone Calls, 5/25/60, Presidential Telephone Calls, 1-6/60 (1), and Phone calls, 5/25/60, CAH Telephone Calls, 3/28/60-6/30/60 (2), Herter Papers, DDE Library.
40. According to Art Lundahl, then the CIA's head of photo interpretation, the plan to use photos went through three "gestations": first, to stage an "extravagant expose" of the "fierce things" the Soviets had been developing; second, to show a few photos of Soviet targets; and third, to show a U.S. installation, which is what was done. Interview with Art Lundahl, Bethesda, Maryland, 31 July 1984.
41. Memorandum of Conference with the President, 16 December 1958, Intelligence Matters (7) [December 1958], Subject Series, Alphabetical Subseries, Records of the White House Office-Office of the Staff Secretary, DDE Library.
42. Memorandum for Record, 12 February 1959, Intelligence Matters (8) [January-February 1959], Subject Series, Alphabetical Subseries, Records of the White House Office-Office of the Staff Secretary, DDE Library.
43. Memorandum of Conference with the President, 7 April 1959, Intelligence Matters (10) [April 1959], Subject Series, Alphabetical Subseries, Records of the White House Office-Office of the Staff Secretary, DDE Library.

44. Memorandum for the Record, 8 February 1960, Intelligence Matters (13) [August 1959-February 1960], Subject Series, Alphabetical Subseries, Records of the White House Office-Office of the Staff Secretary, DDE Library.
45. Memorandum for Record, 25 April 1960, Intelligence Matters (14), Project "Clean Up," Box 40, DDE Library.
46. Memorandum of Conference with the President, 11 July 1960, State Department-1960 (June-July) (3), Alphabetical Series, State Department Subseries, Records of the White House Office-Office of the Staff Secretary, DDE Library.
47. Interview with Art Lundahl, 31 July 1984.
48. For an excellent discussion of the "Missile Gap" controversy, see Walter Laqueur, *A World of Secrets: The Uses and Limits of Intelligence* (New York: Basic Books, 1985), chapter 5.
49. Department of State *Bulletin*, 6 June 1960, 899.
50. Ibid.
51. Ibid., 900.
52. Ibid.
53. Ibid.
54. Ibid., 901.
55. Draft dated 22 May 1960, 6, Speeches of DDE, Box 35, Bryce Harlow Papers, DDE Library.
56. Ibid.
57. *Bulletin*, 6 June 1960, 901.
58. Ibid.
59. Outline, dated 19 May 1960, 3, Speeches of DDE, Box 35, Bryce Harlow Papers, DDE Library.
60. Draft #2, 5/20/60, 5, Speeches of DDE, Box 35, Bryce Harlow Papers, DDE Library.
61. Department of State *Bulletin*, 6 June 1960, 903.
62. Robert H. Ferrell, ed., *The Eisenhower Diaries* (New York: W. W. Norton & Co., 1981), 271.
63. Robert H. Ferrell, ed., *The Diary of James C. Hagerty* (Bloomington: Indiana University Press, 1983), 25.
64. Robinson, William E.-1960 (1) [politics, the U-2 incident], Box 29, Name Series, Whitman File , DDE Library.
65. George H. Gallup, *The Gallup Poll: Public Opinion 1935-1971* (New York: Random House, 1972), vol. 3, 1672.
66. George C. Edwards III with Alec M. Gallup, *Presidential Approval: A Sourcebook* (Baltimore: The Johns Hopkins University Press, 1990), 29.
67. "The Accounting," *Washington Post*, 26 May 1960, reprinted in *Congressional Record*, 23 June 1960, S13950-13951.
68. Robert A. Divine, *Foreign Policy and U.S. Presidential Elections* (New York: New Viewpoints, 1974), 208.
69. Memorandum of Conversation-Bipartisan Leaders Breakfast-26 May 1960. Staff Notes May 1960 (1), Box 32, DDE Diary Series, DDE Library.
70. Minutes of Cabinet Meeting, 26 May 1960, declassified 12 January 1981; and Record of Action, 6/2/60, Schedules, May 1960 (1), Box 32, DDE Diary Series, Whitman File, DDE Library. Someone thought better of the idea; a draft of the statement wasn't declassified until 1981.
71. *Executive Sessions of the Senate Foreign Relations Committee (Historical Series)*, vol. 12 (Washington: U.S. Government Printing Office, 1982), 287.

72. *Executive Sessions,* 466.
73. Colin Seymour-Ure, *The American President: Power and Communication* (London: The Macmillan Press Ltd., 1982), 33-34.
74. Fred I. Greenstein, *The Hidden-Hand Presidency: Eisenhower as Leader* (New York: Basic Books, Inc., 1982), 58-65.
75. Ibid., 66-76.
76. Ibid., 96.
77. Ibid., 99.
78. Martin J. Medhurst, "Rhetoric and Cold War: A Strategic Approach," in Martin J. Medhurst, Robert L. Ivie, Philip Wander, and Robert L. Scott, *Cold War Rhetoric: Strategy, Metaphor, and Ideology* (Westport, Conn.: Greenwood Press, 1990), 20.
79. Dwight D. Eisenhower, *At Ease: Stories I Tell to Friends* (Garden City, N.Y.: Doubleday and Co., 1967), 52.
80. Department of State *Bulletin,* 6 June 1960, 900-901.
81. George B. Kistiakowsky, *A Scientist at the White House: The Private Diary of President Eisenhower's Special Assistant for Science and Technology* (Cambridge: Harvard University Press, 1976), 375.
82. Andrew Berding, *Foreign Affairs and You* (New York: Doubleday, 1962), 95.

Ike delivers his farewell address, January 17, 1961

Charles J. G.
Griffin

# New Light on Eisenhower's Farewell Address

On 17 January 1961, Dwight D. Eisenhower bade farewell to the presidency and to more than a half century in the service of his country. Speaking from the Oval Office, Ike expressed his gratitude to the American public for its confidence and support over the years, and voiced his hopes—and his fears—for the nation's future. Included among the latter was a now-famous admonition:

> In the councils of government, we must guard against the acquisition of unwarranted influence, whether sought or unsought, by the military-industrial complex. The potential for the disastrous rise of misplaced power exists and will persist.

> We must never let the weight of this combination endanger our liberties or democratic processes. We should take nothing for granted. Only an alert and knowledgeable citizenry can compel the proper meshing of the huge industrial and military machinery of defense with our peaceful methods and goals, so that security and liberty may prosper together.[1]

Despite their indelible association with Eisenhower in later years, the president's words of warning came as something of a surprise to many in his immediate audience. Some were surprised to hear "a professional military man bracket the military with big business as potential enemies of the national interest." Others, having expected "a more sentimental leave-taking" from the Old General, were startled by the jeremiadic cast of his final message.[2]

Three days later, Eisenhower was succeeded in office by John F. Kennedy. With attention now focused upon the New Frontier and its eloquent young leader, Eisenhower's prophecy, however troubling, might have been expected to fade from the public mind. But there was something "curiously yeasty" about Ike's phrasing, as Bryce Harlow observed in a letter to the former President two months later.[3] And that "yeast" worked its way through the nation's political

---

•Reprinted with permission from the Center for the Study of the Presidency, publisher of *Presidential Studies Quarterly*.

273

consciousness during the ensuing Vietnam years, until the extent and influence of the military-industrial complex became central issues in the debate over the means and ends of American power. Critics continue to dispute these same issues today.[4]

Although the farewell address is among the best remembered and most influential of Eisenhower's speeches, efforts to account for the origin and development of its famous admonitory passage have been hampered by a relative lack of primary source information. However, with the recent addition of an oral history taken from Captain Ralph Williams (United States Navy, Retired) to the archives at the Eisenhower Library in Abilene, Kansas, it is now possible to develop a more complete picture of the farewell's evolution. Williams, who served as a staff speech writer during the final two years of the Eisenhower administration, worked closely with the president's head speech writer, Malcolm Moos, on the farewell address. His recollections, along with those of the late Dr. Moos, shed new light on a significant episode in the rhetorical history of the Eisenhower administration.

This essay examines currently available information on the composition of Eisenhower's farewell address in order to: 1) clarify the origin of its famous admonitory passage; and 2) disclose how the military-industrial complex warning illustrates Eisenhower's "hidden hand" rhetorical style at work. Specifically, the essay argues that the idea of a presidential warning against the dangers of a "military-industrial complex" originated during a meeting of speech writers Moos and Williams in late October 1960; it further contends that Eisenhower embraced the idea because he realized that—within the rhetorical context of his farewell—such an admonition would convey his legitimate concerns about an expanding defense establishment and score a tactical blow against his political adversaries, even while enhancing his ethos as a statesman "above politics."

## Evolution of the Farewell Address

According to Moos, Eisenhower first indicated his desire to make some sort of farewell speech as early as two years before leaving office.[5] "The President," he states, "was in a philosophical mood one day, and turned to me and said, 'By the way Malcolm, I want to say something when I leave here and I want you to be thinking about it' . . . And I think the statement was prompted by a book . . . [which said] that Alexander Hamilton drafted Washington's farewell address."[6] Moos, a political scientist on the faculty of Johns Hopkins University, had joined the administration on a full time basis in late summer 1958, succeeding Arthur Larson as head speech writer. He was assisted by his student, Stephen Hess, and these two shortly were joined by Williams, who was brought on board to help with matters relating to national security and military policy.[7]

Originally, the president's farewell remarks were to have been included in his final State of the Union message. According to Williams, "Moos wanted the President's last State of the Union message to be something special. . . . We started out with the intent that what we perceived to be the President's last platform was not going to be just another laundry-list recitation of past achievements and future expectations in the traditional pattern of State of the Union messages." But as Williams and Moos began to talk about the speech during the summer and early fall of 1960, it became ever more apparent to them that the 1961 State of the Union would necessarily be "a sort of lame duck effort in any event" and a poor vehicle for the kind of personal leave-taking that Eisenhower had in mind. Consequently, the two decided to develop separate speeches; one, a technical document would eventually become the 1961 State of the Union Address (which Eisenhower never delivered, but sent to Congress in written form); the other, a more personal message, would evolve into the farewell address.[8]

Work on the farewell address thus began in the early autumn of 1960 and, according to Williams, proceeded in fairly typical fashion. It was Moos's habit to meet with Williams and Hess to discuss ideas for upcoming speeches. Promising ideas then were drafted independently by their originators, after which Moos, who styled himself a "carpenter," would piece them together with his own to construct a speech draft for the president. As for Eisenhower's role in the process, Williams recalls that

> . . . for the most part [Eisenhower] wanted his speeches to come up to him as, to use the military definition, "completed staff work": the whole thing laid out, tailored to the audience with everything in there that should be said to that audience, and to be said to the public, at that particular time. He would look at it and at this point he would begin to think about it. But he needed the full text version to stimulate his own thought processes. The more he would read, the more involved—and intensely involved—he would get. He would get completely immersed in the speech before it was over, and the thing would go anywhere from ten to fifteen drafts.

Williams adds that during this process, Ike would

> . . . find some things that he would throw out and other ideas that he would think about, and he would scribble them into the marginal notes. He'd call in Ann Whitman and he'd dictate maybe two or three pages of new material. And so, draft by draft, it literally became his very own speech from the beginning to the end.[9]

It was not uncommon for the president to consult with his brother, Milton, at some point in the drafting process; and it appears that this was true in the case of the farewell address. The extent of Milton Eisenhower's input into the speech, however, remains unclear.[10]

Williams suggests that the drafting process on the farewell began in early November 1960, although archivists have been unable to locate any drafts of the speech dated before the end of the year. However, at least seven drafts of the speech dated between 6 and 16 January 1961, do exist and the relatively finished state of these drafts suggests that work on the speech began well before the new year.[11]

Moos and Williams met on 31 October to discuss the farewell speech. According to a memo that Williams prepared for his own files that same day, three "preliminary guidelines" for the speech emerged from this meeting. One of these called for a review of the president's past major addresses, presumably as a source of material for the proposed speech. The other two guidelines identified specific concerns that Eisenhower might address during the proposed speech. The first of these was "the worldwide tendency for orderly societies to break down into mob-ridden anarchies." The Williams's memorandum noted that even at home "we see instances where political decisions are [made] first on the barricades instead of normal governmental processes," and asserted that "it is easy to wave banners to riot, to protest, but the difficult thing is to work a constructive change so that society is strengthened rather than weakened and divided." Apparently, this idea dropped out early in the composition process, for it does not appear in any of the surviving drafts of the farewell address.[12]

The other idea mentioned in Williams's memo of 31 October concerned the "problem of militarism":

> . . . for the first time in its history, the United States has a permanent war-based industry. . . . Not only that, but flag and general officers retiring at an early age take positions in [a] war-based industrial complex shaping its decisions and guiding the direction of its tremendous thrust. This creates a danger that what the Communists have always said about us may become true. We must be careful to ensure that the "merchants of death do not come to dictate national policy."[13]

It is not possible to be certain which of the two men, Moos or Williams, initiated this particular line of thought, nor does it really matter. For it is amply clear that both agreed that a problem existed with what Williams, for the moment, referred to as a "war-based industrial complex."

Indeed, there seems to have been a good deal of discussion about this issue among the president's staff during the administration's waning months. Moos notes at least three sources for his own concern. First, Eisenhower's naval attaché, Pete Aurand, would drop by to chat and sometimes leave copies of his aerospace journals with Moos, who was astounded "to go through them and see some 25,000 different kinds of related companies in this thing." Second, Moos's student, Stephen Hess, had been working on a study of the growing number of retired military personnel who were entering careers in defense-related private industries. Third, as a professional academic, Moos had grown increasingly conscious of the role that defense dollars played in the growing domination of "scientific research and university life by federal grants and directives. It wasn't the solitary investigator tinkering in the laboratory, but these huge grants and team research . . . and that this is a significant kind of combination."[14]

In any event, Moos instructed Williams to work up a draft of the idea for possible inclusion in the farewell, and the latter set to work without delay. Williams recalls that the concept of a "war-based industrial complex" had originally been a thought "off the top of my head," but

> as I got into writing the thing, it looked like what we were really talking about was a military-industrial complex rather than war-based. I think the "complex" part of it came—you know, you get to the end of a sentence and you don't know how to end it up and this word comes to you and you write it in and that's the way it fits and that's the way it came out. But I remember specifically very well the phrase, "the military-industrial complex" It seemed to describe what it was I was complaining about.[15]

Moos was apparently pleased with Williams's phrasing, as was the president, who, according to his head speech writer, first viewed a completed draft of the speech in early December. "I think you've got something there," Ike told Moos after he had examined the speech. Both Williams and Moos contend that the version of the speech that went up to the president remained substantially unchanged through the remainder of the drafting process, a view supported by the fact that relatively few changes appear in the surviving drafts of the speech.[16]

## EISENHOWER'S DECISION TO INCLUDE THE MIC WARNING IN HIS FAREWELL

Given the level of his involvement in the speech writing process generally, and in view of the personal interest he had expressed in the farewell, it is unlikely that Eisenhower's assent to the military-industrial complex passage was casual or unthinking. Indeed, those closest to the president, including brother Milton and former speech writer Elmo Richardson, along with scholars such as Parmet and Litfin, agree that Eisenhower's concerns about the potential threat posed by a large peacetime arms lobby extended back to World War II.[17]

Eisenhower's conviction that good government required a careful balance among competing interests was one source of his dismay at the rise of a military-industrial complex. As his presidency progressed, Ike felt "more and more uneasiness about the effect on the nation of tremendous peacetime military expenditures" and "the almost overpowering influence" that defense-related interests could bring to bear upon the federal government. "Unjustified military spending," Eisenhower felt, "is nothing more than a distorted use of the nation's resources."[18] In his farewell, Eisenhower would voice his concern that the sheer weight of interests involved in the military-industrial complex might overwhelm the checks and balances so essential to wise decision making during moments of international tension. "Crises there will continue to be," he said:

> In meeting them, whether foreign or domestic, great or small, there is a recurring temptation to feel that some spectacular and costly action could become the miraculous solution to all current difficulties.
>
> . . . But each proposal must be weighed in light of a broader consideration: the need to maintain balance in and among national programs—balance between the private and the public economy, balance between cost and hoped for advantage—balance between the clearly necessary and the comfortably desirable; balance between our essential requirements as a nation and the duties imposed by the nation upon the individual; balance between actions of the moment and the national welfare of the future. Good judgment seeks balance and progress; lack of it eventually finds imbalance and frustration.[19]

What is more, Eisenhower's experiences during the campaigns of 1956 and 1960 could only have intensified his suspicions about the arms lobby. According to Williams, Eisenhower had come to the White House with two objectives in mind. One of these was to accomplish substantial force reductions in the military as the Korean conflict wound down. The other was to balance the budget. But Eisenhower's plans ran afoul of "people who wanted more money for defense," especially those who advocated vast outlays for the newly independent United States Air Force. Williams recalls that the Air Force "came out of the Army with a bee in their bonnet" and "with all the energy of a new organization, with a new mission, and nothing was going to stop the U.S. Air Force."[20] Moreover, the Air Force had

> a tremendous network of help among aerospace suppliers, and the congressional people . . . whose districts benefitted from these contracts. They cultivated the newspapers, and worked the media for all it was worth, and politicians. So they had this great complex if you will, to support the programs that the United States Air Force thought it needed.

Another obstacle standing in the way of Eisenhower's budgetary goals, according to Williams, was that "these cutbacks were proceeding at a time when much of the public was caught up in the Reds-under-the-bed hysteria of the McCarthy era." And so

> the Democrats figured they had a live one: here was a miserly president pinching pennies at the expense of the nation's security, and wasn't it just awful, folks? And, with the appropriate coaching from the Air Force and its supporting industries this angst eventually came to focus on the yawning "gap" that was supposed to exist between the long range bomber capabilities of the U.S. and the Soviet Union.[21]

After the election of 1956 and the launching of Sputnik in 1957, the "bomber gap" re-opened as the "missile gap." The administration was assailed throughout the campaign of 1960 for allegedly letting the nation's missile effort "go to pieces." Although Eisenhower considered the charge spurious (and, indeed, the missile gap miraculously closed soon after the White House changed hands), the issue was politically damaging and no doubt contributed to the Republicans' defeat in the November election.[22]

In the aftermath of the 1960 election, Ike's resentment toward those who had fueled and exploited the missile gap issue could only have intensified his long-standing concerns about the growing power of the defense lobby. Still, the president had never before expressed those concerns in forceful terms to the American public. Why should he do so now, on the eve of his departure from the White House? The answer, I believe, lies in Eisenhower's appreciation of the unique rhetorical opportunity presented by the farewell address itself.

Although he was assailed by some early critics as "an aging hero who reigned more than he ruled," a number of recent studies have shown Eisenhower to have been a subtle and effective leader with a genius for consensus building.[23] Indeed, Greenstein argues that what critics derided as Ike's bland and casual leadership style was in fact a deliberately crafted image, whose careful maintenance allowed Eisenhower to balance successfully the conflicting demands of his office.

Every president, Greenstein contends, is called upon to carry out two roles so contradictory in nature that in most democracies they are assigned to separate individuals. On the one hand, he must be chief of state, "the equivalent of a constitutional monarch," and thus, the symbol of national unity. On the other hand, as "political head of the executive branch, he has the intrinsically divisive responsibilities of a prime minister." According to Greenstein:

> The unique characteristic of Eisenhower's approach to presidential leadership was his self-conscious use of political strategies that enabled him to carry out both presidential roles without allowing one to undermine the other. . . . On

the assumption that a president who is primarily viewed in terms of his political prowess will lose public support by not appearing to be a proper chief of state, Eisenhower went to great lengths to conceal the political side of his presidency.

Greenstein argues that Eisenhower's ability to pursue political objectives without compromising his stature as a symbol of unity enabled him to "bridge the contradictions of the presidency" and to lead the nation effectively. [24]

Eisenhower's military-industrial complex admonition illustrates just this sort of marriage of principle and pragmatism. That he was able to wed the two so effectively is a tribute to Eisenhower's ability to appreciate and exploit the rhetorical opportunities implicit in his farewell. Eisenhower was well aware of the unique role of the farewell address in the literature of any presidency. Like most schoolboys of his generation, Ike had studied Washington's farewell address with its famous warnings against factionalism at home and entangling alliances abroad. Indeed, Eisenhower's well known admiration for Washington was in part inspired by the heroic character and legacy of the first farewell. In *At Ease*, Ike wrote of the attributes that he admired in Washington:

> Washington was my hero. . . . The qualities that excited my admiration were Washington's stamina and patience in adversity, first, and then his indomitable courage, daring, and capacity for self sacrifice.

> The beauty of his character always impressed me. While the cherry tree story may be pure legend, his Farewell Address, his counsel to his countrymen on the occasions such as his speech at Newburgh to the rebellious officers of his Army, exemplified the human qualities I frankly idolized.[25]

Washington's farewell, written largely by Alexander Hamilton, had deftly combined high-minded appeals to patriotic unity with some very down-to-earth political bloodletting. Gilbert notes that Washington's lofty reputation as one "above politics" made such a combination possible:

> Despite the attacks against Washington in the last years of his second term, the President enjoyed still greater authority and reputation than any other American political leader; the thoughts which he would express when he announced his final retirement from office were bound to make a deep impact on American political thinking. Hamilton must have been well aware that participation in the drafting of Washington's valedictory gave him a unique opportunity to impress on the minds of Americans some of his favorite political ideas.[26]

Perhaps it is not too much to suggest that Ike (who, if Greenstein is correct, combined something of Washington's high-mindedness and Hamilton's craft), saw his own farewell as an opportunity to emulate the rhetorical precedent of his hero by striking back at his foes without compromising, indeed, while enhancing, his stature as a man of principle.[27]

Because he was still president, and an immensely popular national figure, Eisenhower could anticipate a large and sympathetic audience for his farewell remarks. And because he knew that the public would be anticipating "a farewell of pleasantries," Eisenhower had good reason to believe that a "sobering message" might have unusual impact.[28] And that impact would be felt at several levels. First, by clearly voicing his concerns about the dangers of an overblown defense establishment, the president would act to preserve the "balance" he felt so necessary to proper government. In his own words, "Only an alert and knowledgeable citizenry can compel the proper meshing of the huge industrial and military machinery of defense with our peaceful methods and goals, so that security and liberty may prosper together." At the same time, by arousing public suspicions against the military-industrial complex, Ike would land a blow against his political tormentors in the defense lobby and the Democratic party, a blow made all the more effective because it was gloved in the statesmanlike aura of a presidential farewell.[29] Finally, by emulating Washington's rhetorical precedent, Eisenhower would enhance his own ethos, invite further comparison with his hero, and help to cement his place in history as a latter-day "Warrior for Peace."[30]

## CONCLUSION

The foregoing study of the evolution of Eisenhower's farewell address supports two conclusions. First, it clarifies and extends our understanding of speech writing in the latter years of the Eisenhower administration. The foregoing investigation confirms both Crable's assessment that Eisenhower favored the practice of having staff present him with completed speech drafts that could then be tailored to his preferences and Greenstein's contention that Eisenhower was nonetheless actively involved in the development of his own speeches.[31] Indeed, Williams suggests that Eisenhower "suffered so much during the press conferences from his extemporaneous utterances" that he may have become *too* involved in the composition of his formal speeches:

> He would edit—not only the textual and substantive material—but he would fiddle with words, and two or three drafts later the same words would be back in that he had thrown out in some draft before.

Williams adds that he "always thought that things got better up until about the fourth or fifth draft, and after that it was straight downhill!"[32]

A second, and related, conclusion of the study concerns the evolution of the farewell and the genesis of the military-industrial complex metaphor for which the speech is so widely remembered. Understandably, most historians have been vague on these subjects. One of the those who has theorized about the evolution of the farewell is Stephen Ambrose, who has suggested that such a speech was not even contemplated until Norman Cousins proposed the idea in a letter to Eisenhower in December 1960. However, the present investigation demonstrates that preparations for the speech were well underway by the time Eisenhower could have received Cousins' suggestion.

Scholars who have speculated about the genesis of the military-industrial complex metaphor are divided in their opinions as to its origin. Richardson, for example, credits Moos with its invention. Litfin favors Moos, but admits that even Moos, when interviewed in 1969 by the *Washington Post*, was no longer sure of the origins of the term. Medhurst leans toward Bryce Harlow as "the man most probably responsible" for the warning's inclusion. While Larson, possibly being diplomatic as would befit a former presidential speech writer, declares that it was Eisenhower's "own in every sense."[33] However, the Williams-Moos memorandum of 31 October 1960 and the oral history taken from Captain Williams in 1988 both point to Williams as the probable author of the phrase.

If not its actual author, Moos was nonetheless instrumental in the genesis of the military-industrial complex warning. It was he who established the inventional procedures followed by the speech writing staff, and who encouraged Captain Williams to give form to the concerns both shared over the potential dangers of an ever-expanding defense establishment. And it was Moos who fashioned Williams's phrase into the framework of the farewell as a whole.

Regardless of its authorship, the military-industrial complex metaphor is indelibly associated with Dwight D. Eisenhower. Americans at the time were intrigued by the spectacle of Eisenhower exiting public life as a Jeremiah. They were sobered by a professional soldier's concern about the dangers of a growing defense establishment. And, as the years went by, they were increasingly impressed by the apparent prescience of those concerns. I have argued that Ike included the military-industrial complex admonition in his farewell speech not simply because he meant it, nor yet because it enabled him to lash back at those who exploited the missile gap issue at the expense of his administration, but because it accomplished both without compromising—indeed, while enhancing—his ethos. Revisionist appraisals of his presidency notwithstanding, it is unlikely that Ike will be remembered as an orator. His rhetorical instincts, however, could be uncommonly good, and they deserve our continuing attention.

## NOTES

1. Dwight D. Eisenhower, "Farewell Address," speech delivered 17 January 1961. *Public Papers of The Presidents of The United States, 1961* (Washington D.C.: Government Printing Office, 1961), 1035-40 (hereafter cited as *Public Papers*).

2. See, for example, "Eisenhower's Farewell: Sees Threat to Liberties in Vast Defense Machine," *The New York Times* 18 January 1961, 1; Elmo Richardson, *The Presidency of Dwight D. Eisenhower* (Lawrence, KS: Regent's Press, 1979), 186; and Stephen E. Ambrose, *Eisenhower The President*, vol. 2 (New York: Simon and Schuster, 1984), 613.

3. Bryce Harlow, Memorandum to Dwight D. Eisenhower and Richard M. Nixon, 17 March 1961, Eisenhower, Dwight D., Papers, Post-Presidential, 1961-1969: Special Name Series, A70-31, Dwight D. Eisenhower Library, Abilene, Kansas (hereafter cited as DDE Library).

4. See, for example, Anthony Lewis, "No Farewell to Arms," *New York Times* 18 January 1981, E23; George Kistiakowsky, "It's Time to Recall a Warning by Ike," *The Boston Globe* 14 January 1981, 15; Stanley A. Weiss, "The Complex Meaning of Ike's Famous Talk," *The Wall Street Journal* 17 January 1986, 18 ; and Norman Cousins, "Ike Was Long Deeply Concerned About the Influence of Military in Government," *Kansas City Times*, 13 January 1986, A6. An even more graphic illustration of the continuing interest as well as controversy generated by Eisenhower's warning can be found in a recent edition of *USA TODAY*, whose editors devoted the paper's entire "Opinion" page to the subject. At the top of the page, columnists such as Edgar Berman and Phyllis Schlafly argued the question of Eisenhower's intentions, while below "ordinary" citizens were asked to respond to the question "What do you think of the USA's military-industrial complex?" Everybody had an opinion. "The Debate: Military Power," *USA TODAY*, 21 January 1986, 8A.

5. Unpublished Oral History Interview with Malcolm Moos, 1972, DDE Library, OH# 260, 33.

6. Ibid.

7. Dwight D. Eisenhower, *Waging Peace, 1956-1961* (New York: Doubleday, 1965), 320; Unpublished Oral History interview with Captain Ralph Williams (USN Ret.), 3 June 1988, DDE Library, OH# 503, 29.

8. Williams, letter to author, 27 April 1990; Williams, Oral History 1.

9. Williams, Oral History, 17-18.

10. See Moos, 35-6; Williams, Oral History, 31-2.

11. Williams, Oral History, 19; Moos, 35-6.

12. Ralph E. Williams, Memorandum for File, 31 October 1960, Ralph E. Williams Papers, 1958-1960, A87-6 Box 1, DDE Library.

13. Williams, Memorandum for File, 31 October 1960.

14. Moos, 34

15. Williams, Oral History, 26-7

16. Moos, 35-6; Williams, Oral History, 25-6.

17. Milton Eisenhower, Oral History Interview, 6 September 1967, Columbia University Oral History Project, vol. 2, 52; Elmo Richardson, *The Presidency of Dwight D. Eisenhower* (Lawrence: Regent's Press, 1979), 185; Litfin, 202-5; Herbert S. Parmet, *Eisenhower and the American Crusades* (New York: Macmillan, 1972), 571. The evolution of Eisenhower's concerns about an emerging "military-industrial complex" has

been carefully traced by Patrick J. Haney in "Eisenhower's Warnings: The Context and Implications of the Military-Industrial Complex and the Scientific-Technological Elite," (senior thesis, The Ohio State University, 1988). A copy of Haney's thesis is available at the Eisenhower Library in Abilene, Kansas.

18. Dwight D. Eisenhower, *Waging Peace, 1956-1961* (New York: Doubleday, 1965), 615-16.

19. Eisenhower, Farewell Address, 1037.

20. Williams, Oral History, 32.

21. Ibid., 33-4.

22. Ibid., 34-5.

23. See, for example, Anthony James Joes, "Eisenhower Revisionism: The Tide Comes In," *Presidential Studies Quarterly* 15 (Summer 1985): 561-71.

24. Fred I. Greenstein, *The Hidden-Hand Presidency: Eisenhower As Leader* (New York: Basic Books, 1982), 5,4.

25. Dwight D. Eisenhower, *At Ease: Stories I Tell to Friends* (Garden City: Doubleday and Co., 1967), 40-41.

26. Felix Gilbert, *To The Farewell Address: Ideas Of Early American Foreign Policy* (Princeton: Princeton University Press, 1961), 127.

27. See George Washington, "Farewell Address," in Ronald F. Reid, ed., *Three Centuries of American Rhetorical Discourse* (Prospect Heights, IL: Waveland Press, 1988), 186-201; see also, Richard E. Crable, 119; Richardson, 185.

28. Eisenhower, *Waging Peace*, 615-16.

29. Taking this argument a step farther, Medhurst argues that the target of Eisenhower's critique in the military-industrial complex passage is, specifically, John F. Kennedy. See Martin J. Medhurst, "Reconceptualizing Rhetorical History: Eisenhower's Farewell Address," paper delivered at the Fall Conference on Public Address (Northwestern University, September 1990), 19. A later version of this essay appears in the *Quarterly Journal of Speech* 80 (May 1994).

30. For a discussion of Eisenhower's ethos as a "Warrior for Peace," see Richard E. Crable, "Ike: Identification, Argument, and Paradoxical Appeal," *Quarterly Journal of Speech* 63 (April 1977), 188-95.

31. Crable, 120. See also Greenstein, 66.

32. Williams, 19, 18, 20.

33. Ambrose, 611-12; Richardson, 185-86; Litfin, 198, note 4; Medhurst, 22; Larsen, 152.

Eisenhower goes over a speech with his television advisor Robert Montgomery

Martin J.
Medhurst

# Eisenhower's Rhetorical Leadership
## An Interpretation

*A*ll leadership—*political, economic, or moral—involves persuading others to do something now that will bring fruit in the future.*

Dwight D. Eisenhower
27 August 1958

Dwight Eisenhower well understood that "presidential power is the power to persuade."[1] What he did not accept, however, was the dominant paradigm of presidential persuasion associated with the Roosevelt-Truman years. Eisenhower did not believe in the cult of personality, in reliance upon rhetorical style to effect persuasion, in the use of speech making as a primary means of policy testing or implementation, in going over the heads of Congress whether by appeal to the masses via electronic media (*à la* Roosevelt) or by personal political barnstorming (*à la* Truman), nor did he believe in using speech making as a symbolic substitute for governing. Eisenhower's idea of rhetorical leadership was different inasmuch as it was based on three interrelated factors: 1) a strategic view of the art of rhetoric; 2) a group-centered view of leadership; and 3) a philosophical commitment to a balanced, middle-of-the-road political stance.

### A Strategic View of Rhetoric

Eisenhower's essentially rhetorical nature escaped most observers in the 1950s and is still poorly understood today. Many scholars of the Eisenhower presidency say little or nothing about his facility as a communicator, perhaps because they find little. Even those who do recognize Ike's rhetorical abilities often seem perplexed by them and unable to explain, with any degree of sophistication, how those abilities relate to Ike's leadership responsibilities. James David Barber, for example, writes that Eisenhower's "remarkable rhetorical success seems to have happened without either great skill or great energy on his part."[2] Barber goes on to note:

This man, who had little use for inspirational blather, whose speeches would not be long remembered for their eloquence, and who continually resisted demands that he lecture his fellow citizens, revitalized national confidence almost in spite of himself. He is a puzzling case. His political habits never stressed rhetoric, yet that is where he excelled.[3]

By "rhetorical success," Barber appears to mean the appeal of Eisenhower's character as capsulized in the slogan, "I like Ike." Clearly, Eisenhower had a public persona that inspired large numbers of people. But beyond this observation about the president's ethos, Barber appears to harbor a restricted view of rhetoric, one that tends to reduce the art to little more than inspirational blather, eloquence, or a lecture. Such a view is not, of course, unique to Barber, but it is a perspective that serves to cloud, rather than clarify, the role of rhetoric in political deliberation and decision making. If rhetoric is nothing more than meaningless words or the ornamentation of language with various figures and tropes so as to produce a sort of stylized eloquence, then Eisenhower certainly does not qualify as a rhetorician. On the other hand, if one adopts a more classical definition of the art, one such as that found in Aristotle's *Rhetoric*, then Eisenhower's persuasive abilities can be understood in a considerably different light.

Aristotle defined rhetoric as "the faculty of discovering in the particular case all the available means of persuasion."[4] Here the "art" of rhetoric centers on one's powers of discovery, or what later rhetorical theorists would call rhetorical invention. Under this view, rhetoric is an art whose central focus is learning how to find and construct the arguments that are most likely to be persuasive in the case at hand. It is a strategic art in the sense that the speaker must analyze the situation, develop a persuasive goal, invent the lines of argument that seem most capable of moving the target audience toward acceptance of that goal, organize the discourse for maximum effectiveness, and select the time, place, occasion, and audience that is most conducive to achievement of the goal. Such an art is not primarily concerned with eloquence, or style, or verbal ornamentation, or wit; instead, the focus of rhetoric as art is on thought, planning, organization, judgment, selection, and analysis. Under this view of rhetoric, Eisenhower was a master practitioner of the art.

Examination of virtually any Eisenhower foreign policy speech will reveal a consistent concern for the strategic dimensions of rhetoric. Failure to understand this dimension leads not only to a view of rhetoric that reduces the art to nothing but verbal style or delivery, but, more important, leads to a view of policy that fundamentally misunderstands Eisenhower's goals and his dominant mode of achieving those goals. J. Michael Hogan points to this problem in his essay on the Open Skies proposal of 1955. So, too, does Robert L. Ivie in his survey of Ike as a cold warrior. But it is not unusual, even in the 1980s and 1990s, to find Eisenhower's three great speeches of 1953—"The Chance for Peace," "Age of Peril," and "Atoms for Peace"—described as efforts to find a *modus vivendi* with the Soviet Union. Even such an astute student of the Eisenhower presidency as Stephen E. Ambrose says of the "Atoms for Peace" speech: "Eisenhower's proposal of atoms for peace was the most generous and most serious offer on controlling the arms race ever made by an American President."[5] It was, of course, nothing of the sort, as close rhetorical analysis demonstrates.[6]

One of the reasons that Eisenhower's leadership qualities have been questioned is that his rhetorical abilities have gone unrecognized. Since there is a close relationship between Eisenhower's theory and practice of rhetoric and his general style of leadership, to misunderstand or denigrate the former is to unintentionally misconstrue the latter. For example, to take "Atoms for Peace" at face value as a plan for reducing the nuclear arms race is to establish the criteria by which Eisenhower is then to be judged: Did the arms race, in fact, decline? So understood, Eisenhower's leadership appears to have been a failure. On the other hand, if one understands "Atoms for Peace" to be an effort to launch a worldwide propaganda campaign that had as its goals placing the Soviet Union in an untenable posture, creating good will among third world countries, and taking the curse off the atom so that implementation of the New Look could proceed unhindered, then one's judgment about Eisenhower's leadership capabilities takes on an altogether different complexion. One's understanding of rhetoric thus affects directly judgments about policy, strategy, and leadership.

Eisenhower considered rhetoric to be a weapon in the arsenal of democracy. Such a weapon was, in fact, one of the most valuable instruments of all for preventing the outbreak of war, testing the sincerity of the enemy, and waging psychological warfare, both at home and abroad. Rhetorical discourse was readily available, cheap to produce, highly flexible, capable of being deployed on a moment's notice, and often effective in achieving the desired end. It was a valuable Cold War weapon and one that Eisenhower employed repeatedly, even before his inauguration.[7]

To Eisenhower, rhetoric was an amoral tool to be used in line with the values and ethics of the speaker. There was no such thing as an ethics of rhetoric per se or principles of the art that would necessarily prevent the use of some kinds of rhetorical practice, not even lying. Rhetoric was a tool, nothing more. Only the end toward which it was deployed and the intent of the deployer presented bases for moral judgment. Fred I. Greenstein is correct, therefore, when he says of Eisenhower that "verbal expression was his instrument."[8] Ike, says Greenstein, "took it as an unspoken axiom that public language was to be adapted to the circumstances at hand and toward the best possible consequences."[9]

The notion of adaptation, central to Eisehower's rhetorical theory, is also a key to his view of leadership generally. Writing to William Phillips on 5 June 1953, Eisenhower said:

> Anyone who accepts a position of responsibility must, by that very fact, exert
> the leadership required in that position. He must, of course, determine and
> employ the methods applicable to his particular situation.
>
> Clearly, there are different ways to try to be a leader. In my view, a fair,
> decent, and reasonable dealing with men, a reasonable recognition that views
> may diverge, a constant seeking for a high and strong ground on which to
> work together, is the best way to lead our country in the difficult times ahead
> of us.[10]

Methods of leadership were to be adapted to the situation at hand and could vary from one situation to the next. Greenstein recognized this aspect of Ike's leadership when he wrote: "Eisenhower held what social scientists call an 'interactionist' conception of leadership. That is, he believed that leadership practices would—and should—vary with the situation and with the qualities of the leaders themselves. He held this belief as part of a world view that took contingencies for granted as a norm of the human condition."[11] Eisenhower's leadership was contingency-based, I shall argue, because it was exercised in large measure through the most contingent art of all—rhetoric. Just as the practice of rhetoric is contingent on such factors as the speaker's goals, the occasion, audience beliefs, values, and expectations, and the speaker's persuasive abilities, so leadership also depends on an accurate reading of the situation, the evaluation of alternatives, cost-benefit analysis, and judgment as to what leadership style seems most likely to be effective in achieving the desired end. Eisenhower clearly recognized these contingencies, for in the same letter to Phillips he wrote:

> [T]he present situation is, I think, without recent precedent in that particular
> legislators who are most often opposing Administration views are of the
> *majority* party. People like to think of Mr. Roosevelt as a leader; in the situa-
> tion where his own party was delighted to hear a daily excoriation of the
> opposite political party, his methods were adequate to his time and to the sit-
> uation. As of today, every measure that we deem essential to the progress and
> welfare of America normally requires Democratic support in varying degrees.
> I think it is fair to say that, in this situation, only a leadership that is based on
> honesty of purpose, calmness and inexhaustible patience in conference and
> persuasion, and refusal to be diverted from basic principles can, in the long
> run, win out.[12]

From this letter, we learn three things: first, that Eisenhower clearly understood his approach to leadership to be different from that of Franklin Roosevelt; second, that the situation which Ike encountered in 1953 was significantly different from that faced by Roosevelt in 1933; and third, that the key element of successful leadership from Ike's point of view was "patience in conference and persuasion." All three of these factors are implicated in Eisenhower's group-centered approach to presidential leadership.

## A Group-Centered View of Leadership

For Eisenhower, leadership meant more than merely being the leader. Leadership implied followership, goal-directedness, and commitment to a cause that transcended the self. That Ike had given serious thought to the problems of leadership over a long period is evidenced in his private papers. As early as 1943, for example, Eisenhower wrote to his son John: "The one quality that can be developed by studious reflection and practice is the leadership of men. The idea is to get people to working together, not only because you tell them to do so and enforce your orders but because they instinctively want to do it for you."[13] The key point is that the leader's main job is to so inspire confidence and loyalty in the followers that *they* will accomplish the task. Over a decade later, Ike expressed much the same idea in a letter to Paul Helms. On 3 June 1954, Eisenhower wrote: "I am more than ever convinced that 'leadership' cannot be imposed; a climate must be created that makes men receptive to and desirous of fighting for the principles of the man currently in the position of the 'leader.'"[14] Under this view, the leader is not set apart from the group but is an integral part of it. The leader's job is to select the goals, set priorities, and give a sense of direction and guidance. If the leader is successful, the group will be so impressed with this direction, so taken with the leader's dedication to accomplishment of the goal, and so convinced of the leader's good will and good intentions toward the membership that the group will pull together to accomplish the task.

In Eisenhower's view, all members of the group played equally important roles. On one occasion, he even referred to "a team of leaders." Such a team should "not be too dependent on the mere presence, words, or even the counsel of the chief," wrote Ike, "but because of its complete solidarity of faith in ideas and ideals, be capable of functioning both collectively and in all of its parts."[15] This was Eisenhower's view of leadership. It was a view predicated on the centrality of the "team," a concept found throughout Eisenhower's speeches and writings. Nowhere was Ike's vision of the team more clearly articulated than in his famous speech at Guildhall, London, on 12 June 1945. Speaking of the recent victory in Europe, Eisenhower said:

> No one man could, alone, have brought about this result. Had I possessed the military skill of a Marlborough, the wisdom of Solomon, the understanding of Lincoln, I still would have been helpless without the loyalty, the vision, the generosity of thousands upon thousands of British and Americans. Some of these were my companions in the high command. Countless others were the

enlisted men and the junior officers that bore the fierce brunt of the fight. Still others were back in the United States and here in Great Britain, in London. Back of us all the time were our two great national war leaders and their civil associates and military staffs that supported, encouraged, and backed us up in every trial, every test. We were one great team.[16]

Terms such as teamwork, cooperation, partnership, and unity run throughout Eisenhower's rhetoric from 1941-1961. The team, not the individual, was the locus of leadership, for it was only the team that could accomplish the goal. As Eisenhower wrote in *Crusade in Europe* (1948):

> The true history of the war . . . is the story of a unity produced on the basis of this voluntary co-operation. Differences there were, differences among strong men representing strong and proud peoples, but these paled into insignificance alongside the miracle of achievement represented in the shoulder-to-shoulder march of the Allies to complete victory in the West.[17]

It was the group that counted, whether international alliance, country, party, or legislative team. That Eisenhower predicated his theory of leadership on group norms seems clear from the available evidence. Small groups were the primary units with which Eisenhower worked: the president's cabinet, the National Security Council, the Joint Chiefs of Staff, the House-Senate leadership, the Council of Economic Advisors, even his "gang" of private businessmen. Much has been written about Eisenhower's penchant for clear organizational structure and how that structure, depending on the writer, either helped or hindered Ike's presidential leadership.[18] While it is true that Eisenhower believed that tight organization promoted both efficiency and effectiveness, it was not at the level of the entire organization that most decisions were made, but at the level of the small group.[19] This was the level at which Eisenhower exercised his presidential leadership most directly.

In all such group settings, Eisenhower's method was similar. He would encourage each member to state his or her point of view and then would listen with a keen ear to what each, in turn, had to say. Since the president received information from multiple sources, both governmental and extra-governmental, Eisenhower was usually the best informed person in the room. Nevertheless, he would listen to what the group members thought, ask a few questions, and then often (though not always) announce what he planned to do with respect to the matter under discussion. On numerous occasions his decisions went against the advice both of the group as a whole and of his most senior advisors, for the group did not make policy, it *advised* in policy making. As with any good leader, Eisenhower listened to that advice, accepting some and rejecting some. In all cases, however, it was accomplishment of the group goal that was paramount, not the leader. This fact, alone, separated Eisenhower from Roosevelt.

Eisenhower found the leadership style of Franklin Roosevelt both conde-
scending and self-centered. Besides, Roosevelt talked too much for Ike's tastes.
There were few worse things, in Eisenhower's judgment, than "talking Generals,"
and he applied the same standard to himself—before, during, and after his presidency. He would speak on behalf of the group's efforts, not to place himself in
the limelight. As he once told his speech writer Emmet John Hughes:

> [Y]ou do not *lead* by hitting people over the head. Any damn fool can do
> that. . . . I'll tell you what leadership is. It's *persuasion*—and *conciliation*—and
> *education*—and *patience*. It's long, slow, tough work. That's the only kind of
> leadership I know—or believe in—or will practice. . . .
>
> I know how good I could make myself look. Everyone who's yapping now
> would be cheering . . . if only I would do my 'leading' in public—where they
> could *see* me. . . . Well, I can't do that.[20]

Eisenhower detested the heroic pose, whether it came from Franklin D.
Roosevelt, Douglas MacArthur, or John F. Kennedy. He also eschewed the
highly stylized rhetoric that often accompanied such a pose. Eisenhower, in the
words of his speech writer Bryce Harlow, was "a meat and potatoes man."[21]
Rhetoric was to do a job, nothing more. Likewise, leadership, to Ike, meant
getting the job done in such a way as to achieve both short-term and long-term
goals. It would not be leadership, for example, to achieve the short-term goal
of reducing the tax burden—a goal dear to the heart of Republican Senate
leader Robert A. Taft—if by doing so one made achievement of a longer-term
goal, such as balancing the federal budget, more difficult. Leadership meant
balance, and perspective, and foresight. By strategically selecting one's rhetoric,
a leader could convince both those within the group and those in the public at
large of his good will, good sense, nobility of character, and superiority of
insight into the problem at hand.[22] It was all a matter of persuasion.

## A Balanced, Middle-of-the-Road Stance

One of the reasons that Eisenhower's skills as a political leader traditionally
have been deprecated is the assumption that the programmatic activism of a
Roosevelt was—for all places and all times—the proper standard against which
to compare a president. As William E. Leuchtenburg notes, "Franklin Delano
Roosevelt continues to provide the standard by which every successor has been
and may well continue to be measured."[23] Such an assumption is inherently
problematic, however, for as Alonzo L. Hamby points out, "the scorecard
[method] cannot speak to the achievement of presidents who come to office
with a felt belief that success means holding the line against change in one way
or another."[24] Dwight Eisenhower was the first Republican president after

twenty years of New Deal/Fair Deal programmatic activism, a goodly portion of which Ike simply accepted as given. Yet Eisenhower was deeply concerned about the growth of the federal government and the systematic loss of state and local autonomy. He was concerned about a government that spent more than it took in, a government in which the twin threats of spiraling defense spending and ever-larger federal largess threatened to turn the country into a "garrison state" where individual liberties might easily be lost.

Eisenhower's answer to the policies of the past and the challenges of the present was slowly to begin to rein in the more extreme measures of his predecessors. His method for doing this was not to proclaim a "revolution" in the tradition of a Ronald Reagan, but rather to pursue a steady centrist course that would assimilate much of the social legislation of the previous twenty years while turning fiscal policy decidedly in the direction of free market economics. Eisenhower consciously chose the middle of the road, even going so far as to argue that "the true radical is the fellow who is standing in the middle and battling both extremes."[25] Likewise, the leader was one who could keep his followers going down the middle of the road while others veered to the right or left. That this is, in general outline, what Eisenhower attempted to do seems clear from the record: in 1952, he steered a middle course between Stevenson and Taft; in 1953, he refused to join McCarthy's witch-hunt while simultaneously refusing to endorse, at least publicly, those who attacked McCarthy; in 1954, he declined to intervene militarily to save the French garrison at Dien Bien Phu while working covertly to assure that the Vietminh would not be able to consolidate their gains. The list could be expanded indefinitely, but the point is clear. For Eisenhower, it was only in the middle of the road that "truly creative" answers could be found.[26]

Part of Eisenhower's middle way philosophy was to pursue "balance" as both method and goal. He acted in a "balanced" manner, not making radical or sudden changes, but he also sought to keep his policies "in balance," for he realized that a change in one area (such as economic policy) would necessarily cause changes in other areas (such as military procurement and consumer confidence). Ike clearly realized that in a complex organization such as the federal government each component was, to some degree, interdependent with every other component. Leadership, then, could not mean taking on single issues and treating them as though they existed in a vacuum. Instead, leadership meant foresight, understanding of interrelationships, and the will to "keep fighting in the middle of the war"[27] until the goal was achieved *in the strategically right way.*

While some scholars have recognized a similarity between Eisenhower's philosophy of the middle way and Aristotle's golden mean, it appears that such a parallel accounts only for Ike's commitment to balance as an operational method. Equally important to Eisenhower's thought, however, is the idea of keeping everything in balance as one advances toward the goal. For Eisenhower, the ultimate goal was to win the Cold War and usher in an era of true peace. That such a goal was not likely to be achieved during his tenure in office, Eisenhower well understood. Even so, the overarching goal of securing a world in which "the future shall belong to the free"[28] functioned for Eisenhower as the end toward which all humanity was moving. In Aristotelian terms, freedom was the entelechic principle that propelled mankind toward its *telos*—the end state that humans, by their very nature, are moving toward. Part of Eisenhower's great "faith" in the future was his belief that it ultimately could not turn out any other way inasmuch as it was in the very nature of man to be free. The task of leadership in a nuclear world, then, was that of preventing outside forces from interfering with the natural evolution of humanity toward peace and freedom. Leadership thus became an exercise in holding constraining forces in check while simultaneously trying to foster those conditions under which human nature could attain its God-ordained end. Eisenhower was under no illusion that the end state would be reached quickly or easily, but he did believe that it would be achieved some day. He well understood that humans were quite capable of setting themselves back, even of engaging in "the annihilation of the irreplaceable heritage of mankind." But he also held that "the whole book of history reveals mankind's never-ending quest for peace" and believed that all humanity could "move forward toward peace and happiness and well being."[29]

Eisenhower's leadership was oriented toward the day of ultimate peace and freedom. Choices made today had to be made in the light of their effects on the situation tomorrow, next year, or ten years hence. Nothing upset Eisenhower more than shortsighted people—isolationists who wanted to withdraw into a "Fortress America," partisan politicians whose concerns extended only to the next election, single-issue constituencies who wanted their particular grievance addressed without regard to other factors, penny-wise but pound-foolish legislators, mostly Republican, who continually tried to slash mutual security funds, and military-industrial lobbyists who failed to understand that too much spending on the military actually weakened American security.

Eisenhower always acted with one eye on tomorrow. He was, in the words of Greenstein, "a very clear-headed man with a long time horizon."[30] Leading Eisenhower biographer Stephen E. Ambrose contends that "one of the greatest strengths, perhaps *the* greatest, was his ability to take a long range view of things," a quality that Ambrose finds "virtually unique in American politics."[31] Taking the long view and attempting to keep things in balance as one progressed toward the goal in a balanced or measured manner was a central component of Eisenhower's leadership philosophy.

By understanding Ike's strategic view of rhetoric, his group-centered view of leadership, and his middle-of-the-road stance, emphasizing balance and a long-range view, one can more readily assess Eisenhower's rhetorical responses to the situations he faced during his presidency. While it is certainly true that

Ike was "no great orator,"[32] what the authors of *Eisenhower's War of Words: Rhetoric and Leadership* have discovered is a president who generally knew what he was doing with language and who used rhetoric as he conceived it—as the strategic art of selection from among various means of persuasion—to try to effect his ends. This he did consciously, regularly, and usually with more success than has commonly been recognized.

Eisenhower was not always a successful rhetorician in the sense that he did not always accomplish his goals. He was, however, always a conscious rhetorician in the sense that he understood the power of language, image, and action to shape audience response and consciously tailored his messages in such a manner as to elicit the responses he desired. Several of the authors of *Eisenhower's War of Words* have raised questions about Ike's rhetorical practices. Some challenge his view of the art as a neutral, amoral tool; others criticize specific rhetorical acts, such as his public discourses on McCarthyism; still others point to the consequences of Eisenhower's rhetorical practices and find much to fault. The point is not that Eisenhower was a perfect rhetorician—a concept which is, itself, oxymoronic—but that he was a president whose leadership cannot be adequately understood without an appreciation of the role played by rhetoric, both in the conception of that leadership and in its execution. Though not a Roosevelt, or a Kennedy, or a Reagan, Eisenhower was nonetheless a rhetorical president and one whose practice of the art deserves continuing scrutiny.

## NOTES

1. Richard E. Neustadt, *Presidential Power: The Politics of Leadership, With Reflections on Johnson and Nixon* (New York: John Wiley and Sons, Inc., 1976), 78.
2. James David Barber, *The Presidential Character: Predicting Performance in the White House,* 2nd ed. (Englewood Cliffs: Prentice-Hall, 1977), 161.
3. Barber, 162.
4. *The Rhetoric of Aristotle,* trans. Lane Cooper (Englewood Cliffs: Prentice-Hall, 1932), xxxvii.
5. Stephen E. Ambrose, *Eisenhower: The President* (New York: Simon and Schuster, 1984), 149.
6. See Martin J. Medhurst, "Eisenhower's 'Atoms for Peace' Speech: A Case Study in the Strategic Use of Language," *Communication Monographs* 54 (1987): 204-20.
7. On Eisenhower's use of rhetoric to wage psychological warfare against the North Koreans see R. Gordon Hoxie, "Eisenhower and Presidential Leadership," *Presidential Studies Quarterly* 13 (1983): 595.
8. Fred I. Greenstein, *The Hidden-Hand Presidency: Eisenhower as Leader* (New York: Basic Books, 1982), 66.
9. Ibid., 69n.
10. Eisenhower to Phillips, 5 June 1953, Whitman File, DDE Diary Series, Box 3, DDE Diary, December 1952-July 1953 (2). DDE Library.
11. Fred I. Greenstein, "Dwight D. Eisenhower: Leadership Theorist in the White House," in *Leadership in the Modern Presidency,* ed. Fred I. Greenstein (Cambridge: Harvard University Press, 1988), 81.

12. Eisenhower to Phillips, 5 June 1953, Whitman File, DDE Diary Series, Box 3, DDE Diary, December 1952-July 1953 (2). DDE Library.
13. Dwight D. Eisenhower to John Sheldon Doud Eisenhower, 19 June 1943, in *The Papers of Dwight David Eisenhower: The War Years II*, ed. Alfred D. Chandler, Jr. (Baltimore: Johns Hopkins University Press, 1970 ), 1198.
14. Eisenhower to Helms, 3 June 1954. Whitman File, DDE Diary Series, Box 7, June 1954 (2). Eisenhower Library, Abilene, Kansas.
15. Eisenhower to Hughes. Whitman File, Administration Series, Box 20, Emmet Hughes, 1945-55. DDE Library.
16. A complete and unedited version of the Guildhall speech can be found in Martin J. Medhurst, *Dwight D. Eisenhower: Strategic Communicator* (Westport, Conn.: Greenwood Press, 1993), 129-31.
17. Dwight D. Eisenhower, *Crusade in Europe* (New York: Doubleday, 1948), 4.
18. See, for example, Phillip G. Henderson, "Organizing the Presidency for Effective Leadership: Lessons from the Eisenhower Years," *Presidential Studies Quarterly* 17 (1987): 43-69; John W. Sloan, "The Management and Decision-Making Style of President Eisenhower," *Presidential Studies Quarterly* 20 (1990): 295-313.
19. On small group communication and its relationship to presidential decision making see Alexander L. George, *Presidential Decisionmaking in Foreign Policy: The Effective Use of Information and Advice* (Boulder: Westview Press, 1980), Chapter 4.
20. Eisenhower quoted in Emmet John Hughes, *The Ordeal of Power: A Political Memoir of the Eisenhower Years* (New York: Atheneum, 1963), 124-25.
21. Personal Interview with Bryce Harlow, 21 March 1984, Arlington, Virginia. Tape recording in author's possession.
22. Good will, good sense, and perception of high moral character are the components of *ethos*—one of the three primary modes of appeal that comprise the art of rhetoric according to Aristotle. The other two modes are *pathos*—the ability to evoke, through one's words, the proper emotional response in the audience—and *logos*—the ability of one's ideas and arguments, as articulated in the speech, to appeal to the audience's sense of rationality.
23. William E. Leuchtenburg, "Franklin D. Roosevelt: The First Modern President," in *Leadership in the Modern Presidency*, 40.
24. Alonzo L. Hamby, "Harry S. Truman: Insecurity and Responsibility," in *Leadership in the Modern Presidency*, 43.
25. Eisenhower to Chynoweth, 20 July 1954. Whitman File, DDE Diary Series, Box 4, DDE Personal Diary, January-November 1954 (1). DDE Library.
26. Dwight D. Eisenhower, "The Middle of the Road: A Statement of Faith in America," reprinted in Medhurst, *Dwight D. Eisenhower*, 133-39.
27. Ibid., 136.
28. Dwight D. Eisenhower, "First Inaugural Address," reprinted in Medhurst, *Dwight D. Eisenhower*, 159-164. For a rhetorical analysis of this speech see Martin J. Medhurst, "Dwight D. Eisenhower's First Inaugural Address, 1953," in *The Inaugural Addresses of Twentieth-Century American Presidents*, ed. Halford Ryan (New York: Praeger, 1993), 153-65
29. Dwight D. Eisenhower, "Atoms for Peace," reprinted in Medhurst, *Dwight D. Eisenhower*, 173-79.
30. Fred I. Greenstein quoted in *The Eisenhower Legacy: Discussions of Presidential Leadership*, ed. Shirley Anne Warshaw (Silver Spring, M.D.: Bartleby Press, 1992), 153.
31. Stephen E. Ambrose quoted in *The Eisenhower Legacy*, 157.
32. Robert G. Neumann, "Leadership: Franklin Roosevelt, Truman, Eisenhower and Today," *Presidential Studies Quarterly* 10 (1980): 16.

# Contributors

**George N. Dionisopoulos** (Ph.D., Purdue) is an associate professor of speech communication at San Diego State University. His research interests include presidential communication and public argument, and his essays have appeared in *The Quarterly Journal of Speech, Communication Monographs, Western Journal of Communication, Communication Studies*, and the *Southern Communication Journal*. He currently serves as an associate editor of the *Western Journal of Communication*.

**Steven R. Goldzwig** (Ph.D., Purdue) is associate professor of communication and rhetorical studies at Marquette University. As a rhetorical theorist and critic, he is interested in politics, religion, and values. His research has appeared in such places as *The Quarterly Journal of Speech, Communication Monographs, Western Journal of Communication, Communication Studies*, and the *Southern Communication Journal*. Formerly an associate editor at *The Quarterly Journal of Speech*, Goldzwig now serves on the editorial board of the *Journal of Communication and Religion*.

**Richard B. Gregg** (Ph.D., Pittsburgh) is professor of speech communication at The Pennsylvania State University. He conducts research in the areas of contemporary rhetorical theory and criticism, with a special interest in contemporary American political rhetoric. He has published essays and book chapters on such topics as protest rhetoric, legislative hearings on the Vietnam War, and the rhetoric of political newscasting. He is co-author of *Speech Behavior and Human Interaction* and author of *Symbolic Inducement and Knowing: A Study in the Foundations of Rhetoric*, for which he won the Winans/Wichelns Award for Distinguished Scholarship in Rhetoric and Public Address from the national Speech Communication Association.

**Charles J. G. Griffin** (Ph.D., Missouri) is associate professor of rhetoric and communication at Kansas State University. In addition to presidential rhetoric, his research interests include American religious discourse and the rhetoric of contemporary social movements. His essays have appeared in *The Quarterly Journal of Speech, Presidential Studies Quarterly, Communication Studies,* and the *Southern Communication Journal.*

**Lawrence W. Haapanen** (Ph.D., Washington State) is head of the communication arts program at Lewis-Clark State College in Lewiston, Idaho. He has authored or co-authored chapters in *The Military-Industrial Complex* (1992), *Oratorical Encounters* (1988), and the *Handbook of Intercultural Communication* (1979). In 1984-85, he served as chair of the Commission on Governmental Communication for the national Speech Communication Association.

**David Henry** (Ph.D., Indiana) is professor of speech communication at California Polytechnic State University, San Luis Obispo, where he teaches rhetorical theory and criticism, political persuasion, and argumentation. His essays on political communication, social movement rhetoric, and public advocacy on behalf of science and technology have appeared in *The Quarterly Journal of Speech, Communication Education, Communication Studies,* the *Southern Communication Journal,* and as chapters in several books. He is co-author of *Ronald Reagan: The Great Communicator* (1992), and serves on the editorial board of *The Quarterly Journal of Speech.*

**J. Michael Hogan** (Ph.D., Wisconsin) is associate professor of speech communication and American studies at Indiana University. He is the author of numerous articles and reviews in speech communication and related disciplines. His 1986 book, *The Panama Canal in American Politics,* won both the Winans/Wichelns Award for Distinguished Scholarship in Rhetoric and Public Address and the Golden Anniversary Prize Book Award from the national Speech Communication Association. He currently serves as an associate editor of *The Quarterly Journal of Speech.*

**Rachel L. Holloway** (Ph.D., Purdue) is an assistant professor of communication studies at Virginia Polytechnic Institute and State University. Her research explores the role of science and scientists in public policy and issue management. She is the author of *In the Matter of J. Robert Oppenheimer: Politics, Rhetoric, and Self-Defense* (1993) and has another manuscript on the debate between Oppenheimer and Teller currently under review.

**Robert L. Ivie** (Ph.D., Washington State) is department chair and professor of speech communication at Indiana University. He is co-author of *Congress Declares War: Rhetoric, Leadership, and Partisanship in the Early Republic* (1983) and *Cold War Rhetoric: Strategy, Metaphor, and Ideology* (1990). He is currently working on a book that examines metaphors of fear as a rhetorical legacy of the Cold War. His research has appeared in various communication journals, including *The Quarterly Journal of Speech* and *Communication Monographs*, as well as in such interdisciplinary outlets as *Social Science History* and *American Behavioral Scientist*. Ivie has served as editor of the *Western Journal of Communication* and presently edits *The Quarterly Journal of Speech*.

**Martin J. Medhurst** (Ph.D., Pennsylvania State) is professor of speech communication and coordinator of the program in presidential rhetoric at Texas A&M University. He is the author of *Dwight D. Eisenhower: Strategic Communicator* (1993) and co-author of *Cold War Rhetoric: Strategy, Metaphor, and Ideology* (1990). In addition to the present volume, he has co-edited *Rhetorical Dimensions in Media* (1984, 1991) and *Communication and the Culture of Technology* (1990). He is a frequent contributor to journals in communication studies and, with co-author Michael A. DeSousa, was the recipient of the national Speech Communication Association's 1982 Golden Anniversary Prize Fund Award for Outstanding Scholarship for his essay on the rhetoric of political cartooning. He has served on the editorial boards of *The Quarterly Journal of Speech*, *Communication Monographs*, and the *Western Journal of Communication*, and currently serves on the advisory board of *Critical Studies in Mass Communication*.

**Gregory A. Olson** (Ph.D., Minnesota) is an assistant professor of communication and rhetorical studies at Marquette University. He is currently expanding his dissertation into a book about Senate Majority Leader Mike Mansfield and the war in Vietnam.

**Thomas Rosteck** (Ph.D., Wisconsin) is assistant professor of communication at the University of Arkansas, Fayetteville. His research interests include the relationship between rhetoric and fictional discourse, especially the uses of narration and figuration. He also writes about rhetoric and popular culture and the role of documentary television in public argument. His essays have appeared in *The Quarterly Journal of Speech* and the *Southern Communication Journal*, among other outlets. He is the author of *See It Now Confronts McCarthyism: Television Documentary and the Politics of Representation* (1993).

**Mark J. Schaefermeyer** (Ph.D., Ohio State) is assistant director of admissions at Virginia Polytechnic Institute and State University. His research interests include computer analyses of political communication, computer-mediated communication, and distance education.

# Index

## A

Acheson, Dean, 98
Adams, John, 4
Adams, Sherman: Chief of Staff, 158; in Suez crisis, 159; on Eisenhower, 185; in Little Rock crisis, 204, 205
Age of peril: 8, 9, 14, 15, 16, 17, 20; "Atoms for Peace" speech, 19, 289; pathology of, 21-22
Age of Vulnerability, 10
Ahlstrom, Sidney, 51, 52
Alexander, Charles: Revisionist, 143; on Geneva, 143; on Open Skies Proposal, 147; on psychological warfare, 150n.11
Alley, Robert S., 47
Allies: and declaration of war, 107-8; in Middle East, 163, 174, 175, 180; and military involvement, 107-8, 109-18; at Paris summit, 255, 260, 261; in the space age, 242; and U-2 affair, 254; unilateral intervention, 110, 112, 113. See also Indochina
Ambrose, Stephen E., 11, 18, 154n.80, 204, 206, 209, 282, 289, 295
American civil religion, 48-51, 53, 70n.12
American "Messianism," 47
American Society of Newspaper Editors, 12
American values (basic ideals), 80-83; American Western myth, 83; anti-Communist subversion, 84, 86; basis of freedom, 82; Eisenhower's "Positive approach," 83, 86; and McCarthyism, 82, 86; and separation of powers, 85; morality of anti-McCarthyism, 83-85, 88, 89, 90

America's "purpose": agency-purpose terms, 56; economic reinforcement, 58; Eisenhower's discourse on, 56, 57, 67-69; "faith in freedom," 60; preservation of freedom, 48, 55, 56, 57-58, 60, 64, 66, 67
Anderson, David L., 8, 117, 121, 134n.75
Anderson, Robert P., 166
Arab-Israeli War: Egyptian aggression, 161; State of Israel formed, 161; United Nations intervention, 161
Arab League, the, 161
Aristotle: defined rhetoric, 288, 297n.22; model for Eisenhower, 288, 294, 295
*Arkansas Gazette*, 197, 201
Arkansas National Guard: activated by Faubus, 196-99, 201, 204-5, 206, 215, 220n.136; federalized by Eisenhower, 194
Arkansas State Board of Education, 198
Arms race, the, 11, 59, 63, 68-69, 289
Arnold, James R., 127
Aswan Dam project, 166-67, 186n.16
*At Ease*, 280
atomic bomb, 53, 63. See also nuclear weapons
Atomic Energy Commission, 53, 63; Chairman, 53; Snapp-Eisenhower briefing, 53-54. See also Hydrogen bomb
"Atoms for Peace," 47, 63, 111; policy, 137, 138, 223; speech, 13, 19-20, 37, 61, 62, 140, 223, 289
Aurand, Pete, 277
Australia: SEATO, 116-17